Strategic Marketing in Practice 2005–2006

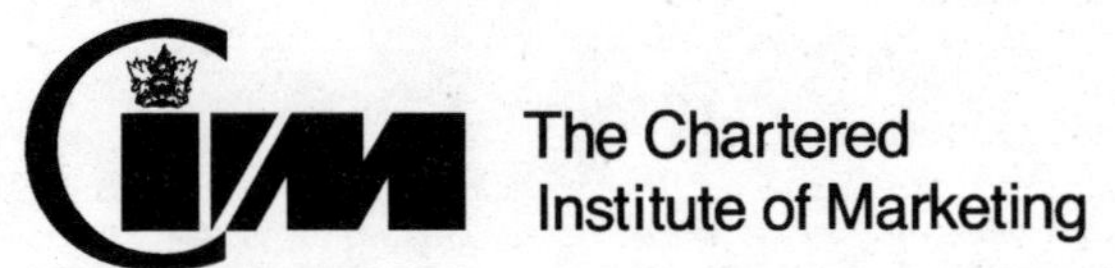

Strategic Marketing in Practice 2005–2006

Ashok Ranchhod and Ebi Marandi

BUTTERWORTH
HEINEMANN

AMSTERDAM BOSTON HEIDELBERG LONDON NEW YORK OXFORD
PARIS SAN DIEGO SAN FRANCISCO SINGAPORE SYDNEY TOKYO

Elsevier Butterworth-Heinemann
Linacre House, Jordan Hill, Oxford OX2 8DP
30 Corporate Drive, Burlington, MA 01803

First published 2005

British Library Cataloguing in Publication Data
A catalogue record for this book is available from the British Library

Library of Congress Cataloguing in Publication Data
A catalogue record for this book is available from the Library of Congress

ISBN 0 7506 6654 4

For information on all Elsevier Butterworth-Heinemann publications visit our website at http://books.elsevier.com

Typeset by Integra Software Services Pvt. Ltd, Pondicherry, India
www.integra-india.com
Printed and bound in Italy

Contents

Preface
welcome to the CIM coursebooks

The CIM has been working behind the scenes for several years to launch the new Professional Postgraduate Diploma in Marketing. As a result four new modules have been introduced (Marketing Analysis and Evaluation, Strategic Marketing Decisions, Marketing Performance and Strategic Marketing in Practice). The Strategic Marketing in Practice module is still based on a major case study. However, now this is a closed book examination and there is an allowance for pre-prepared analyses. This paper encompasses the multidisciplinary nature of marketing, drawing on a range of concepts studied at the Certificate, Professional Diploma and Professional Postgraduate Diploma levels of the CIM qualifications. The paper is a test of the requisite skills in marketing as well as an indepth and contemporary knowledge of marketing. The emphasis of this book is very much on developing a 'balanced' marketing individual who is both practically adept at marketing but one who can also interweave this skill with sound theory and innovative ideas.

Professor Ashok Ranchhod, BSc, MSc, MBA, PhD, FCIM, Chartered Marketer Senior Assessor, Strategic Marketing in Practice

About the authors

Ashok Ranchhod is Faculty Professor in Marketing at Southampton Business School. Ashok has published extensively on e-marketing in Journals such as the *International Journal of Advertising* and the *Journal of Information Technology*.

He has undertaken consultancy work for major organizations and has written case studies on companies in several different sectors of industry for the Chartered Institute of Marketing. Prior to his work in academia, he was the managing director of a small biotechnology company based in Derbyshire.

In addition to the published papers he has received prizes for his papers at the Academy of Marketing and The British Academy of Management. Currently his research is into e-commerce and the marketing of biotechnology companies. He leads a team of research students. Ashok is a Senior Examiner for the Chartered Institute of Marketing (CIM) and is a Visiting Professor at the University of Angers in France. He is also a Fellow of the Chartered Institute of Marketing. He has generated substantial research funds for the Business School.

Ebi Marandi is a Senior Lecturer and the Programme Leader of MA International Marketing Management at Bournemouth University. He is also the Deputy Senior Examiner for CIM's SMiP paper.

An introduction from the academic development advisor

In the last 2 years we have seen some significant changes to CIM Marketing qualifications. The changes have been introduced on a year-on-year basis, with Certificate changes implemented in 2002, and the Professional Diploma in Marketing being launched in 2003. The Professional Postgraduate Diploma in Marketing was launched in 2004. The new qualifications are based on the CIM Professional Marketing Standards developed through research with employers.

Study note © CIM 2005

As a result the authoring team, Elsevier Butterworth-Heinemann and I have all aimed to rigorously revise and update the coursebook series to make sure that every title is the best possible study aid and accurately reflects the latest CIM syllabus. This has been further enhanced through independent reviews carried out by CIM.

We have aimed to develop the assessment support to include some additional support for the assignment route as well as the examination, so we hope you will find this helpful.

There are a number of new authors and indeed Senior Examiners in the series who have been commissioned for their CIM course teaching and examining experience, as well as their research into specific curriculum-related areas and their wide general knowledge of the latest thinking in marketing.

We are certain that you will find these coursebooks highly beneficial in terms of the content and assessment opportunities and a study tool that will prepare you for both CIM examinations and continuous/integrative assessment opportunities. They will guide you in a logical and structured way through the detail of the syllabus, providing you with the required underpinning knowledge, understanding and application of theory.

The editorial team and authors wish you every success as you embark upon your studies.

Karen Beamish
Academic Development Advisor

About MarketingOnline

Elsevier Butterworth-Heinemann offers purchasers of the coursebooks free access to MarketingOnline (www.marketingonline.co.uk), our premier online support engine for the CIM marketing courses. On this site you can benefit from:

- Fully customizable electronic versions of the coursebooks enabling you to annotate, cut and paste sections of text to create your own tailored learning notes.
- The capacity to search the coursebook online for instant access to definitions and key concepts.
- Useful links to e-marketing articles, provided by Dave Chaffey, Director of Marketing Insights Ltd and a leading UK e-marketing consultant, trainer and author.
- A glossary providing a comprehensive dictionary of marketing terms.
- A Frequently Asked Questions (FAQs) section providing guidance and advice on common problems or queries.

Using MarketingOnline

Logging on

Before you can access MarketingOnline you will first need to get a password. Please go to www.marketingonline.co.uk and click on the registration button where you will then find registration instructions for coursebook purchasers. Once you have got your password, you will need to log on using the onscreen instructions. This will give you access to the various functions of the site.

MarketingOnline provides a range of functions, as outlined in the previous section, that can easily be accessed from the site after you have logged on to the system. Please note the following guidelines detailing how to access the main features:

1. *The coursebooks* – Buttons corresponding to the three levels of the CIM marketing qualification are situated on the home page. Select your level and you will be presented with the coursebook title for each module of that level. Click on the desired coursebook to access the full online text (divided up by chapter). On each page of text you have the option to add an electronic bookmark or annotation by following the onscreen instructions. You can also freely cut and paste text into a blank word document to create your own learning notes.
2. *e-Marketing articles* – To access the links to relevant e-marketing articles simply click on the link under the text 'E-marketing Essentials: useful links from Marketing Insights'.
3. *Glossary* – A link to the glossary is provided in the top right hand corner of each page enabling access to this resource at any time.

If you have specific queries about using MarketingOnline then you should consult our fully searchable FAQs section, accessible through the appropriate link in the top right hand corner of any page of the site. Please also note that a *full user guide* can be downloaded by clicking on the link on the opening page of the website.

unit 1 introduction

Introduction

The Marketing Strategy in Practice is part of the new Professional Postgraduate Diploma in Marketing that has been developed at the Chartered Institute of Marketing. It replaces the old Analysis and Decision paper. It carries many of the same hallmarks, but the format is now slightly different and students are expected to prepare analyses before the examination. The examination will also now be a *Closed Book Examination.* It is likely that this will be the final paper that students studying for CIM qualifications undertake. It requires students to have a good knowledge of all the subjects covered at all levels. It is particularly important that candidates have a good knowledge of subject areas at Certificate, Professional Diploma and Professional Postgraduate Diploma levels. The assessment constitutes questions based on a major case study. For this reason, there is no specific syllabus for this paper and much of the rationale for this module lies in developing suitable outcomes for candidates considering a career in Marketing. It is expected that candidates will have passed the other Postgraduate Diploma modules: Marketing Analysis and Evaluation, Strategic Marketing Decisions and Managing Marketing Performance. Each of these modules covers a wide array of Marketing topics that are important for a thorough understanding of marketing at higher levels. The paper requires the application of all the marketing knowledge and experience that students would have gained over several years.

As the title of the paper 'Strategic Marketing in Practice' (SMiP) suggests, candidates need to be able to *apply* their marketing knowledge and skills to a real-life case study. Also as in real life, candidates are expected to analyse the case study prior to the examination and to utilize this analysis in their answers. The case study may take a number of formats. It may be a long case study divided into sections or themes, or it may be in the form of a number of mini cases with a common theme running through it. Comparative mini cases may also be set. This type of flexibility allows the Examiner to test the candidate's ability to be flexible, creative and innovative when asked to tackle a range of differing types of marketing problems and issues. For this reason, good analytical and implementation skills within a marketing context are required. Strategic marketing plans also may not always feature in the examination questions, but the students knowledge of key marketing issues will always be tested. Marketers always need to have good analytical capabilities in order to develop marketing strategies. Once these strategies have been developed, clear and sensible decisions need to be made. Candidates need to be conversant with all aspects of marketing, especially contemporary issues. Cases are by their very nature set in different sectors, have different contexts and require knowledge from different areas of marketing. Marketing problems are rarely neatly packaged. Candidates, therefore, have to have the capability to draw from their wealth of experience and knowledge and also to demonstrate flexibility and creativity by being able to tackle problems in a variety of contexts set in a variety of sectors in different areas of the globe. As we enter the new millennium, marketing is undergoing many changes and marketers need to be able to develop a range of skills. The module sits within the overall Professional Postgraduate Diploma scheme as outlined below:

	Entry modules	Research and Analysis	Planning	Implementation	Management of marketing
Professional Postgraduate Diploma	Entry module – Professional Postgraduate Diploma	Analysis and evaluation	Strategic marketing decisions	Managing marketing performance	Strategic marketing in practice
Professional Diploma	Entry module – Professional Diploma	Marketing research and information	Marketing planning	Marketing communications	Marketing management in practice
Professional Certificate		Marketing environment	Marketing fundamentals	Customer communications	Marketing in practice
Introductory certificate			Supporting marketing processes (research and analysis, planning and implementation)		

Marketing drives the business agenda

Marketing is a set of activities concerned with creating value for shareholders and other stakeholders by creating and capturing exceptional value for customers. Marketers are the people, business as well as marketing professionals, who make decisions about marketing.

Research undertaken to support the development of this syllabus found that organizations expect professional marketers to take increasing ownership for the whole customer experience. This requires them to become more aware of the operational business agenda, more commercial, more strategic and more innovative. They have to develop an even deeper understanding of customers and take a more integrated approach to marketing, both internal and external. This syllabus is an early step in equipping strategic marketers of the future to fulfil these expectations. Professional marketers in publicly quoted or limited companies have to:

- *Focus on the long term* – The focus for marketing is the generation of economic profit (operating adjusted for the cost of capital invested in a business or activity), which is how shareholders measure value. While other business functions can maximize economic profit through efficiency, marketing is the only way to create value. Marketing typically creates three times more value than other functions.
- *Create and capture value for customers* – Marketers create value by increasing the value perceived by customers in an organization's products and services. The key is positioning which, in today's competitive markets, requires deeper insights (into customers' needs and behaviours) and innovation. By increasing perceived value, marketers create the opportunity for premium pricing through which economic profit is increased.
- *Take charge of the business agenda* – Marketing uses its activities and assets (such as brands and relationships) to create customer value. At the same time, these activities and

the use of the marketing assets generate results which are consolidated with other financial results and reported. Shareholders measure the value that the business has created for them as the sum of dividends paid and the increase in price of the shares they own. Marketing has to take charge of investment in marketing assets and all the marketing activities that create value. In short, they must take charge of the business agenda.

'Models' of marketing

The type, or 'model', of marketing practised in any organization depends on a number of factors, not least of which are the nature of the business context and the organization's dominant orientation. Marketing activities in organizations can be grouped broadly into four models:

1. *Sales support* – The emphasis in this model is essentially reactive: marketing supports the direct salesforce. It may include activities such as telesales or telemarketing, responding to inquiries, coordinating diaries, customer database management, organizing exhibitions or other sales promotions, and administering agents. These activities usually come under a sales and marketing director or manager. This form of marketing is common in SMEs and some organizations operating in a B2B context.
2. *Marketing communications* – The emphasis in this model is more proactive: marketing promotes the organization and its product/service at a tactical level, either to customers (pull) or to channel members (push). It typically includes activities such as providing brochures and catalogues to support the salesforce. Some B2C organizations may use marketing to perform the 'selling' role using direct marketing techniques and to manage campaigns based on a mix of media to raise awareness, generate leads and even take orders. In B2B markets, larger organizations may have marketing communications departments and specialists to make efficient use of marketing expenditures and to coordinate communications between business units.
3. *Operational marketing* – The emphasis in this model is for marketing to support the organization with a coordinated range of marketing activities including market research, brand management, product development and management, corporate and marketing communications, and customer relationship management. Given this breadth of activities, planning is also a function usually performed in this role but at an operational or functional level. Typically part of fast-moving consumer goods (FMCG) or B2C organizations, the operational marketing role is increasingly used in B2B organizations.
4. *Strategic marketing* – The emphasis in this model is for marketing to contribute to the creation of value and competitive customer strategy. As such, it is practised in customer-focused and larger organizations. In a large or diversified organization, it may also be responsible for the coordination of marketing departments or activities in separate business units. Strategic marketing decisions, when not made by professional marketers, are taken by business leaders.

Professional marketers are likely to be responsible for strategic marketing only in those organizations with a strong market (note, not necessarily *marketing*), or customer orientation or with separate marketing departments in business units that require coordination. In organizations with a weak customer orientation (typically those with a production, sales, product or technology orientation), the role of marketing is likely to be limited to one of sales support or marketing communications.

Marketing contexts

Organizations operating in a variety of contexts use different marketing activities. There is no 'one size fits all' approach. Organizations and their marketers have to select and use techniques appropriate to their specific context. Typically marketing contexts are summarized as:

Context	Characteristics
FMCG	Used in organizations with a strong market orientation, the 'standard' model of marketing is based on identification of customers' needs and techniques of segmentation, targeting and positioning supported by branding and customer communications.
B2B	The model of marketing adopted depends on factors such as the importance of face-to-face selling, the dominant orientation and power of buyers. Markets are often less information-rich than FMCG markets, which constrains marketing decisions.
Capital projects	A variant of the B2B model where opportunities for positioning are few and the value of any single order constitutes a significant proportion of turnover in a period.
Not-for-profit	The organization is not driven by shareholder value and competition may not be a significant factor in strategy.
SMEs	Operating in any of the above sectors, SMEs are characterized by their limited marketing resources and the limited use of marketing techniques.

Not-for-profit organizations are driven not by shareholders but by other stakeholders, such as government (public sector), beneficiaries (charities) and volunteers (voluntary sector). The concept of shareholder value may not be relevant in these organizations where instead concepts such as 'best value' (public sector) and the level of disbursements to beneficiaries operate. The element of competition may not be explicit in the strategy of these organizations, whose strategies may be more collaborative. Such organizations may use a narrower and more tactical repertoire of marketing techniques than larger commercial organizations with a strong market orientation and driven by shareholder value. It is important, therefore those students studying the SMiP paper can explore the application of marketing in a range of different contexts utilizing the syllabi from the various linked modules and also drawing from current Contemporary Issues in Marketing.

Strategic marketing activities

The full spectrum of strategic marketing activities is illustrated in the statements of marketing practice on which the syllabi of the three modules link to the summative SMiP module. They include:

- Research and analysis
- Strategic marketing and planning
- Brand management
- Implementing marketing programmes
- Measuring effectiveness
- Managing marketing teams.

It goes without saying that strategic marketing operates in a global context. This is not to say that the syllabus has nothing to offer the organization pursuing a domestic strategy or entering its first foreign market. Even if an organization is not operating across borders, it is likely to be working in a market in which competitors based in other countries are operating – in other words, a global context. Throughout this syllabus, the term 'global context' embraces domestic and international activities as well as true global activities of the largest organizations.

Plans and planning processes

The planning processes used in organizations are typically geared to the annual operating and financial reporting cycle. In those organizations in which annual or longer term plans are produced, these plans are usually at three levels:

1. Corporate level
2. Business level
3. Functional level.

Marketing contributes to corporate and business plans and develops its own functional plan at an operational level. In organizations with strong strategic management practices (often those with a strong customer orientation), plans are likely to contain the strategies of the organization or business. In organizations where plans are effectively 'budgets', strategy is unlikely to be explicit. It is therefore important to recognize that

- The terms 'strategy' and 'plan' may not be the same.
- Strategy making and planning may be different processes in organizations.
- Organizations approach strategy formulation in a range of formal and informal ways.

What is sometimes referred to as the 'strategic marketing plan' can take different forms in different organizations. For example:

- It may be the name given to the plans that coordinate the marketing activities of the different businesses or units throughout an organization.
- It may be synonymous with the term 'business plan' or 'corporate plan' in an organization with a strong customer focus or responsibility only for marketing products made elsewhere and bought in.
- It may simply be the name given to the marketing plan, which specifies the objectives or targets, activities, resources and budgets of the marketing function.

However, it should be recognized that the majority of organizations do not produce a strategic marketing plan. The major plans that specify and control the organization's strategy are corporate or business plans, into which strategic marketing should have an input.

The role of strategic marketing

In organizations where strategic marketing does not exist as a function, the process or decisions are still undertaken by senior managers or business leaders. Where it is an explicit function, the strategic marketing role will usually be performed by a marketing function in a business unit and by a corporate level marketing function, which may also have responsibility for coordinating the activities of marketing departments in business units.

The primary role of strategic marketing is to identify and create value for the business through strongly differentiated positioning. It achieves this by influencing the strategy and culture of the organization in order to ensure that both have a strong customer focus. When this role is carried out by a marketing specialist, it is called 'marketing director' or 'strategic marketing manager', sometimes based in a department called 'marketing' rather than 'strategic marketing'. Strategic marketers should champion the customer experience and exert a strong influence on the organization to adopt a customer orientation, contribute along with other directors and senior managers to its competitive strategy, align the organization's activities to the customer, and manage the organization's marketing activities.

During strategy formulation, strategic marketing is about choices that customer-focused organizations make on where and how to compete and with what assets. It is also about developing a specific competitive position using tools from the marketing armoury including brands, innovation, customer relationships and service, alliances, channels and communications, and increasingly price. Strategic marketing does not own the business strategy but, like other departments and functions, should contribute to it and control the operational levers that make a strategy effective. However, marketing has an exceptional contribution to make in identifying opportunities and determining ways to create value for customers and shareholders.

During implementation, strategic marketing is the 'glue' that connects many aspects of the business. It will often manage one or a portfolio of brands. Increasingly, it works with HR to ensure that the culture and values in the organization are consistent with the brand and to ensure that marketing competencies are part of the overall framework for staff development across the business. Strategic marketing also has responsibility for directing the implementation of marketing activities needed to execute the organization's strategy. Other key tasks of strategic marketing in today's organizations are:

- Contributing to strategic initiatives being undertaken by the organization, for example marketing input to a 'due diligence' evaluation of a prospective merger or acquisition. In some cases, strategic marketers will be managing multi-disciplinary teams.
- Coordinating and managing customer information across the organization within the data protection and privacy legislation. This involves close relationships with the IT function.
- Developing and driving the business case for investment in brands, new products and services.
- Championing and developing innovation and entrepreneurship within the organization.
- Ensuring that the marketing function is appropriately skilled and resourced.
- Providing input with finance on the valuation of brands for reporting and disclosure.

This concept of strategic marketing draws heavily on the theory and practice of strategic management, not just of marketing. This is an important distinction since strategic marketing is as much a part of directing how the organization competes as it is a part of marketing itself. Professional marketers engage in relationships with most functions within the organization and are 'business people' rather than 'technical marketers'. This is particularly so at the strategic level. It requires participants at this level to embrace a wider range of management theory and practice than has been the case in the past. In addition to traditional marketing theory, strategic marketing also embraces:

- Business and corporate strategy
- Investment decisions
- Culture and change management
- Quality management
- Programme and project management.

Marketers still have an essential role to play in contributing their specialist marketing skills to the formulation, implementation and control of strategy. These specialist marketing skills are of vital importance to organizations.

The syllabus at Professional Postgraduate Diploma has been divided into four modules:

1. *Analysis and evaluation* – covers the concepts, techniques and models involved in developing a detailed understanding of the market, customers and competitive environment externally and internally the organization, its capabilities and assets, the opportunities available to it and its current performance.
2. *Strategic marketing decisions* – covers the concepts, techniques and models involved in formulating a customer-focused competitive business or corporate strategy and developing a specific and differentiated competitive position. It includes investment decisions affecting marketing assets.
3. *Managing marketing performance* – covers the implementation stage of the strategy. This encompasses managing marketing teams, managing change, implementing strategy through marketing activities and working with other departments, and using measurement as the basis for improvement.
4. *Strategic marketing in practice* – provides the opportunity to explore strategic marketing in a practical setting. It also incorporates the latest trends and innovations in marketing. This module will draw on all the preceding modules and their syllabi.

Figure 1.1 Strategic marketing in practice and links with the other modules at Professional Postgraduate Diploma

Aims and outcomes for strategic marketing in practice

In coming to understand the range of outcomes that are defined for SMiP it is useful to consider the range of skills that students will be expected to exhibit in this module. This is indicated in Table 1.1.

Table 1.1

Key skill unit: Personal skills development	Analysis and evaluation	Strategic marketing decisions	Managing marketing performance	Strategic marketing in practice
Communication				
Interpret and evaluate information	✓	✓		✓
Synthesize and structure information	✓	✓		✓
Present information	✓	✓		✓
Problem-solving				
Select and use strategies to solve problems		✓		✓
Establish what is needed to get results		✓		✓
Monitor progress		✓	✓	✓
Working with others				
Gain commitment			✓	✓
Brief others			✓	✓
Lead implementation			✓	✓

Aim

Marketing has to be firmly rooted in both theory and practice. Practice informs theory and vice versa. The Strategic Marketing in Practice module is designed to allow participants to put strategic marketing into practice. As the final module at Professional Postgraduate Diploma level, it not only builds on the knowledge and skills developed in all the preceding modules, but also looks for an overall competence in marketing that encompasses all the various subject areas covered in Certificate and Professional Certificate level. As marketing is constantly evolving, continuously informed by both academic and business research, one of the aims of this module is to explore the latest trends and innovations relevant to marketers who are operating at a strategic level within organizations. One of the other aims is to understand marketing as an activity, which is important in all contexts (profit, not-for-profit, societal, global). It is expected that participants undertaking this module will be able to add value to both their marketing experience and marketing knowledge. This module therefore does not have a specific syllabus and draws from all the preceding modules and syllabi.

Related statements of practice

- Ad.1 Define intelligence requirements and lead the intelligence gathering process.
- Ad.2 Develop a detailed understanding of the organization and its environment.
- Bd.1 Promote a strong market orientation and influence/contribute to strategy formulation and investment decisions.
- Bd.2 Specify and direct the marketing planning process.

- Cd.1 Promote organization-wide innovation and cooperation in the development of brands.
- Cd.2 Distil the essence of brands and direct/coordinate a portfolio of brands.
- Dd.1 Develop and direct an integrated marketing communications strategy.
- Dd.2 Lead the implementation of the integrated marketing communications strategy.
- Ed.1 Promote corporate-wide innovation and cooperation in the development of products and services.
- Ed.2 Direct and maintain competitive product/service portfolios.
- Fd.1 Promote the strategic and creative use of pricing.
- Fd.2 Lead the implementation of the strategic and creative use of pricing.
- Gd.1 Select and monitor channel criteria to meet the organization's need in a changing environment.
- Gd.2 Direct and control support to channel members.
- Hd.1 Promote and create a customer orientation and infrastructure for customer relationships.
- Hd.2 Direct and control information and activities that deliver customer relationships and service.
- Jd.1 Establish and maintain a project management framework in line with strategic objectives.
- Jd.2 Direct and control the delivery of programmes and projects.
- Kd.1 Establish and promote the use of metrics to improve marketing effectiveness.
- Kd.2 Create a system of critical review and appraisal to inform future marketing activity.
- Ld.1 Provide professional leadership and develop a cooperative environment to enhance performance.
- Ld.2 Promote effective cross-functional working linked to brands and the integration of marketing activities.
- Ld.3 Promote and create an environment for career and self-development.
- Ld.4 Contribute to organizational change and define and communicate the need for change within the department.

Learning outcomes

Participants will be able to:

- 9.64.1 Identify and critically evaluate marketing issues within various environments, utilizing a wide variety of marketing techniques, concepts and models.
- 9.64.2 Assess the relevance of, and opportunities presented by, contemporary marketing issues within any given scenario including innovations in marketing.
- 9.64.3 Identify and critically evaluate various options available within given constraints and apply competitive positioning strategies, justifying any decisions taken.
- 9.64.4 Formulate and present a creative, customer-focused and innovative competitive strategy for any given context, incorporating relevant investment decisions, appropriate control aspects and contingency plans.
- 9.64.5 Demonstrate an understanding of the direction and management of marketing activities as part of the implementation of strategic direction, taking into account business intelligence requirements, marketing processes, resources, markets and the company vision.
- 9.64.6 Promote and facilitate the adoption and maintenance of a strong market and customer orientation with measurable marketing metrics.
- 9.64.7 Synthesize various strands of knowledge and skills from the different syllabus modules effectively in developing an effective solution for any given context.

Knowledge and skill requirements

There is no formal specification of knowledge and skills requirements for this module. Participants are required to demonstrate a full understanding of, and to satisfy the knowledge and skills requirements specified in, the syllabus modules at Certificate, Professional Diploma and Professional Postgraduate Diploma levels. The emphasis in this module is more on applying the knowledge and practical skills acquired in the previous modules. The essential skills assessed as part of this module are:

- Analysis, interpretation, evaluation and synthesis of information, including the ability to draw conclusions.
- Identification, exploration and evaluation of strategic options.
- Selection and justification of an appropriate option using decision criteria.
- Establishing the activities, resources and schedule needed to implement the chosen strategy.
- Working with others to implement and control the strategy.

Participants will be expected to demonstrate their awareness of current issues and an ability to make recommendations for a given context. From time to time CIM will publish a list of trends and innovations to guide tutors and participants in their preparation for assessment. Participants will be expected to read widely in the area of strategic marketing as part of their studies at this level.

The links with other syllabi

The syllabus aims of the three modules within Professional Postgraduate Diploma level are as shown below. They provide a link with Key Skills and show the linkage between the learning outcomes for each module and the Statements of Marketing Practice. All these are linked to the outcomes for SMiP as indicated.

1. Contribute research and insights to inform strategic marketing decisions. This encompasses:

   (a) Identifying the organization's business intelligence requirements.
   (b) Understanding organizational culture and its consequences for strategy.
   (c) Developing and synthesizing a detailed understanding of an organization's customers, internal and external environments and its current business performance from the relevant stakeholders' perspectives.

2. Influence strategic decisions in an organization to create value for customers and other stakeholders. This encompasses:

   (a) Contributing specialist marketing input to strategic decisions to achieve competitive advantage and customer preference.
   (b) Influencing decisions within the organization concerning priorities for marketing activities and investment in marketing assets.
   (c) Promoting a strong market orientation and consistency with the values of the brand.

3. Manage and measure marketing activities undertaken as part of the implementation of a customer-focused strategy. This encompasses:

   (a) Evaluating the techniques available to organizations for integrating teams and activities across the organization.
   (b) Identifying the barriers to effective implementation of strategies and plans and developing measures to prevent or overcome them and effect change.
   (c) Explaining techniques for managing a marketing team, including assessing the organization's need for marketing skills and resources and developing strategies for acquiring, developing and retaining them.
   (d) Initiating and critically evaluating systems for control of marketing activities.

4. Formulate, present and justify a creative, customer-focused and innovative strategy for any given context. This encompasses:

   (a) Identifying and critically evaluating relevant marketing issues and opportunities, including trends and innovations in marketing and business.
   (b) Identifying and critically evaluating the various options available to achieve the desired goal(s).

Points to ponder

- Marketing as a subject area is undergoing major changes. These changes are taking place as a result of dramatic shifts in technology, demographics, globalization, systems of production, logistics and ecological issues. The papers, therefore, are designed to reflect more of these contemporary issues in addition to the knowledge base mentioned above.
- The case studies will also be designed to develop strategic marketing issues which can be operationalized and implemented within realistic constraints. It is often forgotten that marketing is not just about positioning and growth, but also about effectiveness within given constraints within most organizations. These constraints mean that strategies have to be sensibly evaluated and chosen with hard decisions being made. When particular strategies are chosen, it is clear that the constraints could be many and varied. Constraints, for instance, could be financial, organizational (both employee and culture related), marketing (image, size of markets, branding, distribution systems, networks) and if, the organization is a division of a larger entity, headquarter imposed constraints.

Globalization

- The rapid changes in technology are far reaching as they are changing the normal paradigms of marketing. The four Ps cannot now be discussed with certainty. The nature and direction of marketing strategies necessarily have to take into account the massive computing power available and the new developments on the Web. Many multi-nationals have operated globally for decades, but technology is changing the patterns of production and consumption.
- For instance, global brands are available anywhere and production facilities may be located in a myriad of different countries. For smaller companies, locked into local markets, the Internet holds the promises and pitfalls of operating in a global arena.
- The introduction of the euro means that pan-European marketing strategies have to be thought through in a different manner. The changing nature and the growth of South Asian markets has an enormous impact on the marketing strategies of organizations. The nature and strength of the American market is often forgotten. The case studies will reflect these changes and will embrace many different sectors of industry.

Organizational issues

- When developing marketing strategies it is important that the culture and nature of the organization is taken into account. Marketing strategies often succeed and fail as a result of inappropriate personnel, inappropriate structures or climates within organizations. Success or failure of strategies can be defined by utilizing a number of different performance measures such as market share growth, return on investment, brand awareness and sales growth among others. Organizations are, therefore, always striving to create the appropriate structures and develop appropriate cultures to meet the demands of the marketplace.
- The customer is king and marketing strategists have to place the level of market orientation at the centre of their thinking.

Sustainability

- With the growing problems related to the general environmental deterioration and the increasing concern over climatic changes, the issues surrounding sustainability are of critical importance to marketers. Marketing literature has for long been concerned with growth and market share. It is important that issues surrounding the constraints imposed by the environment are taken into account. The world is facing an enormous challenge in terms of the availability of resources and the needs of the population.

Constraints

- In some respects a challenge posed to marketing strategists is the need to consider constraints and responsibility. Constraints can be financial or related to the human resource capabilities of an organization. In many instances constraints can be imposed by the external environment and these are particularly important for the growth of a company's markets.

Financial issues

- Financial issues will always play a key role in developing strategies. A good knowledge of basic financial statements such as profit and loss accounts, balance sheets and cash-flow statements is required.

Knowledge of contemporary marketing issues

- Each case is different and will therefore test some knowledge of contemporary issues. Students therefore need to be encouraged to read journal articles pertaining to the case study.

Application of previous knowledge

- The need to apply models for analysis will continue. However, a more critical approach in applying these techniques will be needed. The paper will reflect the need for both academic and practical knowledge, as true marketers need to have experience in both areas for developing sensible strategies.

Issues of implementation and control

- An awareness of the clear decision-making and implementation strategies will be tested. As will be strategic positioning, innovation and branding in the context of implementation and control.
- Formulating an appropriate strategy, incorporating investment decisions, control aspects and contingency plans.

Assessment methodology for the module

- Students will receive a case study – normally between 30–60 pages (including company/industry data) four weeks prior to the examination date.
- The examination on the case study will be a closed book examination, however, students will be allowed to bring in six sides of A4 prepared analysis and a copy of their case study which may also be annotated. The examination questions will remain unseen until the start of the examination.
- The marking scheme will allocate 25 per cent of marks for the six pages of prepared analysis as follows:

  – 10 per cent awarded for originality and appropriateness of analysis in the context given.
  – 15 per cent awarded for appropriate application of analysis within the questions.

Guidelines for pre-prepared work

Candidates chosen for the pilot study should be given the following advice:

(a) Write or print pre-prepared analysis on *six single-sided* pages. Examiners will be looking for tables, diagrams and key issues. Tables such as SWOT, though helpful do not show deep analytical thought.

(b) If candidates use the available sheets for writing 'crib' material, such as models or plans they will penalize themselves as there will be less space for good analysis that counts towards the final marks.

(c) The diagrams should be clearly visible and the writing should be clearly legible. Typing should be no less than font size 11.

(d) Data given within the case should be analysed clearly and effectively.

(e) All the work should be on CIM paper which will be issued two weeks before the examination.

(f) Please note that it will be totally unacceptable for students to present standardized group analysis/appendices and they will therefore be penalized accordingly.

During the examination

(a) The answers should reflect the use of the pre-prepared material as necessary. Candidates, when writing answers should cross reference the work to guide the Examiner to a particular table or chart or piece of analysis.
(b) Examiners do not expect students to use ALL the pre-prepared material to augment their answers. Obviously, they should only use whatever is necessary for answering the questions as set.
(c) Candidates should attach the pre-prepared work as an appendix. *All papers must be hole punched and include the student registration and centre number.*
(d) Please note that Fifteen marks are allocated *for the application* of the pre-prepared work.
(e) *Only the pre-prepared analysis can be taken into the examination room, therefore no textbooks, journals or other pre-prepared work will be allowed.*

Summary

This chapter gives you an idea of the marketing skills that SMiP module aims to develop and test. It also shows that learning outcomes are more important than specific syllabus regurgitation. In order to reach the desired outcomes, students need to be able to critically assess and absorb the key concepts in the other areas of the Professional Postgraduate Diploma, and their applications to real marketing problems. When studying previous cases students should attempt to list the key outcomes that they have achieved, together with some of the key skills that they have used in order to reach a satisfactory level of competence.

unit 2 what is meant by case study analysis?

Outcomes

Relationship to outcomes

- Identify and critically evaluate marketing issues within various environments, utilizing a wide variety of marketing techniques, concepts and models.
- Identify and critically evaluate various options available within constraints and apply competitive positioning strategies, justifying any decisions taken.

Candidates should also be familiar with the Analysis and Evaluation module and the Strategic Marketing Decisions syllabi.

A brief overview

A case study is an account of the major events taking place in a business within an industry sector over a number of years. A case usually features many of the key events in that it chronicles the events that have been dealt with and have to be dealt with by marketing managers. Issues pertaining to the competitive environment, changes in the business definition and the main areas of the served market segments have to be dealt with by marketing managers.

Cases give students a chance to understand some of the problems faced by organizations and be able to analyse them in detail.

Cases allow students to utilize their understanding of key concepts. Their meaning is made clearer when applied to case studies. Theory and concepts help to analyse a company's situation. Analysing a case requires great powers of deduction. Facts and figures are often hidden in the different areas of the case. The conceptual tools help to probe the case and gather evidence of events. In the real world, it is important to understand that there are no right answers. For most companies, strategic marketing management is difficult. Developing strategies is generally an uncertain game, making it more important to develop a careful diagnosis. All that managers can do is to make the best guess.

As different individuals have differing ideas, case studies provide students with the opportunity to participate in class and to learn from others. Tutors often act as facilitators in this process of enquiry and analysis. In actual businesses, this is exactly the way decisions are made. It is important therefore, that students can analyse the situation and be confident of their solutions.

Analysing a case study

One of the purposes of the case study is to let you analyse the situation that the company finds itself in. In doing this, you will need to apply many of the key concepts that you would have learnt in the other modules. A case study has to be read several times before a clear idea of the key issues can be established. This enables you to establish a picture of the environment in which the company is operating as well as the company's position within it. Eventually, based on this analysis you will make a series of decisions to take the company forward into the future. A detailed and effective analysis of a case should include the following:

1. The key historical events that have contributed to the development of the company.
2. A PESTLE analysis, which looks at Political, Economic, Social, Technological, Legal and Environmental issues surrounding the case.
3. A SWOT analysis and its evaluation.
4. Product market analyses and the links to strategic marketing.
5. Analyses of a range of issues that pertain to the particular case study. Often case studies are not straightforward and different types of analyses are required. These may be more contemporary in nature.
6. Any constraints that the company faces from a resource point of view. These could be human, financial, technical or environmental.
7. Any structural features or control systems.
8. A list of key issues that emanate from the above.

The analyses

The key historical events that have contributed to the development of the company

Cases often contain a history of the company. It is important to analyse this history and to list the key critical events that helped to shape the company's development. At the same time an analysis of the history will also offer insights into the evolution of a particular industry as in the case of Acclaim Incorporated. Historical analysis and charting can help in understanding product market decisions and any development and diversification decisions that have been made by the company.

A PESTLE analysis

A PESTLE analysis looks at Political, Economic, Social, Technological, Legal and Environmental issues surrounding the case.

Cases will contain some or all of the key PESTLE factors. This type of analysis allows you to understand the macro-environment facing the industry sector that the company is immersed in. The Porter five forces framework allows a structured analysis of the environment and the competitive pressures on companies within the industry sector. The PESTLE factors also help to highlight key trends within the markets. Amongst others, these could be demographic profile trends, sociological issues, branding trends in different markets or ethics and sustainability issues (as in December 2004 case). Some of the technological factors may show up the lifecycle stages and any special factors affecting the lifecycle model. Analysing each of the factors gives some idea of the opportunities and threats facing a company.

A SWOT analysis and its evaluation

In addition to the PESTLE analysis, a review of the company's strengths and weaknesses is required. This is an internal audit of the company allowing you to examine each function in which the company is currently strong or weak. Companies could have a weakness in their branding strategies or new product development, yet may have current products which are well positioned in the market. Is a company in an overall strong position? Can it operate profitably in its current market sectors? How can the company minimize the threats to its position and expand on its opportunities? Can the company turn its weaknesses into strengths? A good SWOT analysis helps you to understand, in a clear and succinct manner, how the company is positioned. As part of this analysis, you may want to use the Porter five forces framework (Figure 2.1).

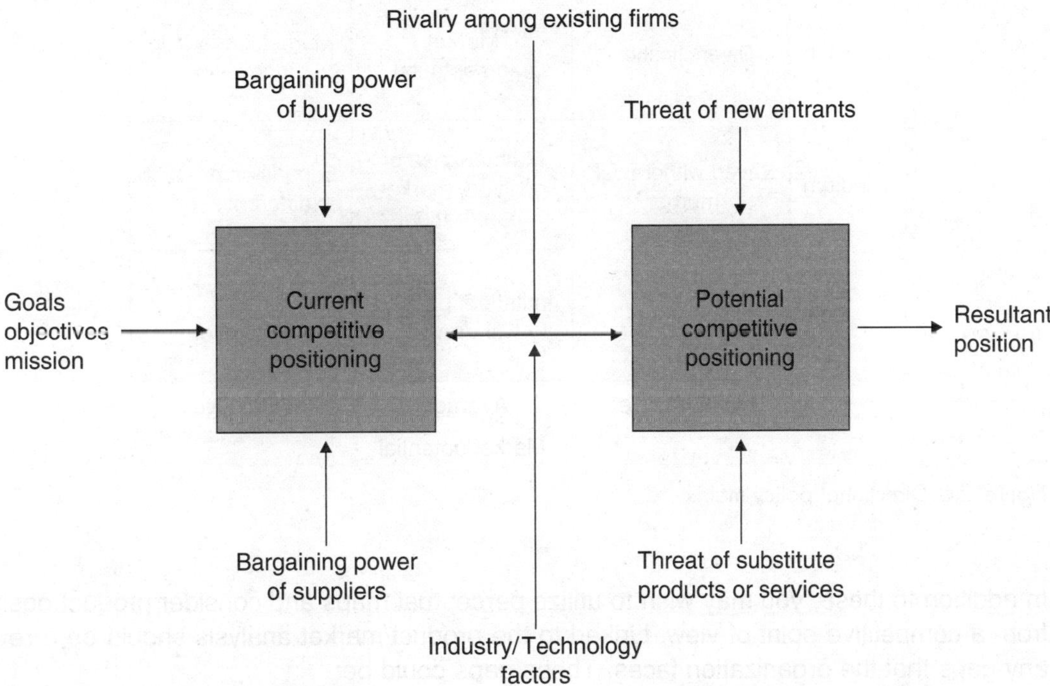

Figure 2.1 Porter framework

Product market analyses and the links to strategic marketing

Following on from the SWOT analysis, an analysis of the products and the markets within which the products and services are sold should be undertaken. This type of analysis will require you to be familiar with the various portfolio models such as the GE Matrix, the BCG matrix, the Ansoff matrix and various other relevant matrices. Below are examples of the expanded Ansoff Matrix (Figure 2.2), and Figure 2.3 shows the Directional Policy Matrix.

Product alternatives

Options	Present products	Improved products	New products
Existing market	Market penetration	Product variants imitations	Product line extention
Expanded market	Aggressive promotion	Market segmentation product	Vertical diversification
New market	Market development	Market extension	Conglomerate diversification

Figure 2.2 Growth vector analyses

Company capability	Unattractive	Average	Attractive
High	Diversification	Market segmentation	Market leadership innovation
Medium	Saved withdrawal; merger	Maintenance of position; market penetration	Expansion product differentiation
Low	Divestment	Imitation; phased withdrawal	Cash generation

Market potential

Figure 2.3 Directional policy matrix

In addition to these, you may wish to utilize perceptual maps and consider product positioning from a competitive point of view. Linked to the product/market analysis should be a review of any gaps that the organization faces. These gaps could be:

- *Product line gap* – Closing this gap entails completion of a product line, either in width or in depth, by introducing new or improved products.
- *Distribution gap* – This gap can be reduced by expanding the coverage, intensity, and exposure of distribution.
- *Usage gap* – To increase usage, a firm needs to induce current non-users to try the product and encourage current users to increase their usage.
- *Competitive gap* – This gap can be closed by making inroads into the market position of direct competitors as well as those who market substitute products.
- *Internationalization gap* – This gap can be shortened through exporting, joint venture arrangements and strategic alliances.
- *Communications gap* – This gap can be shortened through advertising strategies, PR, or proactive use of the Web.

SPACE analysis

All these analyses can be tied together by using SPACE analysis as discussed by the BCG group. SPACE stands for Strategic Position and Action Evaluation. This analysis is based on the following:

1. The company's Financial Strength (FS)
2. The company's Competitive Advantage (CA)
3. The Industry strength (The strength of the industry sector in which the company operates (IS))
4. The stability of the environment in which the company operates (ES).

This analysis is based on your ability to analyse key aspects of the case study, pertaining to the company. The analysis depends on answering a range of questions and then taking an average.

Step one analyses each aspect as shown above.

Financial strength (FS)

Factors determining financial strength									
Return on investment	Low	0	1	2	3	4	5	6	High
Leverage (Debt to equity ratio)	Low	0	1	2	3	4	5	6	High
Liquidity (cash held)	Low	0	1	2	3	4	5	6	High
Capital required/capital available	High	0	1	2	3	4	5	6	Low
Cash flow	Weak	0	1	2	3	4	5	6	Strong
Ease of exit from the market	Difficult	0	1	2	3	4	5	6	Easy
Risk involved in the business	Low	0	1	2	3	4	5	6	High
Other (your own factor)	Low	0	1	2	3	4	5	6	High
Average:									
Critical factors and your assessment of this area of the organization									

Competitive advantage (CA)

Factors determining competitive advantage									
Market share	Low	0	1	2	3	4	5	6	High
Product/Service quality (compared to competitors)	Low	0	1	2	3	4	5	6	High
Product life cycles stages (for range of products/services)	Similar	0	1	2	3	4	5	6	Different
Product/service replacement cycle	Variable	0	1	2	3	4	5	6	Fixed
Customer loyalty	Low	0	1	2	3	4	5	6	High
General utilization of capacity by the competition	Low	0	1	2	3	4	5	6	High
Technological knowledge and competence	Low	0	1	2	3	4	5	6	High
The degree of vertical integration of the company	Low	0	1	2	3	4	5	6	High
Other (your own factor)	Low	0	1	2	3	4	5	6	High

Average −6 =

Suppose the total score comes to 36. This divided by 8 factors = 4.5 take away 6 = −1.5 (So you will get a negative score for this factor)

Critical factors and your assessment of this area of the organization

Industry strength (IS)

Factors determining industry strength									
Growth potential	Low	0	1	2	3	4	5	6	High
Profit potential	Low	0	1	2	3	4	5	6	High
Financial stability (within the sector)	Low	0	1	2	3	4	5	6	High
Technological know-how (needed to operate within the sector)	Simple	0	1	2	3	4	5	6	Complex
Resource utilization (generally within the sector)	Poor	0	1	2	3	4	5	6	Good
Capital intensity (requisite capital for operating in the sector)	High	0	1	2	3	4	5	6	Low
Ease of entry into the market	Easy	0	1	2	3	4	5	6	Difficult
Level of productivity and capacity utilization	Low	0	1	2	3	4	5	6	High
Other (your choice of factor)	Low	0	1	2	3	4	5	6	High

Average:

Critical factors determining industry strength

Environmental stability (ES)

Factors determining environmental stability									
Technological changes	Many	0	1	2	3	4	5	6	Few
Rate of inflation	High	0	1	2	3	4	5	6	Low
Variability of demand	High	0	1	2	3	4	5	6	Low
Price range of competing products	Wide	0	1	2	3	4	5	6	Narrow
Barriers to entry into the market	Few	0	1	2	3	4	5	6	Many
Competitive pressure	High	0	1	2	3	4	5	6	Low
Price elasticity of demand	Elastic	0	1	2	3	4	5	6	Inelastic
Other (a factor of your own choice)									
Average −6 =									

Again for this assessment, suppose the average is 40, this divided by 8 = 5. Then 5 − 6 = −1 (a negative figure)

The key critical factors that determine environmental stability

Your analysis should then be plotted on the following axes in order to determine the strategic position of the company under question (Figure 2.4).

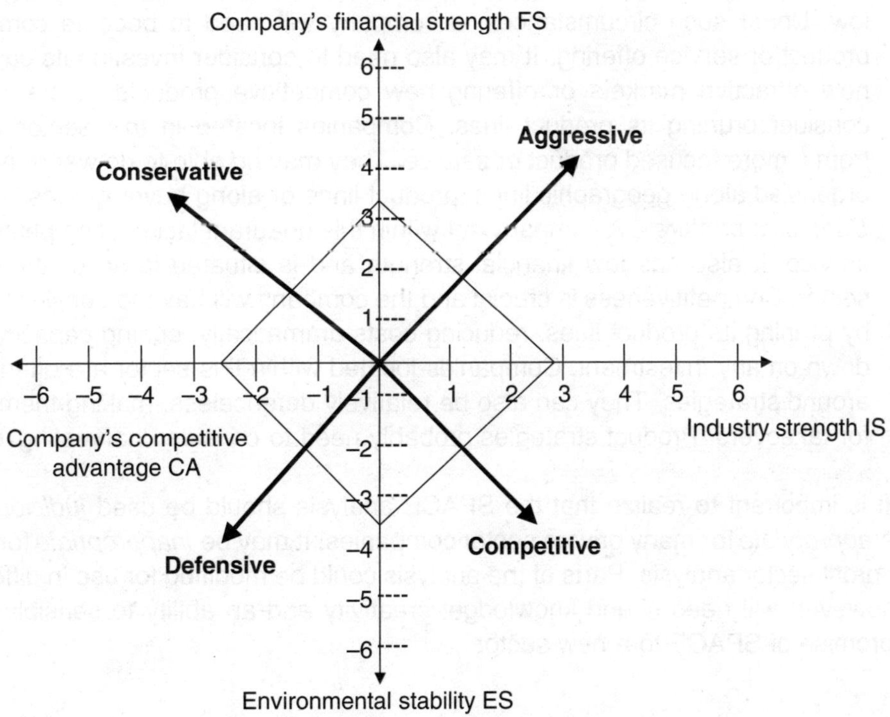

Figure 2.4 Strategic position and action evaluation space matrix

Once this analysis is done, you can plot the actual position of the company by just getting two points (one for the X axis and one for the Y axis). This can be easily obtained by adding CA and IS (you will either get a negative point or a positive point) and adding FS and ES (you will either get a negative point or a positive point). These two points will then determine the overall quadrant in which the company will fall.

The implications for falling within particular sectors are these: (always remember that this exercise should be quite objective and be based on as much real information that you can obtain as possible. Like any other real-life analysis you may also have to make certain assumptions).

(For all the examples it is assumed that the company positions are in the middle of each quadrant.)

1. *Aggressive posture* – In this quadrant, a company is set within an attractive industry which faces little environmental turbulence. The company enjoys a good competitive advantage which it can protect with good financial strength. As this sector is attractive, it is likely to attract new entrants. The company needs to protect its position through acquisitions, by increasing market share or by extending its lead in specific products and services in which it is the market leader. Companies in this sector have the potential to be cost leaders if they are in an FMCG market.
2. *Competitive posture* – In this quadrant, the industry is attractive and the company enjoys competitive advantage within a turbulent environment. The company needs to acquire financial strength. It needs to do this in order to improve its marketing and improve its product lines. It may also need to reduce costs and protect competitive advantage in a declining market. In such a quadrant, a company may need to look for cash resources either through merger or through being acquired. Companies in this area need to differentiate their product offerings and utilize their marketing skills as much as possible.
3. *Conservative posture* – If a company is positioned within this quadrant, it has a focus on financial stability within a stable market. The chances are that the growth is fairly low. Under such circumstances, a company will need to become competitive in its product or service offering. It may also need to consider investing its cash in entering new attractive markets or offering new competitive products. It may also need to consider pruning its product lines. Companies located in this sector would benefit from a more focused product or service. They may be able to do well in niche markets, organized along geographic lines, product lines or along buyer groups.
4. *Defensive posture* – A company set within this quadrant lacks a competitive product or service. It also has low financial strength and is situated in an unattractive industry sector. Competitiveness is crucial and the company will have to consider retrenchment by pruning its product lines, reducing costs dramatically, cutting capacity and slowing down on any investment. Companies located within this sector are often ripe for turnaround strategies. They can also be relatively defenceless, making them easy targets for takeovers. Product strategies probably need to consider 'harvesting' cash cows.

Note: It is important to realize that the SPACE analysis should be used *judiciously* as it may only be *appropriate* for many private sector companies. It may be *inappropriate* for public sector or non-profit sector analysis. Parts of the analysis could be modified for use in different sectors. This, however, will need sound knowledge, creativity and an ability to sensibly translate the basic premise of SPACE to a new sector.

Any constraints that the company faces from a resource point of view

Companies face a variety of constraints when developing their strategies. These constraints could be market constraints (size and growth potential of a market), financial constraints (the ability to finance marketing campaigns, foster new product development, cash flow, ability to raise money, etc.), technical (the ability to develop new products, to market products, manage information systems, Web capability) and finally environmental (these could be pollution management capability, or public concerns as in the case of GM Foods in Biocatalysts).

Any structural features or control systems

Analyses should include an understanding of the present structural pattern of the organization and the way in which this contributes to or detracts from developing its marketing strategies. For instance, is there a defined marketing structure? Are there systems for monitoring marketing effectiveness or orientation? Are the systems rigid or flexible?

Key issues

As a result of these analyses, you should be able to list a number of key issues which are facing the company described in the case study. These key issues form a valuable resource when answering the questions set in the examination.

These type of analyses can then be linked to any *strategic plan* that you may have considered developing.

A generalized approach to formulating strategies would probably contain the following:

1. *Statement of the problem* – This will contain a situation analysis of the company, its problem areas and its general capability.
2. *Analysis of data*

    (a) *Industry* – This would cover an analysis of the growth potential, SWOT, market structure and competitive pressures.
    (b) *Product/Service analysis* – This would consider areas such as market share, pricing, promotion, new product development, distribution, branding and level of market orientation of the company.
    (c) *Financial analysis* – The financial performance of a company gives guidelines on its profitability, return on investment, shareholder value, liquidity, inventory levels and possible resource requirements for growth (see section on Financial Analysis).
    (d) *Management* – If organization charts are available, any gaps in the marketing structure should be ascertained. Also, issues such as mission, values and objectives should be taken into account.

3. *Generation of options and an evaluation of these* – In this section, the options regarding entry into different product/market sectors, strategic alliances, branding strategies, R&D development, internationalization, joint ventures, diversification, vertical or horizontal integration.
4. *Recommendations (Decisions) and strategies* – This should be the crucial element of the plan, encompassing key decisions that may be taken, giving reasons for choosing these, understanding the possible reactions to these by competitors and the justifications for these. Resource implications also need to be considered. Clear and decisive objectives must be set.
5. *Implementation, contingency and control* – This section should look at how easily the recommendations could be adopted, taking into account resource allocation, cost implications, budgets and timetables. This section should also envisage contingency requirements in case of difficulties regarding implementation strategies. When considering implementation, it is also important to develop monitoring systems for ascertaining the success of the recommended strategies.

Summary

When evaluating a case, it is important to be systematic. Analyse the case in a logical fashion, beginning with the identification of operating and financial strengths and weaknesses and environmental opportunities and threats. Move on to assess the value of a company's current strategies only when you are fully conversant with the SWOT analysis of the company. Ask yourself whether the company's current strategies make sense, given its SWOT analysis. If they do not, then what changes need to be made? What are your recommendations? Above all, link any strategic recommendations you may make to the SWOT and GAP analyses. State explicitly, how the strategies you identify take advantage of the company's strengths to exploit environmental opportunities, how they rectify the company's weaknesses, and how they counter any of the threats from the PESTLE factors. It is also important that you consider the strategic options that may be available to the organization. Some of the options may not be feasible, suitable or acceptable in the light of the points you will have covered above. Make sure that you outline the strategies that need to be adopted to implement any recommendations that you make. Many company strategies fail as a result of poor implementation or unrealistic expectations of market growth and demand. You, therefore, have to be aware that your recommendations are sensible and fit the existing resource base and capability of the firm. Remember that this chapter only gives you an indicative and not a comprehensive range of analytical tools. You need to read widely and use other new analytical tools that may be available, including your own ideas. In the first SMiP case, candidates needed to utilize new types of analyses to bolster their arguments and examples of these are incorporated in the book. You must also be familiar with all aspects of the syllabi in the other Professional Postgraduate Diploma modules. Further ideas are given in Chapter 4. Finally, remember that for the SMiP syllabus, you have to prepare analyses *before the examination* (as explained in Unit 1).

unit 3 understanding the direction and management of marketing activities

Outcomes

- Demonstrate an understanding of the direction and management of marketing activities as part of the implementation of strategic direction, taking into account business intelligence requirements, marketing processes, resources, markets and the company vision.

Introduction

This outcome knits together a range of different areas of marketing. Marketing is a complex area of business and for successful implementation it is important for marketers to develop strategic direction for an organization, taking into account marketing intelligence in conjunction with company resources and processes. The importance of developing a vision is also very important when developing a strategic focus. This helps an organization to develop a clear direction. Strategy in marketing involves harnessing a company's resources to meet customer needs through market analysis – an understanding of competitor actions, governmental actions and globalization, together with consideration of technological and other environmental changes.

Business Intelligence

The development and organization of Marketing Intelligence Systems has always been an important aspect of marketing. Market Intelligence can be gathered in several ways. Companies can gather information from secondary sources and reports produced by companies such as Mintel and AC Neilson or commission primary research. An example of primary research is provided by the following mini case (taken from a previous CIM Case Study – Titan).

Case study

Titan's Brand Image in India

Over the last 5 years, consumers have consistently regarded Titan as one of the top brands in India. In 1998, Titan was regarded as the most admired consumer goods company in a survey carried out by Advertising Marketing in India. Titan's history in the polls has been outstanding as Tables 3.1 and 3.2 indicate.

Table 3.1 Company rankings over 6 years in India 1993–1999

Company	1999	1998	1997	1996	1995	1994	1993
FMCG companies							
HLL	1	1	1	1	1	1	1
Coca-Cola	2	7	9	11	13	16	–
Cadbury	3	8	3	3	6	7	6
Pepsi foods	4	3	5	4	7	6	11
Colgate	5	9	6	5	4	5	5
Durables' companies							
Titan	1	1	2	1	1	1	1
BPL	2	2	1	5	3	3	5
Maruti	3	4	5	2	–	–	–
Intel	–	–	–	–	–	–	–
LG Electronics	5	11	–	–	–	–	–

Source: Advertising, Marketing, e-Commerce, India

Table 3.2 Most admired durable brands in India 1998/1999

Rank 1999	Rank 1998	Company	Score	Rank 1999	Rank 1998	Company	Score
1	1	Titan	7.96	19	26	Compaq	6.62
2	2	BPL	7.76	20	21	Eureka Forbes	6.6
3	4	Maruti	7.55	21	24	Carrier Aircon	6.51
4	–	Intel	7.47	22	9	Ericsson	6.5
5	11	LG Electronics	7.39	23	12	Philips	6.5
6	7	Godrej-GE	7.13	24	15	Modi Xerox	6.43
7	3	MRF	7.07	25	29	Videocon	6.41
8	13	Bajaj Auto	7.05	26	23	Chloride India (Exide)	6.38
9	13	Hero Honda	6.96	27	20	HCL Infosystems	6.22
10	5	Asian Paints	6.95	28	21	LML	6.16
11	24	Hewlett-Packard	6.9	29	27	Mahindra and Mahindra	6.1
12	18	Samsung	6.82	30	31	Hero Cycles	6.07
13	18	Whirlpool	6.81	31	33	Onida	5.93
14	15	TVS Suzuki	6.79	32	17	Bausch and Lomb	5.92
15	6	Nokia	6.78	33	30	Goodlass Nerolac	5.86
16	–	Telco	6.67	34	9	Motorola	5.85
17	–	Infosys	6.63	35	8	Baron International	5.82
17	28	Wipro Infotech	6.63	36	32	Blow Past	5.61

Source: Advertising, Marketing, e-Commerce, India

In 1999, the Advertising and Marketing Survey was carried out by IMRB, along the same lines as the previous 7 years in order to maintain continuity and establish the survey's validity in enabling comparisons with previous years. The surveys were carried out exclusively among professional marketers in companies marketing FMCG and durables. Respondents were drawn from all levels and conducted in the major cities of Delhi, Calcutta, Chennai and Bangalore. The company received top positions when the following questions were asked:

1. Products are designed to meet customer needs (7.88).
2. Products are different from competitors (7.25).
3. Better than average at new product launches (7.59).
4. Brands provide long-term stability (7.52).
5. Products are market leaders (7.91).
6. Products are innovative (number 2 slot) (7.32).
7. Products are consistently superior to competitors (7.51).
8. Products offer value for money (7.66).
9. Company's Marketing personnel are of high calibre (7.20).
10. Company's advertising is consistently superior (number 2 slot) (7.53).
11. Company keeps in touch with market constantly (7.4).
12. Company has a superior distribution network (7.78).
13. Provides good after-sales service (number 2 slot) (7.43) (figures in brackets are scores out of 10).

As can be seen, Titan retained its leadership position. Working in its favour was its product launches into new segments, including the Dash! Range for children. In 2000, an Economic Times survey of top Indian companies revealed that Titan was regarded as the top brand in India, ahead of all FMCG companies. A consumer brand is much more than a bundle of tangible and intangible benefits. For this particular survey, seven attributes were considered:

1. The quality of the brand
2. Value for money
3. The future of the brand
4. Distinctiveness
5. Uniqueness
6. The feelings that the brand evokes amongst the consumer
7. How inclined the consumers were to purchase the brand.

The target audience for the survey were, chief wage earners, housewives and young adults between the ages of 15–45 years belonging to the A/B/C households in urban India. In general, the brands are less well known in rural India. A ten-point scale was applied and a total of 3164 interviews were conducted, in the following locations: Mumbai (537), Delhi (520), Calcutta (423), Chennai (409), Rajkot (345), Allahabad (300), Cuttack (300) and Vijayawada (330). The brand received such success because it appeals to the youth segment and is aspirational. Titan, in India, is also known for its classy elegance, while being a popular mass-market brand with a strong presence at the lower end. The brand is regarded as 'mass with class' by brand consultants. It is a brand that is also equally popular with both men and women. The company is consistent in its brand expenditure and spends, on average, around Rs. 25/30 crore on brand building. Although this is small compared to others within the top 10, the amount spent appears to be highly effective.

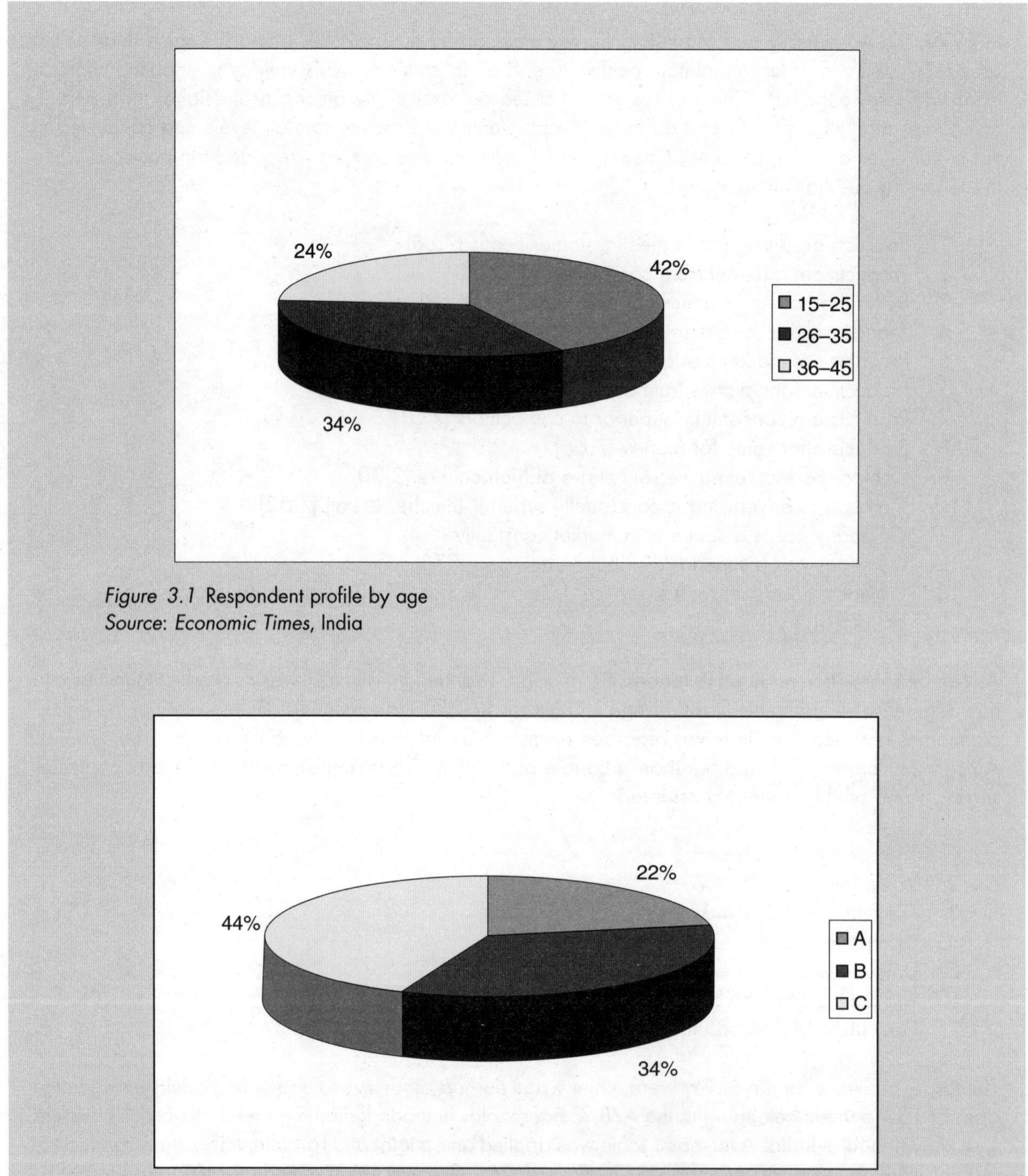

Figure 3.1 Respondent profile by age
Source: *Economic Times*, India

Figure 3.2 Socio-economic classes surveyed

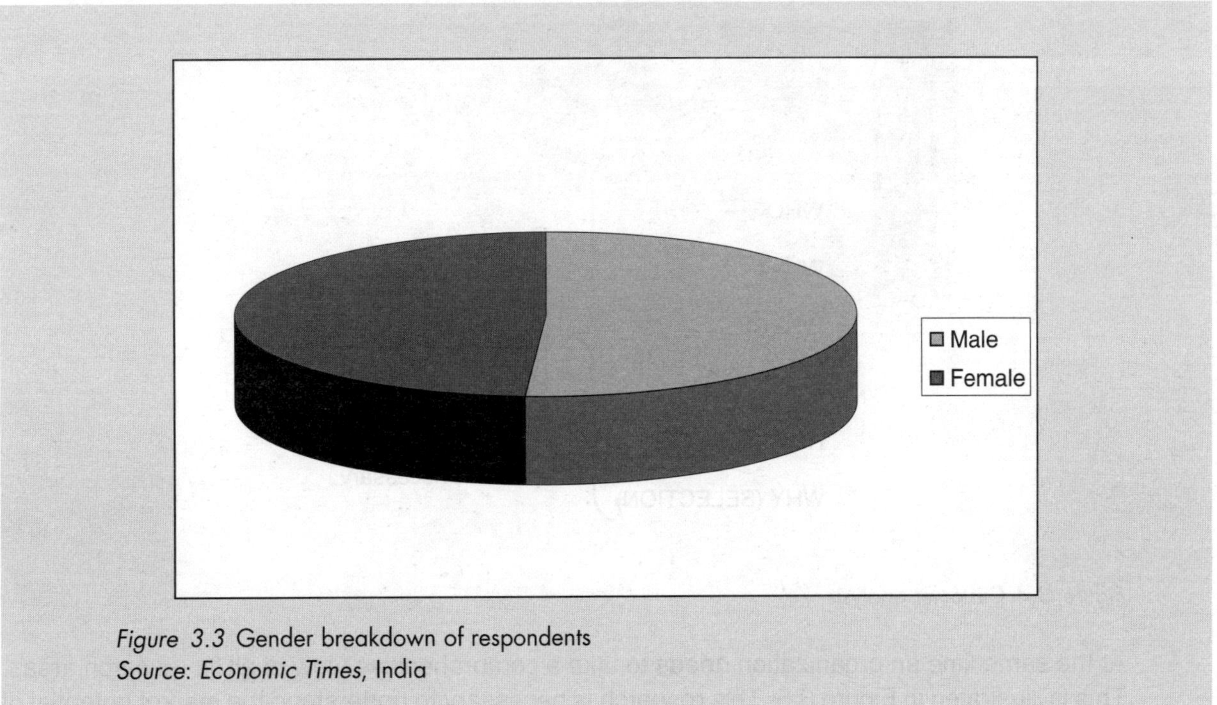

Figure 3.3 Gender breakdown of respondents
Source: *Economic Times*, India

The above excerpt shows the usefulness of primary research carried out by various agencies to Titan. The company could also carry out its own primary research by commissioning agencies to carry out work on customer satisfaction or design of the watches.

Primary research

Good market research provides a good foundation in formulating successful marketing strategy. Conducted carefully, qualitative primary market research studies can yield insights on issues such as product usage patterns, unmet needs, product positioning, and pricing – all of which are central to strategy formulation and decision-making.

Effective qualitative primary market research

The effectiveness of qualitative primary market research depends on how it is carried out and it can be improved by concentrating on the following issues:

Focus on strategic marketing decisions

All aspects of the research study, from questionnaire design to recruitment and analysis, should fit together and be focused clearly on developing information, insights and understanding for strategic decision-making.

Quality of respondents

Data collected in any primary research is only as good as the respondents interviewed. In this respect, respondents should be identified and screened carefully to ensure that each interview increases confidence in the findings.

Building confidence

In all market research studies it is important to develop confidence in the study's findings. In qualitative research such confidence is achieved, as data accumulates to build a believable 'picture' of the study area, and findings from different respondents are in substantial agreement. It may be advisable to conduct both quantitative and qualitative research so that each area complements the other. Figure 3.4 illustrates the key points that need to be understood when researching customers.

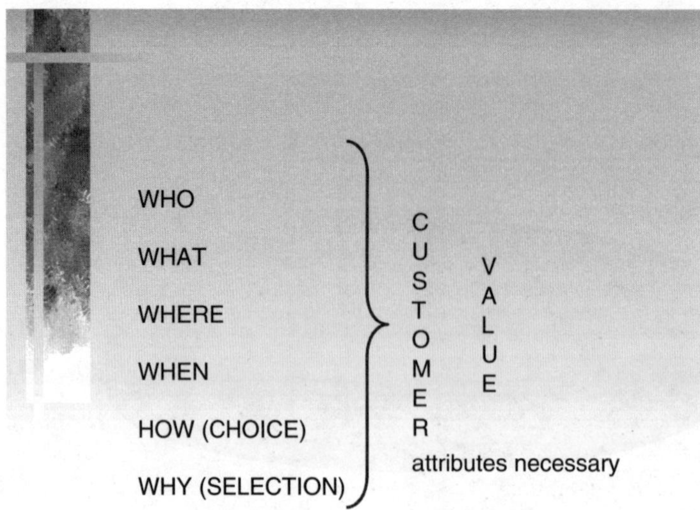

Figure 3.4 Customer analysis

At the same time an organization needs to take a comprehensive view of all its research areas. This is illustrated in Figure 3.5. This research is necessary to understand the market potential of products and services. Market Research in conjunction with market intelligence helps an organization to develop effective marketing strategies. Success depends on information about a particular market segment, a geographic area or customer preferences, enabling better targeting.

Mini case

Marketing campaigns impact on consumer habits

Andy Farquarson looks at the way partnerships between business and charities leave their mark on the consumer.

Cause-related marketing campaigns are having a significant impact on consumer habits and are bringing benefits to both businesses and the charities they link up with, according to new research. This latest study looks for the first time at how people respond to such campaigns – rather than how they think they would.

The key finding is surprisingly high public awareness of campaigns such as Tesco's donation of computers to schools, Avon's support for breast cancer research, or the Andrex puppy appeal in association with the National Canine Defence League. Almost 90 per cent of those surveyed had heard of at least one cause-related programme and almost half could spontaneously name a specific company or brand involved in a campaign. Two in three people believed more businesses should get involved. Against this, however, a small percentage felt cause related marketing was exploitative, or that it was inappropriate for business to become involved in social issues.

Until now, research into the effectiveness of cause related marketing campaigns has focused on consumers' attitudes, rather than their actions. The new study, Profitable Partnerships, was commissioned by Business in the Community (BITC) and is based on a survey of 2000 adults by the British Market Research Bureau. While previous work has established that a majority of people support the concept of cause related marketing, and would probably express that support in their purchasing choices, the fresh research indicates that this broad approval is affecting consumers' choices.

More than 65 per cent of respondents said they had participated in a cause related marketing campaign. Of them, three-quarters had either switched brand, tried out a product or increased their usage; and four in five had felt more positive about certain purchases, more loyal to a company or brand, and more inclined to look out for further cause related campaigns. Although 30 per cent of respondents were regular Internet users, comparatively few had found cause related marketing campaigns on the web. Old media predominated, with awareness of campaigns garnered through in-store promotion (23 per cent), television commercials (18 per cent) and advertisements in print media (11 per cent).

Cause related marketing is defined as any partnership between a business and charity which markets an image, product or service for mutual benefit. 'This is not about corporate philanthropy,' says Sue Adkins, BITC's director of marketing. 'It's about commercial benefit for both cause and company. Any business which tries to project this sort of campaign as strings-free giving is heading for a fall; the public is not gullible.' A good match between partners is also vital, says Adkins. Unless campaigns are properly managed, and based on integrity and transparency, they can be counter-productive.

The new report does not specify what constitutes a 'good' campaign. Among a wide variety of factors cited by those surveyed were schemes that supported local community activity, a high level of donation or support for the project or charity and clearly communicated, unambiguous benefits. Tesco's 'computers for schools' initiative is a good example of such clarity, argues Adkins. It has delivered more than £30 million of computer equipment to schools, raised Tesco's profile (more than 40 per cent of adults know about the initiative), and bolstered public perception of the company as a good corporate citizen.

Unsurprisingly, Tim Mason, Tesco's marketing director, welcomes the BITC findings. 'Successful marketing is all about meeting customer needs and most consumers expect companies to be socially responsible,' he says. 'That's what is driving the rapid growth of cause related marketing and I am sure that growth will continue for the foreseeable future.' Marketing departments may formulate corporate strategies, but it is the advertising industry that gets the messages across to consumers. So it is hardly surprising that advertising agencies are establishing specialist teams to provide cause related marketing expertise to their clients.

One of the longest established is Saatchi & Saatchi's 'cause connection', set up in 1997 by Marjorie Thompson (who worked both in the public and voluntary sectors before joining Saatchis). 'There are huge opportunities to develop cause related marketing in the UK,' says Thompson. 'For instance, government could provide much more in the way of match-funding and tax breaks to encourage good corporate citizenship. That would help charities gain long-term funding and exploit the expertise of the communications profession to promote their missions and messages.'

Note: Profitable Partnerships is available at £75, or £50 to registered charities, from BITC, 44 Baker St, London W1M 1DH. Further information at www.bitc.org.uk.

Source: *The Guardian*, Wednesday, 15 November 2000.

This article indicates the way in which market research can be utilized by companies to boost their corporate image.

Secondary research

This type of research is based on information gleaned from studies previously performed by government agencies, chambers of commerce, trade associations and other organizations. This includes Census Bureau information and Nielsen ratings. Such information is now readily available through the World Wide Web. In some instances, detailed reports are produced for industry sectors by major agencies such as the Gartner group. However, these are quite expensive to purchase.

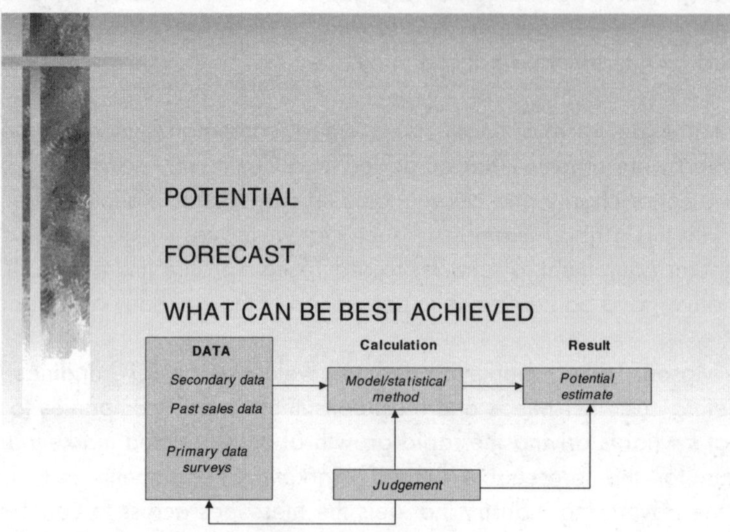

Figure 3.5 Market potential and forecasting

Although secondary research is less expensive than primary research, it is not as accurate, or as useful, as specific, customized research. For instance, secondary research may help a shoe manufacturer to understand the number of shoes sold within a country. However, pricing data, the impact of shoe design or how well the brand is accepted, may not be available. This is where primary research can be used to obtain more specific information. Organizations rely on information systems and this aspect is summarized in Figure 3.6. An organization, as it develops and grows has much historical information that it can draw from its archives. Often interesting information lies hidden until it is analysed. Market Intelligence is drawn from company sources, customers, salesforce, secondary information, commissioned research and the Internet. All the information has to be drawn together to form a Marketing Decision Support System.

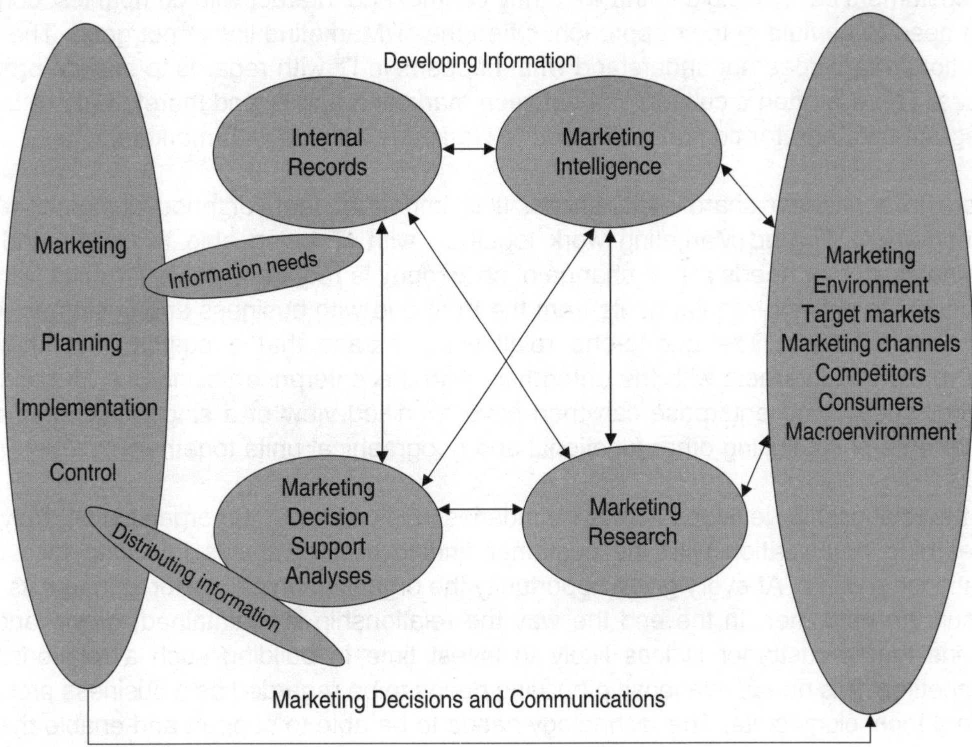

Figure 3.6 Marketing information system
Source: Adapted from Kotler (1992)

The role of information technology

In the last decade, information technology has become a very important part of a marketer's armoury. There is little in marketing that does not incorporate information technology. Market intelligence can therefore be gathered in many ways (Ranchhod, 2004):

(a) Salesmen, on the road, can be updated on customer requirements as necessary. This information can be used for enhancing CRM and logistics.

(b) As mobile devices become more sophisticated, customers will be able to access inventories of their suppliers. This means that they can place orders and specify delivery times. This can be done via links to an intranet or the Internet. Well-organized companies can gather and store this information.

(c) Individuals, apart from talking to others, will also be able to communicate with machines. This is already a reality with consumers being able to buy soft drinks, chocolates and car washes via mobile devices. Data on consumption patterns can be stored.

(d) Consumers will be able to pay for restaurants, meals via secure transactions through a mobile device.

(e) The 'blue-tooth' devices can enable retailers to market special offers to customers on their mobile devices if they are within a twenty-metre radius. This will also allow customers to undertake transactions with shops and restaurants.

(f) Radio will become an integral part of the mobile device, allowing an individual access to a myriad of radio stations. This also has implications for advertising and branding.

(g) The incorporation of GPS into mobile devices (Ground Positioning Systems, via satellite) means that individuals will be able to easily locate their positions and also the nearest outlets or services that they need.

As customers become fluid in the way they contact and interact with companies, companies in turn need to be fluid in their approach. Often the IT/Marketing link is not good. The marketing function, often, does not understand what happens in IT with regards to service provision and prices. There is often a cultural gap between marketing and IT and therefore there is a need to integrate data and for computer experts to work side by side with marketers.

There is a need to share experiences. It is important that for good customer relationship management, IT and Marketing work together, with IT being able to understand what the internal customer needs are. A change of philosophy is required, where IT shifts from 'building solutions' to defining requirements from the front end with business and customers in building the best solutions. The one-to-one relationship means that a customer is known to the enterprise and interacts with the enterprise, with the enterprise flexing and changing to meet his/her needs. The enterprise can then have a unified view of a single customer across the entire enterprise, linking other functional and geographical units together.

As the relationship develops across boundaries, it is clear that the organization, truly becomes a learning organization with the customer finding that he/she is investing in a continuing relationship with it. At every given opportunity the organization can 'tailor' and refit its behaviour to suit the customer. In the end the way the relationship is maintained, grown and nurtured means that a customer is less likely to invest time in building such a relationship with a competitor. This needs relationship building needs to be regarded as a business process rather than a technology suite. The technology needs to be able to support and enable this process.

The learning organization and market-based learning

The learning organization can 'learn' in different ways. An organization can be adaptive to its environment, thereby learning from the subtle changes taking place in the marketplace. In other instances an organization can become efficient in the way it utilizes information, developing information processing patterns that can enable it 'read' the changes taking place in the marketplace and change its behaviour patterns accordingly. Authors such as Senge (1990) view a learning organization as a continuously creative, innovative organization, where each member is an active participant within the learning process. This allows for continuous learning and flexibility.

Learning is often constrained (single-loop learning) at a low level or it is of a higher, creative order where cognitive learning takes place (double-loop learning).

Single-loop learning

It is easy for organizations to be conditioned by single-loop learning. In many instances, companies have to adjust to specific demands in the market and often they will have well-developed strategies to cope with this. Single-loop learning is also prevalent within functional areas of businesses as bureaucratic systems are in place to deal with orders and demands. These are routine patterns and are triggered by particular stimuli within the environment. The marketing function in a chocolate company, for instance, will respond to low demand by spending more on advertising. In general short-term tactical issues are dealt with efficiently. Single-loop learning does not stretch to questioning the phenomena that create the response (i.e. why are the chocolate sales low?), it merely sets in motion patterned responses to external pressures.

Single-loop learning is often constrained by a learning 'boundary'. This is not unusual or undesirable. In many instances, companies serve particular markets and they have to focus on these markets to deal with them efficiently and to give customers satisfaction. This efficiency in the marketplace can create rigid adherence to organized approaches and leave little to the imagination. The way in which the business is conceptualized guides core capabilities. However, in many instances these could become 'core rigidities' and can just concentrate on the served market, fostering quite a narrow perspective. Therefore an adaptive approach (single-loop) is usually sequential, incremental and focused on issues or opportunities within the traditional scope of the organization's activities. This leaves little room for imagination and for any moves towards more interesting and potentially lucrative areas of business.

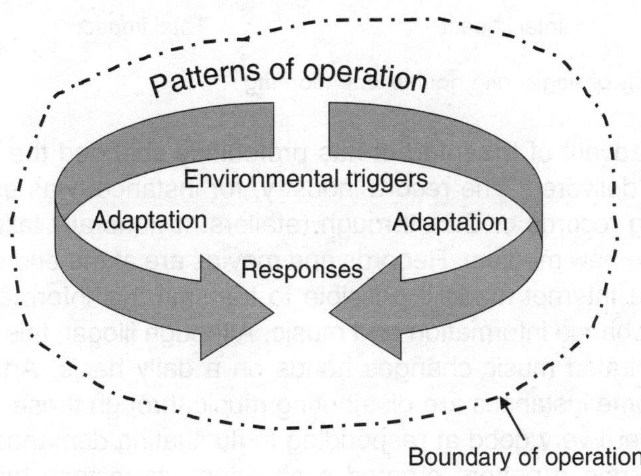

Figure 3.7 Single-loop learning

Double-loop learning

This higher level of learning affects the whole organization and is rarely contained within functional areas. It entails a deeper challenge to routine practices and rules. This type of generative learning shows a willingness to question long-held assumptions about mission, customers, capabilities or strategy. Often this is based on systems thinking and works through existing relationships, linking key issues and events. When an organization begins to embrace 'double-loop' learning, interrelationships and dynamic processes of change are important. Often a learning organization adept at double-loop learning can take advantage of 'windows' of opportunity that may be available to organizations. Often slower moving organizations that have 'fixed' views of markets and their role within them may fail to take advantage of these opportunities.

Higher-level learning usually occurs during some types of crisis, for example: new strategy, new leader, and significant changes in the market. It corresponds to the development of a new frame of reference(s). One of the consequences of a double-loop learning organization is the necessity to 'unlearn' an old process as old frames are longer efficient in coping with the new reality.

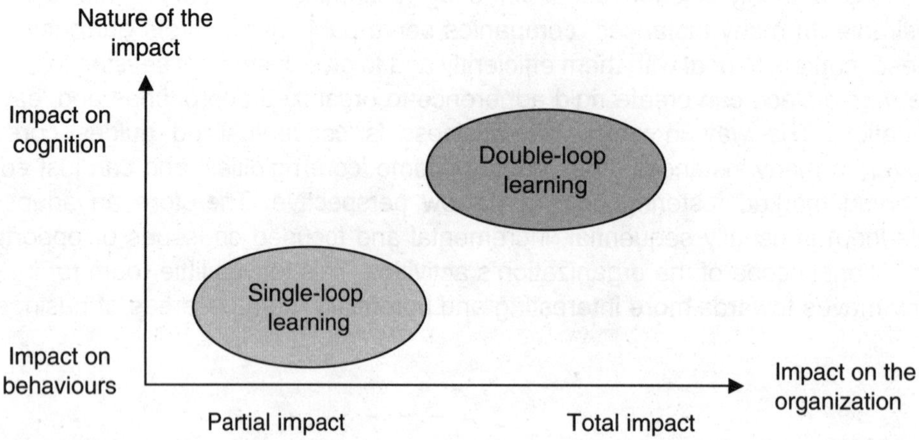

Figure 3.8 The impacts of single- and double-loop learning

For instance, the advent of the Internet has profoundly changed the way in which music and entertainment are delivered. The record industry, for instance, was essentially stuck in its old paradigm of selling records or CDs through retailers. It generally failed to grasp the opportunities offered by the new medium. Records and movies are at the end of the day essentially bits of information. The Internet made it possible to transmit this information globally. Individuals began to freely exchange information and music. Although illegal, this still occurs regularly and vast amounts of pirated music changes hands on a daily basis. Artists now have their own websites and in some instances are distributing music through these sites. The music companies, in general, were very good at responding to fluctuating demands in the marketplace, but the single-loop response pattern created a situation where they failed to see the changes beyond their own self made 'boundaries'. No sensible Internet strategies were therefore developed. This has led to much heartache and refocusing within the sector. Music can now be stored on CDs, mobiles, Mpeg players, memory sticks and computer hard disks, making the one-dimensional approach to music sales obsolete. The same is true for television programmes and films.

A company's intelligence gathering system needs to be flexible and wide ranging so that old paradigms are constantly challenged. A true learning organization, therefore will, place great value on information transmission contributing to general learning. This will depend on the following:

- *Knowledge acquisition* – Converting data into knowledge that can be understood and assimilated.
- *Information distribution* – Distributing information and knowledge throughout the organization.
- *Information interpretation* – Understanding the information and interpreting it so that sensible opinions can be formed.
- *Organizational memory* – Understanding the new knowledge and embedding it in the organization's memory.

Organizations need to learn from the markets that they operate in so that the organizational memory consists of market-based learning (see Figure 3.9).

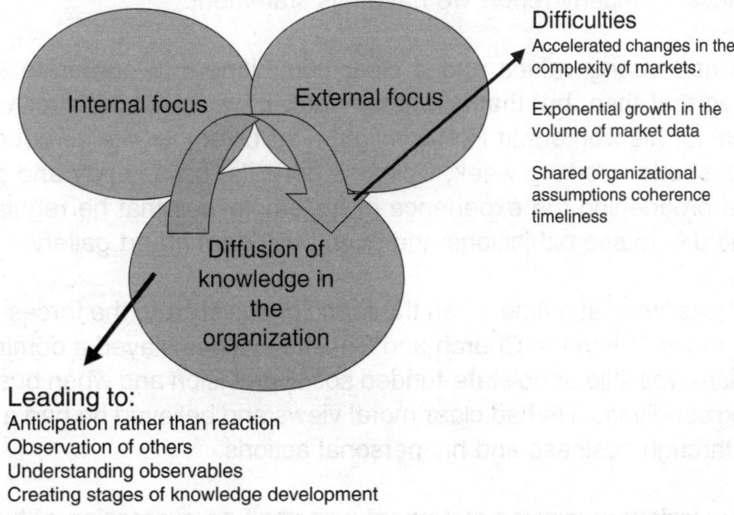

Figure 3.9 Market-based learning

In order to achieve some sort of shared purpose so that organizations benefit from learning, a mission statement can be of benefit, provided its scope is not too narrow and constricting. Pearce and David (1987) suggested that a mission statement should contain the following aspects:

1. Customers (the target market)
2. Products/services (offerings and value provided to customers)
3. Geographic markets (where the firm seeks customers)
4. Technology (the technology used to produce and market products)
5. Concern for survival/growth/profits (the firm's concern for being financially sound)
6. Philosophy (the firm's values, ethics, beliefs)
7. Public image (contributions the firm makes to communities)
8. Employees (the importance of managers and employees)
9. Distinctive competence (how the firm is better or different compared to its competitors).

Each of these points covers aspects of the organization where information and learning are important. A broad encompassing statement can, therefore, be quite helpful to an organization.

Some examples of Mission statements:

The Co-operative Bank have this as their ecological statement:

However, we undertake to continually assess all our activities and implement a programme of ecological improvement based on the pursuit of the following scientific principles:

- Nature cannot withstand a progressive build-up of waste derived from the Earth's crust.
- Nature cannot withstand a progressive build-up of society's waste, particularly artificial persistent substances which it cannot degrade into harmless materials.
- The productive area of Nature must not be diminished in quality (diversity) or quantity (volume) and must be enabled to grow.

Society must utilize energy and resources in a sustainable, equitable and efficient manner.

We consider that the pursuit of these principles constitutes a path of ecological excellence and will secure future prosperity for society by sustainable economic activity.

The Co-operative Bank will not only pursue the above path itself, but endeavour to help and encourage all its partners to do likewise.

From the Unilever company report we have this statement:

Our founders had strong values and a clear commitment to corporate social responsibility, (it wasn't called that then, but that is what it was). It was William Lever who famously built a 'garden village' for his workers at Port Sunlight near Liverpool. He introduced such pioneering initiatives as a shorter working week, sickness benefits, holiday pay and pensions. He felt so strongly about broadening the experience of his employees that he regularly took them all to London for the day to see exhibitions and even built them an art gallery.

William Lever was living at a time when the fabric of society and the forces in society were very different from today. When the Church and Christian values played a dominant role in people's lives, when there was little or no state-funded social provision and when businesses operated in often appalling conditions. He had clear moral views and believed he had a moral responsibility to help, both through business and his personal actions.

Indeed his very visionary mission statement was itself an expression of his values:

> *'To make cleanliness commonplace; to lessen work for women; to foster health and contribute to personal attractiveness, that life may be more enjoyable and rewarding for the people who use our products.'*

From Cadburys we have the following:

- Promote social housing of good quality which enhances the environment
- Manage all their housing and estates to the highest standards for all residents
- Encourage residents to share in decisions affecting their communities.

Each of the above examples are very good examples of mission statements where Corporate Social Responsibility is taken into account. Mission statements can be quite varied and address different issue. Often all the issues discussed by Pearce and Webb are rarely addressed.

Summary

This chapter considers the importance of having a mission for an organization and subsequently organizing for information acquisition and dissemination. It is clear that an organization with a well-developed sense of direction has the opportunity to create learning situations. Organizations have to learn and grow and base their learning on particular insights gained from the market. Technology also has an important role to play in the dissemination of knowledge and organizational learning.

References

Ranchhod, A. (2004) *Marketing Strategies: A Twenty-first Century Approach*, Harlow: Pearson Education Ltd.

Senge, P.M. (1990) 'The leader's new work: Building learning organizations', *Strategic Management Review*, Fall, pp. 7–23.

unit 4 contemporary issues in marketing

Outcomes

This unit is concerned with aspects of the outcome:

- Assess the relevance of opportunities presented by contemporary marketing issues within any given scenario including innovations in marketing.

In attempting to look at this outcome, this unit offers an insight into several Contemporary Issues, such as Relationship Marketing, Key Account Management, Sustainability in Marketing, branding and Corporate Identity.

Introduction

Several environmental factors are combining to bring pressure upon companies to adopt more elaborate strategies to differentiate themselves from close competitors. There are many reasons for this. The following section makes brief references to some of them.

Similarity of core products

Compared to a few decades ago there now numerous suppliers of goods and services offering identical or very similar products. Most consumer products, and consumer goods in particular, can now be made not just by so many companies but by so many nations. There is a fierce competition in the marketplace for customers of most products.

International trade and globalization

Barriers to international trade are constantly coming down and coupled with the adoption of free trade and business practices by most of the previously socialist/communist countries, an increasing number of companies are entering the international trade arena adding to competition in the marketplace. Monopolies, state subsidies and protected industries are becoming things of the past, and almost every company must now fight for its share of customers. The work of the World Trade Organisation (WTO) and also creation of trading blocs, for example the EU, are major drivers of this process.

Increasing customer awareness

Customers are now much better positioned than ever before to collect information on companies, products, prices and all that they are interested in with respect to their purchases. Today information technology brings the world markets into consumers' homes at the touch of a button, making them more aware and more demanding.

Additionally, customers, or at least some of them, are showing increased awareness of the impact of capitalism and marketing on the environment and on consumers. Corporate social responsibility, with its many branches, for example green marketing, are contemporary issues that organizations have to deal with.

Increasing consumer protection legislation

In response to pressure groups, and consumers in general, governments are increasingly putting legal measures into place to protect consumers, as well as the environment. In many instances such measures are international or regional, for example labelling laws emanating from the EU.

Increased mergers, alliances and takeovers

Increasing number of mergers, alliances and takeovers means that organizations are in danger of losing their identities and consequently many of their customers.

As a response to the circumstances described above, many companies are making serious attempts to differentiate themselves and to gain or maintain competitive advantage. To these companies the issues relating to branding, relationship building, corporate social responsibility and developing a strong corporate identity are of vital importance, since these are key tools in differentiation. This chapter discusses these topics.

Relationship marketing

The last couple of decades witnessed the growing importance of relationship marketing within both the academic and practitioner fields. Numerous authors enthusiastically sang the praises of the so-called 'new approach' to marketing, some even calling it a new paradigm. The 1990s, in particular, saw the adoption of the term, if not the real practice, by many organizations. In the early years there were many different interpretations of the concept and it meant different things to different people. While the plethora of different definitions still exist and it cannot be claimed that there is a unanimous agreement about the concept, there is slowly a form of consensus appearing. Authors and practitioners are finding common ground as to what relationship marketing is and what it is not.

Misconceptions about relationship marketing

Many of the practitioners who attempted to adopt relationship marketing, particularly those in the fields of database and direct marketing, now realize that putting a customer's name on a communication does not mean you are in a relationship with that customer. Nor does holding customers' details and profiles and sending them regular mail shots herald the dawn of a relationship. Even a customer who comes back on a regular basis is not necessarily in a relationship of any significance with the organization. You may visit your local supermarket because it is convenient to do so but not want any dialogue or partnership or relationship of any kind with that supermarket. A relationship, in business terms, requires a voluntary patronage of a supplier by a customer over time, when there are other choices available to that customer. In addition, a relationship has to be seen as such by both parties and a company's perceived relationship with its customers is hollow if the latter do not consider themselves to be loyal to, or in a relationship with, that organization.

Many organizations have also begun to recognize that relationship marketing is not an add-on to their existing strategy and ways of doing business, but that it is a philosophy which has to be embraced in its totality and that this, particularly in the case of IT-enabled relationship marketing, that is CRM, requires a great deal of financial investment with the cost of software, interactive websites, call centres and other systems proving to be prohibitive for some organizations. Perhaps even more difficult than meeting the costs, is the fact that relationship marketing requires a total change in organizational culture where so many practices have to be changed, for example adoption of a customer orientation by the whole organization, long-term thinking, new re-numeration and reward structures. The business world traditionally assesses success on a short-term basis, in terms of monthly, weekly or even daily sales and market share figures. To begin to think in terms of customer share, as required in a relational strategy, instead of market share; to think of share of a customer's wallet rather than the number of customers coming through the door; and to reward your sales people for re-selling to existing customers and for looking after them rather than paying commission only for new sales, requires a massive cultural shift.

Additionally, despite some misconceptions, it is not recommended that companies engage in relationship marketing with all their customers, nor that relationship marketing is suitable for all companies in all sectors. Companies should contemplate investing in a long-term relationship with those customers whose lifetime value they calculate to be worth the investment. Also, it has to be recognized that different customers have different desire levels and propensity to engage in a long-term relationship with suppliers. According to Gronroos (2000), for example customers may be segmented into three groups, where those in 'transactional mode' do not seek contact from supplier; those in 'active relational mode' actively look for contact with suppliers and service providers; and those in 'passive relational mode' would like to know that they can contact suppliers if they so wished, but seldom do.

While, generally it is the relationship with customers that is often in focus, the importance of the organization's relationship with other stakeholders should not be forgotten. The success of a relational strategy with customers depends on the quality of an organization's relationship with all those that it is involved with in creating and delivering value. Different authors have referred to a large number of stakeholders. The following is one model depicting markets of concern for the organization in its relationship marketing strategy.

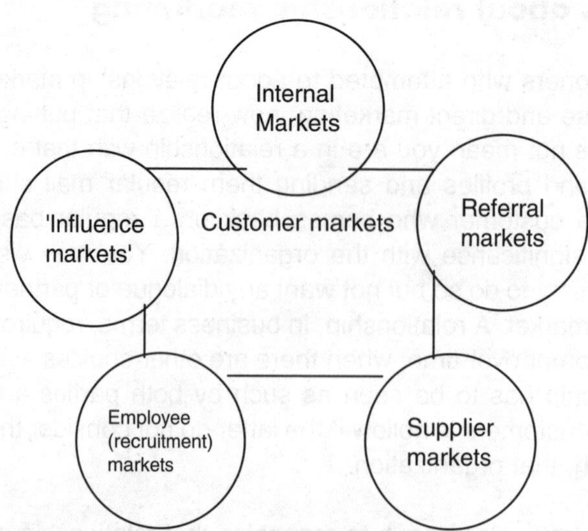

Figure 4.1 The six markets model: a broadened view of marketing
Source: Christopher *et al.* (2000) *Relationship Marketing: Bringing Quality, Customer Service and Marketing Together*, Oxford: Butterworth-Heinemann, p. 21

In the above model:

Referral markets – include customers, intermediaries and any source that may refer customers to the organization.
Employee markets – this refers to the potential employees of an organization, for example recent graduates.
Influence markets – this includes government and regulatory bodies.
Internal markets or internal marketing – is thought to be of great importance in implementing a relationship marketing strategy, but there is no universal consensus as to what it means. It may be fair though to suggest that most people would agree internal marketing implies the application of the marketing concept internally within the organization. Put simply, this involves promotion of the company mission, objectives, and a customer orientation philosophy amongst all staff so that they all buy in and pull in the same direction. It also involves identifying and satisfying employee needs in terms of self development, participation and promotion. Communications play a significant role in internal marketing. The use of regular appraisals, briefing meetings with staff, team-building exercises, suggestion boxes, staff development programmes, equal opportunity initiatives, and the use of in-house news letters, Intranet, and so on are all tools used in internal marketing.

Finally, relationship marketing is not advocated for all companies and all industries. It is thought that the most suitable sectors for relationship marketing are service industries, where customer anxiety is high during the purchase, where either regular or periodic transactions are required, and where there is a good opportunity for customization of products and communication. Also, complexity of service and the need for reassurance and uncertainty (Berry, 1983; Lovelock, 1983), turbulence in the Market environment (Zeithaml, 1981) have been suggested to create fertile grounds for relationship marketing.

What is relationship marketing?

Many definitions of the concept are offered in the literature. For example, Berry's (1983) definition emphasizes 'enhancing customer relationships' in 'multi-service organizations', while Gummesson's (1994) definition views RM as 'relationships, networks and interaction', and Ballantyne's (1994) definition refers to 'exchange relationships' which evolve to provide 'continuous and stable links in the supply chain'. It seems, however, that most textbooks and academics are adopting the definition offered by Gronroos. According to him, in a relational sense:

> *Marketing is to establish, maintain and enhance relationships with customers and other partners, at a profit, so that the objectives of both parties are met. This is achieved by a mutual exchange and fulfillment of promises* (Gronroos, 1994)

From the above definition it is possible to deduce that the following are some of the essential characteristics of relationship marketing:

Long-term orientation

Long-term orientation of the relationship marketing concept as opposed to the short-term orientation of transaction marketing has been stressed by numerous writers (Gronroos, 1990; Gummesson, 1987; Palmer, 1996; Christopher *et al.*, 1991). Comparing transaction marketing with relationship marketing within the service sector, Storbacka *et al.* (1994) suggest that 'In a relationship perspective the focus is not on service encounters (or transactions) as such' and that 'the encounter is rather seen as an element in an ongoing sequence of episodes between the customer and the service firm'. Relationship marketing aims to close the loop between getting of customers and keeping them (Christopher *et al.*, 1991).

Communication and achievement of mutual objectives

The traditional marketing concept views the supplier as active and the buyer as passive, while the relationship approach 'clearly views marketing as an interactive process in a social context where relationship building and management are a vital cornerstone' (Gronroos, 1994). Whereas traditional marketing emphasizes competition as the driving force of a market economy, relationship marketing puts collaboration in focus (Gummesson, 1996). The idea of collaboration as an alternative strategy implies that in return for the loyalty of the customer the supplier listens to, and cooperates with, the customer to provide individual and customized solutions for problems. This new approach to marketing, 'enables marketers to mass-customize products, tailor services and personalize dialogue with consumers' (Peppers and Rogers, 1995).

The relationship marketing concept places heavy emphasis on the importance of communications between the customer and supplier as well as emphasizing mutual satisfaction of objectives. This essentially requires an ongoing two-way communication between the customer and the supplier, where customers are able to take the initiative in communicating. In consumer markets, where individually tailored products are often not a viable option, due to the large number of customers involved, mass-customized products are modified and offered to micro-segments of the market, supplemented by one-to-one communication which is made possible using modern technology. Today, this is possible not only in face-to-face encounters but also through well-designed websites, call centres and so on making two-way communication a reality.

It is suggested (Payne *et al.*, 1996) that relationship building should follow an elaborate process whereby suppliers move Prospects up on the ladder of loyalty turning them into Customers, then Clients, followed by Supporters and Advocates and finally into Partners. The Advocate stage is where the supplier begins to reap the benefit of word of mouth or voluntary promotion by customers, and Partnership is relationship marketing at its perfect form. It would be fair to propose that different types of communications and messages will be required for each stage of the process as well as for different individual or micro-segments of customers.

Fulfilment of promises by all the parties involved

This characteristic can be examined mainly in the context of trust and commitment. Indeed, it may be proposed that the trust and commitment theories of relationship marketing best explain how long-term mutual exchange relationships can be created, maintained and enhanced. If a long-term relationship is to be created and successfully maintained, it would be safe to assume that, there has to be trust between the parties involved. Long-term relationships and keeping of promises require investment in time, resources, emotional bonding and forsaking of others. Gronroos (1996) advocates a trusting relationship with customers as opposed to an adversarial one, while Grossman (1998) defines trust as 'the degree of confidence one feels in a relationship' and goes on to add that trust has three elements: predictability, dependability and faith. Moorman *et al.* (1992) define trust as 'a willingness to rely on an exchange partner in whom one has confidence'.

Morgan and Hunt (1994) define commitment as 'an exchange partner believing that an ongoing relationship is so important as to warrant maximum efforts at maintaining it'. Bejou and Palmer (1998) assert 'commitment implies that both parties will be loyal, reliable and show stability in relation to the agreement they have with the other party'. The extent to which the principles of relationship marketing could be imported from the business-to-business sector and applied to the consumer markets has been much debated, as have the conditions which are pertinent to the development of customer-supplier relationships, as discussed earlier. There is, however, widespread agreement that a relationship marketing strategy could help with differentiating a company and result in customer loyalty. This in turn would reduce the company's costs of recruiting new customers, enable it to cross sell more easily to existing customers and also help it to benefit from favourable word-of-mouth advertising.

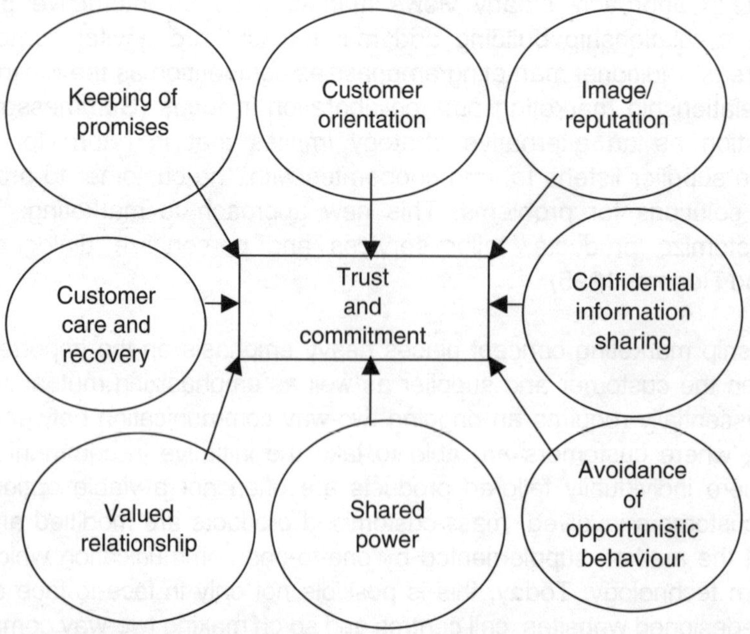

Figure 4.2 Creating trust and commitment
Source: Little and Marandi (2003)

The concept of relationship marketing is mainly concerned with the customer-supplier interface and is, to a large extent, distinct from branding relationships (for example, you could be loyal to a particular brand of perfume but not be bothered as to where you buy it from). For a discussion of brand relationships see Ranchhod (2004).

References

Ballantyne, D. (1994) 'Marketing at the crossroads' Editorial, *Asia-Australia Marketing Journal*, **2**(1) August.

Bejou, D. and Palmer, A. (1998) 'Service failure and loyalty: An exploratory empirical study of airline customers', *Journal of Services Marketing*, **12**(1).

Berry, L.L. (1983) 'Relationship Marketing', in L.L. Berry *et al.* (eds), Emerging perspectives of services marketing, *American Marketing Association*, Chicago: IL.

Christopher, M., Payne, A. and Ballantyne, D. (1991) *Relationship Marketing: Bringing Quality, Customer Service and Marketing Together*, Oxford: Butterworth-Heinemann.

Gronroos, C. (1990) 'Relationship approach to marketing in service contexts: The marketing and organizational behaviour interface', *Journal of Business Research*, **20**.

Gronroos, C. (1994) 'From marketing mix to relationship marketing: Towards a paradigm shift in marketing', *Management Decision*, **32**(2).

Gronroos, C. (1996) 'The rise and fall of modern marketing and its rebirth', in S.A. Shaw and N. Hood (eds), *Marketing in Evolution: Essays in Honour of Micheal J. Baker*, Macmillan: New York.

Gronroos, C. (2000) *Service Management and Marketing – A Customer Relationship Approach*, 2nd edition, Chichester: John Wiley and Sons.

Grossman, R.P. (1998) 'Developing and managing effective consumer relationships', *Journal of Product and Brand Management*, **59**, January.

Gummesson, E. (1987) 'The new marketing-developing long-term interactive relationships', *Long Range Planning*, **59**, January.

Gummesson, E. (1994) 'Making relationship marketing operational', *International Journal of Service Industries Management*, **5**(5).

Gummesson, E. (1996) 'Relationship marketing and imaginary organizations: A synthesis (Nordic Perspective on Relationship Marketing)', *European Journal of Marketing*, **30**(2).

Little, E. and Marandi, E. (2003) *Relationship Marketing Management*, London: Thomson Learning.

Lovelock, C.H. (1983) 'Classifying services to gain strategic marketing insight', *Journal of Marketing*, **47**, Summer.

Moorman, C., Zaltman, G. and Deshpande, R. (1992) 'Relationships between providers and users of market research: The dynamics of trust within and between organizations', *Journal of Marketing Research*, **29**, August.

Morgan, R.M. and Hunt, S.D. (1994) 'The commitment-trust theory of relationship marketing', *Journal of Marketing*, **58**, July.

Mulvany, S. (1998) 'New you: Improving listening skills', *Journal of Property Management*, Chicago, July/August.

Palmer, A. (1996) 'Relationship marketing: A universal paradigm or management fad?', *The Learning Organisation*, **3**(3), 18–25.

Payne, A., Christopher, M. and Peck, H. (1996) *Relationship Marketing for Competitive Advantage-Winning and Keeping Customers*, Butterworth-Heinemann.

Peppers, D. and Rogers, M. (1995) 'A new marketing paradigm: Share of customer, not market share', *Managing Service Quality*, **5**(3).

Ranchhod, A. (2004) *Marketing Strategies: A Twenty-first Century Approach*, Harlow: Prentice Hall.

Storbacka, K. Strandvik, T. and Gronroos, C. (1994) 'Managing customer relationships for profit: The dynamics of relationship quality', *International Journal of Service Industry Management*, **5**(5).

Zeithaml, V.A. (1981) 'How consumers' evaluation processes differ between goods and services', in H.H. Donnolly and W.R. George (eds), *Marketing of Services*, AMA: Chicago, IL.

KEY ACCOUNT MANAGEMENT

***Source*: Little, E. and Marandi, E. (2003) *Relationship Marketing Management*, London: Thomson Learning, Reproduced with kind permission from Thomson Learning.**

Introduction

Key Account Management (KAM) is a common manifestation of relationship marketing in business-to-business markets. With its roots in selling, the theory and practice of KAM is narrower in scope than that of relationship marketing – it can be seen as the application of 'external' RM principles in a business-to-business context, predominately from a supplier's perspective. Nevertheless, the subject offers valuable insights into the practical considerations of implementing RM, and hence can, in turn, inform the development of the broader theory.

This chapter begins by defining KAM, its costs and benefits, before looking at the nature of the business-to-business relationships and the key stages in their development. Decision-making frameworks for identifying key accounts and developing KAM programmes are then considered. After considering the subsidiary topic of Global Account Management (GAM) the chapter ends with a discussion of the contribution that KAM can make to the wider theory of RM, and whether KAM practices in turn can be informed by more general work on RM.

What is key account management?

KAM defined

Key Account Management is a management practice aimed at optimizing the relationship between a supplying organization and a buying organization. As is usual in the marketing literature, there is some debate over the precise meaning of the term 'Key Account Management' (KAM). Further confusion is created by the fact that KAM is used interchangeably with National Account Management (NAM), Strategic Account Management (SAM), and Account Management (AM), although there appear to be no significant distinctions between the meanings of the four terms. Nevertheless, there is general consensus that KAM consists of three elements. Kempeners and van der Hart (1999) represent these elements well by defining [Key] Account Management as follows:

> *the process of building and maintaining relationships over an extended period, which cuts across multiple levels, functions and operating units in both the selling organization and in carefully selected customers (accounts) that contribute to the company's objectives now or in the future.* (Kempeners & van der Hart (1999: 311))

As reflected in this definition, the practice of KAM is characterized by:

- *The conscious selection of key accounts* – the starting point of KAM is the identification of customers which will equate to strategic partners. All KAM programmes must, therefore, employ a mechanism for selecting these key accounts, based on the strategic objectives of the organization.
- *The development and maintenance of long-term relationships* – having identified the key customers, the organization must have strategies and systems in place to build and maintain a business relationship with that customer.
- *The establishment of cross-functional processes for servicing accounts* – this is a common feature of all definitions and examples of KAM. In order to enable the other two features of the KAM programme, the organizational structure and systems must enable multi-functional processes based around individual accounts.

KAM activities

Homburg *et al.* (2002) identify KAM by the activities that the suppliers undertake in order to build and maintain relationships. These include:

- Special pricing
- Customization of products and services
- Development of special products or services
- Joint coordination of workflow
- Information sharing
- Taking over the customer's business processes.

McDonald (2000) focuses on the communication ties between the two companies, which move from the 'bow-tie' formation shown in Figure 4.3 to a 'diamond' structure (Figure 4.4). Such a shift in structure can be both a response to and a stimulus for relationship development.

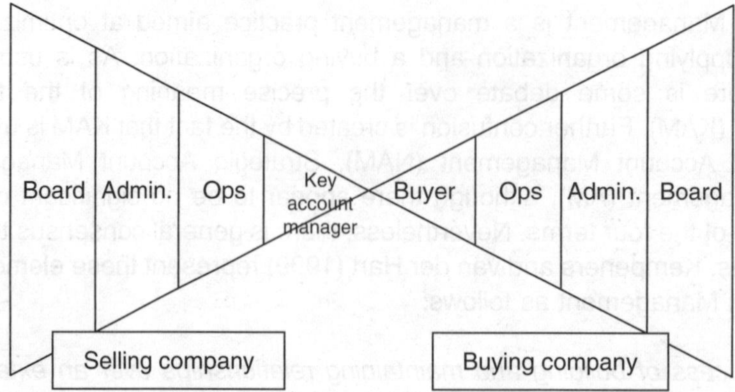

Figure 4.3 The bow-tie structure (evident early in KAM relationships)
Source: McDonald, M. (2000) 'Key account management – a domain review', *The Marketing Review*, 1, 15–34, Reprinted with permission of Westburn Publishers Ltd

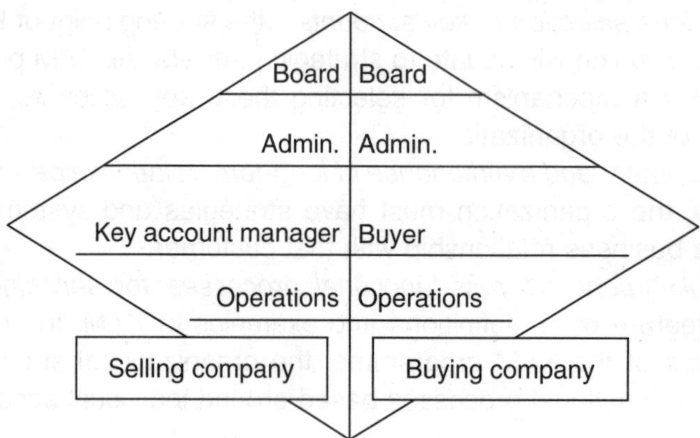

Figure 4.4
Source: McDonald, M. (2000) 'Key account Management – a domain review', *The Marketing Review*, 1, 15–34, Reprinted with permission of Westburn Publishers Ltd

The rationale for KAM

Before examining the mechanics of KAM and its implementation, it is worth considering the advantages (and penalties) of the practice. These are summarized in Figure 4.5. The supplier benefits from increased turnover, since the proper selection and development of accounts implies, amongst other things, the cultivation of the high volume, high value customers. At the same time, costs associated with the winning of new customers, such as marketing research and communications, are reduced. Ellram (1991) further notes that the long-term relationships give the supplier the opportunity to plan its production and logistics with greater certainty, perfecting repetitive operations. Hence, both production and transaction costs may be reduced. The buyer, in turn, benefits from products and services that are specifically tailored to its needs, whilst receiving some of the benefit of the supplier's cost reductions in the form of price discounts.

It is the mutual benefits, however, that bring the greatest strategic advantages to the parties involved. Both parties enjoy reduced risk, alleviating the threat of both short-term crises in supply and demand, and long-term planning uncertainty. By pooling their resources, the two companies not only make efficiency gains, but are able to explore business opportunities that might require a prohibitively high investment were they operating individually. Resources here refer to intangible assets, such as brand image, skills, information and organizational competences as well as to tangible assets. By sharing information, for example, the two parties may be able to develop products, process or strategies that could not have been developed individually. Similarly, one party may be able to capitalize on the brand image of its partner by association to gain access to new markets or buyers. Finally, Ojasalo (2001) notes that the benefits of KAM may occur at the individual as well the organizational level, through the enhanced social interaction arising from the bonds that inevitably form between individuals in the two companies. Given the effect, this has an employee satisfaction and motivation, this would have indirect benefits at the organizational level.

It should be stressed, however, that these benefits arise from the successful implementation of KAM, and represent the greatest benefits which can accrue. It will be seen that the development of KAM infrastructure involves a significant investment in terms of management time, staffing and training; an investment that will probably not create a return during the early stages of the relationship. The proper selection of key accounts, and the proper development and maintenance of these relationships is critical to the long-term profitability of the any KAM programme.

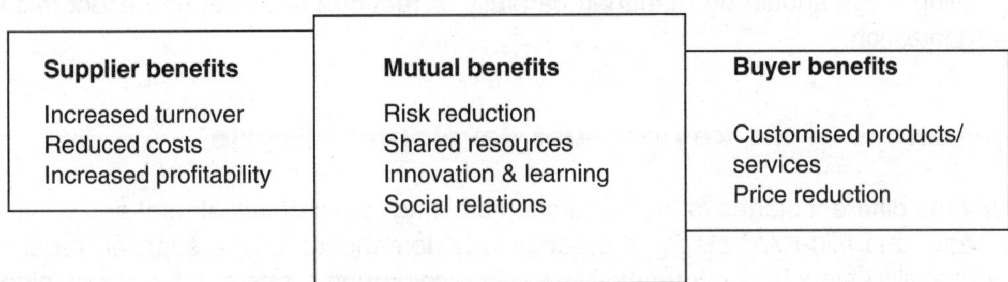

Figure 4.5 Benefits of key account management

The key account development cycle

Stages in the key account development cycle

As with all relationships, key account relationships develop over time and require different treatment at different stages in this development. The literature offers two competing models of key account development, though the differences between are nominal. The explanation offered below is a synthesis of the two.

Pre- and early-KAM

These stages are described by the McDonald *et al.* (1997) as the 'scanning and attraction stages'. Here the supplier is concerned with the identification of potential key accounts, and gaining information by which the selection decision can be made. The move into early-KAM is characterized by the willingness of the supplier to make adjustments to its standard offering. The types of information needed to select key accounts are discussed in the next section. Given the fact that customers in the pre- or early-KAM stages of development are of relatively low importance to the organization, sales representatives play the central role in this process, with no special infrastructure or resources being devoted to the customer (Millman and Wilson, 1995). The focus of the relationship remains on the product, and on a set of relatively discrete (albeit repetitive) transactions.

Mid-KAM

Here the focus of the relationship begins to shift to process, as trust and commitment develop between the two parties. Hence the range of value-added services offered by the supplier assume as great an importance in the eyes of the buyer as the product and its price. Both begin to view the relationship as long term, though the buyer will still maintain contact with alternative suppliers. The number of contact points between the two companies will increase, and the management of the account will tend to shift towards more senior levels of the organizations, as it takes on greater strategic importance.

Partnership and synergistic KAM (mature KAM)

At this point in the relationship, the boundaries between the two companies reduce as the structural and social bonds between them strengthen. The sharing of sensitive information and joint problem-solving will be common practice, and both formal and informal contacts will occur regularly at all levels of both the organizations. Synergistic KAM is described by McDonald *et al.* (1997) as 'quasi-integration' – a state in which the two organizations operate jointly.

Uncoupling KAM

Relationship disintegration may occur at any stage. McDonald *et al.* find that relationship breakdown is most frequently attributed to a breach of trust. Millman and Wilson stress, however, that relationship dissolution should not necessarily be viewed as a failure, since it may be in the interests of a party to end a relationship. Whether intentional or not, the uncoupling stage should be managed carefully to reduce the social and economic impact on the organization.

Implications of the key account development cycle

Clearly the different stages of the cycle bring differing levels of investment and varying returns. The early- and mid-KAM stages are particularly demanding for the supplier, requiring investment in activities such as information gathering, communications and the developing of value-added services in an attempt to gain the confidence of the buyer. The major benefits of KAM, however, occur in the later stages. The supplier must, therefore, ensure that the balance of its relationship portfolio is maintained, so that the superior returns from mature relationships can fund the development of those in the early- or mid-KAM stages.

Identifying key accounts

The need for selection criteria

Given the cost/benefit implications of the key account development cycle, the need for the careful selection of potential key accounts is critical. Millman and Wilson (1995) describe the example of a business relationship between two multinational companies agreeing to develop jointly an advanced pigmentation system. Whilst the selling company saw the project as the start of a long term, strategic relationship, the buyer viewed it as a one-off project. The buyer terminated the arrangement after 2 years, leaving the seller shocked and bitter, with no resulting sales gain to soften the blow. If a selling company is to profit from KAM, it must minimize the likelihood of such strategic failures. Although research in the field of KAM is limited, it has been found that companies that explicitly define and identify key accounts are more successful in targeting resources, and show a more sophisticated understanding of their customers (Millman and Wilson, 1999). The remainder of this section reviews various criteria for the selection of key accounts suggested by research into KAM.

Relationship history

Obviously, this criterion presumes that KAM is being implemented against a background of established accounts, and cannot be easily applied to new prospects. The literature commonly points to longevity as an indicator of the strategic importance of an account, constituting evidence of commitment and trust, both of which are important ingredients of strategic relationships (McDonald, 2000). Ojasalo (2001) points out, however, that longevity is no guarantee of profitability.

Volume

Theorists are virtually unanimous in identifying sales volume as a key determinant in the selection of key accounts (Krapfel *et al.*, 1991; McDonald *et al.*, 1997; Campbell and Cunningham, 1983). Research suggests that practitioners also find this criterion simple to apply, since it is easily quantified and readily accepted by key players within the organization. When 'selling' the importance of the account internally, key account managers found that sales turnover was well recognized throughout the business (McDonald *et al.*, 1997). It should be stressed that potential sales volume is as important as current – the same research found that achieving links with fast growing companies, or companies in developing markets was also a prime strategic consideration.

Profitability

Ojasalo (2001) points out that high sales volume does not always lead to profitability, and to be of value, the total revenue from an account must exceed its servicing costs within a given timeframe. The quantification of profitability, however, is not straightforward. The majority of costs associated with the servicing of key accounts involve services, management time, and the resolution of day-to-day problems. Intangible activities such as this are difficult to cost, particularly in organizations where a single team or manager handles more than one account. Similarly, the benefits accruing from a relationship may be equally nebulous and difficult to quantify – gains in areas such as innovation, learning and reputation are hard to assess in anything but qualitative terms. Hence, Millman and Wilson (1999) found that the assessments of the net value of business relationships tended to rely on the subjective judgement of those involved in their operationalization.

Status

Ojalaso (2001) identifies the fact that organizations often derive benefit from association with a reputable partner. Research by McDonald *et al.* (1997) found that some selling companies actively targeted national or multinational or 'blue-chip' companies, since the prestige associated with these organizations facilitated the winning of further customers. It was also noted that companies with a good reputation were more likely to focus on long-term value creating activities rather than short-term cost issues, and hence were more receptive to KAM initiatives.

Ease of replacement

This criterion is relevant to the decision to develop rather than to initiate a key account relationship, since it applies to existing customers only. Krapfel *et al.* (1991) recommend that by calculating the cost of replacing an exiting customer or supplier, an organization can obtain a useful quantitative measure of the relationships value.

Resources synergies

Campbell and Cunningham (1983) identify this as a separate criterion, whilst Millman and Wilson (1999) subsume it within broader considerations of 'strategic fit'. The selling organization will be able to service the account more effectively if it is able to leverage any resources or competences that distinguish it from its competitors. Hence it should look for partners amongst organizations that would benefit particularly from its unique strengths. Similarly, it should ensure that these partners command resources that may in turn benefit the selling organization.

Strategic compatibility

Millman and Wilson's (1999) notion of strategic fit also encompass the alignment of organizational goals, *modus operandi*, culture and relational norms. Similarly, McDonald *et al.* (1997) note that not all organizations seem willing or able to maintain long-term relationships, so receptivity to a KAM programme is an important consideration. More practical considerations such as compatibility between present and intended product and market arenas, and even such mundane issues as the physical location should not be ignored.

Criteria for selecting a key supplier

The literature tends to view KAM from the perspective of the supplier, and most of the criteria outlined above have been formulated with the supplier in mind. Many apply equally well to the buying company that is considering the development of strategic relationships with its supplier – the volume criterion, for example, becomes a question of whether the supplier can reliably fulfil current and future orders in the volume needed by the buyer. Similarly, issues of strategic compatibility or resource fit are mutual concerns. In addition, the McDonald *et al.*'s research identified that the buying company is likely to weigh the following factors in its choice of strategic partner:

- *Product quality* – Whether goods or service, the quality of the product and the relevance of value-added service will be of prime importance to the buying organization.
- *Ease of doing business* – Aggravation and problem-solving are significant costs to the buying organization, and purchasing officers look very favourably on those suppliers that minimize these costs.
- *People quality* – Purchasing officers took account of the personality and skills of key contacts in the selling company, valuing such qualities as *honesty, integrity and, above all, 'a spirit of understanding'* (McDonald *et al.* (1999: 748)).

By understanding the criteria that the customer will apply in selecting suppliers, the supplier will be in a better position to design a KAM system that suits their needs.

Serving key accounts: KAM activities

Adding value for key accounts

Having identified the key accounts, the next stage in the KAM process is to identify the means by which the relationship can be developed (Cann, 1998). This can in part be addressed by the installation of special resources dedicated to the servicing of the account, as discussed in the next section. However, before investing in such resources, the organization must have a clear idea of the activities to which they will be applied. There is a clear, though tacit, consensus in the literature that such activities involve adding value rather than cutting prices. Homburg *et al.* (2002) refer in passing to 'special pricing' and Ojasalo (2001) implies the use of discounting by listing cost savings as one of the benefits to buyers of key account relationships. Otherwise, the KAM literature is silent regarding the potential of pricing as a tactic in relationship development, focusing instead on the means by which added value can be generated – McDonald *et al.* (1997) even found that suppliers actively targeted non-price-sensitive accounts so that the investment made in the account could be recouped through premium pricing.

Figure 4.6 summarizes the key activities or tactics that may be employed. These are arranged as a hierarchy of measures. Although the position of each element in the hierarchy is not definitive, it serves as a rough indicator of those elements that are basic pre-requisites of any strategic relationship, and those which characterize highly developed partnerships.

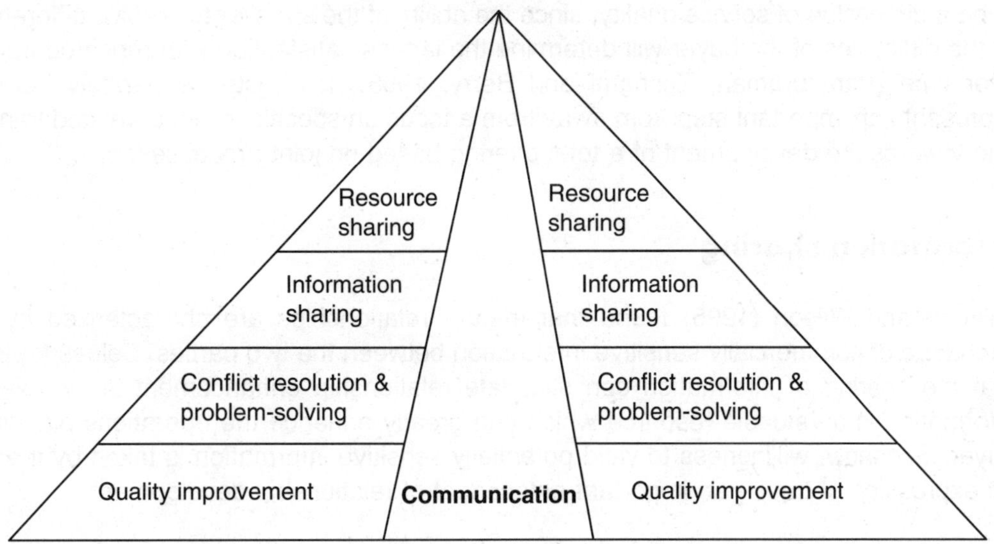

Figure 4.6 Adding value to key accounts

Quality improvement

This is perhaps the fundamental element of KAM, and the pre-requisite of a strategic relationship most commonly cited by buyers (McDonald *et al.*, 1997; Millman and Wilson, 1995). In the words of Millman and Wilson: *The desire to serve key customers better must be matched by the capability to do so* Millman and Wilson (1999: 332). Given the long-term focus of strategic relationships, product excellence at any one moment is less important than the capability to continuously develop product offerings in response to market conditions, buyer requirements and competitor activity. Since, in all but the earliest stages of the relationship, the supplier's total offering is likely to involve a significant service element, even suppliers of manufactured goods must be able to reassure buyers of the quality of their processes and people, as well its manufacturing capability (McDonald *et al.*, 1997). Hence the focus from the outset is on internal process quality rather than product quality.

Customization

Again, this can be seen as a pre-requisite of any relationship. In order to initiate any degree of exclusivity in the relationship, the supplier must be able to offer the buyer something that its competitors cannot. Customization may derive from the physical modification of tangible goods, or from the development of tailored services or transaction routines.

Conflict resolution and problem-solving

Selnes (1998) found that the flexibility of the supplier in accepting responsibility for resolving the buyer's problems was a key determinant of a buyer's trust in their supplier, which in turn was a key antecedent of motivation to enhance the relationship. Responsiveness is often considered to be a dimension of service quality, since the ability of the supplier to resolve differences with, or the difficulties of the buyer will determine the latter's satisfaction with repeated transactions over time (Parasuraman, Zeithaml and Berry, 1988). It is listed separately here since it represents an important step from away from a focus on specific, product-related transactions, and towards the development of a total offering based on joint processes.

Information sharing

Millman and Wilson (1995) found that mature relationships are characterized by the free exchange of commercially sensitive information between the two parties. Selnes (1998) states that the sharing of information can stimulate relationship enhancement in two ways. First, information is a valuable resource which can greatly enhance the operations planning of the buyer. Secondly, willingness to yield potentially sensitive information is taken by the buyer as an expression of trust – an important antecedent of relationship development.

Resource sharing

Perhaps the pinnacle of key account relationship building is the ability of the two parties to share resources for mutual advantage. Whether through temporary joint ventures, or the development of permanent systems or structures, the sharing of resources is both a result of, and a stimulus for, very close bonds between organizations.

Communication

Communication occupies a special place in the servicing of key accounts, since it underpins all of the other tactics, and is universally cited as being of central importance to the initiation, development and maintenance of key accounts. The two major models of KAM development identify the various stages by the nature and extent of the communication channels existing between the two companies (McDonald, 2000). A key tactic for relationship development is therefore the development of communication channels between buyer and supplier.

Research by Schultz and Evans (2002) suggests that the nature of communication is important:

- *Informality* – Customers are heavily concerned with interaction efficiency, and found informal methods less cumbersome than formal channels. Perhaps more important, informal communication is strongly linked to trust, suggesting that it is perceived to be more open and frank than carefully managed interaction.
- *Bi-directionality* – In order to add value to the relationship, communication must be two way, with suppliers both listening to and acting on feedback from the customer, and keeping them informed.
- *Frequency* – In keeping with customers' preference for informal modes of communication, frequent, short episodes of interaction make customers feel they are being 'kept in touch with'.
- *Strategic content* – The content of communication is just as important as the mode and frequency. Customers respond better to communication which they feel to be of strategic importance, reacting badly to being bombarded with trivial detail.

Servicing key accounts: Developing a KAM infrastructure

Identifying the type of KAM system

Having identified the key accounts, the next stage in the development of KAM is the design of the system through which they will be serviced. Shapiro and Moriarty (1984) describe five major types of key account 'programme':

1. *No programme* – no formal system or infrastructure is developed.
2. *Part-time programme* – people with other roles take on the additional responsibility of managing the account.
3. *Full-time programme (unit level)* – the system is operated by fully dedicated staff, but decentralized at business unit or division level.
4. *Corporate-level programme* – the system is run centrally by dedicated staff.
5. *National account division* – a separate operating unit is dedicated to the account.

From a study of some 400 German and US suppliers, Homburg *et al.* (2002) identified eight distinct types of KAM system:

1. *Top-management KAM* – involves highly formalized KAM programmes. As the label suggest, such programmes exhibit the highest degree of top-management involvement, and are usually located at the organization's headquarters. Most have dedicated sales managers responsible for key accounts, and make extensive use of key account teams. Collaborative activities, such as the coordination of the manufacturing schedules are of high intensity, and the supplier is proactive in developing such activities. Despite this positive picture, access to function resources such as functional resources is low.
2. *Middle-management KAM* – is also highly formalized, but attracts less involvement from senior management. The intensity of collaborative activities and the proactivity of the supplier are only of medium level. Key account managers tend to be locally based, and enjoy less prominent positions in the corporate hierarchy than their counterparts in top-management KAM systems. Access to functional resources is low.
3. *Operating-level KAM* – is also relatively formalized, involving standardized procedures, and contributing significant value to the key accounts. Senior management involvement, however, is lower still, and a still greater proportion of account managers are based at local level. Access to functional resources is low.
4. *Cross-functional, dominant KAM* – offers the most positive picture against all criteria. Access to resources is high, and senior management involvement is significant. Processes and structures are well developed, and key account managers enjoy a prominent role. Proactivity and intensity of collaboration are both high. Of all the organizations surveyed, those employing this form of KAM system key account managers spend the greatest proportion of their time on external activities.
5. *Unstructured KAM* – systems are characterized by a lack of formality and standardization, and a reactive stance to collaborative activity. With little top-management involvement, account managers in this group spend the lowest proportion of their time on external activities.
6. *Isolated KAM* – is a system in which KAM activities are instigated by local sales effort, but lacks support from the central business units. Although the involvement of senior management is medium, access to functional resources is limited, and selling centre *esprit de corp* is low.

7. *Country-club KAM* – systems exhibit a high degree of involvement from top management, but little else. Structures and processes are poorly developed, and teams are hardly ever formed. Special activities are neither intense nor proactive. The authors suggest that this form of KAM amounts to little more than representation by senior managers.
8. *No KAM* – operators may pay lip-service to a KAM system, often by awarding sales or general managers the title account coordinator or similar. However, no special activities of any significance are undertaken for their key customers.

Homburg *et al.* took a number of measures of the success of the various companies, both at the account level (i.e. how well the particular relationships were performing) and at the organizational level (how well the business as a whole was performing). Perhaps predictably, the No KAM and isolated KAM approaches performed the worst, whilst cross-functional, dominant KAM companies performed particularly well against organization-level outcomes. Top-management KAM Systems were found to be associated with the most profitable companies, suggesting that greater gains from other approaches are offset by higher costs.

This research offers valuable insights into the range of KAM system that may be applied. It is also possible that the various systems, rather than being alternatives, are stages in the development of KAM system. The key conclusion arising from the research is the desirability that senior management be actively involved in the design and implementation of KAM systems, rather than delegating the task to local sales managers.

The role of the account manager

The role of the key account manager will vary considerably depending on the nature of the organization, its environment and the KAM system in force. Millman and Wilson (1995), however, tentatively suggest a list of functions which are commonly associated with such posts:

- Maintaining the sales/profitability of key accounts
- Customizing the seller's total offering to key accounts
- Facilitating inter-level or inter-functional processes that add value to the total offering
- Promoting the KAM concept within the organization
- Promoting the interests of the account within the organization.

Based on the research by Homburg *et al.* described above, and work by other authors (e.g. Millman and Wilson, 1996; McDonald *et al.*, 1997; Schultz and Evans, 2002), it is clear that the key account manager plays a crucial role in the implementation of KAM. Decisions on the responsibility, authority and resources allocated to key account managers will be critical in determining the effectiveness of the programme. Kempeners and van der Hart (1999) suggest the following checklist:

- *Full or part-time system* – should account managers be dedicated full time to the servicing of key accounts, or should they also have other responsibilities?
- *The position of account managers in the system* – should they be integrated into the sales department or should a new organizational layer be created? Should they be physically located at head office or locally? Should different levels of key account management be created?
- *Allocation of responsibility* – how many accounts should each manger control?
- *Allocation of authority* – what resources should the account manager control? Should these be held centrally, or dedicated entirely to the account manager?

These questions have significant implications for the organization's structure, since the KAM framework will have to be integrated with existing structures and processes. Homburg *et al.*'s research indicates that, if medium-term profitability is the chief focus, a centralized, highly developed key account executive function is not always the optimum solution, due to the cost of installing and maintaining such a system. It is possible, however, that the superior returns of such a system pay dividends in the longer term.

Skills of the key account manager

Given the importance of the key account manager, a significant amount of research has been conducted into the skills necessary to perform this function. According to Millman and Wilson, the demands of the role require:

> *High calibre people who not only sufficiently 'rounded' to be able to diagnose/analyse complex commercial and technical situations; but also equipped to cope with highly politicized interaction, together with personal tensions and ambiguities inherent in the boundary-spanning role.* (Millman and Wilson (1995: 17))

Shultz and Evans (2002) also single out communication skills as *the* key competence required of key account representatives, particularly the ability to share information of a strategic nature, rather than communicating predominantly on tactical issues. McDonald *et al.*'s research adds the following requirements:

- Integrity
- Product service knowledge
- Understanding the buying company's business and business environment
- Selling/negotiating skills

Possession of these skills and competences is understandably rare, and organizations seeking to implement KAM must be prepared to invest heavily in the selection, retention and development of suitable candidates.

The key account team

The use of key account teams to support the manager varies considerably between different examples of KAM systems, with account managers in some companies having no support from teams (Kempener and van der Hart, 1999; Homburg *et al.*, 2002). Homburg *et al.* (2002) found that the companies that performed best at the operational or account level made extensive use of teams. Shultz and Evans (2002) recommend the use of key account teams. Not only do they enable frequent contact with the customer, but they also help the flow of information in the selling organization, so that relevant information about the customer and the account is transferred to all points of customer contact.

According to Kempener and van der Hart, key account team decisions relate to the constitution and control of teams:

- *Constitution of account teams* – The role of the account team is to support cross functional activities. To be of value, therefore, the teams should comprise members from all functions that have a hand in servicing the account. Team members may be full or part-time, and certain members (or indeed entire teams) may be involved only on an *ad hoc* basis, to solve a particular problem.
- *Control of account teams* – The most formalized control structure involves the key account manager with line-management responsibility for a dedicated, full time team. Where part-time or *ad hoc* members are involved, however, line management responsibility may be shared, or rest wholly with a manager in a functional department.

Clearly there are significant trade-offs here between efficiency and effectiveness, as demonstrated in Homburg *et al.*'s finding that the most formalized and 'successful' systems were not necessarily the most profitable. Moreover, the development of a permanent structure would be inappropriate in the early stages of a relationship – it is implicit in the notion of the account development cycle that supplier investments increase as trust develops between the two parties, and the chance of exit reduces (McDonald, 2000; Millman and Wilson, 1995). As with the various options for designing the role of the key account manager, so the different account team structures might be used by the same organization at different stages of the account's development.

The relevance of KAM to relationship marketing

A specific application of RM

Theories of KAM have been developed in high value, low volume, business-to-business markets, usually as an extension of theories of personal selling. This naturally sets limits on the applicability of KAM to RM practices in other types of market, particular to mass markets. Nevertheless, the KAM literature illustrates some important general principles of RM.

The need for senior management support

Both the empirical research and theoretical work provide strong evidence to suggest that KAM strategies will not work without the active support of senior management. This reinforces the general principle that RM requires a fundamental change in the values, goals and resource priorities of the organization, and will not be successful if viewed as a tactical issue. In the early stages at least, RM initiatives must be championed by influential members of the organization's management if they are to succeed.

The need for cross-functional coordination

KAM programmes appear to work better when they are supported by teams arranged around customers rather than functional areas. The development of KAM relationships involves a move away from the focus on rigid structures producing standardized offerings, and towards a more flexible, network structure which can adapt to changing customer requirements, calling on new members and resources as circumstances require. This mirrors the consensus in the more general literature that RM is best supported by a network structure based on process rather than functional areas (see Chapters five: Structure and Chapter six: internal marketing).

The importance of communication

Finally, the KAM literature underlines the central role of communication in building and maintaining the trust on which relationships depend. Whether dealing with customers, employees, channel members or referral markets, the management of relationships hinges on the development of open, dialogue between the parties involved. This is as true for mass, consumer markets as for business-to-business sectors.

References

Campbell, M. and Cunningham, M. (1983) 'Customer analysis for strategic developments in industrial markets', *Strategic Management Journal*, **4**(4), 369–481.

Cann, C. (1998) 'Eight steps to building a business-to-business relationship', *Journal of Business and Industrial Marketing*, **13**(4/5), 395–405.

Ellram, L.E. (1991) 'Supply chain management', *International Journal of Physical Distribution and Logistics Management*, **21**(1), 13–22.

Homburg, C., Workman, Jr. J., Jensen, O. (2002) 'A configurational perspective on key account management', *Journal of Marketing*, **66**(2), 38.

Kempeners, M. and van der Hart, H. (1999) 'Designing account management organizations', *Journal of Business and Industrial Marketing*, **14**(4), 310–355.

Krapfel, Jr., Salmond, D. and Spekman, R. (1991) 'A strategic approach to managing buyer-seller relationships', *European Journal of Marketing*, **25**(9), 22–48.

McDonald, M. (2000) 'Key account management – a domain review', *The Marketing Review*, **1**, 15–34.

McDonald, M., Millman, T. and Rogers, G. (1997) 'Key account management: Theory, practice and challenges', *Journal of Marketing Management*, **13**, 737–757.

Millman, T. and Wilson, K. (1995) 'From key account selling to key account management', *Journal of Marketing Practice: Applied Marketing Science*, **1**(1), 9–21.

Millman, T. and Wilson, K. (1996) 'Processual issues in key account management', *Journal of Business and Industrial Marketing*, **14**(4), 328–337.

Millman, T. and Wilson, K. (1999) 'Processual issues in key account management: Underpinning the customer-facing organization', *Journal of Business and Industrial Marketing*, **14**(4), 328–337.

Ojasalo, J. (2001) 'Key account management at company and individual levels in business-to-business relationships', *Journal of Business and Industrial Marketing*, **16**(3), 199–218.

Parasuraman, A., Zeithaml, V. and Berry, L. (1998) 'SERVQUAL: A multiple item scale for measuring consumer perceptions of service quality', *Journal of Retailing*, **64**(1), 12–40.

Schulz, R. and Evans, K. (2002) 'Strategic collaborative communication by key account representatives', *Journal of Personal Selling and Sales Management*, **22**(1), 23–32.

Selnes, F. (1998) 'Antecedents and consequences of trust and satisfaction in buyer-seller relationships', *European Journal of Marketing*, **32**(3), 305–322.

Shapiro, B.P. and Moriarty, R.T. (1984) 'Organising the National Account Force', working paper, Marketing Science Institute, MA.

Using the KAM contemporary issue within case studies

KAM has become increasingly important for many organizations as they attempt to develop effective strategies for dealing with the various segments that they operate in. For instance, in Business-to-Business marketing, KAM is highly relevant. In past cases such as WCI and Enzymes Ltd, growth was possible and sustainable through KAM. In business to consumer markets each account is an important account, especially in a case such as Reiss. In this instance some of the more tangible aspects of relationship marketing such as acquisition, retention and adaptation come into play. So a better understanding of KAM for the B2B markets can also help with trying to understand wider issues surrounding relationship marketing.

SUSTAINABILITY AND STRATEGY

***Source*: We are grateful to Pearson Education for granting us the permission to use Chapter 4 from *Marketing Strategies: A 21st Century Approach* by Ashok Ranchhod.**

Sustainability: Limits to Growth.

Introduction

As the world's population grows and some 90 million more individuals are added to the planet each year, many marketers are questioning some of the basic tenets of marketing. Is it right to expect continued growth? Should we be marketing goods that are likely to harm the planet? Should marketing concentrate on products that are 'green'? These and many other questions are being asked not just by marketers but by the general consumers themselves. In recent surveys, it has been shown that consumers are concerned about the products that they purchase, however cost may be a factor in purchasing products as well.

Nonetheless, in Germany, 88 per cent of consumers are ready to switch brands to greener products, the corresponding figures in Italy and Spain were 84 per cent and 82 per cent respectively (Wasik, 1996). In the US, the green market is estimated to include 52 million households (Ottman, 1993). In 1996, MORI categorized 36 per cent of its British poll respondents as 'green consumers' on the basis of their claim to have 'selected one product over another because of its environmentally friendly packaging, formulation or advertising' (Worcester, 1997). This compared with 19 per cent in 1988 (although it continued the steady decline from a peak of 50 per cent in 1990). This makes it important that marketers actually understand and respond to customer needs.

Furthermore, are the provisions of certain products and services sustainable? Sustainability is about understanding the interactions of the various stakeholders in an organization. Maximizing profits and looking for short-term gains in market share may, in the long run be so harmful to certain groups of stakeholders that the company itself may suffer bad publicity. These stakeholders are the employees, the local community and government agencies. The main stakeholder is probably the planet itself and increasingly the public feels that business firms should take responsibility for environmental damage inflicted on parts of the earth in the pursuit of profit. An example of this is the cost to General Electric Company in the USA for removing two million cubic metres of contaminated sludge from the Hudson River (New Scientist, 2001). For 35 years the company poured some 500 000 kilograms of Polychlorinated biphenyls (PCBs) into the river, before they were banned in 1977. Residents living near the river bank claim to have suffered from a variety of PCB-related illnesses ranging from cancer to physical deformities. As a result of this, the US Environmental Protection Agency has decided to remove the sludge and have asked GEC to foot the $500 million bill.

In a situation like this, the factors are complex however, the fact remains that the consumers of the period actually bought electrical equipment that was manufactured by GEC, generally unaware of the pollution problems. The onus, therefore, remains on companies to ensure that their products and services are environmentally friendly or not and whether their practices are environmentally sustainable or not. This information also needs to filter through to the consumer. In this chapter, therefore we will explore various notions of sustainability, ranging from 'green' products to sustainable production. The aim of this chapter is to understand the implications of being environmentally friendly and how by taking such a stance, a company could create a sustainable competitive advantage in marketing.

Understanding environmental marketing

For many consumers, the term 'green' may evoke a range of different emotions and understanding. For some, it may mean products that do not harm the environment, for others it may mean products that have been made without harming the environment. Many may consider ethical and moral considerations such as fair trade with the developing nations. For some it could be charitable ventures such as Oxfam. From these examples, it can be seen that the term environmentally-friendly, encompasses a myriad of meanings for individuals, depending on their range of experiences and perspectives. The main issue here is the merging of the social concerns as well as ecological concerns. Many in marketing would argue that these are now Inseparable (Peattie, 1995). Others argue that simply being green is not enough and that ethical issues also need to be taken into account. This is backed up by research into the notion of 'environmental justice' within the USA (Oyewole, 2001). The main contention is that many companies site chemical plants and dump toxic waste near poor or deprived communities. This is also part of a global concern where some products are cheaply made by communities who are too poor to complain about environmental issues, needing jobs and money to sustain themselves.

Hand in hand with this, crisis-ridden governments such as Indonesia, the Philippines, South Korea and Thailand cut back on environmental spend (French, 2000). For instance, in Russia, the budget for protected areas was cut by 40 per cent. The globalization of commerce is intensifying the environmental agenda, with many countries, increasingly concerned about the effect of global consumption trends on the environment. This is shown in the diagrams below (Worldwatch Institute, 2000). The quotes are provided by the Institute.

Energy and climate

As our growing population increased its burning of coal and oil to produce power, the carbon locked in millions of years worth of ancient plant growth was released into the air, laying a heat-retaining blanket of carbon dioxide over the planet. Earth's temperature increased significantly. Climate scientists had predicted that this increase would disrupt weather. Indeed, annual damages from weather disasters have increased over 40-fold.

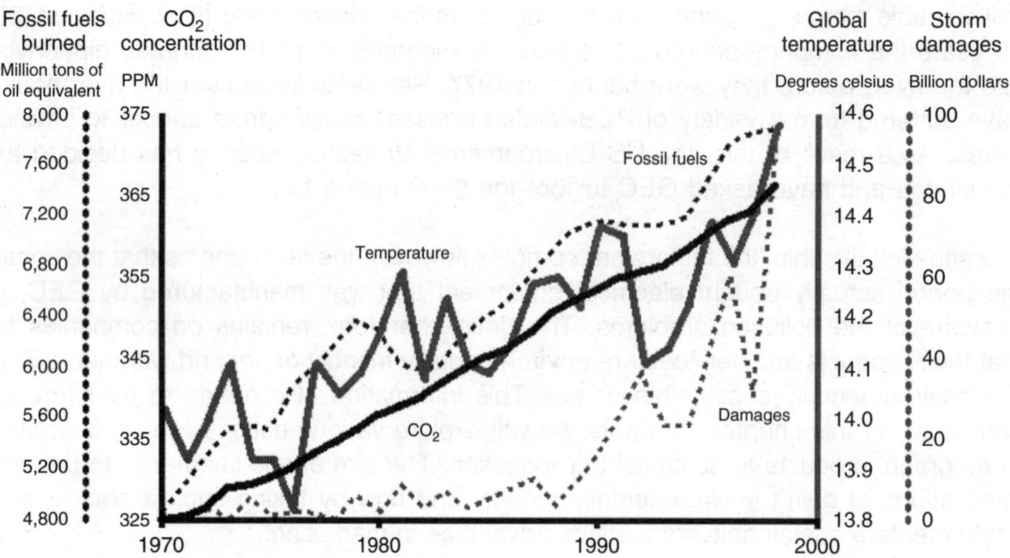

Figure 4.7 Energy and the climate

Chemicals and the biological boomerang

Our consumption of chemicals has exploded, with about three new synthetic chemicals introduced each day. Almost nothing is known about the long-term health and environmental effects of new synthetics, so we have been ambushed again and again by belated discoveries. One of the most ominous signs of this is the evolution of pesticide resistant pests as the use of pesticides increases.

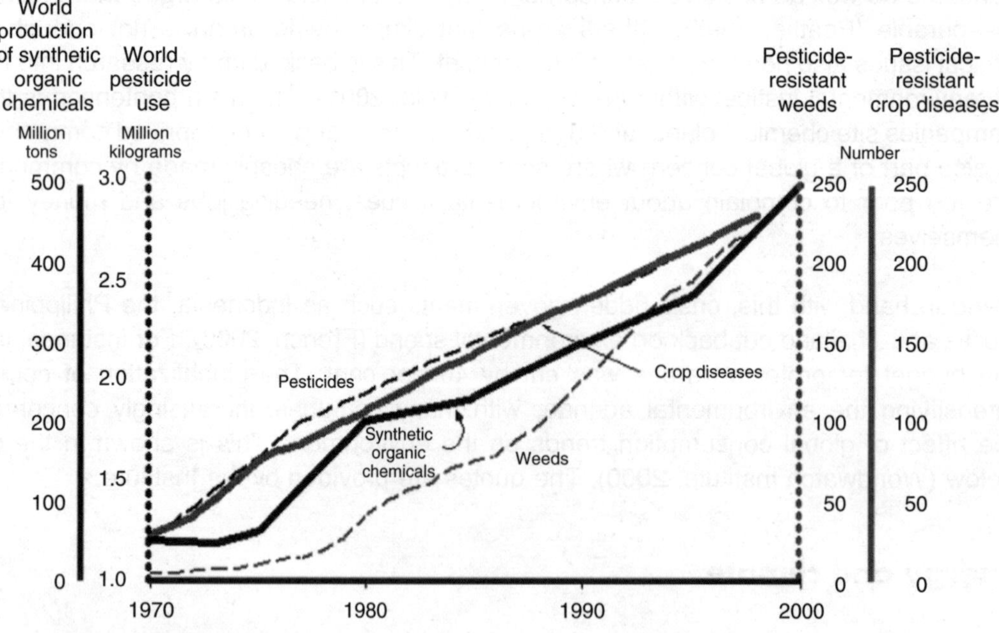

Figure 4.8 Chemicals and the biological boomerang

Commerce and the oceans

The global economy has more than doubled in the past 30 years, putting pressure on most countries to increase export income. Many have tried to increase revenues by selling more ocean fish – for which there is growing demand, since the increase in crop yields no longer keeps pace with population growth. Result: over fishing is decimating one stock after another, and the catch is getting thinner and thinner.

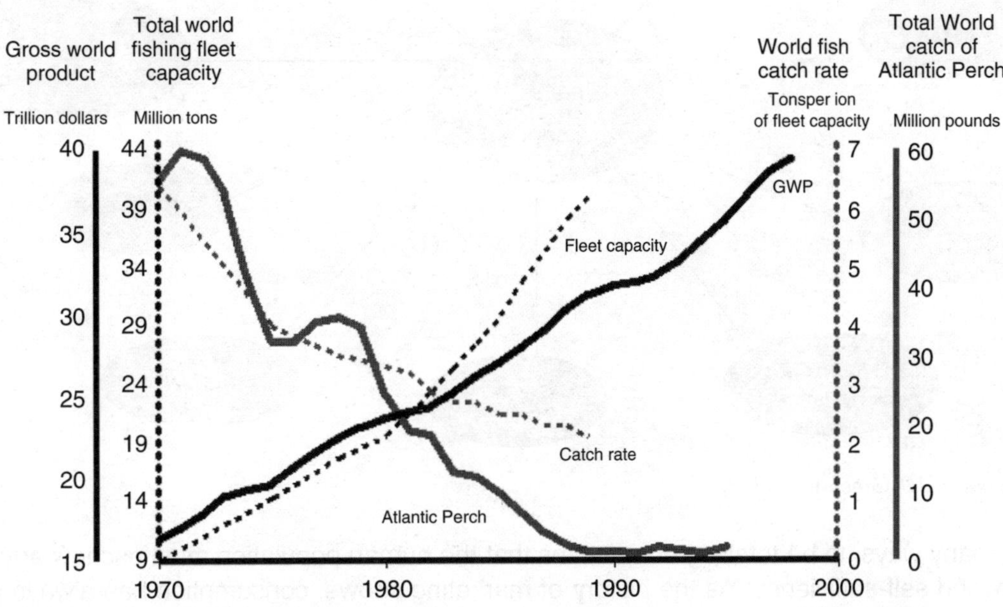

Figure 4.9 Commerce and the oceans

As production, marketing and consumption become increasingly global environmental issues affect every one of us. For marketers, who are often concerned with single products or brands, it is often difficult to disentangle the various interconnecting strands affecting the production of a single product. A complex piece of machinery such as a car, may well have certain products which, have not been either ethically or environmentally produced. Some marketers would even say that the production and use of a car itself is environmentally unfriendly, as each car in use adds to local and global pollution. Given this range of views, we need to understand the different ways in which green marketing is perceived.

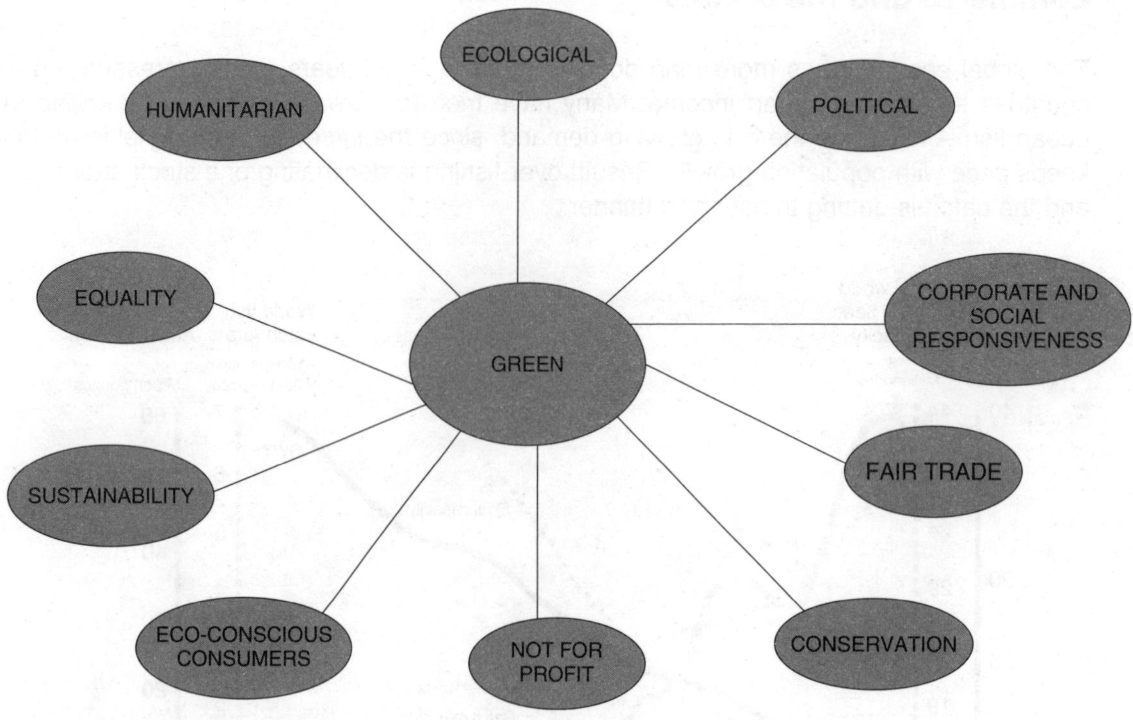

Figure 4.10 Green marketing

In many ways, to be totally green, means that the human population must eschew any luxuries beyond self-sufficiency. As the history of marketing shows, consumption has always played a large part in human existence. For this reason, many marketers feel that being totally green is unattainable, therefore the term 'greener' should be used (Charter and Polonsky, 1999). Figure 4.11 also shows the way in which many products are now global and the way in which consumption at the local level also has global implications.

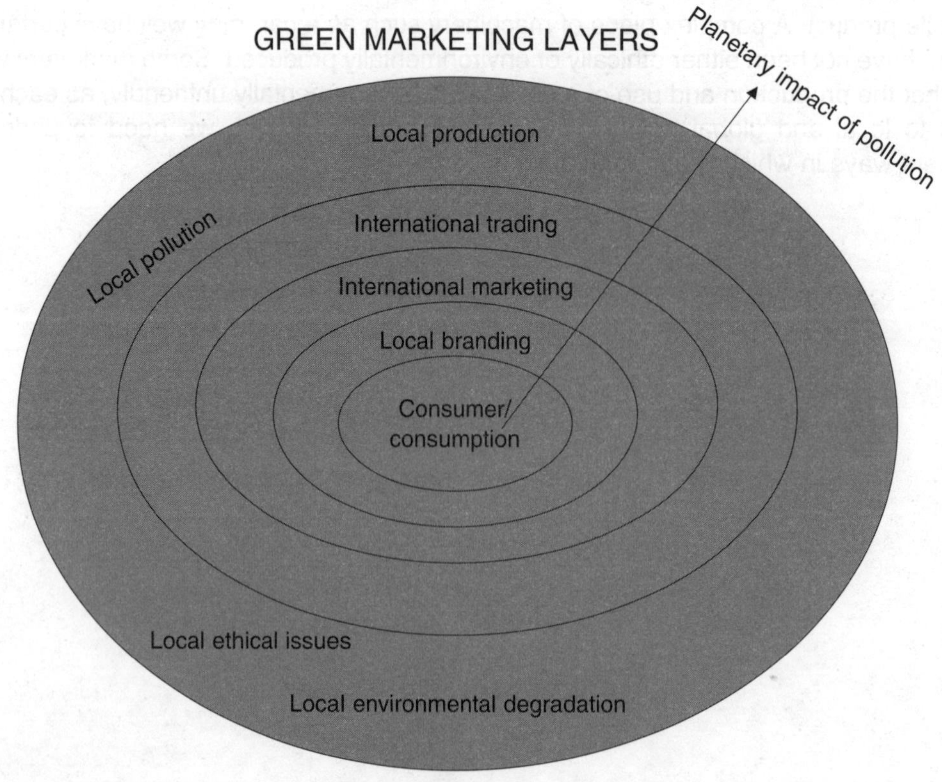

Figure 4.11 Global implications of green marketing

In order to understand how products can be understood as being green, many complicated systems have evolved over the years and many multinationals are now taking the green issues more seriously. MacDonald's for instance has spent a great deal of money on improving their ability to recycle of its materials, but has been quiet on discussing the impact the company has on the environment as a result of the mass production of beef. McDonald's for instance have instituted the following programmes in order to combat energy wastage (Wasik, 1996):

(a) *McRecycle USA programme* – The company claims to purchase over $100 million of recycled packaging. Switching from white to brown bags has saved bleaching costs and prevented a greater degree of chemical pollution.
(b) *Recycled materials in construction* – The company sets aside 25 per cent of its construction budget for recycled materials for construction.
(c) *Energy efficiency* – In partnering with the US Environmental protection Agency, the company instituted a 'Green Lights' Programme. Eco-efficient lighting was used in stores. The stores themselves were made more energy efficient. The energy saved has resulted in preventing over 30 tons of carbon dioxide being released into the air.
(d) *Waste reduction action plan (WRAP)* – The focus of this programme was to cut the amount of waste materials going to landfill sites by using recycled materials and paper.

Interestingly, the biggest failure of the many programmes instituted was in the recycling within the shop environment. Consumers were generally oblivious to this! So the final question is, is McDonald's a green product? This a difficult question to answer because the company has obviously tried hard to improve its products and services through the various ecologically efficiency programmes. On the other hand the morality of mass-producing beef remains unresolved. Some would argue that even this brings necessary employment in poorer areas, others would argue that such farming is harmful to the environment. In the light of these fundamental questions, we can only argue for greener marketing.

Greener marketing may well colour different companies in different shades of green (see Figure 4.12). Again, it is important to note that both social and ecological issues are inextricably intertwined and a truly green company should address both issues simultaneously. Addressing both these issues are the correct routes to creating sustainable businesses and environments. The Nike case illustrates the particular problems faced by an organization caught exploiting workers and then as a result of public pressure, attempting to set things right.

Case example

Nike Corporation

Consider Nike, the $8 billion footwear and apparel company, which has become a lightning rod for activists, consumers, the media, and others, who have taken aim at the company's workplace, environmental, and human rights practices. According to its critics, Nike has engaged in a variety of practices that have exploited Third World workers and the communities where they live. The images proffered by Nike's critics are vivid: women and young children toiling for long hours for low pay in squalid conditions, breathing fumes of toxic chemicals, unable to protest for fear of losing their jobs, manufacturing goods whose price tags exceed their monthly pay.

Nike acknowledges that in the past it was less than vigilant in monitoring the practices of its factories – although nearly all of which are contracted to independent manufacturers. It has now launched an aggressive and ambitious effort not only to correct such situations but to also set a shining example for its industry. The company has begun using sustainability as a design criterion to reduce the use of toxic materials and generation of waste in its manufacturing process. Nike cut the use of solvents in its adhesives by 800 000 gallons in one year and has a goal of reducing its use of volatile organic compounds per unit of production by 90 per cent by 2001. The company also supports organic cotton farming by providing incentives for farmers to switch to organic production.

None of this seems to have stemmed the tide of criticism. In recent years, Nike has been named among the ten 'worst' international corporations by Multinational Monitor magazine. It had an Indonesian factory looted and burned by protesters and suffered criticisms by US women's groups, who pilloried the company for commercials that call for empowering women while poorly paying its predominantly female overseas workers. Its hometown, Portland, Oregon adopted a resolution urging its troubled school district to 'respectfully decline' a $500 000 cash donation because of the company's alleged human rights abuses.

The experiences of Nike and other companies that have come under intense public scrutiny because of perceived wrongdoings suggest that consumers' expectations of brands are changing. It is no longer enough that a company delivers good- quality products. In the search for differentiation, the battleground shifts from the tangible – pounds of chemicals and other wastes released into the environment – to the intangible – ethics, values, and corporate culture.

So ethics are part of understanding sustainable marketing strategies. The other part of understanding sustainability lies in taking a different view on the commonly quoted product life cycle.

The life cycle analysis (LCA) concept – life cycle thinking

One way of considering the creation and utilization of products and services which are environmentally friendly is the LCA concept. The LCA is recognized both as a concept and an analytical environmental management tool (SPOLD, 1995). This concept, sometimes termed lifecycle thinking, helps everyone (consumers and producers alike) to understand the overall environmental implications of the services required by society. This promotes the consideration of the cradle-to-grave implications of any actions taken, forcing, thinking to move beyond the narrow vestiges of supply chains and sector-based considerations of the environment and considers the wider implications of our activities.

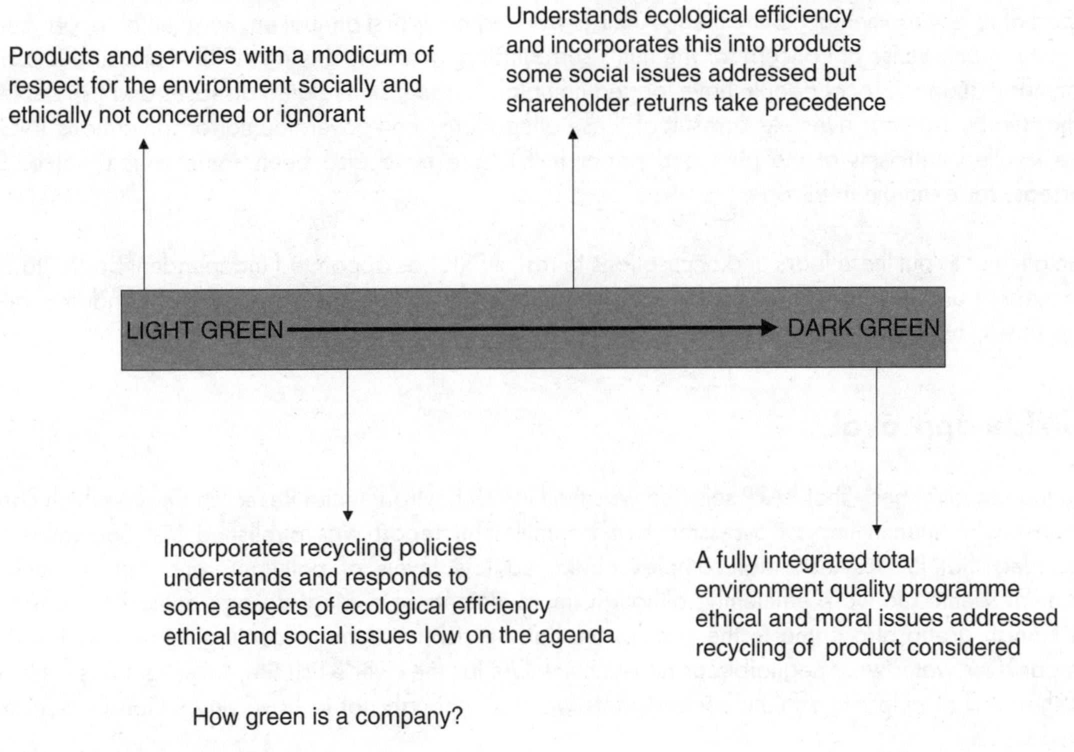

Figure 4.12 Measuring the green policy of organizations
Source: Ranchhod (2001)

Case study

MINI CASE

APRIL takes a leaf out of the green book by Anna Jenkinson

Asia is not renowned for being the most advanced region as far as environmental awareness goes. Just think of the car-clogged, highly polluted streets of many of Asia's big cities, the lack of paper recycling systems throughout much of the region or even the poor quality of drinking water in some places further off the beaten track.

But a mixed track record is no excuse for Asian industries today and many of the region's major pulp and paper manufacturers are facing up to the 'green challenge'. One such company is Indonesia's Riau Andalan Pulp and Paper (RAPP), part of the Asia Pacific Resources International (APRIL) group. On the environmental front, RAPP was arguably helped along by its cooperation, albeit short lived, with Finland's UPM-Kymmene. 'The presence of a European company helped raise environmental awareness and performance,' according to Canesio P Munoz, the company's environmental manager. But since the alliance broke down and RAPP was left standing on its own two feet, there has been no let-up in the company's momentum for greener and cleaner operations.

At present, RAPP is constructing a second pulp line at its Kerinci mill in the Riau province on the Indonesian island of Sumatra. As the company starts to expand towards a two million ton/yr pulp capacity target, the mill is becoming increasingly aware of the need to meet stringent environmental targets to satisfy both local and international demands. The company is targeting a first quarter 2001 startup date for the new line at the Riau mill.

As part of its environmental commitment, APRIL is working on its first annual environmental report. But it is not just a moral sense of concern for the mill's surroundings which is driving APRIL – pressure is coming from many quarters. Local people have lodged complaints about skin-related diseases and fish depletion in the nearby Kampar river. As a result of these allegations, non-governmental organizations (NGOs) have levelled criticisms at the pulp and paper mill. There have also been some critical voices from overseas, for example in Europe.

In an attempt to put these fears and accusations to rest, APRIL has appointed independent bodies to carry out research and help prove that the Indonesian mill operates in line with international standards, and in some cases, beats these targets (Table 4.1).

Outside approval

One independent body that RAPP selected was the Finnish Environmental Research Group which carried out an environmental impact assessment at the mill. The report was published last September and concluded that RAPP's industrial complex contained low levels of pollutants and that the external treatment seemed to work efficiently, although improvements of nutrient dosage could be carried out. The Finnish group also came to the conclusion that the risk for humans coming into contact with the Kampar river water was 'negligible or non-existent'. As for the river's fish life, investigations suggested that the level of pulp mill effluent contaminants was low enough not to have any serious effect on the animals.

Table 4.1 RAPP-effluent load as compared to international standards (kg/ton)

Parameter cluster rules		**Indonesian**		**Canada**		**Sweden**
		RAPP				
	(Early 2000)		(BC)			Existing mills
New mills	(Oct 1999)					
BOD5	8.5	4.5	8.7	8.05	5.5	2.93
COD	29.75	No Spec	31	No Spec	No Spec	11.22
TSS	8.5	7.0	4.0	16.4	9.5	4.41
PH	6–9	5–9	5–9	5–9	5–9	7.1–8.2
AOX	No spec	1.5	0.23	0.623	0.272	0.12

No Spec = No Specification

Soon after the Finnish report, RAPP launched a one-year program with local NGOs to carry out further studies into the effects of the pulp and paper operations on the quality of the local river. The gist of these investigations is to sample biodata from the Kampar river every three months and compare examples taken from upstream, downstream and at the point of effluent discharge from the pulp mill.

The research is a three-pronged effort, with local NGO Riau Mandiri assessing the water quality, the Fisheries department of the University of Riau in charge of the river biology/ecology and the University of Singapore investigating health-related matters.

The preliminary results are good news for RAPP, with no strong condemnations being thrown in its direction. The water quality is described as 'generally good', although Riau Mandiri is looking further into the COD (chemical oxygen demand) and BOD (biological oxygen demand) readings which have recently started to rise. The University of Riau has not noticed any significant difference to the natural river life either. In fact, fish stocks actually increased due to higher nitrogen and phosphorous levels in the effluent treatment. The university team continues to assess the quality of the fish stocks as it seems that sulphur levels are slightly higher than normal, though.

On top of that, the reports from local people about skin irritations are not being blamed on RAPP and it is thought that plants may be the problem. The findings of one Riau University study suggest that it is 'unlikely' that river water is a cause of inflammatory skin problems among villagers. Monitoring will continue, though, until a more conclusive verdict is reached.

It is certainly in RAPP's interests to cooperate with the NGOs and prove the mill's case wherever possible, as the NGOs can act as a powerful lobbyist. As Riau Mandiri spokesperson, Anny Hardiyanti, says, 'After a year's monitoring, if we find negative results, we will urge the company to address the problem. And if the problem is not addressed, we will launch a campaign against the company responsible.' Added to that, the NGO is not afraid of carrying out threats of action. It has already launched several campaigns against other companies, which were found to be polluting another nearby river in the region.

Forest sustenance

A key tenet of APRIL's environmental policy is striving towards fully sustainable forest management. The Indonesian mill's long-term goal is to achieve sustainable forest management certification. But as an interim step, the mill is focusing on an ISO 14001 certificate for its forestry operations, which it hopes to receive by the end of this year. If the company sticks to the timetable, certification would come just a few months after RAPP was awarded ISO 9002 for its pulp and paper operations.

ISO 14001 is an environmental management system, which provides criteria for assessing a company's use of air, water, soil and resources. The drive towards this certification comes from RAPP's customers around the globe, and particularly from European consumers.

Part of the company's efforts towards full sustainability is the development of its acacia plantations. Planting started back in 1993 and some of the plantations are already mature, but the company is waiting until next year before harvesting the area for strategic reasons. RAPP aims to make a full switch from mixed tropical hardwood to acacia plantations by 2008.

The company has also carried out extensive tests on the plantations and is extremely pleased with the yield and quality results. The plantations are expected to yield 210 m^3/ha at harvest and achieve a wood to pulp conversion rate of 4.5 m^3/ton/ib. As a result, RAPP hopes to gain the double advantage of higher yields and limiting any adverse effects on the environment.

By RAPP's calculations, the mill will need 127 500 ha of plantations to supply pulp line #1 which has an 850 000 ton/yr capacity (Table 4.2). Pulp line #2A is due to come on line by the first quarter of 2001, bringing total capacity up to 1.3 million tons/year. RAPP calculates that it will need 195 000 ha/yr of acacia plantations to meet this pulp capacity, and it is no surprise perhaps that the company happens to have exactly this amount available. Originally the government allocated 280 000 ha of land to RAPP for conversion into plantations. The area chosen by the government was so-called 'non-productive land' – in other words the land had already been logged over and exploited. Some of this area must be maintained as a greenbelt area to protect wildlife and ensure biodiversity in the area, leaving the company with the magic number of 195 000 ha/yr for converting into plantations.

Indonesia's social scene

On paper, the land transfer sounds like a relatively simple procedure – the government allocates land and the company decides to convert the area into plantations. In practice, though, there are many more hurdles to be cleared. For example, some of the allocated land is next to local settlements and the communities claim that the ground is theirs in accordance with 'community rights'. Companies such as RAPP are only able to operate effectively by avoiding conflicts with these local communities. This involves talking with the people, suggesting alternative sources of income and convincing them that they will not lose out. As environmental manager, Munoz, says, 'We don't drive people out. Resolutions are always reached by consensus.'

Of the total area allocated to RAPP, some 60 000 ha of land were termed so-called 'problem areas'. So far, the company has resolved approximately half of the issues. RAPP is all too aware of the need to work with the local people to avoid potentially serious problems. For example, last December the Kerinci mill was brought to a standstill as demonstrators took to the streets in protest over a labour dispute. And in the new era of 'reformation' which is flourishing in Indonesia, local communities are becoming increasingly aware of their rights and companies such as RAPP clearly want to avoid conflicts wherever possible.

To date, RAPP has employed a host of community development (CD) projects to try and keep the peace with the locals. The CD programs have existed since 1993, although the initiative was significantly expanded in 1998. Last year alone, the company implemented programs in six local villages. RAPP has carried out initiatives such as building a mosque, providing drinking water, building bridges to overcome transportation difficulties and training the villagers to cultivate unused land for productive and profitable uses.

RAPP's budget for CD programs in 2000 is $2 million and the company's management believes that it is money well spent. Not only does it benefit the local people, but it also promotes good relations with neighbouring communities and improves the skills of potential employees for the pulp and paper mill.

One village called Gunung Sahilan chose to develop oil palm plantations with the company's CD program funds. As a result, APRIL teamed up with an associated company, Asian Agri, which is active in the oil palm industry. The alliance has worked well and the villagers seem extremely pleased with the project's success. But when asked if he was satisfied, the village chief replied, 'We don't need more, but we want more.' A note of warning to RAPP, perhaps, that it cannot sit back and relax. The company must constantly remain attentive to the demands of the local people just as much as, if not more than, those of the international community.

Table 4.2 Plantation supplies at RAPP

		Line 1	**Line 1 + 2A**	**Line 1 + 2A + 2B**
Pulp mill capacity		850 000	1 300 000	2 000 000
Acacia growth rate				
Mean annual increment	m^3/ha/a	30	30	30
Rotation	Yr	7	7	7
Yield at harvest	m^3/ha	210	210	210
Wood to pulp conversion				
Acacia species	m^3/t/ib	4.5	4.5	4.5
Wood and HTI requirement				
Annual acacia input	m^3/yr	3 825 000	5 850 000	9 000 000
Total net HTI area required	Ha	127 500	195 000	300 000
Land resources for tree				
Plantation development				
RAPP HTI concessions area	Ha	195 000	195 000	195 000
Associated companies/jvs	Ha	0	0	85 000
Tree farms	Ha	0	0	20 000
Total area	ha	195 000	195 000	300 000

HTI = hutan tanaman industry

The case illustrates the various factors involved in a company striving to be green. The chain to the final consumer however, can be quite long.

Paper/Pulp production → Packaging, Printing (newspaper/books), Paper products → Consumer → Disposal/Recycling

Consider the life cycle of the products taking into account the various stages of responsibilities.

According to SPOLD, lifecycle thinking reflects the acceptance that key company stakeholders cannot strictly limit their responsibilities to those phases of the lifecycle of a product, process or activity in which they are actively involved. It expands the scope of their responsibility to include environmental implications along the entire lifecycle of the product, process or activity. The implication of this type of thinking is that all processors, manufacturers, distributors, retailers, users and waste managers in the life cycle share responsibility.

The individual share of responsibility for each of them will be greatest in the parts of the lifecycle under their direct control and least in the other stages of the cycle. Life cycle thinking has been applied to much of the legislation emanating from the European Commission, especially with regards to product and waste policy. The concept of producer responsibility is at the heart of waste strategy, and it follows life cycle thinking. An example of this is given in Figure 4.13.

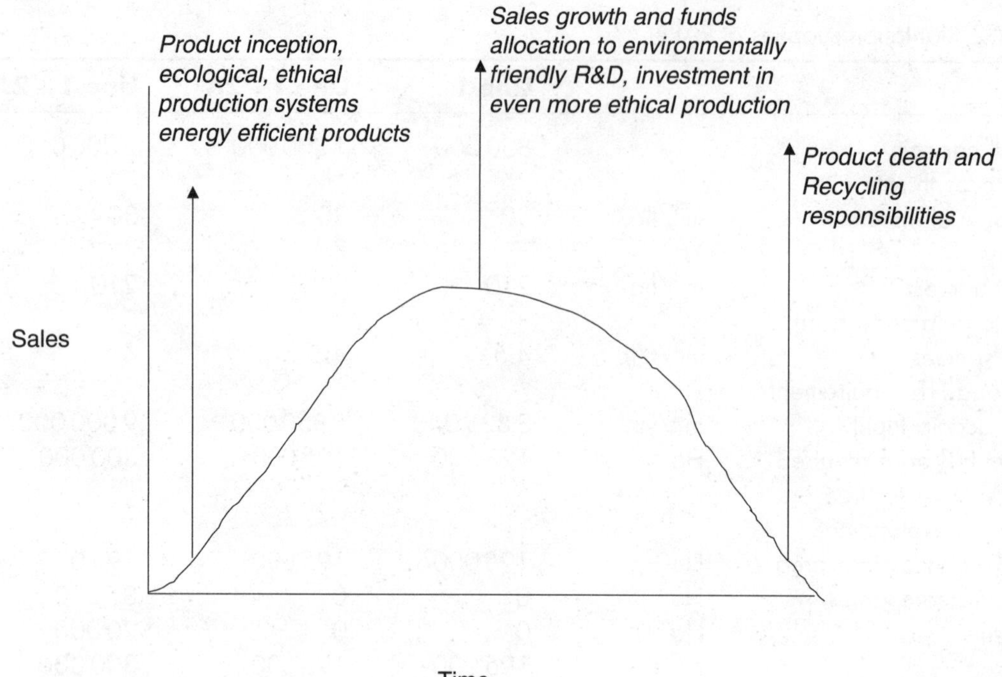

Figure 4.13 Green Lifecycle Analysis
Source: Ranchhod (2001)

Currently there are various different concepts that are related to developing ecologically sound products. Some of these are as follows:

(a) *Design for the environment* – There are many initiatives for reducing the various environmental impacts that a product may unleash. These could be at the production stage, the usage stage, or the disposal stage. In designing for the environment, technologist are concerned with reducing energy consumption (both in the production of an item as well as when it is in use) and generally conserving resources. The main trends are:

1. The incorporation of information from LCA into design.
2. The definition of environmental objectives.
3. A focus on the relationship between the product and the consumer and how the design can encourage environmentally responsible behaviour in the consumer.

According to the US EPA (1992) Life Cycle Design is

A systems-oriented approach for designing more ecologically and economically sustainable product systems which integrates environmental requirements into the earliest stages of design. In LCD, environmental performance, cost, cultural and legal requirements are balanced

(b) *Clean technology* – A definition of Clean Technology is that it is the means of providing a human benefit which, overall, uses less resources and causes less environmental damage than alternative means with which it is economically competitive (Clift, 1995).

(c) *Industrial ecology* – This is generally concerned with the evolution of technology and economic systems in such a way that human activities mimic mature biological systems with regards to being self-contained in their material and resource use (Allenby, 1994). Governments and non-governmental organizations often use this idea when they assess industrial processes.

(d) *Total quality environment management* – This concept synthesizes Environmental Management and Total Quality Management (TQM) (GEMI, 1993). TQEM relies on the following basic parts:

1. *Identify customers* – The definition of quality dependent on what the customers want (a broader definition of customers is taken and they include consumers, legislators, environmental groups and society at large.
2. *Continuous improvement* – A systematic approach at continuously improving processes all the time.
3. *Do the job right the first time* – In terms of the environment, eliminate problems at the outset. Quality failures may be detrimental to the environment and also incur financial costs, without providing benefits to the consumer.
4. *Take a systems approach* – Each part of environmental management is considered to be a 'system'. This includes people, equipment and processes. Weak links in the system are addressed.

In general the Plan-Do-Check-Act (PDCA) cycle is followed in common with typical TQM programmes.

All these concepts are inter-linked and there is now a concerted approach to take a more holistic view and incorporate each of these concepts into a general framework for sustainable development (SETAC, 1998).

Implications for organizations

For organizations it is becoming increasingly important to incorporate green thinking into their processes and products. Organizations need to consider very carefully how much their activities impact on the planet. Any improvement creates a net benefit for both the consumer and the planet. There are charges against companies that they embrace a green attitude at a superficial level and are generally engaged in 'greenwashing' the public through clever advertising and Public Relations activities. In fact even companies like Body Shop have been criticized for exaggerating their claims with regards to promoting sustainable development and the purity of their ingredients (Stauber and Rampton, 1995) In many cases, companies even pursuing a modicum of green policies are not rewarded in the marketplace (Wong *et al.*, 1996). Such criticisms could be levelled at almost every corporation. Nonetheless, it is important to realize that corporations can, even, by implementing some of the concepts discussed above, have a major impact on the environment. For instance:

- Anheuser-Busch has developed an aluminium can that is 33 per cent lighter. This reduced use of aluminium combined with an overall recycling plan saves the company $200 million a year.
- Ford Motor Company used more than 60 million two-litre plastic soda bottles in the manufacturing of grille reinforcements, window frames, engine covers, and trunk carpets. In 1999, this effort accounted for 7.5 million pounds of plastic.
- Kellogg's plant in Bremen, Germany employs a wastewater recycling operation that reduces water consumption and wastewater effluent. In India, a Kellogg vapour-absorption system is used to provide plant air conditioning, eliminating the use of ozone-depleting substances. Fluorescent bulbs at the Kellogg plant in New Jersey are sent for recycling, removing potentially hazardous materials from landfills (Rand Corporation, 2000).

In spite of cynical views, these efforts, not only save the companies concerned millions, but also save resources. These types of savings are not easily obtainable through individual customers. It is important that companies pursue such strategies. This is especially important when you consider that a study showed that of the 100 largest economies in the world, 51 were global corporations – only 49 were countries (Anderson and Cavanagh, 1996). Mitsubishi was larger than the fourth most populous nation on Earth, Indonesia. General Motors was bigger than Denmark, and Toyota bigger than Norway. Often large chunks of world trade are actually transactions between different parts of organizations. Companies therefore, have to be proactive in pursuing ecologically friendly processes and also in producing such products. In addition to this, they are also under pressure from consumers and non-governmental organizations (NGOs such as Greepeace). Companies have become much more sensitive to such pressures because of (Bennet and James, 1999):

- The growing economic value of a good corporate reputation and a strong positively regarded brand. These can be put at risk by adverse criticism of environmental and social performance (Fomburn, 1996).
- The growing number of customers who are becoming more 'green conscious' (this is discussed later), taking social and environmental criteria into account when purchasing goods or services.
- The tremendous flow of information, at unprecedented levels, through satellite TV stations such as CNN and the Internet. In the future, it is likely that information will also be transferred 'on the move' through mobile communication devices such as WAP phones. This flow of information increases the visibility of any enterprise.
- Companies are also dependent on workforces who are highly educated and are often more environmentally literate than their older counterparts.

Interestingly, a recent survey of ethical funds shows that they have performed strongly over the past 3 years. Many funds have shown growth ranging from 73 to 50 per cent (Bien, 2001). These are early days, but the current results bode well for ethical and green investments. What, then should companies strive to achieve? Some of the key questions that companies should be addressing are given at the end of the chapter. In many ways, companies have to strive to get into a virtual circle and constantly look forward to the future with their R&D (Figure 4.14).

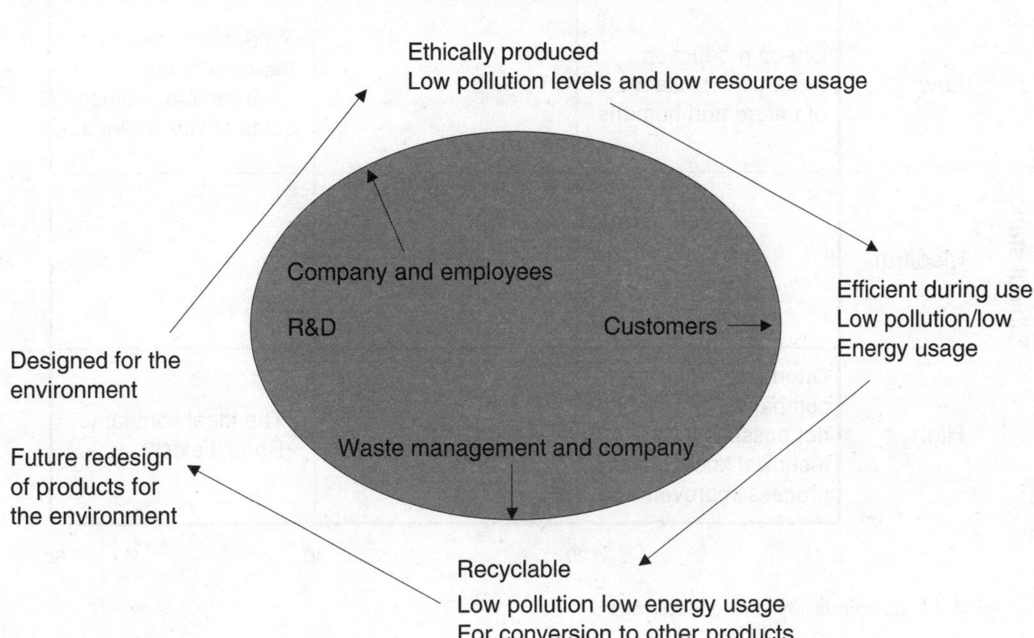

Figure 4.14 Assessing green credentials

Given this type of virtual way, in which companies could operate, the competitive advantages that could be gained are considerable. Various authors have tried different types of categorizations, for instance Hart (2000) has developed the Sustainability where companies can rate themselves on the following scale for each quadrant (1-nonexistant; 2-emerging; established; or 4-institutionalized). Based on this assessment each individual organization can look for gaps and attempt to understand their sustainability credentials and begin to plan both internal and external strategies for the future.

Another way of assessing the total commitment of a company to sustainability and ethical consideration is to utilize the matrix shown below. The questions help in understanding the box in which a company falls.

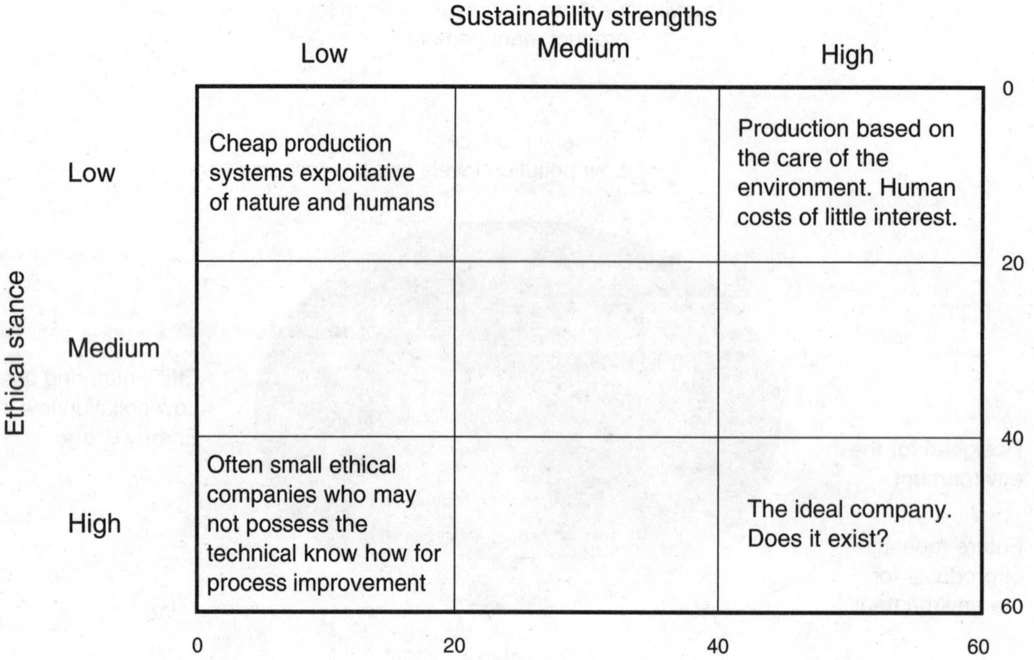

Sustainability strengths

Ethical stance	Low	Medium	High
Low	Cheap production systems exploitative of nature and humans		Production based on the care of the environment. Human costs of little interest.
Medium			
High	Often small ethical companies who may not possess the technical know how for process improvement		The ideal company. Does it exist?

Horizontal scale: 0, 20, 40, 60; vertical scale: 0, 20, 40, 60

Figure 4.15 Sustainability and ethical matrix

The following questions were formulated by understanding the various cases for greener organizations (Peattie and Charter, 1997; Piasecki *et al.*, 1999; Crosbie and Knight, 1995). Look at the questions set. Companies scoring 12 points in both sets of questions fall into the top left-hand quadrant. Companies scoring 60 in both sets of questions fall into the bottom right hand quadrant. The set of questions is designed to show the quadrant in which a company falls (Figure 4.16). It also then points the way for future improvement and the opportunities that may be available.

Green Management questions

	Very poor	Poor	Adequate	Good	Very good
	1	2	3	4	5
1. Design for the environment					
2. Energy efficiency in manufacturing					
3. Waste in manufacturing					
4. Pollution during manufacturing					
5. Recyclability of packaging					
6. Lifespan of product					
7. Energy efficiency during use					
8. Recyclability of product					
9. Total quality environmental management					
10. Search for new green product opportunities					
11. Use of pollution control equipment					
12. Compliance consulting					

Ethical considerations

	1	2	3	4	5
1. Working conditions					
2. Staff welfare and health care					
3. Limitation of exposure to pollutants					
4. Sustainability of operations within local ecology.					
5. Involvement of stakeholders in environmental issues					
6. Continuous pollution monitoring					
7. Management of the end of the life cycle without affecting others (prevention of dumping in poor areas)					
8. Respect for fauna and flora					
9. Adequate compensation to local suppliers					
10. Honesty in advertising					
11. Discussions with NGOs					
12. Environment restoration post production					

Figure 4.16 Green management questions

Companies scoring in the medium/medium range (middle of the matrix) can be prone to resorting to strong advertising campaigns and PR in order to 'greenwash' the public. Consumers often have to rely on specialist journals or articles in newspapers for a true indication of a company's policy. There is a great danger for companies to pay lip service to green strategies and not necessarily address the key issues involved. These issues are explored in detail in the hard hitting book by (Stauber and Rampton, 1995). As discussed before, a company that is truly following sustainable principles has to be both ethically and environmentally sound. Customers too are realizing that we do not live in a world with infinite resources. In fact the new-world paradigm reflects the fact that we are *a part* of nature and not *apart* from it (Wasik, 1996). The Postmodern consumer is more concerned about nature and is likely to look at issues holistically, Table 4.3 illustrates this. For a further discussion of the postmodern consumer, see chapter 2.

Table 4.3 Old versus new paradigms

Old World View	New World View
Continuous unbridled growth	Sustainable, green economics
Conquer nature, reap resources	Biophilia (affinity for nature)
Environmental compliance	Eco-auditing
Marketing to fill needs	Marketing to sustain life
Materialism	Personalism
Industrial production	Industrial ecology
Design for obsolescence, disposal	Design for environment
Cost accounting (profit/loss statements)	Full cost accounting
Departmentalism, reductionism	Holism

Green consumer behaviour

According to a survey carried out by the Wirthlin Group (Wirthlin Worldwide, 2000), two thirds of American consumers agreed that 'environmental standards cannot be too high and continuing improvements must be made regardless of the costs'. In 1999, a Gallup poll survey found that 68 per cent of Americans worried a great deal about the pollution of drinking water and 53 per cent about the contamination of soil and water by toxic waste. Understanding the complexity of the human/ecological interface requires a degree of scientific understanding. Yet surveys conducted by the National Science Foundation suggest that, even using lenient standards, only about 11 per cent of citizens understand enough of the vocabulary and concepts of science in general, in order to be considered scientifically literate (National Science Foundation, 1998).

This is an especially important issue when companies are advertising the green benefits of their products. How many consumers will actually understand the claims made? Are they likely to understand the scientific reasoning behind particular policies or are they likely to be emotively manipulated by the press in a simplistic manner? Quite often, people are very likely to understand simple cause-and-effect relationships. According to Coyle the NEETF president (NEETF/Roper, 2000):

'...[P]eople understand that cars pollute, or that species become extinct when habitat is destroyed. But when there are two or more steps involved...such as energy production from fossil-fuelled power stations contributing to climate change, thereby warming ocean waters sufficiently to inhibit the production of plankton for fish, thus impairing the survival of marine life...public understanding drops precipitously.' Each year, The National Environmental Education & Training Foundation (NEETF) issues a 10-question survey on environmental awareness; in a typical year, Americans averaged fewer than 25 per cent correct answers to basic environmental literacy questions. Furthermore, myths and misconceptions persist. Surveys indicate that many Americans still believe that trash bags can be made to biodegrade in landfills (virtually nothing degrades in landfills). Many people still believe aerosol cans contain ozone-destroying ingredients (chlorofluorocarbons were banned from aerosols in 1978) and that landfills are brimming with plastic (plastic accounts for just 9 per cent of municipal solid waste, paper and cardboard four times as much).

This can be illustrated by an Energy and Environmental Profile Analysis of Children's Single-Use and Reusable cloth diapers carried out by Franklin Associates in 1992 and explained in Fuller (1999). For many consumers, the intuitive understanding is that plastic/paper diapers are vastly energy consuming and polluting. The comparative scientific analysis however shows that the environmental answers are not clear cut. The results show that:

- Home cloth diapers consume 33 per cent more energy than single use diapers and 12 per cent more energy than commercial cloth diapers.
- Single-use diapers produce about twice the total solid waste by volume of home or commercial cloth diapers.
- Home cloth diapers produce nearly twice the total atmospheric emissions of single-use diapers or commercial cloth diapers.
- Home or commercial diapers produce about seven times the total water-borne waste of single-use diapers.
- Home or commercial cloth diapers consume more than twice the water volume of single-use diapers.

Many criticisms can be levelled at such an analysis and indeed, some authors argue that single use diapers also contribute to air pollution, via incineration. They may also be the cause of allergic skin reactions. Nonetheless the case illustrates the complexity of issues involved when undertaking some sort of Life Cycle Analysis for products. Consumers, too, need to be able to follow complex arguments in order to make valid judgements.

Roper Starch (Rand Corporation, 2000) who produce the Green Gauge Report on the environment and environmentally conscious purchase decisions, showed how consumer attitudes broke down in the 2000 survey:

11 per cent True-Blue Greens – The recyclers, composters, letter-writers, and volunteers of the world, the ones most likely to go out of their way to buy organic foods, recycled paper products, rechargeable batteries, less toxic paints and other goods with environmentally preferable attributes.
5 per cent Greenback Greens – Those who will contribute to environmental organizations or spend more for green products, but not consider changes in lifestyles or housekeeping due to environmental concerns.
33 per cent Sprouts – Those who care about the environment, but who will only spend slightly more for environmentally sensitive products.
18 per cent Grousers – These are people who care about the environment but view it as someone else's problem; Grousers don't seek environmentally sensitive goods or consider green-minded lifestyle changes.
33 per cent Basic Browns – People who are essentially unconcerned about the environment.

There is another way of slicing the consumers and that is the traditional method of classifying consumers as:

(a) *Traditionalists* – Those who believe in the nostalgic image of small towns and conservative churches.
(b) *Moderns* – These are individuals who are more materialistic and consumer oriented. They are generally individuals who see life through the same filters as Time magazine.

(c) *The cultural creatives* – This is a new category, discussed by Dr Paul Ray (Rand Corporation, 2000) as a result of market research studies in consumer behaviour. The cultural creatives (CCs) have often been involved in or care about three to six social movements. These are:

(i) Very strong environmentalism
(ii) The condition of the whole planet
(iii) Civil rights
(iv) Peace
(v) Social justice
(vi) New spiritualities
(vii) Organic food
(viii) Holistic health.

Many follow personal paths an spiritual goals. These individuals account for a high proportion of people using alternative healthcare and every other Lifestyle of Health and Sustainability (LOHAS) product and service. The individuals are very good at putting their own big picture together from a diverse range of sources of information. They compare and contrast and are adept at understanding the real issues. They are the least likely to be 'greenwashed'. In addition to this, to fully appreciate the sustainable lifestyle, the Natural Business Communications and the Natural Marketing Institute believe that the greater paradigm of such existence is LOHAS, or Lifestyles of Health and Sustainability. The LOHAS market comprises five core market segments – Sustainable Economy, Healthy Lifestyles, Personal Development, Alternative Healthcare and Ecological Lifestyles. The five segments combined represented a $226.8 billion US market and an estimated $546 billion global market in 2000. Within each of these five segments are many specific categories of products and services across a vast array of businesses and industries. The chart below shows the total size for the five key LOHAS segments and the associated industry categories:

Table 4.4 Key LOHAS Segments and Industries

LOHAS market segment	**Total in $ millions**
Sustainable economy	$76 470
Healthy lifestyles	$27 811
Alternative healthcare	$30 698
Personal development (mind, body, spirit)	$10 628
Ecological lifestyles	$81 178
TOTAL US LOHAS MARKET	$226.8 billion

Source: Rand Corporation, 2000

The 'Ecological Lifestyles' and 'Sustainable Economy' segments represent nearly 75 per cent of the global market, if the US breakdown is emulated around the world. In the light of this complexity of what exactly is a green consumer, several interrelated factors have to be taken into account as shown in Figure 4.17. The complexities surrounding the definition of a green consumer are indeed great. However, the examples above and the discussions show that a new breed of consumer is indeed emerging. This new consumer is influenced by many factors. These factors are generally concerned for a need to protect the environment and to lead ethically correct lifestyles. The market trends show that these consumers are growing in numbers. Companies wishing to understand this growing band of potential customers' need to address their marketing offer in a sensible and honest manner. They also need to consider the way in which markets may move in the future.

Green marketing strategies

In many cases, companies often take reactive stances to green issues. These reactive stances often damage the credibility of a company and the products that are sold. It is therefore important for companies that are seriously concerned about green issues to be more proactive and pursue a market orientation that is green in its design. In order to gain competitive advantage, companies have to exhibit the following characteristics:

(a) Offering products that address the ethical, moral and sustainability issues described above.
(b) Producing goods which are not only commercially viable, but which also meet consumer needs.
(c) Using some of the profits for environmental and social improvement at the source of production.
(d) Segmenting the markets effectively, so that the complexity of the niche markets and the 'new' consumer are understood and targeted accordingly.
(e) Communicating honest and credible messages to the customers. These messages should be transparent and should be understood by internal stakeholders, external stakeholders and the consumers.
(f) The transportation and logistics systems should mirror the company's aims and objectives of lessening pollution, being environmentally friendly, etc.
(g) Developing a marketing perspective that takes a cradle-to-grave approach for products.
(h) In cases where products are complex, offering certain levels of educational marketing literature.
(i) Presenting advertising in a clear and concise manner.
(j) Understanding the *future* needs of the customers and stakeholders.

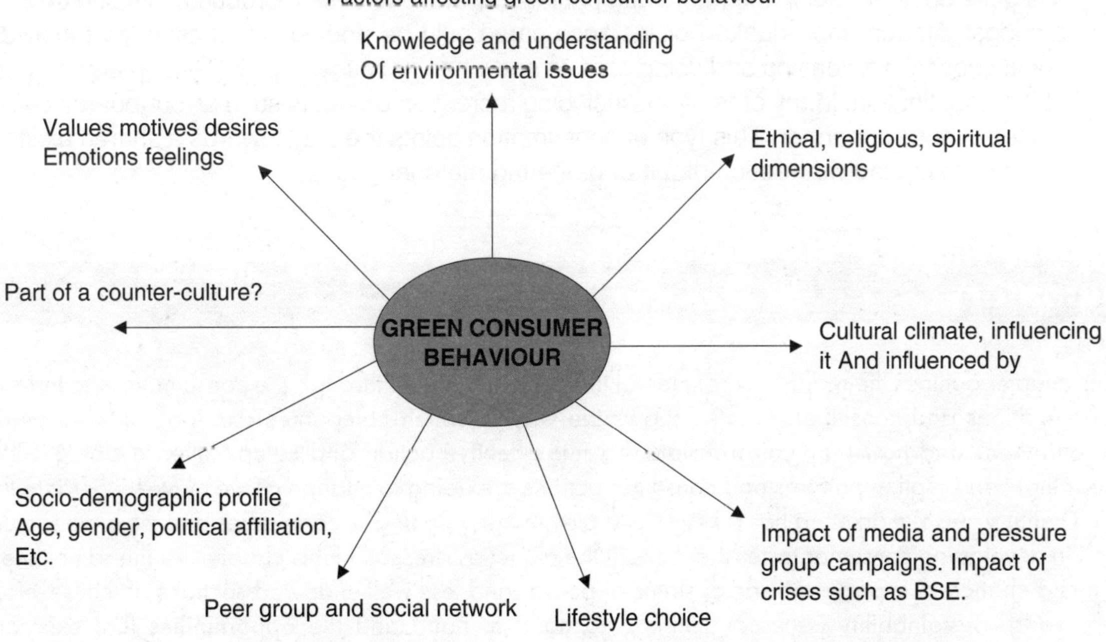

Figure 4.17 Inter-related green consumer factors
Source: Adapted from Wagner (2001)

Anticipating the *future needs* of consumers are of vital importance as the 21st century dawns. Future technological and biotechnological advances could spell either triumphs or disasters for the environment. Already there is considerable disquiet over the introduction of GM Foods. The way in which Foods are produced, distributed, commercialized and perceived has been radically changed in the last 20 years by the advent of new technologies such as Genetic Engineering.

The creation of genetically modified foods and organisms has increased the general public awareness about the elements and the quality of foods. The main concern over GM Foods centres on the fact that they have not conclusively been tested in people's diets using rigorous standards (Cottrill, 1998). The negative perceptions surrounding GM Foods lie deep in the myths and fears of the modern civilization (the expression Frankenstein Foods is a good example) (MacMillan, 2000). Given these negative and in many cases serious concerns about the possible consequences of the environmental spread of 'rogue' genes via cross-pollination, the public are concerned about clarity of messages and clear labelling. As a reaction against GM foods and continuing health scares, organic food sales have grown rapidly. The growing and consumption of organic foods, by many, is seen as ecologically friendly and sustainable.

According to Datamonitor, organic sales in the United States reached $5.4 billion in 1998 and were estimated at $6.4 billion in 1999. Datamonitor (1999) projects sales will continue to grow at approximately 20 per cent per year, reaching $7.76 billion in the year 2000, $9.35 billion in 2001, slightly more than $11 billion in 2002, and slightly more than $13 billion in 2003. Sales during the 1990s grew by 20–24 per cent per year. Organic produce still remains the leading category, although such categories as organic frozen foods, organic dairy, organic bakery items/cereals, organic baby food, and organic ready meals are growing at a faster rate. Another aspect of future consumer trends may be the need for convenience, access to product use and a desire to be free from material possessions.

It is quite possible that in the future companies may have to design products that can be shared amongst different individuals. For instance cars could be pooled within cities and individuals could subscribe to leasing and using cars as and when necessary, pick them up and drop them at their destination. Many other items including recreation products such as surfboards could be leased in such a manner. This type of consumption points the way towards a shared existence, away from the individualistic pursuit of gathering material goods.

Summary

This chapter outlines the major environmental threats to the planet through the consumption patterns of organizations and consumers. It also shows the way in which companies can look at what being green means and how they can translate this into effective action and competitive advantage. It is clear that consumption patterns and consumer actions are going to change as we move further into the 21st century. Also, marketing has a key role to play in the greening of companies and the environment and in developing consumer tastes that benefit the planet as stressed in this chapter. At the same time it offers a chance to improve the social status of poorer and less well-endowed sections of the developing world. Sustainability issues and ethics go hand in hand and the opportunities that exist are immense for companies that can think and act holistically in meeting the growing demand for greener products.

References

Allenby, B. (1994) 'Industrial ecology gets down to earth', *IEEE Circuits and Devices*, **10**(1), 20–24.

Anderson, S. and Cavanagh, J. (1996) 'Top 200: The Rise of Global Corporate Power', Institute for Policy Studies, Washington DC.

Anonymous (2000) 'The State of the World', Worldwatch Institute.

Anonymous (2001) 'Clean me a river', *New Scientist*, **171**(2303), 17.

Bennet, M. and James, P. (1999) *Sustainable Measures: Evaluating and Reporting of Environment and Social Performance*, Sheffield, UK: Greenleaf Publishing.

Bien, M. (2001) 'Ethical investing, even a blue chip share can be green', *The Independent*, February 25 (Foreign Edition), UK.

Charter, M. and Polonsky, M.J. (1999) *Greener Marketing: A Global Perspective on Greening Marketing Practice*, Sheffield Greenleaf.

Clift, R. (1995) 'Clean technology: An introduction', *Journal of Chemical Technology and Biotechnology*, **62**, 321–326.

Cottrill, K. (1998) 'Out of the lab and onto the table', *Journal of Business Strategy*, **19**(2), pp. 38–39.

Crosbie, L. and Knight, K. (1995) *Strategy for Sustainable Business: Environmental Opportunity and Strategic Choice*, Maidenhead, UK: McGraw-Hill Book Company Europe.

Datamonitor (1999) Organic Trade Association and Datamonitor (Datamonitor's 1999 US Organics Report).

EPA (1992) Life Cycle Design Guidance Manual. Environmental Protection Agency (EPA), EPA 600 1R-92/226, Cincinnati, USA. http://www.epa.gov/.

Fomburn, C. (1996) *Reputation, Realising Value from the Corporate Image*, Cambridge, MA: Harvard Business School Press.

French, H. (2000) 'Coping with ecological globalization', *The State of the World*, W. Institute, New York and London: W.W. Norfton and Company, pp. 184–211.

Fuller, D.A. (1999) *Sustainable Marketing: Managerial-Ecological Issues*, Industrial Examples Sage Publications Ltd.

GEMI – Global Environmental Management Initiative (1993) *Total Quality Environmental Management*, GEMI, Washington.

Hart, S.L. (2000) 'Beyond greening: *Strategies for a sustainable World*', *Business and the Environment*, Boston, MA: Harvard Business School Publishing.

Jenkinson, A. (2001) 'APRIL takes a leaf out of the green book', *Pulp and Paper International*, **42**(8), 19–21.

MacMillan, A. (2000) Genetically Modified Foods: The British Debate, http://cbc.ca/news/viewpoint/correspondents/mamillan_gmf.html.

Makower, J. (1994) Beyond the Bottom Line: Putting Social Responsibility to Work for your Business and the World. Simon Schuster.

National Science Foundation (1998) Science and Engineering Indicators (1998) http://www.nsf.gov/sbe/srs/seind98/frames.htm.

NEETF/Roper (2000) The Ninth Annual National Report Card on Environmental Attitudes, *Knowledge and Behaviours*, NEETF/Roper.

New Scientist (2001) 'Clean me a river', **171**(2303), 17.

Ottman, J. (1993) *Green Marketing: Challenges & Opportunities for the New Marketing Age*, Lincolnwood, IL: NTC Books.

Oyewole, P. (2001) 'Social costs of environmental justice associated with the practice of green marketing', *Journal of Business Ethics*, **29**, 239–251.

Peattie, K. (1995) *Environmental Marketing Management*, London: Pitman.

Peattie, K. and Charter, M. (1997) 'Green Marketing', in P. McDonagh and A. Prothero (eds), *Green Management: A Reader*, London: Dryden Press, pp. 388–412.

Piasecki, W.B., Fletcher, K.A. and Mendelson, F.J. (1999) *Environmental Management and Business Management: Leadership Skills for the 21st Century*, John Wiley and Sons.

Rand Corporation (2000) Consumer Power and Green Consumption, http://www.rand.org/scitech/stpi/ourfuture/Consumer/Section6.html.

SETAC (1998) Evolution and development of the conceptual framework and methodology of life-cycle impact assessment, http://setac.org/files/addendum.pdf.

SPOLD (1995) Synthesis Report on the Social Value of LCA Workshop, SPOLD/IMSA obtainable from Proctor and Gamble Services Company, Temsalaan 100, 1853 Strombeek-Bever, Belgium (Fax +32 2 568 4812) Spold terminated its activities at the end of 2001. Its history may be obtained on http://www.spold.org/whatis.html.

Stauber, J. and Rampton, S. (1995) *Toxic Sludge is Good for You: Lies, Damn Lies and the Public Relations Industry*, Monore, ME: Common Courage Press.

Wagner, S.A. (2001) *Understanding Green Consumer Behaviour*, London and New York: Routledge.

Wasik, J.F. (1996) *Green Marketing and Management: A Global Perspective*, Cambridge, MA: Blackwell.

Wirthlin Institute (2000) Environmental Update, Vol. 10, No. 8, http://209.204.197.52/publicns/Twr1100.pdf.

Wong, V., Turner, W. and Stoneman, P. (1996) 'Marketing strategies and market prospects for environmentally-friendly consumer products', *British Journal of Management*, **7**(3), 263–281.

Worcester, R. (1997) 'Public opinion and the environment', in Jacobs, Michael (ed.), *Greening the Millennium? The New Politics of the Environment*, Oxford: Blackwell.

World Watch (2000), 13, March/April.

Corporate identity

Attempt at improving public image and creating a public identity is an ancient practice witnessed not least of all in flags and other symbols used to rally the masses and unite them. In recent times businesses have adopted the practice of nations by adopting a consistent name, logo and tagline. The practice of corporate identity began to assume significant importance in the 1970s, but still confusion exists over the meaning of corporate identity, image and personality. The concept also overlaps with branding, but is nevertheless a separate subject area. This section will attempt to provide some understanding of the subject though definitive conclusions can yet not be reached.

The concept of corporate identity is important for the same reason as for branding and relationship marketing – the increasing competition in the marketplace and the need to differentiate. It is also related to the increasing recognition of the importance of integrated marketing communication and associating the organization with certain values that would be appealing to the target audience. This is thought to be helpful in building long-term relationships with customers and other stakeholders. Organizational identity and values are, perhaps, particularly relevant with more politically/ideologically motivated consumers who are interested in social and political issues and encourage some organizations, at least, to consider corporate social responsibility and cause-related marketing. Corporate identity strategy is a systematic attempt at using effective integrated communications to build relationships between an organization and its stakeholders. Corporate identity is the manifestation of an organization's mission statement, values, corporate objectives plus a plethora of visual and behavioural elements that help the organization to project its personality.

Corporate identity – a graphic design approach

Examining the concept in more detail reveals that the original notion of corporate identity was more closely linked to visual identity: logos, organizational nomenclature, buildings, design, stationery and so on. This approach was basically a graphic design approach, and was hugely influential in brining to the fore the basic elements of importance in designing corporate identity.

One of the influential writers on corporate identity, Olins (1978, 1995) has proposed that visual identity can reflect an organization's personality, strategy, branding and communication policies. Olins stresses that in the recent graphic design literature, symbolism has become the focal point and moved from promoting corporate visibility to communicating corporate personality. The graphic design paradigm defines corporate identity as 'an assembly of visual clues-physical and behavioural by which an audience can recognise a company and distinguish it from others and which can be used to represent or symbolise the company' (Abratt, cited in Stuart, 1999).

Corporate identity – integrated communications approach

Integrated communications approach to corporate identity embraces the concept from a public relations viewpoint. This approach believes that corporate identity is a tool for the organization to communicate effectively with all of its stakeholders (e.g. Schulz *et al.*, 1994). Emphasis is placed on those processes which are used to strategically create, change and manage an organization's corporate identity and improve its public image. Such processes may begin with the mission statement and positioning of the organization.

Synthesis approach

This approach assumes that corporate identity is created through both behavioural and communications strategies, as well as through symbolic elements and visual manifestations. The viewpoint stipulates that image is an expression of corporate personality and as such an externalization of an organization's unique traits, capacities and competencies on a mental, physical and emotional level (Olins, 1995). This approach is a holistic one and regards the organization as an evolving entity.

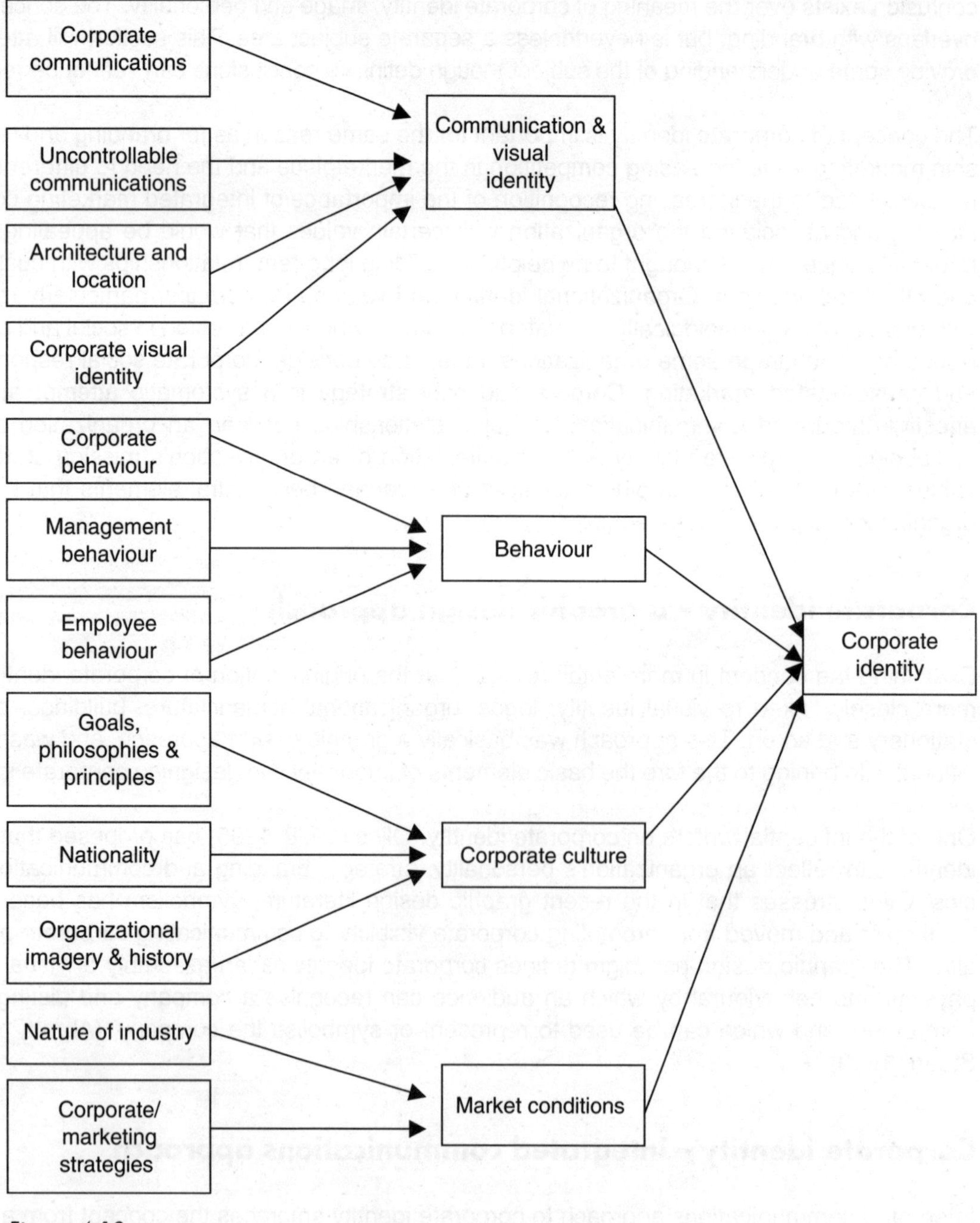

Figure 4.18

Corporate identity and its sub-constructs

Melwar, T.C. and Jenkins, E. (2002) 'Defining the Corporate Identity Construct', *Corporate Reputation Review*, 5, 1, 76–90.

Defining corporate identity

From the above discussion it may be discerned that there is not a universal definition of corporate identity. The definition adopted here will be that by Olins (1978) who proposes that corporate identity is 'the tangible manifestation of a corporate personality' and involves the management of all the means that a company uses to present itself through experiences and perceptions to its various publics (Olins, 1995).

Corporate personality

It is suggested that corporate personality is the soul, the spirit of the organization and is unique for every organization (Olins, 1995). It should be pointed out that some authors (Albert and Whetton, 1985) have referred to an organization's character instead of personality.

Corporate/public image

Identity may be suggested to refer to content while image refers to form. When an identity is projected an image is formed in the individual's mind and this is how a corporate image is formed (Moffit, 1994).

The role of communications

It is essential that the senior level management effectively communicate the desired corporate identity to all employees and monitor employee behaviour towards customers and other stakeholders. Company's behaviour through its products, services and processes need to be monitored too. Additionally, intentional external communications including advertising, PR, promotions and visual identity elements need to be carefully thought out. While, the communications discussed so far are within the control of the company, other types of communications, for example competitor claims, media interpretation, rumours and word of mouth are outside company's direct control but will need to be dealt with effectively by the company. Here, the role of public relations becomes apparent.

Integrated communications and consistency are the cornerstones of success in creating and maintaining the desired corporate identity and reputation. Synthesis must exit not just between messages conveyed by different communications tools, used on different occasions, but also between corporate identity and corporate strategy.

References

Albert, S. and Whetton, D. (1985) 'Organisational identity', *Research in Organisational Behaviour*, **7**, 263–295.

Moffit, M.A. (1994) 'Collapsing and integrating concepts of "public" and "image" into a new theory', *Public Relations Review*, **20**(2), 259–2170.

Olins, W. (1978) *The Corporate Personality: An Inquiry into the Nature of Corporate Identity*, London: Design Council.

Olins, W. (1995) *The New Guide to Identity*, London: Gower Publishing.

Shultz, D., Tannenbaum, S.J. and Lauterborn, R.F. (1994) *Integrated Marketing Communications: Pulling it Together and Making it Work*, Chicago: NTC Business Books.

Stuart, H. (1999) 'Exploring the corporate identity/corporate image interface: An empirical study of accounting firms', *Journal of Communication Management*, **2**(4), 357–371.

Branding

Brands are the major enduring assets of a company, outlasting the company's specific products and facilities (Kotler *et al.*, 2005). A typical definition of branding would be that branding is the process used by a company to distinguish its products from those of its competitors through assigning a name, term, sign, symbol, packaging and design. In reality, though, simply allocating a name to a product and printing a symbol on the package does not really turn a product into a brand, not successfully anyway. Marketing research has to be carried out in order to determine the physical and emotional needs of target customers, as brands are essentially about emotions, and satisfying of psychological needs. The driver looking proudly at the Mercedes badge on the bonnet of his car is looking at more than a means of transportation, he/she is looking at the vehicle through which the desire to be 'successful' has reached its point of satisfaction. Hence, brands are much more than just names and symbols. They are about feelings, emotions and perceptions and lifestyle statements. To build a successful brand, marketing research should help to make the right decisions about the following:

Product benefits – What are the physical and emotional benefits of buying a brand?

In what tangible ways is brand A better than brand B?

In what ways and which psychological needs of the target market will brand A satisfy better than brand B?

Core values – Successful brands are built on clear core values, important to the target market, and consistently reinforced through integrated marketing communications. Relevance of such values may be widely different depending on the product category and the target markets and can be revealed through marketing research. Examples of core values are Volvo: safety; BMW: performance, technology, innovation; Pretty Polly: sexy, middle class, young female; Levi: young, sexy, American, original denim jeans; Asda: value for money.

Brand associations – All that is directly, or indirectly linked to the brand in the customer's perception. These could include locations, sounds, colours, faces, story lines, attributes, and so on. Creating the right associations in the customer's mind is a key aspect of successful branding. Cadbury, the British chocolate manufacturer, keen to promote its two-hundred-year heritage and its emphasis on quality and tradition uses colour purple in its packaging (royal), as well as a picture of one-and-a-half-pints of milk (quality) and sponsors the longest running TV soap in the UK-Coronation Street (tradition, way of life).

Brand image and brand identity – Brand identity refers to the message sent by the brand owner about the brand. Brand image, on the other hand, is how the target audience perceives the brand. Successful branding implies a great degree of closeness between the two. 'Images surrounding brands enable consumers to form a mental vision of what and who brands stand for. Specific brands are selected when images they convey match the needs, values and lifestyles of consumers' (de Chernatony and McDonald, 1988).

Brand personality – This is the 'character of the brand described in terms of other entities such as people, animals or objects' (Jobber, 2001). For example, a Volvo could possibly be described as a white, middle age, middle-class accountant, while a Renault Clio may be described as a young, modern, upwardly mobile woman.

Brand names – Brand names ought to be selected carefully. Ideally a brand name should be short, distinctive, memorable and easy to pronounce. Additionally, a brand name should say something about the product and its benefits and also not have negative meanings in other languages.

Branding types (**also referred to as branding strategies, and branding policies by different authors**) – Companies may choose one or more of the following options:

1. *Individual branding* – This is when a company uses different brand names for different products (or different versions of the same product), enabling it to position each brand differently in the market, for example up market and down market, (Seiko and Pulsar). Here the failure or success of each brand is of no consequence to other brands of the company, but promotional costs might be high.
2. *Corporate branding* – This allows a new brand to benefit from the corporate reputation, but a new brand failure can damage that reputation. Also, this approach does not leave much flexibility regarding the positioning of the brand.
3. *Multi-branding* – Individual differentiation of brands is made possible in this approach, and allows for different positioning of the company's different brands with the failure of one not necessarily affecting others. However, promotional costs are normally higher than in corporate branding.
4. *Range branding* – All the products in a range carry the same brand name, and promotional costs are spread through the range. All the brands within the range may enjoy the same strength while successful, but a failure may affect all the brands in the range. Again, positioning and marketing mix decisions for individual brands are limited as there has to be consistency throughout the range.
5. *Private branding/own label brands* – In this case the manufacturer produces under the supplier's own brand name passing all the responsibility for promotion to the supplier. This approach reduces promotional costs but also creates a barrier between the company and the customer.

6. *Generic branding* – Refers to a brand that that does not carry a company name or other distinguishing terms, and merely indicates the product category. This option reduces promotional and packaging costs and hence the final price to the customer. This approach means competition is mainly on price and customer service and psychological elements play a smaller role in differentiation.
7. *Brand licensing* – This refers to when a company grants permission to another company to use its brand name, in return for a payment or percentage of turnover. This is a good way of earning royalties/fees and expanding the brand quickly. However, problems could arise with regard to such issues as quality control and damage to the brand.

Brand development strategies

Brand extension/stretching – This involves using an existing successful brand to launch new or modified products in a different product category, for example a hi-fi/electronics manufacturer stretching its brand to mobile phones as in the case of Sony. This is a risky option if consumers find it hard to associate the brand with the new product category. On the other hand it has the advantage of giving the new product instant recognition through the brand name.

Line extension – This is when new items are added to the product line under the same brand name. This works best if the extension competes with other brands rather than take the market from the existing items in the line.

New brand development – New brands may be developed for existing, or for new markets. Ideally a new brand ought to be capable of real differentiation rather than more or less a copy of existing brands in the market.

Brand revitalization

Every brand has its life cycle and at some stage revitalization and re-positioning of the brand may be necessary. Revitalization may be in four shapes (Doyle, 1998):

1. *Develop new markets* – Saturation of existing markets may be compensated by finding new markets for the brand in geographic areas where the brand may be able to enjoy growth.
2. *Enter new segments* – This involves attempting to promote the brand to new consumer markets (e.g. different age groups, or industry sectors).
3. *Find new applications* – Finding new uses for existing brands can help revitalize them, for example baking soda used as de-odouriser in refrigerators.
4. *Increase brand usage rate* – There are many ways that a company can attempt to increase the usage of its brands, for e.g. by making it easier to use a brand, by providing incentives to use (loyalty rewards, etc.).

Brand positioning

When deciding on the positioning of a brand, various factors need to be taken into consideration. These include: the target market in terms of consumers and the competition; the culture and history of the brand-how it has developed over the years; brand assets and attributes in terms of what makes the brand different from competitors; brand values, images and personality; and finally physical and psychological benefits to consumers.

Brand re-positioning

As successful brands take a long time and a large investment to establish themselves, it is not possible to re-position a brand over night and to change consumers' perceptions. Given adequate marketing research and sustained and integrated marketing communications, however, it is possible to successfully re-position a brand. There are many different types of re-positioning. The two main ones are:

1. *Real repositioning* – This is achieved as a result of product modification and updating.
2. *Psychological repositioning* – This is about changing consumer beliefs about a brand through advertising and other forms of communications. A recent example of this is Skoda's positioning in the car market which has over a decade moved from being a very poorly regarded car to a relatively respectable one.

Brand equity – is the value of a brand, based on the extent to which it has high brand loyalty, name awareness, perceived quality, strong brand associations, and other assets such as patents, trademarks and channel relationships. A brand with strong brand equity is a valuable asset (Kotler, 2005). The value of a brand may be shown on a company's balance sheet, although in practice it is very difficult to measure.

Global brands – These are brands that are marketed across national boundaries with the same strategy, the same positioning with little or no change in the marketing mix, e.g. Coca-Cola. Successful global branding is much more difficult than domestic branding, not least of all due to cultural differences which still exist despite globalization gradually eroding such differences. Branding is essentially built around the concept of core values, and values are the most fundamental components of culture. Cultural differences basically refer to differences, first and foremost, in values and also in attitudes, beliefs and customs. Values are enduring beliefs about right or wrong, good or bad which we hold as members of society as well as consumers, and which shape our behaviour. Culture will therefore affect whether consumers desire a brand in the first place, how strongly they desire it, to what use they will put it and how often will use it. Culture will also heavily influence the promotion of brands. As brands are built through associations and images, careful thought will have to be applied to such matters as nudity, gender roles, respect for elders, religious symbols and so on. For example, recently Harrods had to withdraw bikinis depicting the image of Buddha after there was uproar among the Buddhist community.

References

de Chernatony, L. and McDonald, M. (1998) *Creating Powerful Brands in Consumer, Service and Industrial Markets*, Oxford: Butterworth-Heinemann.

Doyle, P. (1998) *Marketing Management and Strategy*, 2nd edition, London: Prentice Hall.

Jobber, D. (2001) *Principles and Practice of Marketing*, 3rd edition, Maidenhead: McGraw-Hill.

Kotler, P., Wong, V., Saunders, J. and Armstrong, G. (2005) *Principles of Marketing*, fourth European edition, Harlow: Prentice Hall.

Case study

Nike

The American giant Nike is the leading global manufacturer of sportswear. According to Greek mythology, Nike was the winged goddess of victory with a mystical presence symbolizing victorious encounters. The Nike 'swoosh', designed in 1971, is meant to embody the spirit of the winged goddess who inspired chivalrous warriors (www.xroads.virginia.education). Today, Nike's name and swoosh are seen on the shoes and clothes of some of the world's most successful sportsmen and women.

Nike began in the 1960s from humble origins, as a result of cooperation between Philip Knight and Bill Bowman, an athletics trainer. Philip Knight is the main owner, CEO and chairman of the corporation. Nike is always at the forefront of design innovation. At the time of writing, for example, Nike's Shox range has taken the market by storm. A Shox trainer incorporates heel columns for cushioning, and is normally available in sizes 3–8 for women and 5–12 for men. It comes in a number of versions and each version has its own colours. These versions include, Shox fsm, Turbo, TL2, GMB for women; and TL2, R4, Turbo 2, Turbo leather, etc. for men. Shox trainers belong to the running shoes lines produced by Nike, who produce many different versions/sub-brands of running and other shoes (e.g. Sohx, Airmax) with each one of them having yet their own various versions (as described earlier in the case of Shox), or for example in the case of women's tennis shoes (Air Max Court Miller, Air Illusion 2, Air Zoom Thrive). Thus, it could be said that Nike offers great 'depth' in its product lines.

Nike product mix also offers great width. Nike offers numerous product lines, with running shoes being only one of those. Lines offered by Nike include: Sports shoes/trainers (running, tennis, golf, football, hockey, etc.); sportswear (shorts, caps, trousers, T. shirts, socks); leisurewear (shirts, trousers, shorts, caps, sandals), sports equipment (footballs, golf balls, racquets, etc.); merchandise (phone covers, watches, bags).

Nike's products in the UK are sold mainly through large sports retailers such as JJB Sport, selected department stores such as John Lewis and direct marketing/catalogue companies, for example Littlewoods. The trainers can also be purchased from Nike's state of the art website (www.Nike.com) and other retailers' websites, for example (www.lxdirect.com). Similar distribution strategy is followed by Nike in most of the countries in which it is operating.

Nike engages in well thought out and massive promotion of its products using a range of tools including television, cinema and print advertising, celebrity endorsement by, and sponsorship of, well known and popular athletes, posters and the Internet. Nike's payments to celebrity's like Tiger Wood is thought by some to be greater than the corporation pays its entire workforce in some Asian countries.

Nike's promotion is based around building the brand on the core values of 'innovation', 'inspiration', and 'speed'. Comparing with the music world Nike are the Rolling Stones or the Oasis of the sportswear world, with an intentional roughness to the brand. They are not sponsors of official events such as the Olympics (that is left to Addidas). They have continued to sponsor controversial stars such as, Michael Jordan and Eric Cantona and they famously advertised that 'You don't win silver, you lose gold'.

The corporation's main target market is the medium to high end of the market in terms of price, and the fashion conscious, casual shoes/clothes wearers and amateur and professional athletes. The non-professional target market of Nike is the 15–25 year old male and female. According to Mintel (2003) however, this target group is not particularly happy with Nike's recent attempts to court older consumers.

A very brief PEST analysis for Nike's UK market reveals:

Political – The country is politically stable, corporation tax is not particularly high, Government is in favour of business expansion and freedom, laws and regulations do not restrict selling of sportswear in anyway.

Economic – UK enjoying long period of boom, unemployment is low, inflation and interest rates are low, consumer spending is high.

Socio-cultural – Casual/sportswear in fashion, trainers in fashion, many people willing to spend money on designer/expensive trainers for themselves or their children, youngsters copying each other and buying latest/expensive trainers (even those from poorer backgrounds).

Technological – Computer designed trainer technology available, advanced spring/air technology for trainers for added comfort and speed. There is also technology available now to engage in direct dialogue with customers (The Internet, mobile telephones, etc.), to take individual measurements even, and to customize products and communication with customers, if a company so wishes.

Nike's main competitors are Addidas, Puma and La Coste. Nike, however, remains just ahead of the competition in terms of innovation and branding.

Nike is a long established global company with a great experience in operating in international markets. It employs top designers and marketing teams. The corporation's annual income is estimated at 8 billion dollars per year. Despite its success, Nike has had to face criticism for exploiting Asian labour in what are alleged to be sweatshops. Nike however, like Gap, Addidas, etc. deny this and argue that it is the sub-contractors in Asian countries who are to blame for ignoring codes of conduct which they have negotiated. Even so, this is an area that Nike has to deal with to improve its public image. Recent donation of 1 million dollars by Nike to Tsunami victims is less than some individuals have contributed.

Questions

1. Recommend ways in which Nike can go beyond having a brand relationship with its customers and develop relationship marketing strategies. Would such a strategy be beneficial to Nike? Explain your answer (whether you agree or not).
2. Examine Nike's corporate Identity and identify its strengths and weaknesses. You may wish to use the model by Melwar and Jenkins (2002) which appears in the section on corporate Identity in this chapter.

References

http://www.lxdirect.com

http://www.nike.com

http://xroads.virginia.edu.html

Mintel (2003) *Footwear-UK-August 2003*, Mintel International group

Source: Roxie Marandi.

Case study

Argos

Argos operates within the so-called variety goods sector in the UK and Ireland. Part of the Argos Retail Group and owned by Gus, Argos is the market leader in its field with over 500 high street, and out of town, catalogue showrooms. Argos's business proposition is that of delivering value and choice at locations that are convenient to customers. The latter visit the showrooms and order products from catalogues and collect within minutes after payment. Argos catalogues offer numerous goods: personal items, homeware, electric appliances, TV, hi-fi, sports and photographic equipment, computers, etc. Argos's closest competitor is Littlewoods/Index . Argos, with an annual turnover of approximately 3 billion pounds (Mintel, 2004) continued to expand the number of its showrooms in 2004, and retailers in the UK, including Argos experienced a prosperous 2004, although Christmas sales figures were not as expected. Argos customers are now able to purchase products on-line or by telephone.

Briefly:

- Argos is the market leader of the non-food mixed goods retailer sector in the UK.
- Argos' core competencies include the successful operation of a multi-channel retailing network.
- Argos, whilst competing with a range of Department and variety stores, only has one competitor in its strategic group, Littlewoods Index.
- Argos' experience of running the catalogue showroom format appears to be its main source of competitive advantage, ensuring its position as market leader.
- Argos' position in the industry enables it to purchase and retail strongly branded products with value-for-money as its primary trading proposition.

Physical and operational assets

- Over 500 catalogue showrooms.
- 20 'Call and Collect' Stores.
- Major modern warehousing and distribution network, including Argos Direct Distribution Service and arrangements for delivery direct from manufacturers.
- State-of-the-art Call Centre facility.
- Argos has undertaken major investment in its operational assets including in its supply chain management, IT systems and warehousing.
- Interactive technologies and plasma screens being introduced to improve customer queuing.

Human resources

ARG has 49 000 employees in UK and Europe (www.gusplc.co.uk).

Systems

- IBM Websphere software provides e-commerce infrastructure.
- New IT and software systems investments in Enterprise and Resource Planning.
- Software to facilitate management information systems and database analysis.

Marketing assets

- Stores in all major towns and shopping locations.
- Around 50 million catalogues distributed annually Argos catalogues present in 70 per cent of households (www.4i.co.uk).
- Consumers are able to select from product lines at home, telephone or use website to check availability and reserve products before travelling to stores.
- Argos is a well-recognized brand name in the UK and Ireland.
- Argos is the UK market leaders in Toys, Jewellery, Watches, Portable Audio, Small Kitchen Appliances, and is also the leading retailer of furniture and home furnishings.
- Multi-channel distribution network ensures rapid distribution of goods to customers through wide range of distribution channels.

Organizational competencies

Strategic:

- Argos has managed to stay ahead of its main rival Littlewoods Index.

Functional skills:

- Marketing campaigns successful in terms of customer recall rates (75 per cent +) (Grant, 2002); 'never out of stock' policy achieved on 500 key lines (accounting for 20 per cent of sales) (Mintel, 2002).
- Money-back guarantee to customers honoured within 16 days of purchase for any reason.

Operational:

- Argos has introduced a successful multi-channel retailing strategy. Its strength is in its experience of operating in the market, where location of stores and distribution network provide access to wide customer base.

Corporate level:

In addition to achieving market leadership from sales in store, Argos has made innovation part of its strategy: Argos was the first chain to launch a satellite T.V. channel, and become the first in the world to introduce a 'Text and Take Home' mobile phone stock check and reservation service (BBC, 2002).

SWOT analysis

Strengths – Argos established as the UK's leading multi-channel retailer, achieving market leadership in many product lines.

Weaknesses – Argos Additions clothing is currently loss making, and sales in mail order Home Shopping are declining.

Opportunities – Improvement of customer in-store experience through introduction of modern technologies to improve waiting times; expansion sales through the Internet.

Threats – loss of market share to large grocery retailers offering one-stop shopping; continued decline in mail order reducing overall group performance.

Value chain analysis

- Investment in latest technologies to improve customer experience in-store, and to ensure purchases may be made in the most convenient way to individual consumers may be considered to be a key value-adding service to consumers.
- Continues to follow an aggressive offensive marketing strategy to ensure it remains the market leader of catalogue and multi-channel retailing in a market in which growth is expanding.
- Latest marketing and promotional campaigns have proved successful.
- Improved inbound logistics are expected to reap benefits of £50m per year to further improve its sales proposition (www.argos.co.uk).

Industry analysis

The industry is one in which there is likely to be intense rivalry between competitors. Although goods sold are strongly branded and therefore suppliers have some control over prices, the size of the buyers, coupled with suppliers' needs for large distribution channels give buyers strength to squeeze suppliers to lower prices. There is growing danger of substitutes from Internet distributors.

Question

Using the information in this case study and any additional information you may be able to find, devise a 3-year strategic marketing plan for Argos. Where information is not available make assumptions.

References

htpp://www.argos.co.uk

http://gusplc.co.uk

http://4i.co.uk/expertise

Mintel (2002) Department and Variety Store Retailing in the UK, February, Mintel International Group Ltd.

Mintel (2004) Variety Stores-UK, August, Mintel International Group Ltd.

BBC (2002) Argos Introduce Shopping by txt msg, BBC I News, 23rd October.

Source: Reshma Ranchhod.

Contemporary issue in the context of the case study

This chapter highlights some of the major issues surrounding company organization and development in an ever-diminishing energy base within a competitive world. Issues of sustainability, branding, corporate identity and responsibility as well as customer loyalty are becoming extremely important for developing marketing strategies. These topics are now at the forefront of many company decisions. Students should become well versed in these contemporary issues.

unit 5 effective customer orientation

Outcomes

- Formulate and present a creative, customer-focused and innovative competitive customer strategy for any given context, incorporating relevant investment decisions, appropriate control aspects and contingency plans.
- Promote and facilitate the adoption and maintenance of a strong market and customer orientation with measurable marketing metrics.

This chapter will build on the concept of relationship marketing within the customer context as already discussed in the previous chapter.

(a) Market orientation and customer orientation.

(b) Details of financial analysis and marketing metrics as control mechanisms.

(c) Discussion and formulation of contingency plans.

Introduction

Being customer-focused is becoming an important plank of many organizations marketing strategies. Being customer-focused largely results from well-developed Customer Orientation Strategies.

Market and customer orientation

For many years there have been discussions about market orientation and its meaning to organizations when producing marketing strategies. Market orientation has as its main constructs:

(a) Intelligence gathering
(b) Intelligence dissemination
(c) Competitor analysis
(d) Customer analysis.

In addition to the above, companies face turbulent environments moderating the strategies they adopt for both customers and competitors. It could be argued that a truly market-oriented company is one that organizes its activities, products and services towards the needs of its customers, in a better manner than its competitors.

However, the essence of all the arguments lies in the following:

(a) *Information generation* – This is the generation of customer, market and competitor-related information as a result of a company's intelligence gathering activities. The information is either from internal or external sources.
(b) *Information dissemination* – Having obtained the necessary information, a company needs to disseminate this information effectively to all the individuals operating within its confines. If information dissemination is poor, it can be difficult for a company to develop the correct strategy for a given market or set of customers.
(c) *Implementation and response to the information received* – A company needs to act on the information received and it needs to act in a clear and precise manner. Therefore, the *type* of information gathered and the *speed* with which it is disseminated within a company play an important role in determining marketing strategies and the implementation of those strategies.

Figure 5.1 encapsulates the key components of market orientation and how they affect the success of a company in the marketplace. In general, there are three main themes which relate to the marketing concept: *Customer focus* – information generation pertaining to customers; *Competitor focus*; and *Responsiveness* – dissemination of information obtained pertaining to customers across the functional departments. This would be with a view to meeting customer needs as quickly as possible by having good inter-functional coordination within the departments.

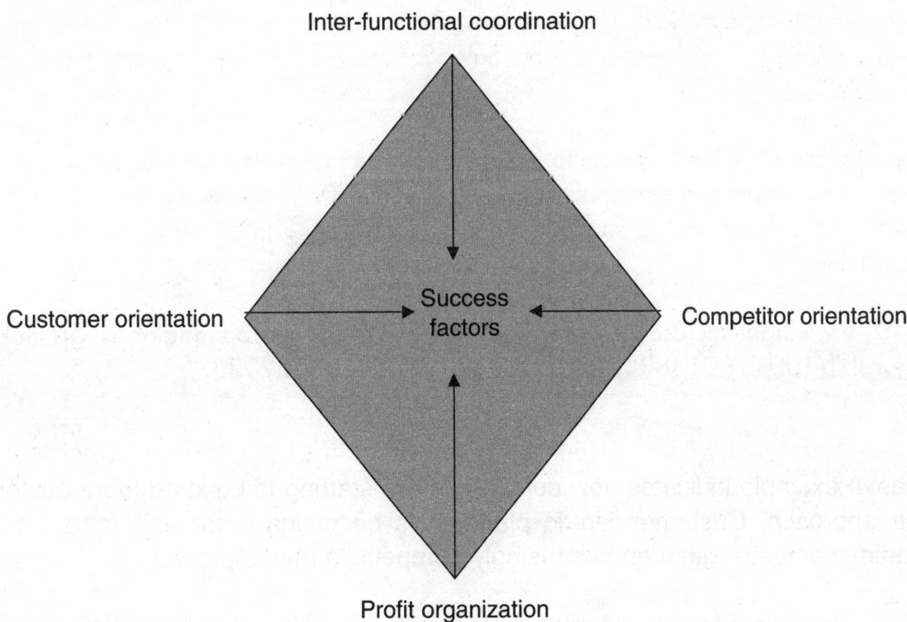

Figure 5.1 Components of market orientation
Source: After Deng and Dart (1994)

Case study

Leica Microsystems increases market orientation

Leica Microsystems has announced sweeping restructuring measures all along the value added chain to improve customer orientation and therefore enhance the market impact and competitiveness of the globally operating company. 'In view of the growing customer demand for integrated digital application solutions for the display and analysis of microscopic structures,' says the manager of the Business Area Microscopy Systems, Dr Roland Zarske, 'we have decided to restructure our Business Units. Instead of the four Business Units we have at the moment, there will be just two: "Compound Systems", where the main emphasis will be on Life Science, and "Stereo Systems", which will continue to make most of its turnover in industry.' Both units integrate various technologies as well as software development, which was previously independent. The aim of this measure is to enhance the intelligence of system developments and make the new units particularly efficient, as an integrated customer solution can only be provided by offering automated microscopes together with digital application solutions. At the same time, the company plans to move capacities from German locations to its factories in Asia for reasons of cost efficiency, or to transfer to business partners.

Simultaneously, Leica Microsystems is to set up a pan-European sales organization reflecting the market segments. This will allow the European Selling Units to market their innovative all-round applications in the segments Research (Life Science), Clinical, Industry, Surgery and Sample Preparation in a more targeted, coordinated and customer-oriented way. Additionally, Leica's presence all over Europe will be consolidated by expanding the existing dealer network, while the teams already existing in each country will continue to provide local after-sales service. 'Through greater customer orientation we can accelerate sales growth and increase profitability, which are key elements of our business strategy,' explains the manager of the European Sales Organization, Dr David Martyr. With centralized organizations, functions such as Marketing and Technical After-Sales Service will be able to operate more powerfully on a European scale.

'With the new structures, we will be able to focus our competences even more accurately on the benefit of the customer and enhance our competitiveness,' says CEO Dr Wolf-Otto Reuter. 'In conjunction with improvements in efficiency, this will enable us to intensify investing in further innovations and assets to safeguard our future.'

Source: http://www.light-microscopy.com/WebSite/SC_MQM.nsf?opendatabase&path=/website/pressrelease.nsf/(ALLIDs)/BD14834D6BDC0CB8C1256E3200522025.

The above example indicates how companies are starting to become more customer-oriented in their approach. Customer-centric planning is becoming more and more useful as many companies compete within an increasingly competitive marketplace.

There is now considerable interest in trying to understand how companies can become customer-centric. Every organization, whether it is profit-oriented or not, has to be able to satisfy its customers. Figure 5.2 shows the gradual evolution in marketing towards customer orientation. In order to be customer-centric, marketers need to be able to assess each customer individually and satisfy their needs either directly or through a third party.

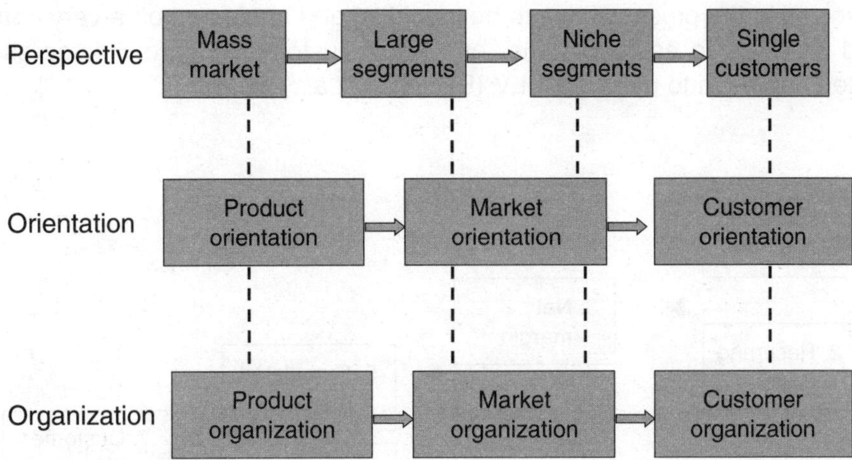

Figure 5.2 Growth of customer-centric marketing
Source: Sheth *et al.* (2000)

In addition to this, technology is rapidly changing the way in which relationships are managed. Customers are able to contact companies through various channels and these need to be understood and managed by an organization. These are shown in the Figure 5.3:

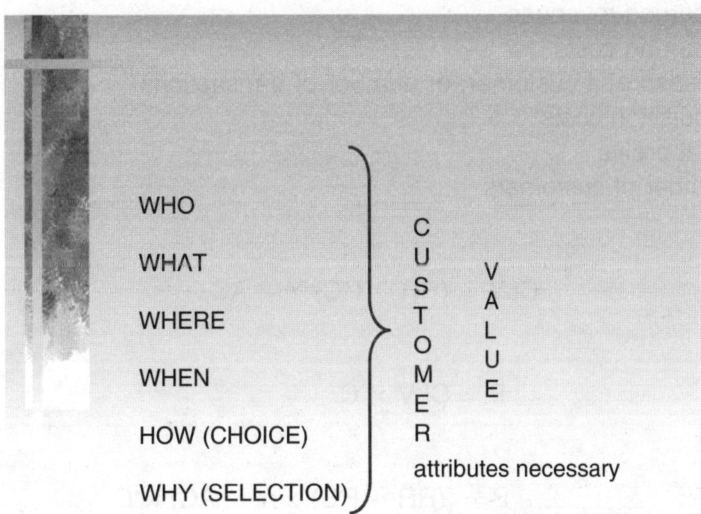

Figure 5.3 Customer analysis

Valuing customers

In calculating customer profitability, most methods start from the customer lifetime value (CLV). Customer lifetime value is a controversial concept among the business specialists (Ranchhod and Gurau, 2003). Some consider it as 'an elaborate fiction of presumed precision' (Jackson, 1992), while other analysts declare that companies should abandon lifetime value theories and take care of the customers now (Ambler, 2001).

In mathematical terms, the CLV consists in taking into account the total financial contribution – that is revenues minus costs – of a customer over his or her entire life of a business relationship with the company. Despite its simplicity, the measurement of CLV requires great care. All cash flows involved in the process have to be identified and measured on a very detailed level, and allocated precisely to each customer or type of customer. Figure 5.4 represents a concise seven-step approach to measure CLV (Bacuvier *et al.*, 2001).

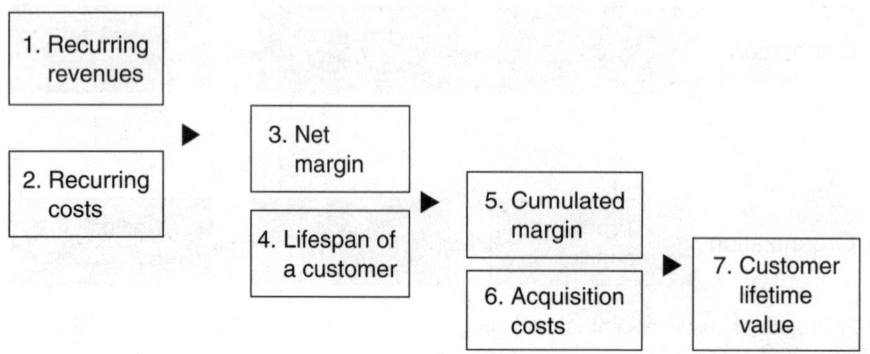

Figure 5.4 Seven-step process to measure customer lifetime value

Translating Figure 5.4 into mathematical formulas, we obtain:

CLV – Customer lifetime value (Profitability)
RR – Recurring revenues
RC – Recurring costs
Y – Lifespan of a customer, or number of transactions
AC – Acquisition costs
P – Total profits
C – Number of customers

$$CLV = (RR - RC)\,Y - AC \quad (5.1)$$

$$P = CLV \times C \quad (5.2)$$

$$P = [(RR - RC) \times Y - AC] \times C \quad (5.3)$$

The mathematical expression of the CLV can represent a sound basis for analysing the existing situation, and for identifying the possible strategies to increase customer profitability. Analysing formula (5.3), five levers of customer value creation can be identified (Bacuvier *et al.*, 2001). These strategies represent only the starting point of a company-wide operational effort. Table 5.1 shows the complexity of implementing customer-oriented strategies based on the analysis of the CLV.

Table 5.1 The operational requirements for implementing customer-oriented strategies based on CLV analysis

Strategy	Tactics	Operation	Requirements
Conquer – increase C – the number of customers	Improve the existing offer in order to attract the potential customers close to the existing customer segments	Improve: o product o price o distribution o promotion	Research Segmentation Investment
	Diversify the offer in order to attract new segments of customers	Increase the product/ service portfolio	Research Segmentation Investment
Increase RR – recurring revenues	Increase the volume of sales	Diversification Stimulate the demand	Research Segmentation Investment
	Increase the value of sales	Upgrade the offer	Research Segmentation Investment
	Increase both the volume and the value of sales	Diversification Stimulate the demand Upgrade the offer	Research Segmentation Investment
Reduce RC – recurring costs	Reduce general costs (administration, maintenance, etc.)	Increased efficiency	Research Segmentation Investment
	Reduce cost of: o product/service o distribution o communication	 Cheaper supplies Cheaper outsourcing Increased efficiency	Research Segmentation Investment
Retain – increase Y – lifespan of a customer	Increase customers' loyalty maintaining and/or increasing customer satisfaction	Improve present offer Better targeting Score better than competition	Research Segmentation Investment
Reduce AC – acquisition costs	Better targeting of potential customers	Improve offer Improve targeting Use the same resources more efficiently	Research Segmentation Investment

Problems in calculating the customer lifetime value

The calculation of the CLV is not problem-free. However, most of these problems can be successfully solved taking into consideration two main issues:

1. The company applying this method has to clearly define from the beginning the purpose of using CLV analysis and the expected benefits.
2. The problems raised by the CLV analysis are often industry and company specific, as a result the company has to select the most appropriate way to apply this concept in its particular situation.

Defining a 'customer'

The first challenge is to define the customer unit (Ness *et al.*, 2001). Is it an individual, an account, a household, or a business address? A second challenge is linking customer information into a single customer record when they leave and return multiple times during their lifetime.

The answer to these questions is industry specific. The business organization has to identify the characteristics of its customer relationship, and, on this basis, to define the customer unit and the customer lifetime cycle. In the present marketplace, a company can be confronted with the following situations:

Table 5.2 The characteristics of customer relationships in different industrial markets

Number of customers	Number of transactions	Level of involvement
Large	Large	High
Medium	Medium	Medium
Small	Small	Low

Table 5.2 shows the possible combinations of customer relationships characteristics, different among industrial sectors and even among companies within the same industry. For example, a company with a small number of customers, which makes a small number of transactions that require a high level of company-customer involvement, will probably define the customer unit as being single customers (individuals or organizations), and the customer lifecycle depending on the business cycles specific for the industry (production cycle, investment cycles, consumption cycles). On the other hand, for a company dealing with a large number of clients, with large number of transactions and low involvement, it might be more appropriate to aggregate the individual customers into particular segments with homogeneous profiles and behaviour. This type of segmentation helps a company to become more customer-focused in a sensible profitable manner (Figure 5.5) illustrates this. It also helps a company to develop feedback loops and a chance to develop contingency plans in case a given situation does not materialize.

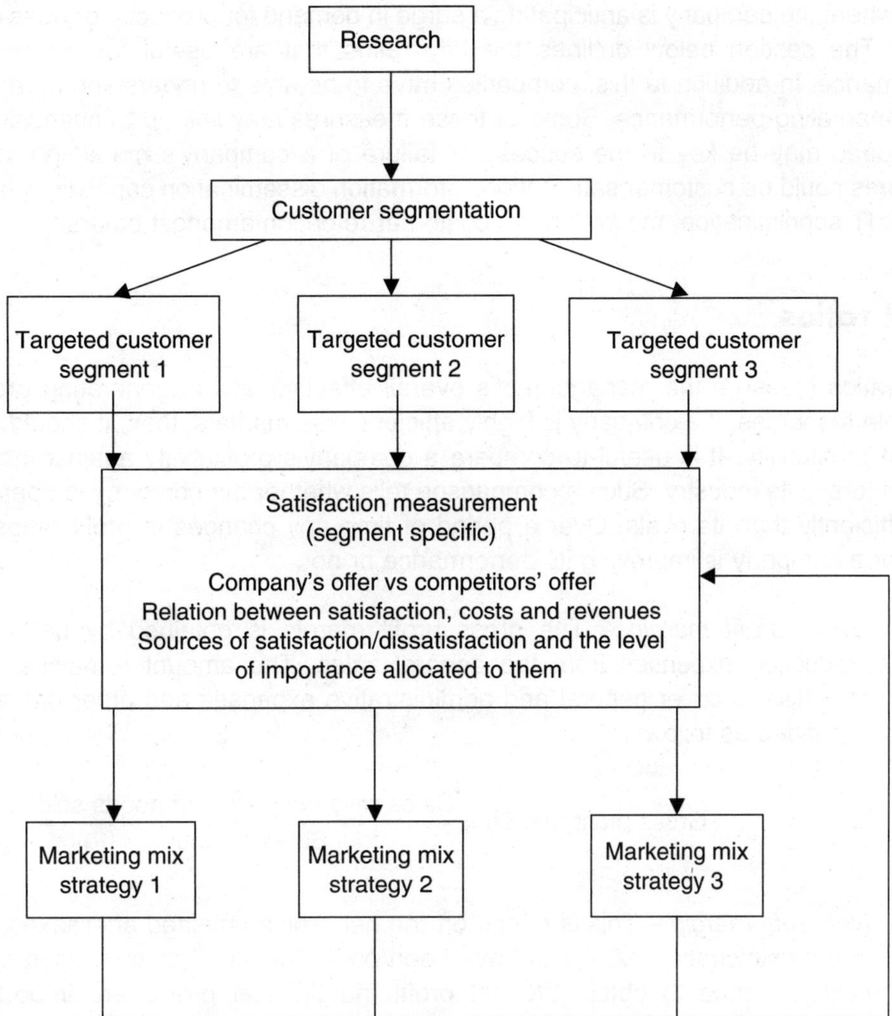

Figure 5.5 The use of customer segmentation and customer satisfaction measurement for designing and implementing targeted marketing mix strategies

Financial analysis and marketing measures

Introduction

Cases are based on real companies which have financial reporting systems. Usually, for the purposes of disseminating information to shareholders and stakeholders, companies produce annual accounts explaining financial flows, profits and losses and balance sheets. Many accounts also contain information on market shares, geographical segmentation and regional segmentation. Recently, there has been considerable interest generated in understanding the use of particular sets of data pertaining to marketing. These can be measurement of brand equity, customer satisfaction, loyalty/retention, share of voice and marketing spend. Some of these measures are shown in the Table 5.3. Interestingly not many companies actually utilize the full range of marketing metrics for measuring their marketing performance. Often we are only left with the age-old financial measures. These measures do help in understanding the position of a company. Quite often they are used by senior managers to gauge trends, especially if data for previous years is available in the same format. In most cases, the analyses are based on financial ratios. These accounting ratios are used in the interpretation of financial statements. Usually, these ratios are at their most useful when compared to ratios for different time periods. This can be helpful in identifying trends and understanding strengths and weaknesses. If, for instance, inventory levels are high in a balance sheet, does it imply that there is a peak, where the company is anticipating a surge in demand for products, or does it imply falling sales? The section below outlines the key ratios that are useful for analysing company performance. In addition to this, companies have to be able to understand measures that are about marketing performance. Some of these measures may link up to financial performance and indeed may be key to the success or failure of a company's marketing strategy. Such measures could be customer satisfaction, information dissemination capability within an organization, IT sophistication, market share, customer retention amongst others.

Profit ratios

Profit ratios measure the management's overall effectiveness in generating profits from the available resources. If a company is highly efficient in its markets, then, it should exhibit a high level of profitability. It is useful to compare a company's profitability against that of its major competitors in its industry. Such a comparison tells whether the company is operating more or less efficiently than its rivals. Over a period of time any changes in profit ratios will indicate whether a company is improving its performance or not.

1. *Gross profit margin* – The gross profit margin is obtained by deducting variable production expenses from the general sales. The amount remaining can then be allocated to cover general and administrative expenses and other operating costs. It is defined as follows:

$$\text{Gross profit margin} = \frac{\text{Sales revenue} - \text{Cost of goods sold}}{\text{Sales revenue}}$$

2. *Net profit margin* – This is based on the net profits obtained after taxes, loan interest and administration expenses have been paid. This net income is then divided by the sales revenue to obtain the net profit margin. Net profits are important because companies need to make profits to survive and also invest in the future to develop and grow markets.

$$\text{Net profit margin} = \frac{\text{Net income}}{\text{Sales revenue}}$$

3. *Return on total asset* – This ratio measures the profit earned on the employment of assets. It is defined as follows:

$$\text{Return on total assets} = \frac{\text{Net income}}{\text{Total assets}}$$

4. *Net income* – is the profit after preferred dividends (those set by contract) have been paid. Total assets include both current and fixed assets.

5. *Return on shareholders' equity* – This ratio measures the percentage of profit earned on the shares held within the company. Companies attractive to shareholders are those that can maximize this ratio. The greater the return, the greater the amount of money that can be distributed to individual shareholders. It is defined as follows:

$$\text{Return on shareholders' equity} = \frac{\text{Profits after taxes}}{\text{Total equity}}$$

6. *Liquidity* – The amount of liquidity refers to ready cash that may be available to a company for immediate use. The lower the liquidity, the greater the danger of a company, not being able to meet its immediate cash commitments or tactical marketing requirements.

(a) $$\text{Current ratio} = \frac{\text{Current assets}}{\text{Current liabilities}}$$

(b) $$\text{Quick ratio} = \frac{\text{Total assets}}{\text{Total liabilities}}$$

(c) $$\text{Inventory to net working capital} = \frac{\text{Inventory}}{\text{Current assets} - \text{current liabilities}}$$

7. *Leverage* – If a company has borrowed little money, then it is possible for it to increase the amount of money it can raise in the marketplace, either through loans or share issues. The money can enable further investments in marketing or new product development.

(a) $$\text{Debt to assets ratio} = \frac{\text{Total debt}}{\text{Total assets}}$$

(b) $$\text{Debt to equity ratio} = \frac{\text{Total debt}}{\text{Total equity}}$$

(c) $$\text{Long-term debt to equity ratio} = \frac{\text{Long-term debt}}{\text{Total equity}}$$

8. *Activity* – This reflects the efficiency with which the company is dealing in the marketplace. High inventory levels could signify flagging sales, indicating poor distribution, lack of advertising or sales efforts.

(a) $$\text{Inventory turnover} = \frac{\text{Sales}}{\text{Inventory}}$$

(b) $$\text{Fixed asset turnover} = \frac{\text{Sales}}{\text{Fixed assets}}$$

(c) $$\text{Average collection period} = \frac{\text{Accounts receivable}}{\text{Average daily sales}}$$

Marketing metrics

These will vary from one company to another. The key points to consider are: 'Who are the main users of company reports, and how important are they as data sources?'

Shareholders will be interested in profitability and long-term growth. On the other hand directors and employees will be interested in issues such as market share, growth in the client base, profitability per customer, distribution costs, customer satisfaction and so on. Thus information usage is very dependent on the functions within an organization.

Marketing metrics have become a point for serious consideration for many organizations that are looking for the best ways in which performance can be measured. Performance varies according to the company characteristics and according to the sector in which it operates. Having standard metrics for all organizations is difficult, so it is useful to consider how metrics model can be developed for each organization. Figure 5.7 offers an idea of how some general marketing measures could be developed for an organization. However, there are many other issues to consider such as:

(a) Brand equity measures
(b) Environmental measures
(c) Customer satisfaction measures
(d) Customer loyalty measures
(e) Customer profitability measures
(f) New product success measures.

amongst a range of others. In all cases, it is useful to categorize the measures according to their acceptability, suitability or feasibility for adoption by a particular organization (Ranchhod, 2004). Table 5.3 indicates the types of metrics that could be considered by companies.

Table 5.3 Marketing metrics for possible use in company reporting

Market data	Market size	Market trend
Relative market performance	o Unit volume trend o Market share (volume) o Market share by mix by major market segment (value)	o Relative price levels and trends o Sales by major brand (value) o Major brand trends (value) o Channel (value)
Customer performance	o Number of customers o Customer loyalty o Customer complaints o Relative quality o Relative value	o Customer service levels o Customer satisfaction o Consumption per capita (value) o Would recommend company or brands to friend
Innovation	o Activity calendar (past year) o New product/service review o New products/services launched in past 5 years as % of this year's sales	o Statement of future opportunities and objectives o Partnerships, acquisitions, licences
Efficiency	o Capacity utilization o R&D productivity	o Awards
People and competency	o % employee turnover o % employees participating in share purchase or profit-sharing	o Training activities, and training spend o Spend as % of sales o Employee satisfaction o Intellectual property
Investment	o R&D priorities and spend as % of sales o Capital expenditure activity and spend as % of sales o Advertising spend as % of sales	o Total marketing spend as % of sales o Technical support to customers
Branding	o Preference o Purchase intent o Brand value o Brand strength	o Awareness o Image o Perceived differential o Brand positioning
Distribution	o Level o Trend	o Channel mix o Channel trend

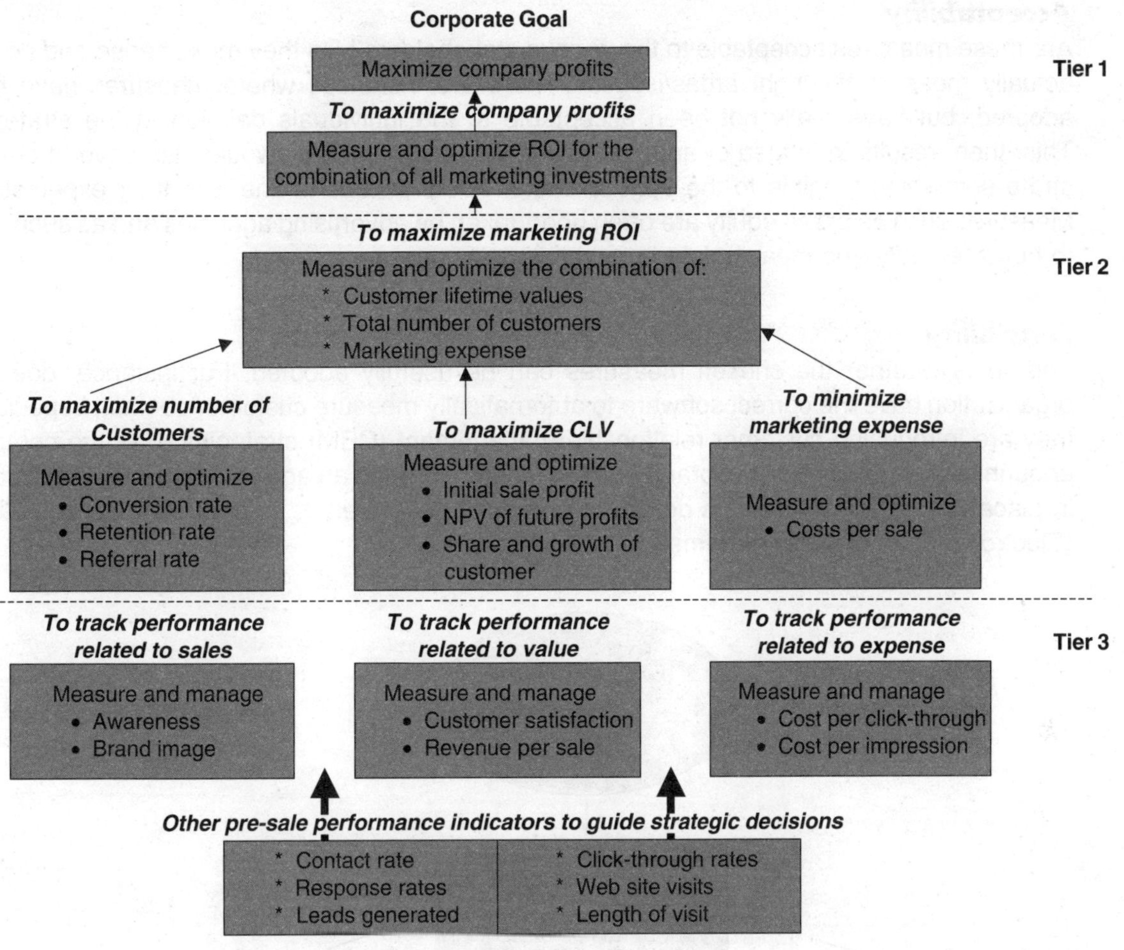

Figure 5.6

Suitability

This provides an assessment of the most suitable measures that could be adopted for a particular company. This is likely to depend on the following:

(a) Industry sector.
(b) Service or product orientation of the organization.
(c) Not-for-profit or a non-governmental organization (NGOs).
(d) The level of technology used for automatic measurement. For instance, on the Internet, transactions can be recorded automatically. When loyalty cards are used, the customer transactions are recorded in a database. These records can then be subsequently used for datamining.
(e) The strategic vision of the company. For some companies there may be an emphasis on rates of return, on others such as NGOs the emphasis could be on the rates of consumer awareness or the level of funds generated.
(f) Is the measure chosen likely to be valuable in the long run and can trends be ascertained?
(g) Can the measures chosen be used to benchmark against competitors?

These measures can then be screened by considering the following criteria:

Acceptability

Are these measures acceptable to the various stakeholders? Do they make sense and do they actually measure the right areas/issues? There are instances where measures have been adopted, but have really not been acceptable to the individuals developing the strategies. This, then, results in fudged or anomalous results. The measures would also have to demonstrate something tangible to the various stakeholders and be in line with their expectations. Measures such as brand equity are often undertaken by advertising agencies and as such need to be acceptable and meaningful to marketing personnel.

Feasibility

This tests whether the chosen measures can be usefully adopted. For instance, does the organization have the correct software to automatically measure customer contact, especially if they are introducing customer relationship management (CRM) strategies. Has the company enough resources to carry out brand equity research through an agency? Does it have systems in place with retailers to obtain details of revenues generated at point of sale through EPOS (Electronic Point of Sale) systems?

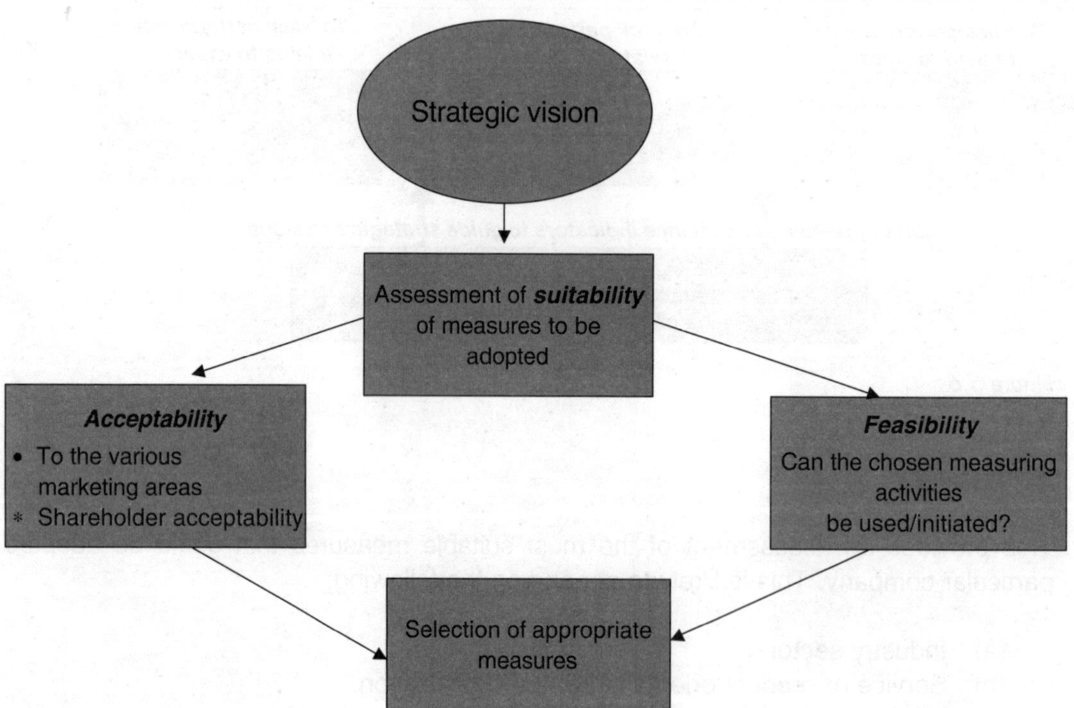

Figure 5.7 A framework for selecting marketing measures
Source: Ranchhod, 2004

Some common measures

Usually in marketing, there are some measures, which are used commonly by organizations. These measures are:

(a) *Customer satisfaction* – Measurement can be complex and depend on attributes measured – internal barriers to measurement.
(b) *Customer loyalty* – A measure of good marketing? Brand purchase measures? Financial performance also affects the situation/'lifetime value' of customers in the base.
(c) *Brand equity* – many academics and managers believe that a powerful brand is probably among the greatest marketing assets a firm can have.
(d) Allow firms to charge price premiums over unbranded or poorly branded products.
(e) Can be used to extend the company's business into other product categories.
(f) Reduce perceived risk to customers (and investors?).

The measures could be behavioural, looking at perceptions or purchase patterns. They could also indicate knowledge of the grand and show the effectiveness of brand marketing within a complex portfolio. Another important measure could be the financial value of the brand to a company's investors. Such measures may be long term rather than short term in nature.

Understanding online metrics

Online companies spent £150 million on advertising last year. Did it work?

Oliver Rowe reports on the business of getting your dot com company recognized in the real world.

It is one of the most important questions you have to face. You are setting up an Internet business. Everybody tells you that marketing and advertising the site will make or break you. There is no point having a good idea if nobody hears about it. So you siphon off a large part of your launch budget for the purposes of building your brand. Domination of your market is what you seek. And to achieve that you pay advertising companies lots of money to tell the world that you have arrived. But does it work? Advertising and media agencies up and down the country have certainly enjoyed a windfall over the past few months. But new figures revealed here show that many companies, whatever they spend on advertising their wares, are not getting the immediate brand recognition they crave. As we all know, brand is king. 'The only effective barrier to entry in e-commerce is branding,' says Simon Murdoch of Amazon. David Taylor, head of digital branding at the Added Value Company, a leading brand consultancy, concurs. 'Dot com companies have a real need to develop a clear positioning and identity to survive and prosper in the long run.' Data from ACNielsen MMS, which records advertising expenditure, shows that online companies spent in excess of £150 million on advertising in 1999 – not including direct mail, sponsorship or promotions. This has all been spent advertising online brands in the real world of traditional media. It represents a threefold increase in what was spent in 1998. However the issue now is whether these companies are getting value for money.

This should cause some alarm for online companies because what naturally preoccupies all advertisers is how effective their advertising spend actually is. One key measure of advertising effectiveness is awareness of the brand amongst the public. Research undertaken in the last two weeks by CIA MediaLab as part of its Sensor study has analysed what the UK's major online companies spend on advertisers and compared it to people's awareness of the brand. What is clear from this analysis is that the public's awareness of your brand and the amount you actually spend on advertising are certainly related. But, more worryingly for those spending precious resources telling the public 'We're here!', some brands have got more recognition bang for their advertising buck.

Let's look at the figures. Four major brands, AOL, Yahoo!, Freeserve and BT, all achieve awareness of over 40 per cent amongst the UK adult population. The amount each has spent on advertising differs hugely, raising the question: who has the most effective advertising? Of course the level of recognition also reflects other factors such as the time since each launched and the amount of press coverage they have received. Looking specifically at Internet service providers (ISPs) we find that AOL has only been outspent by Freeserve. The two have very similar awareness levels despite the fact that AOL has been around much longer than Freeserve. AOL's recent merger with Time Warner will certainly have helped general awareness levels. What is clear is that Freeserve has been more aggressively going after market share, but AOL has decided to fight back with a spend of around £1.4 million in the past 2 months.

It should be made clear that advertising needs to play a different role in the marketing mix as the brand moves through its cycle from an initial launch, to growth to maturity. These ISPs are still growing but are using advertising to help attract both existing and new Internet users. The fascinating part of all this is not only trying to work out why differing levels of advertising spend have delivered different results, but also why so many companies are spending so much on advertising. The perception is that there is currently an opportunity to build online brands, and thus market share, more quickly and easily (and cheaply) than in a year or two's time when the Internet will be a bigger place. When a market is being launched it is cheaper to buy a share while it is still small than try and steal it off competitors once the market has matured. It is for this reason that venture capitalists are keen to give promising young Internet start-ups large sums of money to spend advertising their brand before someone else gets into that sector of the market.

A prime example of the advantage of being first to market can be seen in the differences in awareness levels and advertising spend between Amazon and BOL. Despite spending nearly £3.7 million on advertising in the last 12 months BOL only has an awareness of 27 per cent amongst people who used the Internet in the past month. This compares to a significantly higher awareness of 75 per cent for Amazon from a slightly smaller spend. Maintaining awareness is an easier job than gaining it in the first place. Also, the amount BOL has spent on advertising does not compare favourably to other online brands such as Lastminute which has a 29 per cent awareness from a £1 million spend. Meanwhile, online retailer Boo has spent more than £750 000 in the past 2 months and has failed to show any significant change in awareness amongst CIA's sample.

To be fair, asking people whether they are aware of a brand at a particular moment in time is a relatively crude measure of advertising effectiveness. However, doing it amongst a pre-defined target audience that has been agreed by the brand owners and the media agency is a good place to start, but media agencies do get judged by the awareness they deliver. Even so, as for AOL and Freeserve, achieving awareness may only be the first part of the advertising process. As well as achieving awareness, advertising needs to communicate some brand values which should help drive share and loyalty. The temptation for brands is to launch with a fanfare to the world, but without any budget left they cannot follow it up. The result is that brand awareness will quickly decay. It could be argued that some brands should use their advertising budget more wisely.

Media agencies could more accurately target the right consumers, possibly using other media and over a longer period of time, thus satisfying the joint media requirements of frequency of advertising exposure and recency. But does this excite investors, or the MD, as much as blowing the annual budget on a few weeks of high-profile TV advertising?

One sector that is moving wholeheartedly online is banking, and its experience with advertising and brand building holds some important lessons. As yet unreleased research by CIA shows that amongst those that have already opened an online bank account or who intend to open one in the next year, 89 per cent of those aware of Egg say it appeals to them as a brand. This compares to only 60 per cent for the parent brand Prudential. The Smile brand appeals to 70 per cent of those aware of it in this target audience compared to 58 per cent for parent Co-operative Bank. Smile has shown impressive awareness growth in the last 2 months on the back of a £1.2 million advertising budget.

Advertising is clearly establishing new values for a new brand while trying not to cannibalise the existing customer base of the parent. As the Internet audience grows, then so the amount brands will be encouraged to spend on advertising will increase until those that can't afford to play the spend game drop out or get bought up. Make sure your brand works. Spend money on advertising. But make sure it works.

Note: Oliver Rowe is operations manager at CIA MediaLab, ORowe@cia-group.com.

The above article demonstrates the use of marketing metrics within the context of the Internet and the difficulties of determining the effectiveness of online advertising.

Source: The Guardian, Monday, 6 March 2000.

Contingencies

With an increasing uncertain and risky environment, the need for developing contingency plans is becoming increasingly important. Unfortunately, often companies develop budgets for marketing plans, with little thought given to 'what if' scenarios. Sometimes subjective assessments of potential growth in market share are made and risks are discounted. Contingency is described as an allowance for unforeseen expenditures or revenues. Contingency, if not applied reasonably, might destroy an otherwise good plan, and if not applied adequately, might create financial problems.

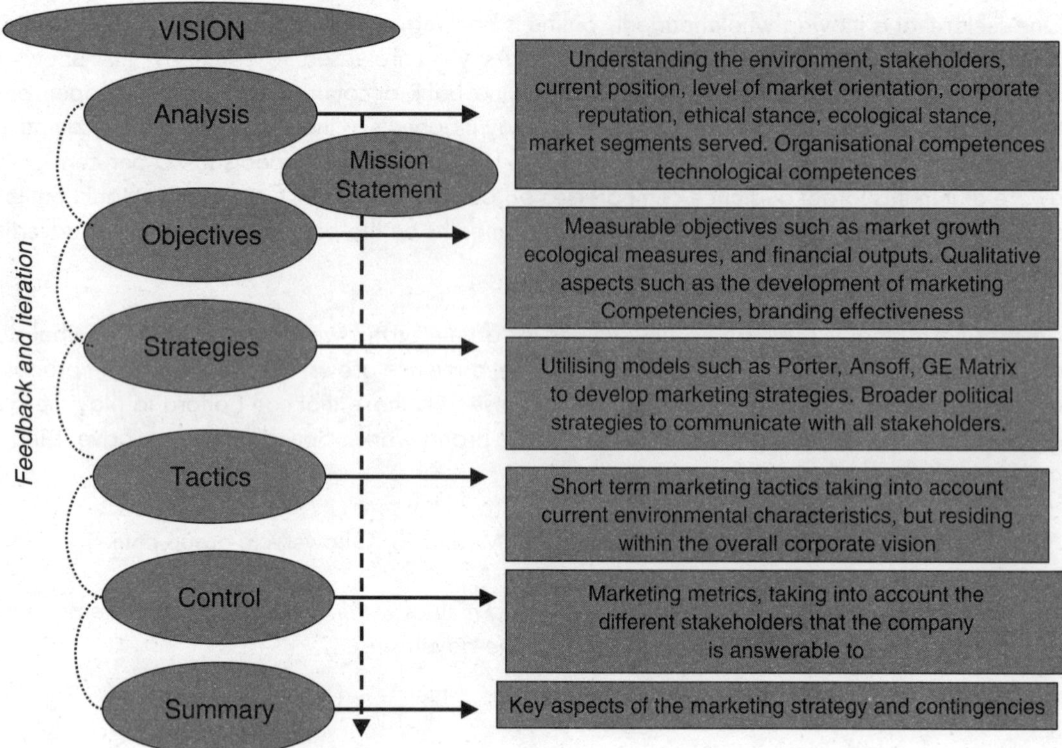

Figure 5.8 Strategic marketing model for the 21st century

As Figure 5.8 shows, the control aspects are important and contingency plans can be taken into account in Figure 5.9. Metrics can help to understand the deviations from given plans and situations. However, when the strategies do not go according to plan, the contingencies come into play. These contingencies can be quite variable in nature:

(a) Greater than expected growth in sales or vice versa.
(b) Greater expenditure on advertising due to failure of set campaigns.
(c) Supply chain cost variations.
(d) Price pressures resulting from customer actions.
(e) Variations in product quality/quality recall.
(f) Poor or good publicity for the company affecting sales.
(g) Changes in economic conditions, for example rise in interest rates.
(h) Changes in technology rendering the current product range obsolete.
(i) Internal production delays affecting sales.

And many others, depending on the nature of the business and the sector in which it operates.

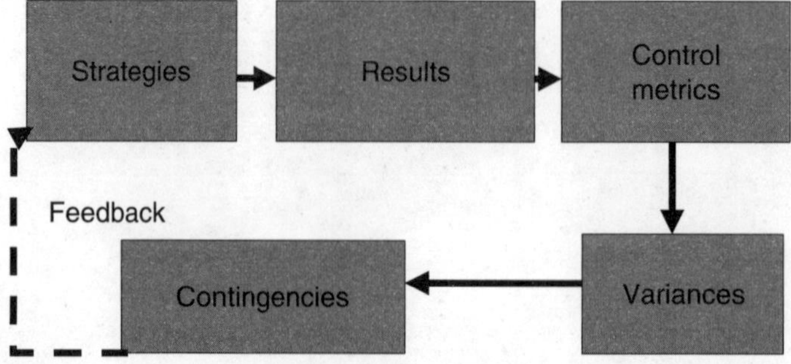

Figure 5.9 Contingencies and control

Summary

This chapter demonstrates the usefulness of understanding customer-related issues when developing marketing strategies. It also shows the importance of developing strategies that take into account measures, which are useful and meaningful within the context of the company under consideration. Every organization, in every sector, has its own key issues that it needs to take into account. These key issues then translate into effective control measures based on their suitability, acceptability and feasibility for adoption. Finally, every plan needs to incorporate contingencies that come into play as a result of the detection of variances within the determined control metrics.

References

Ambler, T. (2001) 'Abandon lifetime value theories and take care of customers now', *Marketing*, July 12, p. 18.

Bacuvier, G., Peladeau, P., Trichet, A. and Zerbib, P. (2001) 'Customer lifetime value: Powerful insights into a Company's Business and Activities', http://www.bah.com/viewpoints/insights/cmt_clv_2.html.

Jackson, D.R. (1992) 'In quest of the grail: Breaking the barriers to customer valuation', *Direct Marketing*, **54**(11), 44–48.

Ness, J.A., Schroeck, M.J., Letendre, R.A. and Douglas, W.J. (2001) 'The role of ABM in measuring customer value', www.mamag.com/strategicfinance/2001/03f.htm.

Ranchhod (2004) *Marketing Strategies: A 21st Century Approach*, Pearson Education FT Knowledge.

Sheth, J.N., Sisodia, R.S. and Sharma, A. (2000) 'The antecedents and consequences of customer-centric marketing', *Journal of the Academy of Marketing Science* , **28**(1), 55–66.

unit 6 the examination

Outcomes

- Putting everything together
  - (a) How to analyse case studies and formulate good analyses in line with the new requirements of SMiP.
  - (b) How to apply and use analyses in the closed book examination.
  - (c) What the examiners will be looking for.

The examination

Examination approaches

The examiners, when looking at answers to examination questions based on the case study, look for:

Analytical and critical thinking

The case study is based on real organizations and we expect candidates to critically analyse it utilizing a range of techniques. The case study is sent to students four weeks before the date of the examination. As this is a closed book examination and we are looking for pre-prepared analyses, it is important that the weeks before the examination, time is spent on understanding and analysing the case. The purpose of a case is to develop the following:

- Analysis and critical thinking
- Decision-making
- Judging between courses of action
- Handling assumptions and inferences
- Presenting a point of view
- Listening to and understanding others
- Relating theory to practice.

Candidates should be able to analyse each case and comprehend the other areas of the Professional Postgraduate Diploma syllabi from where they may need to draw their underpinning knowledge. Although candidates need to demonstrate their underpinning knowledge in the context of the case study, it is important that they show some creative flair and innovation in their answers. Candidates will also be expected to show an understanding of contemporary marketing issues. Examples of these are given in Unit 4.

The examiners are looking for the candidates to demonstrate analytical ability, interpretive skills, insight, innovation and creativity in answering questions. They are also looking for candidates to take clear and sensible decisions within the context of the case study. A critical awareness of the specific issues involved, relevant theoretical underpinning, attention to detail, coherence and justification of strategies (within the context of the questions set) adopted will also be assessed.

Answering questions within the set context

The SMiP paper asks for special understanding of the case within the context of the questions set. As this is a closed book examination, the only material allowed in the examination will be the pre-prepared analysis. The title of the paper Strategic Marketing in Practice (SMiP), means that we are looking for an understanding of strategic issues involved in developing specific strategies within a company. The candidates need to be competent enough to analyse problems within a marketing context and subsequently take appropriate decisions to implement marketing strategies for an organization. In order to achieve competence in this area, prospective candidates will need to be conversant with all aspects of marketing, as strategic marketing problems do not come in neat packages. A comprehensive grasp of the basic subjects at the Certificate and Advanced Certificate level together with the syllabi for the Professional Postgraduate Diploma modules is needed. Decisions made have to reflect the fact that candidates have thoroughly understood the key marketing issues impinging on the case. They have to make decisions which are realistic and justifiable and above all actionable within the given constraints.

Judging between courses of action

When analysing a case study, it would be surprising if only one course of action was possible. Often there are several alternatives to a problem and a company has to weigh up the chances of success and pursue a particular course of action. As an examination candidate, you are expected to pursue courses of action which are possible, realistic and sustainable. The examiners are not looking for right or wrong answers, they are searching for solutions that will work within the given scenario of the case study.

Handling assumptions and inferences

All cases are based on real-life information that may have gaps within it. No company works in a perfect environment or with perfect information. This would not only be impossible, but would be outside the capability of any human being. The result is that we all create an image of the way in which a company is operating. In creating that image and understanding it, there may be gaps that need filling. These can be done by the projection of trends or by making certain assumptions about market demand or product suitability. In most cases, students will need to make certain assumptions. As long as these are not wildly off the mark and help to augment the case and your arguments, they are perfectly acceptable. In some cases, candidates may wish to point out that further market research is necessary.

Presenting a point of view

All cases are about presenting a point of view. Examiners expect student answers to vary. It is therefore important, when preparing for the case, that you do not get hung up on thinking that your friend or colleague has the right answer. If you have analysed the case thoroughly and you feel that you have a clear view of the strategies that should be adopted by the company then you should put these forward. At all times you should consider the detail, coherence and strategic aspects of arguments, justifying them fully.

Relating theory to practice and vice versa

In order to be a good practising marketing manager, you need to be able to seamlessly knit marketing theory to practical solutions. I see this as a symbiotic process. Too often we see managers who only emphasize the practical aspects and by doing that, deny their companies the benefit of marketing frameworks and any new knowledge that may be available. By the same token, simply propounding theoretical frameworks, with little or no thought given to the practical application of these frameworks to real problems is also unacceptable. In order to formulate sensible solutions to cases you will need to be knowledgeable about both practical marketing aspects and theoretical issues and contemporary marketing thinking.

How to pass the case study paper

In general, candidates are expected to allocate some study time at a centre in order to prepare for the case study. The notional study time is 45 hours over a period of 10–12 weeks. Roughly half of this time should be allocated for work on previous cases and the rest for developing analyses and scenarios for the new case and preparing for the examination that candidates will be sitting.

The paper

The SMiP paper is the culmination of all the marketing subjects covered at all levels, but especially the Diploma and the Advanced Diploma. For this reason, there is no specific syllabus for this paper. This type of expertise will be needed to tackle the Case Study paper. It is also clear that it will not be possible to tackle the Case Study without a clear grasp of the fundamentals of Analysis and Evaluation, Strategic Marketing Decisions and Managing Marketing Performance. In this sense, for all students the case study is a culmination of the application of all the marketing knowledge that you have gained over several years.

Closed book examination

For all the students, the SMiP paper is a *closed* book examination. This means that candidates are only allowed to take their pre-prepared analyses into the examination. Used judiciously, this material can be useful for referencing when answering questions. Fifteen marks are also allocated for the *application* of the analyses to the question set. Many candidates think that excellent analyses, with poor answers will enable a pass. This is misguided as no matter how good the analyses are, they have to be applied within the context of the case. Skimpy answers relying on analyses will almost certainly fail. It is, therefore, important for candidates to spend time developing good answers and using the analyses to augment these answers.

It is highly important, therefore, that a considerable amount of time is spent on developing tables, undertaking detailed analyses, producing diagrams and assembling this information on six A4 sides. This is helpful for quick referencing during the examination. It also leaves candidates free to think about which bits of information may be useful to use in framing answers.

Allocation of marks

The marks will be allocated in the following manner:

Marks for analysis: 10

Marks for the application of the analysis: 15

This methodology:

1. Rewards students for work done in the 4 weeks between the release of the case and the day of the examination.
2. Enables students to concentrate on the case and utilize the analyses effectively in their answers.

Candidates should undertake the following advice (repeated from Unit 1):

(a) Write or print pre-prepared analysis on *six* sides of A4. Examiners will be looking for tables, diagrams and key issues. Tables such as SWOT, though helpful, do not show deep analytical thought.
(b) If candidates use the available sheets for writing 'crib' material, such as models or plans they will penalize themselves as there will be less space for good analysis that counts towards the final marks.
(c) The diagrams should be clearly visible and the writing should be clearly legible. Typing should be no less than font size 11.
(d) Data given within the case should be analysed clearly and effectively.
(e) All the work should be on CIM paper which will be issued two weeks before the examination.
(f) Please note that it will be totally unacceptable for students to present standardized group analysis/appendices and they will therefore be penalized accordingly.

(*During the Examination*)

(a) The answers should reflect the use of the pre-prepared material as necessary. Candidates, when writing answers candidates, should cross reference the work to guide the examiner to a particular table or chart or piece of analysis.
(b) Examiners do not expect students to use ALL the pre-prepared material to augment their answers. Obviously, they should only use whatever is necessary for answering the questions as set.
(c) Candidates should attach the pre-prepared work as an appendix. *All papers must be hole punched and include the student registration and centre number.*
(d) Please note that Fifteen marks are allocated *for the application* of the pre-prepared work.
(e) *Only the pre-prepared analysis can be taken into the examination room, therefore no textbooks, journals or other pre-prepared work will be allowed.*
(f) *You will be allowed to bring an annotated copy of the case study into the examination.*

Notes to candidates

These notes are modified from time to time, depending on the context within which the cases are set. The following is an example of what was used in the June 2003 case study.

Extended knowledge

Notes to candidates, June 2003. The examiners will be marking your scripts on the basis of questions put to you in the examination room. Candidates are advised to pay particular attention to the *mark allocation on the examination paper and budget their time accordingly.*

Your role is outlined in the candidates' brief and you will be required to recommend clear courses of action.

You will be awarded marks for analysis, but poor application may mean the difference between a pass and a failure. The analyses should have been undertaken before the examination day in preparation for meeting the tasks which will be specified in the examination paper.

Candidates are advised not to waste valuable time collecting unnecessary data. The cases are based upon real-life situations. No useful purpose will therefore be served by contacting companies in this industry and candidates are *strictly instructed not to do so* as it would simply cause unnecessary confusion.

As in real life, anomalies will be found in this case situation. Please simply state assumptions where necessary when answering questions. The CIM is not in a position to answer queries on case data. Candidates are tested on their overall understanding of the case and in key issues, not on minor details. There are no catch questions or hidden agendas. In addition, for this particular case, the CIM is not prepared to answer any financial queries.

Additional information will be introduced in the examination paper itself which candidates must take into account when answering the questions set.

Acquaint yourself thoroughly with the case study and be prepared to follow closely the instructions given to you on the examination day. To answer examination questions effectively, candidates must adopt a report format.

The copying of pre-prepared 'group' analyses written by consultants/tutors is strictly forbidden and will be penalized. The questions will demand analysis in the examination itself and individually composed answers are required to pass.

From case to case, there may be minor modifications to the candidates' notes depending on the type and style of case.

The candidate's brief

This brief is an integral part of the case study. It gives some idea of the role you are expected to play in solving the case study. The candidate's brief gives individuals a position either as an external consultant or an internal manager. On the day of the examination, they are expected to answer the questions set from the point of view of the role that has been allocated. The brief is likely to contain the following:

- A brief analysis of the company situation
- Some idea of the deliberations within the company
- An attempt to place you at the centre of the action, asking you to prepare reports on some critical strategic issues/problems facing the organization
- Some statement on incorporating any contemporary issues of your choice into the answers that you propose.

The use of additional information

Cases will vary in nature and from time to time additional information may be provided. It is important therefore for you to incorporate this material in your answers, as and when it is needed.

The additional information is something that you should take into consideration when answering the questions set, as it is likely to have some bearing on the market conditions or on some areas of the case. The additional information will not invalidate all the work that has been undertaken over the 4 weeks. The additional information is introduced to test the ability of candidates to be flexible in their thinking and to test the ability to assimilate and effectively incorporate new material into the development of their strategies.

Gauging performance

To perform well on the paper, candidates will have to exhibit the following:

- A need to concentrate on the strategic aspects of marketing underpinned by the necessary detail.
- The ability to identify 'gaps' in the case study and to outline the assumptions made.
- The ability to critically apply relevant models for case analysis.
- The ability to draw and synthesize from any of the diploma subject areas as relevant.
- Concentration on the question set rather than just the pre-prepared analysis.
- The ability to answer in the report format with comprehensive sentences rather than providing simplistic lists.
- The judicious use of diagrams for illustrative purposes.
- The ability to draw disparate links together and give coherent answers.
- The use of interesting and useful articles from journals in their answers.
- Developing strategic ideas, centred around contemporary marketing issues.
- Innovation and creativity in answering the questions.
- Demonstration of practical applications of marketing knowledge.
- Sensible use of time and an ability to plan the answers within the set time.
- A good understanding of the case study set.

The best way to prepare for the case would entail the following considerations:

- Practice on previous examination papers.
- Reading and digesting the senior examiner's report.
- Reading books, newspapers, relevant marketing and academic journals.
- For each examination case ascertaining the relevant knowledge base that will be required.
- Being flexible and critical when using analytical models instead of being prescriptive.
- Depending on the case study, utilizing a range of different analytical models and tools appropriate to the context of the case (see Figure 6.1 for an illustrative schedule for preparing for the examination).

In addition to the above, candidates should also be prepared to undertake the following:

- The use of relevant models for the sector in which the case study is based.
- The use of each candidate's practical and business experience using any illustrative examples.
- The use of diagrams.
- A thorough marketing and financial analysis of each case study within the given context of the case study.
- An awareness and application of strategic marketing ideas and solutions.
- Revisiting relevant syllabi from the Diploma and Advanced Diploma within the given context of the case study.

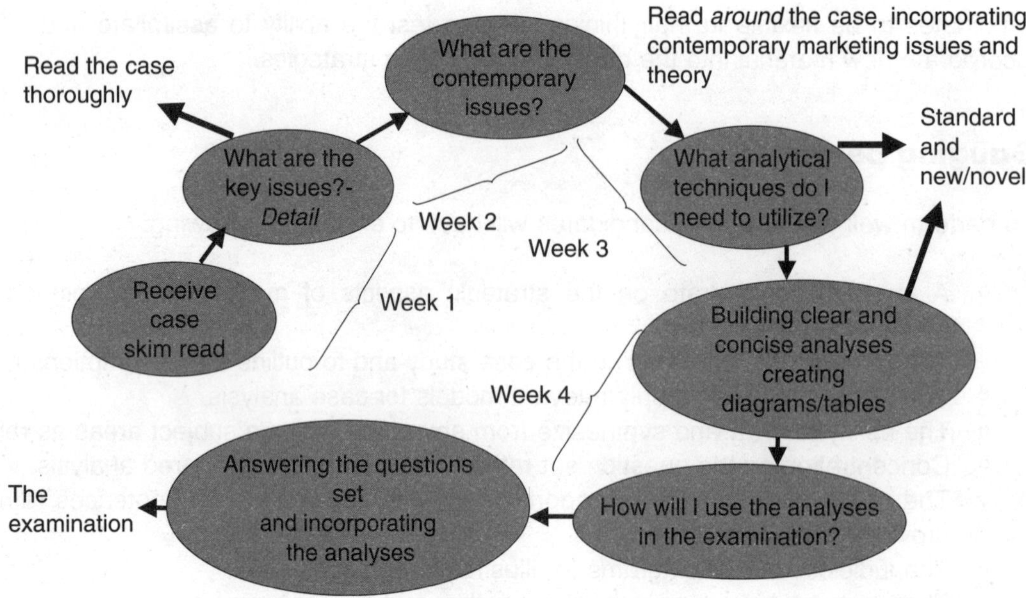

Figure 6.1 Approaching the SMiP case

An examiner's point of view

It would be of help if candidates would briefly wear an Examiner's hat when preparing for the exam and imagine their scripts and answers as perceived from the other side. This section has been written by an experienced A & D, and now SMiP, Examiner and feedback writer for failed scripts. It provides very useful advice for candidates.

Presentation

It is a fact that most of us are forgetting the skill of handwriting. While, no CIM Examiner expects or rewards beautiful handwriting, it is expected that he/she must be able to read what the candidate has written. Unfortunately, increasingly Examiners are confronted with truly awful handwritings which are difficult, and sometimes impossible, to read. If your handwriting is bad, try to practice handwriting large amounts of work without a break, as in the exam situation.

Another problem with many scripts, sometimes in addition to bad handwriting, is the number of words or lines crossed out, or parts of an answer written on one page with additional parts on another with instructions to the Examiner where to find the missing parts. Messy presentation does not help you. Some scripts contain diagrams/illustrations with so many tiny words written in bad handwriting that even a magnifying glass is not enough to make sense of what is presented. Then there are those answers that last several pages without a paragraph break, with no, or very few, sub-headings.

All of the above makes an Examiner's job difficult, and while it is the duty of all Examiners to read the scripts carefully and reward candidates for correct answers, there is also an onus on the candidates to present their work in such a way that it can be marked with reasonable effort and within a reasonable period of time. Make sure your handwriting is legible, and use headings, sub-headings and paragraphs. Leave a reasonable gap between different answers and mark each answer clearly. Underline sub-headings, if you wish and use highlighters too to make important words, terms or figures stand out, but do not overdo it.

Read the question

This may sound too obvious to mention but experience shows otherwise. Candidates must read each question several times and break each question to its constituent parts. Some candidates see a familiar word or two and start answering the question right away. For example, the Senior Examiner can ask dozens of different questions on branding. Seeing the word branding in the question and starting the answer is dangerous. You must make it clear to yourself what exactly the question wants you to do. This is closely linked with another type of answer which Examiners are sometimes confronted with. That is, candidates writing everything they know about a concept either hoping to impress the Examiner or hoping the Examiner, somewhere in the long answer, will be able to find parts that relate to the question.

Read each question carefully, understand what it requires and give concise and to the point answer. The Examiner will be more impressed with a compact and precise answer that is three to the four pages long than with one that is a whole answer book long but not relevant for most part.

Messages to examiners

Examiners will mark the answer that is in front of them. They will ignore your messages about running of time and so on. Do not write messages and, as in the case of a recent candidate, please do not mark your script either!

Prepared answers

Some of the answers from a number of centres are often very similar, if not identical. While, themes and ideas may be discussed in advance, and may be similar, the actual answers are not expected to mirror each other. The candidates are expected to write answers individually during the exam. There is a consensus amongst Examiners for SMiP that in future very similar/identical answers may be penalized.

Another form of prepared answer is where candidates guess what the questions will be and rehearse or prepare answers which they then include in their scripts, sometimes clearly giving the wrong answer because they have guessed incorrectly. This approach became common with some centres taking the A & D paper, and has partly been responsible to the changes made to SMiP paper where advance guessing of questions will be more difficult.

Prepare for different scenarios but do not limit yourself by guessing the questions exactly.

Understanding of marketing theory and its application

The SMiP paper requires a demonstration of both academic theory and application of that theory to real-life situations. Unbalanced answers stand to lose marks. While you are not required to engage in pure theoretical discussion, you should use definitions, and particularly models and theories in your answers, where appropriate. Sometimes, such models are included in the case study – use them! The answer to a question requiring a marketing plan does not require any theoretical discussion at all, but even there theoretical models, for example Boston Matrix, Porter's Five Forces, should be included when relevant.

The SMiP paper will require an understanding of contemporary issues in marketing, as well as questions on branding, internationalization and communication that A & D candidates came to expect. It would be useful to keep abreast of contemporary issues in marketing. Contemporary issues, by their nature, are subject to change, but currently, it may be suggested, include: corporate social responsibility, relationship marketing/CRM, mobile and e-marketing, corporate identity, public relations and added value.

The importance of analysis and justification

The marking scheme for the SMiP paper allocates a significant portion of the total mark to analysis and application. Good recommendations can only be based on a thorough analysis, with the latter helping the justification of the former. Where the relevant analysis is included in the appendices make clear references, in your answer, to the relevant diagram/table/illustration giving page number and title. Remember that the maximum number of pages you are allowed to attach to your script is six (and no more). These must be single sided.

Additionally, always justify your recommendations/opinions. While bullet points are allowed in answers, those that are so short as not to mean much will not gain you any marks.

Finally, remember that analysis means breaking down the given information and making sense of it, or determining its significance. Merely repeating what is in the case study does not equate to analysis and does not get any marks.

It must be pointed out here that a large percentage of SMiP, and also A & D, candidates in December 2004 passed their exams, many with good grades. This means that the majority of candidates and their tutors are well aware of good exam techniques.

Summary

When working on the case and in the examination, do not repeat in summary form large pieces of factual information from the case. The examiners are fully aware of the case. It is better to use the information in the case to illustrate your statements, to defend your arguments or to make salient points. Beyond the brief introduction to the company, you must avoid being descriptive; instead, you must be analytical.

You will need to ensure that the sections and sub-sections of your discussion flow logically and smoothly from one to the next. Try to build on what has gone before so that each analysis builds on the previous one. A piecemeal approach to analysis results in fragmented writing lacking coherence. This is because the parts do not flow from one to the next, and this becomes apparent to the examiners. Sometimes this happens when intensive group and individual approaches are put together.

It is important to write in a report format using clear English, avoiding grammatical and spelling errors. Clarity of approach and the judicious use of diagrams helps examiners to follow your arguments easily.

Finally:

- Practice on previous cases and to see how you would have approached the case differently from the specimen answers given.
- Read and digest Senior Examiner's reports.
- Read books, newspapers and relevant marketing and academic journals.

Be flexible and critical when utilizing analytical models and steer away from being prescriptive in your approach. More practice will result in better insights and help you with being creative and innovative when framing your answers.

The unit that follows gives you an indication of the way that students have approached examinations. This has been done through the usage of specimen questions for this NEW module with a general examination brief for answering the set questions by the Senior Examiner. As the first examination for this paper was in December 2004, you have been provided with the questions set for the examination and actual specimen answers.

unit 7 case study

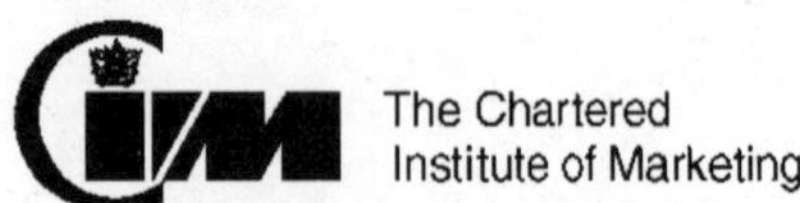

Professional Postgraduate Diploma in Marketing

Strategic Marketing in Practice

64: **Strategic Marketing in Practice**
Time: **14.00 - 17.00**
Date: **10th December, 2004**

3 Hours Duration

This paper requires you to make a practical and reasoned evaluation of the problems and opportunities you have identified from the previously circulated case material. From your analysis you are required to prepare a report in accordance with the situation below. Graphing sheets and ledger analysis paper are available from the invigilators, together with continuation sheets if required. These must be identified by your candidate number and fastened in the prescribed fashion within the back cover of your answer book for collection at the end of the examination.

Read the questions carefully and answer the actual questions as specified. Check the mark allocation to questions and allocate your time accordingly. Candidates must attempt ALL parts. Candidates should adopt a report format; those who do not will be penalised

Professional Postgraduate Diploma in Marketing

64: Strategic Marketing in Practice

As the individual who is being considered for a strategic marketing manager's position for a large multinational you have been asked to address the following questions by the Board:

Question One

Drawing from your examples, critically assess key ways in which an established company can implement CSR strategic marketing policies.

(25 marks)

Question Two

Marketing communications play an important role in developing company reputation. Explain how the case examples illustrate the various ways of developing communication strategies meeting the needs of differing customers.

(25 marks)

Question Three

Show and explain in detail the main marketing metrics that could be developed by companies wishing to develop Corporate Social Responsible strategies.

(25 marks)

A further 25 marks are available for candidates prepared work.

(Total 100 marks)

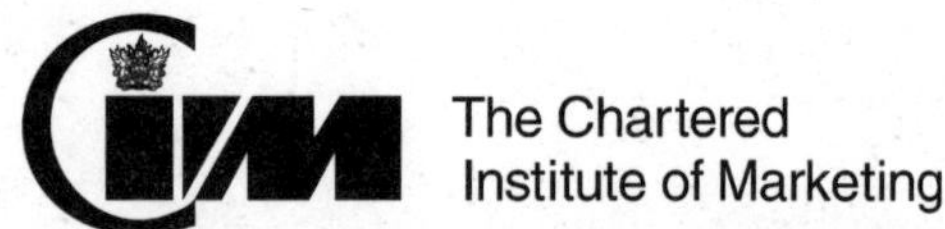

Case Study December 2004

Strategic Marketing in Practice

Candidate's Brief for Strategic Marketing in Practice

You are Alan Walker, with a career in companies marketing Fast Moving Consumer Goods (FMCG). You have recently been approached privately by a large multinational operating in this sector to consider developing their marketing strategy incorporating Corporate Social Responsibility (CSR) policies. As a first step, you have been asked to compile a portfolio of examples to offer the clients, together with some ideas of your own that you have developed concerning this area. The company is particularly interested in exploring how to develop communication issues and has also expressed concerns about measuring how successful CSR strategies are. On 10th December 2004, you will be presenting your report to the board, outlining the key points that you have gleaned from your research so far. The board will then ask you some specific questions that you will have to be prepared to answer.

Candidate's Brief for Analysis and Decision

You have been appointed by a company working in retailing to understand the role of CSR in developing marketing strategies. In order to help the organisation you have put together a number of case studies. You may be asked to put together a strategic plan for one of the cases. You will also be asked to consider communication and internationalisation issues.

These specific questions will be set to you at a proposed board meeting on the 10th December 2004.

Important Notice

The material within this booklet has been reproduced by kind permission of The World Business Council for Sustainable Development (WBCSD).

This Case material is based on an actual organisation and existing market conditions.

Candidates are strictly instructed NOT TO CONTACT WBCSD or any other companies in the industry. Additional information will be provided at the time of the examination. Further copies may be obtained from The Chartered Institute of Marketing, Moor Hall, Cookham, Maidenhead, Berkshire, SL6 9QH, UK.

Sustainability and Marketing

As the world slowly begins to embrace the new millennium, it is clear that issues surrounding resources, climate change and pollution are high on the agenda of most governments, some companies, and many individuals. Recent surveys suggest that awareness of green issues is currently running at very high levels in most of the developed world. According to the The World Business Council for Sustainable Development (WBCSD), if consumption rates in developing countries matched those of the developed world, it would need three earths to sustain the current world population. Instead of lowering living standards in one part of the world and improving them in other parts, the business idea is to create sustainable development by creating goods and services that improve the quality of life in all parts of the world. If a holistic view is taken of the marketplace, supply and demand are viewed as part of a system rather than disparate parts of the business equation. Companies have the opportunity to improve people's lives through what they do, how they do it, and who and what they affect. Furthermore, are the provisions of certain products and services sustainable? Sustainability is about understanding the interactions of the various stakeholders in an organisation. Maximising profits and looking for short-term gains in market share may, in the long run, be so harmful to certain groups of stakeholders that the company itself may suffer bad publicity. These stakeholders are the employees, the local community and government agencies. The main stakeholder is probably the planet itself, and increasingly the public feels that business firms should take responsibility for environmental damage inflicted on parts of the earth in the pursuit of profit (Ranchhod, 2004).

One way of considering the creation and utilisation of products and services that are environmentally friendly is the LCA concept. The LCA is recognised both as a concept and an analytical environmental management tool (SPOLD, 1995). This concept, sometimes termed life cycle thinking, helps everyone (consumers and producers alike) to understand the overall environmental implications of the services required by society. This promotes the consideration of the cradle-to-grave implications of any actions taken, forcing thinking to move beyond the narrow vestiges of supply chains and sector-based considerations of the environment, towards acknowledging the wider implications of our activities.

According to Dr. H.N.J. Smits, CEO and Chair of Rabobank:

Sustainable development, far from being a new and restrictive condition to industrial and financial progress, provides the keys that will unlock all the major markets of the future.

According to WBCSD it is important that:

Market attributes that can serve the purpose of sustainability (such as freedom of choice, competition, and innovation) should be more fully engaged. Markets can also provide the poor with more opportunities and can better reflect the values of environmental goods and services crucial to our quality of life.

In doing this it is important that the seven keys to success are followed:

SUSTAINABILITY THROUGH THE MARKET	
Seven keys to success	**Seven value propositions**
1. Innovate	Novel technical and social resources – new ways to improve lives while boosting business.
2. Practice eco-efficiency	Economic benefit and environment performance.
3. Move from stakeholder dialogues to partnerships for progress	Shared understanding, aligned action and social inclusion.
4. Provide and inform consumer choice	A different type of demand by enhancing appreciation for values that support sustainability.
5. Improve market framework conditions	A stable, corruption free, socio-economic framework that facilitates positive change.
6. Establish the worth of Earth	Environmental conservation and promotion of resource efficiency.
7. Make the markets work for everyone	Economic benefit and social cohesion.

Table 1

Stakeholder issues are very important in the current business climate and companies that ignore the wide range of stakeholders may encounter difficulties in particular situations. Companies for instance that flout environmental issues may find that they are exposed by NGOs (Non-Governmental Organisations) such as Greenpeace. The complex web of interactions is depicted in Figure 1.

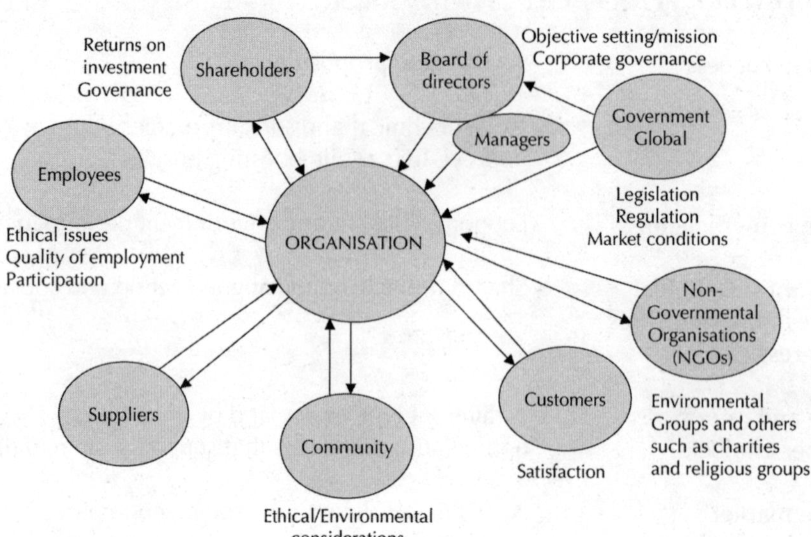

Figure 1 (Ranchhod, 2004)

Organisations now have a chance to develop and practice socially responsible marketing strategies that take into account various stakeholder issues and offer ethical and environmentally-sound products and services. According to the latest Business in the Community Report, produced in collaboration with the UK Department of Trade and Industry (DTI), it was noted that the total value of ethical consumption in the UK was £19.9 billion, and the recorded sales of ethically marketed goods and services was £6.9 billion – a 13 per cent increase from 2001. The key findings indicated:

- Ethics plays a role in the purchasing choices of the majority of consumers. However, when asked, a significant number tend not to label themselves as ethical consumers. Their behaviour does not conform to the traditional definitions of ethical consumption. Rather, they are engaged in what is termed "ethical invisibles", such as shopping to support the local community and avoidance of "unethical" brands.
- These "invisibles" contributed £5.6 billion to the £19.9 billion ethical marketplace in 2002.
- The total value of ethical banking increased to £3.9 billion (a rise of 16%), while the value of ethical investments fell back to £3.5 billion, (a contraction of 8% against a market decline of 17%).
- Boycotts by ethically motivated consumers cost big brands £2.6 billion a year.
- Ethical consumerism has crossed into the mainstream with some ethical products now close to being the product of consumer choice in their respective sectors.

However, the total market share for ethical goods and services represents only around 2 per cent of the total market. This shows that although consumers can act as innovators, government and other influences are necessary to grow this market.

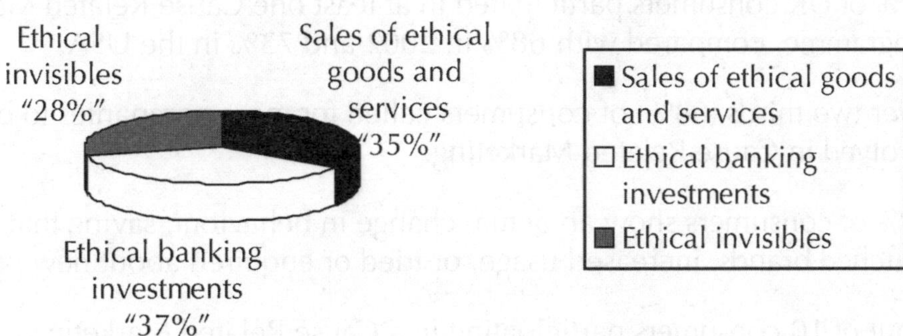

Figure 2

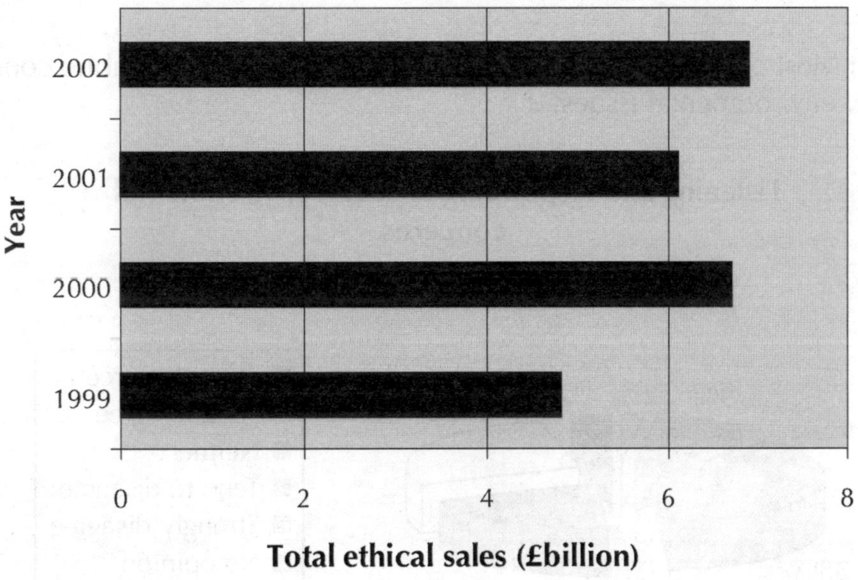

Figure 3

In terms of brand benefits, research undertaken by Research International, shows Lightspeed and Dunhumby, clearly the benefits of Cause Related Marketing. The results indicate:

- 98% of consumers in the UK and the USA are aware of at least one Cause Related Marketing programme, compared with 88% in 2000.
- 83% of UK consumers participated in at least one Cause Related Marketing programme, compared with 68% in 2002 and 73% in the USA.
- Over two thirds (68%) of consumers called for more companies to be involved in Cause Related Marketing.
- 48% of consumers show an actual change in behaviour, saying that they switched brands, increased usage, or tried or enquired about new products.
- 7 out of 10 consumers participating in a Cause Related Marketing programme report a positive impact on their behaviour or perceptions.

(This report is based on an investigation of the perceptions and buying behaviour of 6,000 consumers in the UK and the USA and was conducted in 2003)

Question: Most companies listen to the public and respond to public concerns on social and environmental issues.

Listening and responding to social/environmental concerns

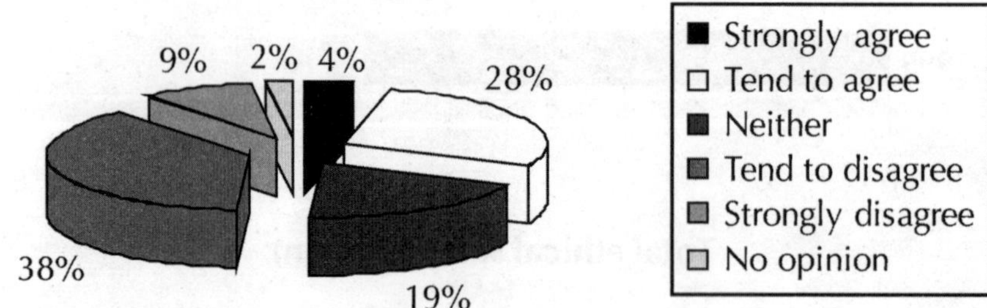

Figure 4

Question: If I had more information about companies' social, environmental and ethical behaviour, this would influence my decision about what to buy.

Impact of increased information on purchase

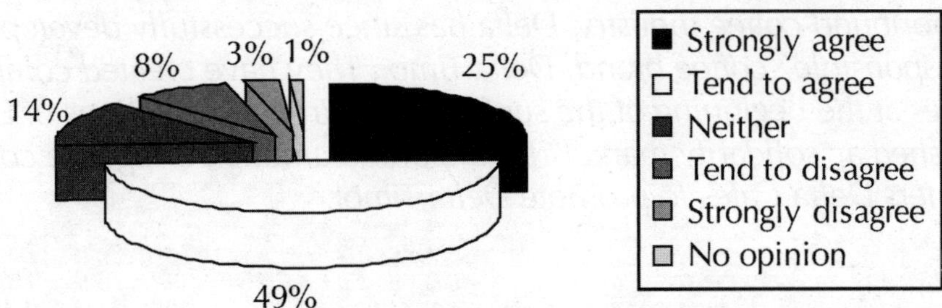

Figure 5 **Base: 1044 GB Adults 16+ (Source: MORI)**

In general most consumers want companies to take a "holistic" view of their CSR strategies instead of fragmented approaches such as Cause Related Marketing. Consumers expect companies to go that little bit extra instead of just concentrating on economic issues.

The following range of case studies illustrate the different ways in which socially responsible marketing strategies can be practiced by different organisations.

Case 1

Sonae: Delta Cafés socially responsible coffee

In 2000, the East Timor government invited Delta Cafés to help resuscitate the country's moribund coffee industry. Delta has since successfully developed a "socially responsible" coffee brand, Delta Timor. They have created competitive communities at the beginning of the supply chain, in the plantations of East Timor, and established a "solidarity market" for the brand among Portuguese consumers. Sonae partners Delta Cafés to promote Delta Timor.

Situation

Delta Cafés was created in 1961 in the village of Campo Maior, Alentejo, in a small 50-metre warehouse, which could only handle two 30kg roasters. In 1998, the Nabeiro/Delta Cafés Group was restructured, giving rise to 22 companies organised into strategic areas, with turnover of 160 million Euros. It is now the market leader for coffee in Portugal, with a market share of 38%. It has 28,000 direct retail clients (among the largest of which is Sonae, a leading Portuguese retailer), and 1,839 employees.

Fiercely loyal to the community in which he grew up, the company's President, Rui Nabeiro, has always resisted a move to a larger commercial centre, because his company is so much a part of the social fabric of Campo Maior. Of a working population of 2,500, 63% work at Delta. It is primarily a coffee roasting operation, so the company's project in East Timor represents a departure into quality control and social engagement all the way back to the origin of the product.

As a result of a brutal war of independence over two and a half decades, East Timor's infrastructure is almost non-existent, and the majority of the population live in poverty. Until 1999, the Indonesian government paid coffee farmers to be idle, in order to keep the Timorese economically disenfranchised. The land, favoured as amongst the best in the world for coffee bean production, was left untended and eroded. Any crop produced was thus of poor quality and could not be sold outside the limited market of Indonesia.

East Timor finally broke away from Indonesia in the country's new president, Xanana Gusmão, saw foreign direct investment as essential to kick-start the economy, and invited Delta to East Timor to assist with the revitalisation of the near moribund coffee business.

Why would a coffee roasting company invest in such an unpromising region? Because the soil, landscape, and climate of East Timor make it among the best places in the world to grow coffee, and Delta sees real opportunity in investing in this potential capacity.

Targets

As there was no certified standard established for coffee growers, which is essential in ensuring a reputation for quality in a global brand, the farming communities of East Timor had no access to the global market.

Delta believed that by investing in a potentially successful product, it could open up new markets and help rebuild the country, whilst generating revenues. To Rui Nabeiro, it also became a personal mission to help improve the living conditions of the people in these communities.

Having analysed the situation, the following co-operation targets were drawn up:

- To create a four-year project for capacity building, to enable coffee growers' coffee to have a certification of origin, "Timor Coffee".
- To promote seminars on coffee growing and help develop coffee growers' technical skills with the aid of specialists from Delta Cafés.
- Social actions, by helping to improve, rehabilitate, and build school infrastructures in the coffee growing regions, contributing directly to the integrated development of the community.

Before the project even officially began, in line with their policy of "do first, speak later," Delta renovated the first of many schools to demonstrate their commitment. They enlisted the help of a Portuguese Non-Governmental Organisation (NGO), Addocere, to monitor the school's use of funds and the quality of education provision. Advisors were sent to hold seminars with local farmers to build their capacity, teaching them the fundamentals of quality coffee production.

Twenty-seven permanent employees were enlisted, with 350 extra for the harvest (April-August). The contract with these workers was simple: follow the process taught to them by Delta, and they would have a guaranteed buyer for their coffee. The company seeks to give these workers and their families the incentive to stay in the mountains and devote themselves to the maintenance of a high quality coffee crop.

Actions

Delta Cafés embarked for Timor with a clearly defined project of solidarity and fair trade. Delta would not only buy the coffee at a fair market price, but would invest a share of the profits in Timor.

This was the beginning of the "One coffee for Timor" campaign. For each 250-gram package of Delta Timor blend produced, Delta would re-invest 0.25 Euros in technology and training for the growers, building of support infrastructures, construction of schools, and the provision of schoolbooks and materials, clothes and toys for the growers families. Civil education is also provided for teachers and parents, and the first kindergarten was opened in 2001.

The coffee carries a special logo identifying it as having been produced in support of sustainable communities.

Work was done to standardise technology and warehouses in line with Portuguese specifications; training was provided for the new machinery and in all the techniques of producing a better coffee crop.

Auditing the programmes is essential to their credibility as socially accountable efforts. In East Timor, as in Brazil, Delta audits the suppliers, checking that they are not violating Delta's principles of the Business of Sustainability and Social Accounting at Source:

- Integrity and transparency.
- Quality.
- Capacity building.
- Fair trade.
- Environmental accountability and eco-efficient practice.
- Social accountability, working conditions and condemnation of child labour.
- Auditing.

To guarantee success, Sonae, the biggest retailer in Portugal, has supported the project since the very beginning through efficient placement, promotion and launching of the coffee Delta Timor in all its stores all over the country.

Results

Co-operatives are now being established, giving communities a stake in their local area. Partnerships with the national government, the UN and NGOs have been essential to the process, and Delta believes more can still be achieved.

The project is already turning a profit, in part due to the marketing strategy and brand's popularity with Portuguese consumers – and their willingness to pay more for a socially responsible branded product.

It was also important to have the retail giant Sonae on board to promote the Delta Timor brand prominently in their stores. The project is also a commercial success for Sonae, increasing their coffee sales and category profit, due to the product origin certification and quality.

While East Timor coffee still has a long way to go before it can produce gourmet coffee, Delta has measured improvement in processes along the supply chain. If 100 is taken as the optimum quality, East Timor's general level is around 31. In two years, Delta's East Timor crop has improved to 58. This is expected to reach the golden 100 in the next 15 years.

The Delta Timor blend has been very successful, and now represents 3.2% of the market for 250-gram pack coffee sales in Portugal. Rather than taking away from the sales of other Delta brands or those of competitors, it has established a new "solidarity market". Connectivity between the producers and the consumers, even at opposite ends of the globe, has been achieved.

Delta hopes that as more communities become educated and develop their capacity to produce coffee along the lines the company has shown, a greater share of the East Timor coffee crop will be worth buying up for export. They have established that there is a demand in Portugal and elsewhere in Europe, and are seeking to expand production of the Timor brand.

Despite the localised nature of this project, the company does see the development of product origin communities as a trend that will continue, and are planning to start similar projects in Angola, Colombia and elsewhere.

Case 2

Procter & Gamble – Providing Safe Drinking Water

Situation

Established in 1837, the Procter & Gamble Company began as a small, family-operated soap and candle company in Cincinnati, Ohio, USA. Today, Procter & Gamble (P&G) markets almost 300 products to more than five billion consumers in 140 countries. Procter & Gamble's corporate tradition is rooted in the principles of personal integrity, respect for the individual, and doing what's right for the long term. More than 98,000 P&G people work every day to provide products of superior quality and value to the world's consumers.

The P&G Health Sciences Institute is dedicated to identifying, developing, and using leading health care technologies in the development of effective products for both the developing and developed world. One aspect of their work is looking at the more than 1 billion people who do not have access to safe water. Diarrhoeal diseases, resulting from a lack of safe water, remain a leading cause of illness and death in the developing world, with about two million children dying every year due to these diseases. The Millennium Declaration Goal (MDG) is to halve the proportion of people unable to reach or afford safe drinking water by 2015.

The P&G Health Sciences Institute has worked in partnership with the International Council of Nurses (ICN) and the Centers for Disease Control and Prevention (CDC) to find alternative, affordable solutions to the problem of safe drinking water.

The ICN is a federation of 124 national nurses' associations, representing millions of nurses worldwide. Operated by nurses for nurses since 1899, ICN is the international voice of nursing, and works to ensure quality care for all and sound health policies globally.

The CDC, located in Atlanta, Georgia, USA, is an agency of the US Department of Health and Human Services. CDC protects people's health and safety by preventing and controlling diseases and injuries, enhances health decisions by providing credible information on critical health issues, and promotes healthy living through strong partnerships with local, national and international organisations.

Targets

A complementary approach to providing piped-treated water is through treatment of drinking water directly in people's homes. This Point-Of-Use (POU) model, combined with safe storage, has the advantages of cost, immediate availability, and ease of distribution to reach rural areas. The World Health Organisation (WHO) and United Nations Children's Fund (UNICEF) have recognised that POU water treatment and safe storage at the household level can provide significant health benefits, by reducing the incidence of diarrhoea in developing countries. Because of the potential to dramatically improve the health of vulnerable populations, this approach is receiving increased attention, including the recent announcement of the collaboration of more than 20 organisations, including P&G, the ICN, and the CDC, in the International Network to Promote Household Water Treatment and Safe Storage.

There is conclusive evidence that simple, acceptable, low-cost interventions at the household and community level are capable of dramatically improving the microbial quality of household stored water, and reducing the attendant risks of diarrhoeal disease and death. The provision of safe water alone will reduce these and other enteric diseases by 6 to 50%, even in the absence of improved sanitation or other hygiene measures. Overall, combined solutions that bring unwanted and harmful matter together in small masses in water, as well as chlorine disinfection systems, have shown considerable promise as microbiological purifiers of household water.

The aim of PuR is to create safe drinking water through the removal of pathogens and the use of disinfectants in turbid waters. P&G believes that if it can provide affordable products that meet a real consumer need, then there will be demand for these products in the developing world.

Activities

A new POU technology, a combination coagulation, flocculation and disinfection treatment system, has been developed through collaboration between the Procter & Gamble Health Sciences Institute and the US Centers for Disease Control and Prevention (CDC).

The PuR product was developed based on tests with thousands of consumers in developing countries. These consumers consistently say they want visible signals that the water is cleaner, at-home control, and affordability.

The PuR product uses the same ingredients as those in municipal water systems, but is reverse engineered to effectively be a mini-water treatment plant in a sachet. The small sachet of powdered product:

- Visibly separates the cleaned water from the murky masses, while providing residual chlorination.
- Uses ingredients used in municipal treatment plants, including ferric sulphate to remove phosphate and calcium hypochlorite as a disinfectant.
- Provides superiority to chlorine alone in performance in turbid waters and reduction of organics, including humic acid (a fertiliser) and DDT (an insecticide), as well as heavy metals.
- Remains stable, providing potential for long-term consumer use, as well as for providing emergency water.

The water purification process involves simple implements that consumers have in their homes:

- Add 1 sachet to 10 litres of water and stir to begin process of separating the cleaned water from the murky masses.
- Stir water for 5 minutes until clear.
- Filter water through a cloth and dispose of separated floc in the latrine.
- Let clear water stand for 20 minutes to allow for complete disinfection.
- Store in a suitable container to prevent recontamination.

Testing

PuR has been tested in the laboratory against model test waters for removal of pathogenic bacteria, viruses, and parasites, as well as a selection of heavy metals and organics. It has been tested in the field in numerous countries for removal of turbidity and fecal organisms. The Centers for Disease Control and Prevention have conducted two large health intervention trials to determine effectiveness in reducing diarrhoeal disease.

Distribution

Previous public health interventions have used a market-based approach to build consumer awareness of the need for the intervention through social mobilisation and mass media. This approach uses existing commercial infrastructures to ensure broad and convenient access. A market-based approach may also be effective for providing POU systems. Initial efforts are underway with the combination treatment system to develop a sustainable market-based approach, and to learn how to best make POU products available. Three separate complementary models are being explored:

(1) A social model led by non-profit organisations.

(2) A commercial model led by the private sector.

(3) An emergency relief model led by relief organisations.

These efforts will use broad public-private partnerships with governments, research institutions, NGOs, professional associations, and the private sector.

Social Model

In some countries a social model may be the most appropriate, due to economic and infrastructure constraints that limit the commercial model. The social model involves the use of established social marketing distribution channels by non-profit organisations, as well as a social network approach with local NGOs and ministries of health. This model is being used effectively in many parts of the developing world to provide important health products.

Commercial Model

The commercial model leverages the technology, innovation, distribution and marketing infrastructure of the private sector, combined with advocacy, education and research efforts by collaborating group,s to build awareness of the need to properly treat and store water. This model is being explored in initial commercial test markets conducted in Guatemala, the Philippines, Morocco and Pakistan. Specific activities include a scientific symposium and outreach to build awareness, local training sessions involving village health workers, and health intervention trials conducted by Medical Entomology and Training Unit (MERTU) and the CDC. Collaboration with the Johns Hopkins University Communications Programme is underway, in order to identify the key factors needed to enable the long-term consumer habit change needed for PCU technologies.

Emergency Relief Model

Every year there are tens of millions of people who lack access to safe drinking water, either because of natural disasters such as floods and earthquakes, or because of armed conflicts resulting in internally displaced people or refugee situations. The emergency relief model involves product distribution along with education materials, typically by a relief agency.

The combined treatment system has several potential advantages for emergencies, including long-term stability, so the product can be stockpiled in areas of frequent disasters, ease of transport, and robustness to treat even very turbid surface waters. Several NGOs, including the International Rescue Committee and the International Committee of the Red Cross, are evaluating the combination system for use in emergency situations. Simple education materials in multiple languages have been developed for the combination system to allow for rapid deployment.

Innovation

The innovation in this project lies in the three different models P&G will use to approach emerging market opportunities. Specifically, P&G will use the strengths of the private sector for its technology, scale, resources and generating capacity, and the NGOs and governments for their programme skills, government ministry access and connectedness, access to public health expertise and resources, as well as education and advocacy programmes.

Packaging

The packaging of the product in small sachets that sell well in poor countries is also an innovation. They are convenient to store over long periods of time, and thus can be kept for emergency use, or consumers can buy many without it being cumbersome. One small sachet, costing about US$0.10 in the commercial model, will treat 10 litres of water (enough drinking water for an average family for two days) – an acceptable price per litre in initial market tests. PuR can also be bought in bulk quantities for use in emergency disasters or as miniature treatment plants.

Challenges

The challenges encountered so far have centred around sustaining a consumer habit change. P&G believes that partnerships will be absolutely essential in making these efforts more efficient, i.e. through partnerships on education about the causes, consequences and ways to treat unsafe water.

Results

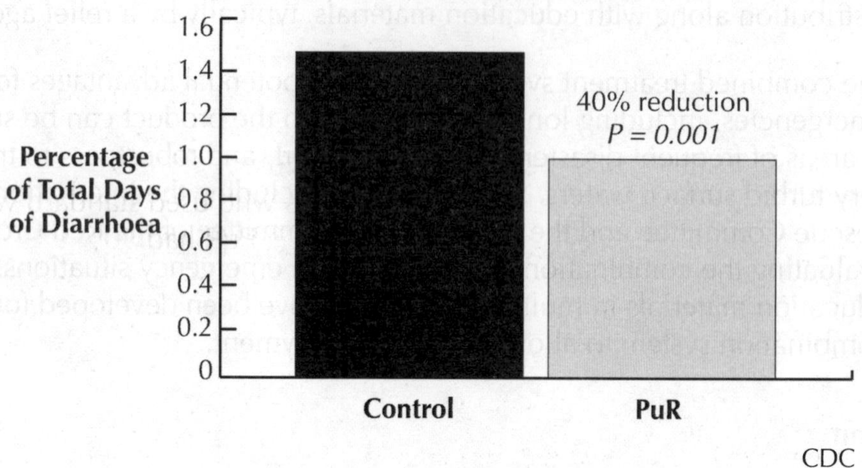

Laboratory evaluations in test waters demonstrate that this treatment system effectively reduces the levels of representative waterborne bacteria, viruses and parasitic pathogens from test waters. Two health intervention trials conducted by the CDC in rural Guatemala demonstrate that the combination system can significantly reduce the incidence of diarrhoea.

In addition to microbial contaminants, the treatment system increases water clearness, and removes a variety of chemical contaminants such as arsenic, making it suitable for treating a wide variety of water sources in developing countries. Because the treatment makes water significantly clearer, the amount of microbes in the water is less than compared to disinfection alone in highly turbid waters, thus providing a strong visual signal to consumers that the treatment is effectively cleaning the water.

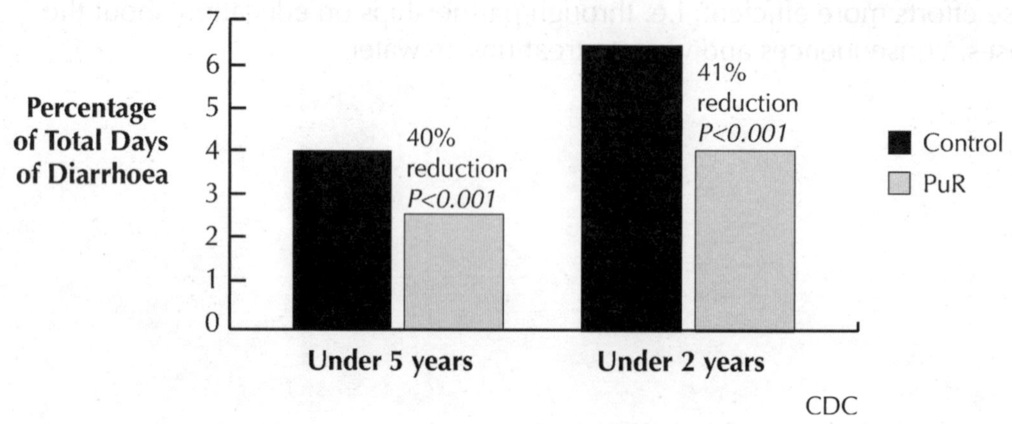

The results of the tests in the 492 Guatemalan households showed that at baseline, 1% of water samples from intervention households were potable. However, 21% were potable at 4 months, and 47% were potable after three rounds of weekly encouragement. After adjustment for week, age, and group interactions, persons in households given the product had significantly less diarrhoea than the baseline by week 31, whereas households given bleach alone had 18% less. Households given the product had less turbid water (51% mean reduction) than baseline.

In another test of 514 households in 14 villages in San Juan Sacatepéquez, Guatemala, where diarrhoea is a leading cause of death, families who used the product to treat their drinking water had cleaner drinking water and 40% less days of diarrhoea compared to neighbouring households who used standard water handling practices. In addition, the households using PuR had 50% less prolonged episodes of diarrhoea in children under the age of 2.

Consumers describing their experience with PuR reported clearer water and find the process simple to use. They also find the pricing ($US 0.01 per litre of treated water) acceptable. It is clear, however, that educational efforts, including product demonstrations, are necessary to encourage a consumer habit change.

Lessons Learned

Point-Of-Use drinking water solutions, using a market-based approach, require broad collaborations involving the private sector, governments, NGOs and research institutions, in order to provide effective education, marketing and product distribution.

A one-off educational programme did not bring about widespread regular use of any of the Point-Of-Use interventions – reinforcement was critical. The visual appeal of clear water and the potential for profit-funded continual promotion of the product could result in sustained use, thereby empowering household to reduce diarrhoeal illness.

Case 3

Procter & Gamble – Combating "hidden hunger"

Established in 1837, the Procter & Gamble Company began as a small, family-operated soap and candle company in Cincinnati, Ohio, USA. Today, Procter & Gamble's (P&G's) 98,000 employees make and market almost 300 products in 140 countries. P&G is looking more seriously than ever at the opportunities presented by the four billion poor people in the world. To meet the company's goal of "developing low income market products and business models", partnerships that leverage vital core competencies are a key ingredient. P&G considers this model of social equity and sustainable business as the best approach for delivering solutions to the world's pressing issues, while at the same time capturing new market opportunities for the company.

P&G decided to focus on consumer needs and to limit that focus to a few countries. Their approach to the needs in emerging markets was informed from the outset by a belief that the company would be able to make money and deliver benefits to the communities they were working in. They focused initially on products that filled critical dietary gaps, while providing consumers with something that was both fun and appealing. UNICEF, the Micronutrient Initiative, and Cornell University approached P&G with a seemingly intractable need in emerging markets known within the development community as "hidden hunger". They chose P&G because of its fortification technology and its expertise in food formulation.

Micronutrients are key

The hidden hunger problem is a simple one. Essential micronutrients like iodine and iron are normally only found in foods such as meat that are typically too expensive for the poor to buy. The lack of these nutrients in diets severely impacts child growth and intellectual development.

According to the World Health Organisation:

- Iron deficiency is the number one nutrition problem worldwide. Two billion people get too little iron. One billion suffer from iron-deficient anaemia. Iron deficiency causes low birth weight, unsafe pregnancy, and impaired growth and mental development.
- Iodine deficiency is the number one cause of preventable mental retardation. One billion people are at risk of iodine deficiency, which impairs mental development, impairs growth and learning, and increases susceptibility to infection.
- Vitamin A deficiency is the number one cause of preventable blindness. 190 million people are at risk. Beyond blindness, vitamin A deficiency causes susceptibility to severe infection and anaemia. It's also linked to increased mortality rates.

Initially, P&G came up with a product called NutriDelight, a low-cost powdered drink mix containing all the vital micronutrients that also tastes great, is stable and accessible for digestion (bio-available). NutriDelight contained GrowthPlus, a patented source of iron, vitamin A and iodine.

As part of the product's development, UNICEF funded a clinical study, conducted among nearly 700 children in Tanzania in 1996. The results showed the unique combination of ingredients in NutriDelight helped kids grow significantly better, while also boosting their mental alertness and performance. The product's development and clinical evaluation benefited from the joint capabilities of scientists at the P&G Nutrition Science Institute and leading health experts at UNICEF, the Micronutrient Initiative and Cornell University. Before the product was launched, WHO, UNICEF and local physicians were engaged to deliver education campaigns to raise awareness about micronutrient deficiency and ways to combat hidden hunger.

P&G, in consultation with leading experts on micronutrient deficiency, decided to launch the product in the Philippines, where the government had begun taking steps to address the problem of hidden hunger. The product campaign used strategies and business components that looked fairly similar to many other P&G product launches in developed markets. Given the nature of the product and its additional benefits, P&G also spent some time educating the population on the public health benefits of micronutrients.

Initially the company sought to distribute the product and deliver public health education itself, but this approach was unsuccessful. P&G found that it had insufficient in-country infrastructure to deliver its product to the poorest communities. The company did not possess the local knowledge and reach. Even when P&G accessed those markets, the product turned out to be mostly unaffordable, partly because of the diversion of funds to education campaigns and away from demand creation for a product that addresses a problem that is widely unknown.

These same health benefits, which were marketed on the packaging, were undermined by the absence of enforced intellectual property rights in the Philippines. Local competitors were soon able to sell similar looking products more cheaply and claimed that their products also contained "micronutrients".

NutriStar, a re-brand of the NutriDelight product, was then launched in Venezuela. This time, building on the lessons learned from the Philippines, P&G decided to do things differently. Focusing on its strengths, P&G shifted away from its "go in and do everything yourself" mentality towards a network approach, looking to engage with new and often unexpected partners who were already well established on the ground.

P&G: Nutritional product

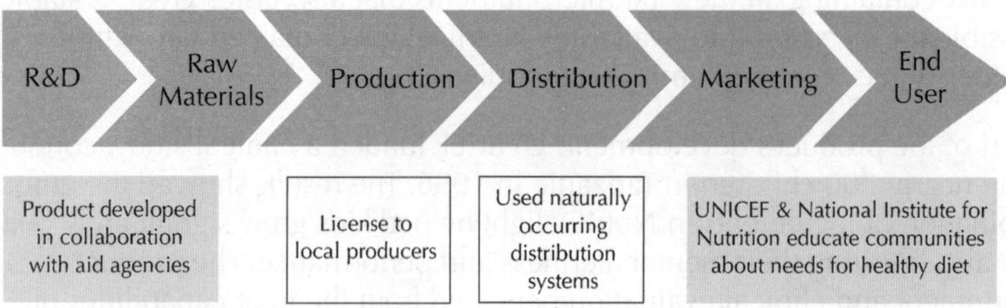

P&G recognised that its own core competencies lay in product marketing, strong science-based product development, quality assurance and up-the-trade distribution. It needed partners that were able to handle local production, ensure down-the-trade distribution, credibly tackle the educational components of the business, and provide trusted sources of third-party verification for benefits marketing.

To develop its information and product awareness, P&G began to build a network of partnerships with NGOs, multilaterals, and local pediatric associations, focusing each partnership around an educational need or an informational resource that would be trusted and recognised by its customers. Without marketing the product per se, the educational campaigns help to raise awareness of the problem of hidden hunger and create demand for a product that addressed the issue among the targeted communities. As part of this effort, P&G donated part of the profits from the sale of NutriStar to fund public service programmes that educate parents and children on proper nutrition. P&G expects to invest about US$1 million in these educational efforts.

In selecting private sector partnerships, P&G looked to use its core competencies of demand creation, strong science-based product development, quality assurance and uptrade distribution as a base. Therefore the company sought partners with expertise in production and downtrade distribution, or who were government or NGO agencies, or involved in education or social marketing.

The innovation for P&G was to get out of the old style "go in and do everything yourself" business model, breaking internal prejudices to find "naturally occurring" distribution systems – not only for products but also for information. Thus P&G partnered with local enterprises, taught them how to make the product, and left them in charge of distribution. Risk was shared between partners: P&G bearing the brand equity risk and local companies the capital risk.

For the public sector, focus was put on programme skills, government ministry access and connectedness, access to public health expertise/resources, and nutrition education and advocacy programmes.

Overall, these partnerships proved valuable in creating a pool of local investment and ensuring that products actually reached the markets they were aimed at. Involving local companies in the value chain was also a good way to create additional sustainable livelihoods around product development.

Creating demand

Public health organisations (WHO, UNICEF etc.) organised awareness raising and education campaigns before the launch of the product. It helped local people realise that they could be affected by a lack of micronutrients in their diets. It also suggested ways to tackle the phenomenon of "hidden hunger". The international organisations teamed up with National Institutes of Nutrition and local doctors who were known and respected by local communities. This added credibility to the campaign and magnified its impact. These campaigns helped create a latent demand for the product, which indirectly provided P&G with a licence to operate. However, there was no public endorsement of the product or mention of the product's name. For US$0.30 (30 cents), the product mostly sold to the middle class. With government subsidies, the product could be made available in schools (bulk quantity and no packaging would reduce costs considerably). NutriStar costs less than soft drinks – and, of course, is much more nutritious.

Innovation has also taken place with regards to packaging. The product is sold in small sachets that sell well in poor countries, but mostly to the richer segments of the populations.

Despite these efforts, it proved difficult to reach all of the levels where the product was needed. This was further compounded by political instability in Venezuela, which prevented P&G from further refining and fixing its business model. This eventually led to P&G pulling NutriStar out of the Venezuelan market.

However, NutriStar is now fully national in Nicaragua, using P&G's partnership/licensing model with a local manufacturer. This is a unique, collaborative business model where USAID played a significant and critical role. USAID initiated connections with key Nicaraguan Ministries and thought-leaders and helped give credence to both P&G's science and P&G as a company.

Benefits

The development of this product has had commercial and social benefits. Commercially it has positioned the P&G brand in new markets and developed a new commercial product designed for a large customer base, while helping the company to think differently about profit margins. It introduced a system for market entry that is faster and less expensive, through the use of local enterprises.

Socially speaking the product has a low pH, thereby improving water quality by killing bacteria, as well as a long shelf life and dry packaging, which are better suited to the needs and conditions of customers. For local companies, its manufacture has meant increased training and competencies, as well as the creation of jobs for manufacturing and distribution.

Case 4

Interface – Sustainability means "business as usual"

For Interface, the past 10 years have been a comprehensive sustainability learning approach for the company; a great deal has been learned along the way and the process has benefited from mistakes and successes. The company is very aware that sustainability means "business as usual" for everyone, and these experiences have provided a solid contribution to successful change. The company is well on course to achieve its core vision of becoming a leading example a sustainable and restorative enterprise by 2020, across five dimensions: people, place (the planet), product, process and profits. This is a daunting task, but Interface embraced the challenge when its Founder and Chairman, Ray Anderson, presented it to the organisation in 1994. As a result, Interface has undergone a considerable transformation in its effort to re-orient the entire organisation.

Interface Inc. is a leading manufacturer of carpet and fabrics for commercial and residential interiors, with 20 facilities on four continents, annual sales of US$923 million, and 5,100 associates worldwide. Interface developed a shift in strategic orientation focused on seven key fronts for approaching sustainability, based on the Four Systems Conditions of The Natural Step. These fronts are:

1. Eliminating waste – not just physical waste, but the whole concept of waste.
2. Eliminating harmful emissions.
3. Using only renewable energy.
4. Adopting closed-loop products and processes.
5. Using resource-efficient transportation.
6. Energising people (all stakeholders) around the vision.
7. Redesigning commerce so that a service is sold that allows the company to retain ownership of its products and to maximise resource productivity.

By heavily engaging its employees in the importance of the Seven Fronts in achieving sustainability, and through its wide array or programmes, many valuable ideas have emerged that enable Interface to move forward with its vision to "lead others forward through power of influence."

Eliminate Waste

Through its waste elimination drive, the company has saved US$231 million since 1995, paying for all its sustainability work. Interface defines waste as anything that does not provide value to the customer. This includes traditional forms of waste such as off-quality and scrap, as well as non-traditional forms of waste such as the overuse of materials, inventory losses etc.

Benign Emissions

Interface has reduced its total global greenhouse gas emissions by 46% on an absolute basis, through improved energy efficiency, the increased use of renewable energy, and a major landfill gas project at the LaGrange, Georgia , USA, carpet manufacturing facility.

The LaGrange manufacturing facility employees were challenged to find local options for the direct purchase of renewable energy, in keeping with the Renewable Energy Front, due to their location in a small, rural Georgia community. The only alternative for increasing their renewable energy usage was through the purchase of Renewable Energy Certificates (RECs) from distant projects. They desperately wanted to find a means for meeting this need more locally.

Through participating in the World Resources Initiative's Green Power Market Development Group, the idea for using landfill gas arose, and was transformed into a project. Interface pitched the landfill gas project idea to the city of LaGrange in 2001, proposing an engineering study to determine the viability of capturing landfill methane gas from the city landfill, for use as an alternative fuel source for the manufacturing plant. Once the engineering project was initiated with the city, Interface began to see greater potential for impacting Front 2 – Benign Emissions. The landfill gas project could greatly reduce greenhouse gas and other emissions, thereby creating a safer environment for community residents, and creating valuable business partnerships with the potential to boost the local economy.

At first the small city-owned landfill gave the impression that there was not much opportunity, but the engineering studies revealed that the city of LaGrange had an enormous untapped resource and revenue stream. On 20 August 2003, Interface Flooring Systems signed a ten-year contract with the LaGrange to purchase the landfill gas, and the city committed to voluntarily construct the gas collection system and the leachate recirculation system, to install the flare, and to construct the ten-mile pipeline between the landfill and the Interface plant. Once complete, the pipeline will be available to a second commercial customer, one of Interface's competitors. The project is a "first" in LaGrange, Georgia, as well as in the American carpet industry. The pipeline is due for completion in the third quarter of 2004, but Interface is already receiving the greenhouse gas emissions credits associated with the flare at the landfill. The flare, combined with improved energy efficiency, and increased use of renewable energy, enabled Interface globally to reduce carbon dioxide emissions on an absolute basis by 46% from their 1996 baseline.

By creating awareness among its employees, and energy and enthusiasm around the sustainability issue, Interface has been able to successfully lead others forward in this important initiative that has multiple environmental, social and economic benefits. Methane is 21 times as potent as carbon dioxide in its contribution to global warming. When methane escapes into the atmosphere, it creates odours and contributes to local smog as well as potential explosion hazards. Its use as an alternative fuel for two heaters and a boiler at the Interface plant provide a much more attractive use.

The project will also boost the local economy. It is estimated that, coupled with other improvements being made in the city of LaGrange, the project will generate an estimated $30 million in revenue for the city over the next 50 years, whilst adding an extra 20 years to the life of the landfill. Interface's cost for retrofitting the two heaters at its plant will be approximately $50,000, but yearly savings from using landfill gas rather than natural gas will be approximately $20,000. The project will have a three-year payback.

The local community will benefit from the project through cleaner air and a reduced need for fossil fuels. By educating its associates on the importance of benign emissions and renewable energy, and then by engaging external stakeholders (local government and community), Interface has been able to take what it has learned and put it into practice, making a positive contribution to the community where its internal stakeholders live and work – core to the company's commitment to social sustainability.

The proven success of this endeavour will give Interface the power to seek and leverage similar projects for its manufacturing facilities around the world, and the initial reactions to the programme by external stakeholders have been favourable. In December 2003, Interface Inc. received the Lone Star Award from the Southeast Green Power Network for "creating a new supply of green energy…and future oriented policies that include the development of a new green energy source that is used on-site and is not connected to the grid."

The cool carpet scale

Along these same lines, Interface introduced the first "climate neutral" carpet product in 2000, and in 2003 it introduced the Cool Carpet™ option, allowing for all of the life cycle impacts of a carpet product (up and down the supply chain) to be completely offset with Emission Reduction Credits (ERCs). The offsets are third-party validated and "Climate Cool" certified by the Climate Neutral Network. Cool Carpet is now available on any modular or broadloom carpet product offered by the Interface companies in the US, Canada, UK and Europe, with expectations to expand the programme into Asia-Pacific later this year. Interface received the US EPA's Climate Protection Award in April 2004 for its development and delivery of climate neutral products and programmes.

Renewable Energy

By educating its employees on the importance of reducing energy consumption, while increasing the use of renewable energy, a new level of awareness was created throughout Interface, resulting in a number of partnerships with government as well as non-government initiatives. As has been true for many of Interface's other sustainability initiatives, it was the "first" in its industry to engage in these external partnerships.

Interface Inc. is a founding corporate member of the Green Power Market Development Group (GPMDG), a collaboration of leading corporations and the World Resources, Institute dedicated to building corporate markets for green power. Its goal is to develop corporate markets for 1,000 MW of new, cost competitive green power by 2010. In 2003, Interface Inc. and other corporate partners in the GPMDG bought Green-e certified Renewable Energy Certificates (RECs) in an amount that broke all prior US records. The combined purchase was enough energy to power 24,000 homes, and avoided an estimated 450 million pounds of carbon dioxide emissions. The development of the landfill gas project in LaGrange, Georgia, is another activity that Interface has participated in through this partnership.

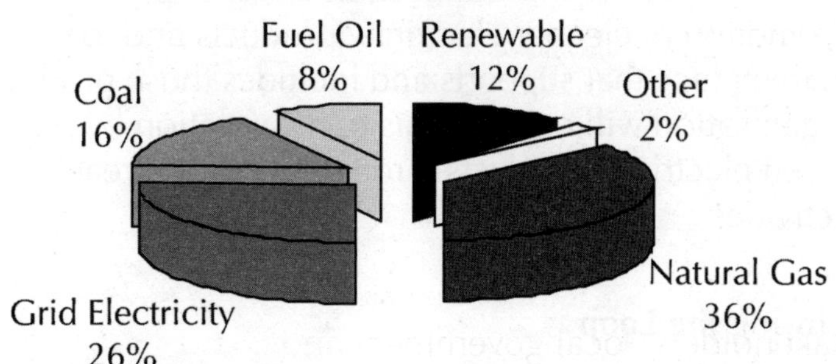

Interface's Bentley Prince Street (BPS) broadloom manufacturing facility also participated in this landmark event by purchasing 30,501 megawatt-hours of RECs over a six-year period. This purchase, in combination with its existing renewable energy sources, allowed BPS to obtain 100% renewable electricity. Interface Flooring Systems participated as well, purchasing 1,224 megawatt-hours of RECs over a three-year period.

In 2004, the Interface companies were publicly recognised by the US EPA for their participation in the Green Power Partnership and for their ongoing commitment to purchase and use renewable energy.

Three Interface manufacturing operations are currently recognised as members of the EPA's Green Power Partnership; Interface Flooring Systems (LaGrange, Georgia – a charter member of the programme), Interface Fabrics (Maine and Massachusetts facilities), and Bentley Prince Street (City of Industry, California). The Partnership is a voluntary programme designed to reduce the environmental impact of electricity generation by promoting renewable energy. The Partnership seeks to demonstrate the advantages of choosing renewable energy, provide objective and current information about the green power market, and reduce the transaction costs of acquiring green power. The EPA recognises organisations that switch to green power as environmental leaders who are establishing the choice for renewable energy as the next step in sustainable business practice.

Interface Fabrics, through its membership in the US EPA's Green Power Partnership, purchased 2,500 RECs, or enough to offset the emissions associated with one million linear yards of Terratex® brand recycled polyester fabric.

Interface Fabrics Group is a founding member of the Maine Green Power Connection (MeGPC), a growing network of businesses, organisations and residents who are working together to create a viable market for greener electric power in Maine. The Connection exists to provide a single-focus entity for the promotion of cleaner electricity products and for the creation of an electricity marketplace that supports and includes those products and their providers. The organisation will catalyse this transformation by building customer demand for green electricity products through public outreach, education and aggregation activities.

Closing the Loop

Industrial systems are linear, take-make-waste systems. Natural, cyclical, living systems are destroyed when resources are depleted and waste accumulates in the biosphere. Interface is redesigning its processes and products into cyclical material flows where "waste equals food." It is reducing its use of raw materials, and working to get the most value out of the materials employed. This includes the careful recycling of synthetic materials, so that waste materials in society become valuable raw materials in industry. It also means keeping organic materials uncontaminated so they may return to their natural systems. In 1994 an average of 13% of the materials used in Interface's products were non-petro-based. As of 2003, the average has increased to 20%.

Resource Efficient Transportation

Interface is dependent on fossil fuels to deliver its products and services to its customers, but this is not a viable model for sustainable transportation. This Front is the one least within Interface's control and the one most difficult to address. A significant portion of Interface's transportation footprint is due to the delivery of raw materials and the transport of finished products. Interface participates in voluntary partnerships focused on reducing pollution and greenhouse gas emissions.

The corporation is a charter partner in the US EPA's SmartWay Transport voluntary partnership and has also partnered the Business for Social Responsibility's Green Freight Group. Interface has also launched a global internal Transportation Working Group that is actively working to establish the corporation's transportation footprint and is developing metrics for measuring its success.

Since 1997, Interface has sponsored the planting of almost 45,000 trees to offset air travel by its associates. The internal programme, called Trees for Travel, has enabled Interface to achieve notable success on two key Fronts: benign emissions and resource efficient transportation.

Associates at Interface Research Corporation and the Troup County (Georgia) manufacturing facilities can opt to offset the CO_2 emissions associated with their daily commutes to and from work through the Clean Co2mmute programme.

Interface also offsets the CO_2 emissions associated with fuel usage in company cars through its Interface Cool Fuel™ programme, using rebates received from a corporate fuel card rebate programme. These programmes were featured in Interface's winning nomination for the US EPA's 2004 Climate Protection Award.

Engaging stakeholders

Interface realises that it must engage its stakeholders in order to best understand sustainability in all of its Fronts, for the challenges that lie ahead. Many of Interface's original initiatives focused on internal stakeholder engagement. Today Interface is focusing heavily on its external stakeholders, constantly broadening its circle of influence, in keeping with its mission. Over the years, Interface has been the "first mover" or "first in its industry" to get involved in those programmes, processes and dialogues that have pushed green development to the forefront. Interface is involved in a number of partnerships, certification programmes, educational initiatives, testing protocols, rating systems and performance tracking programmes related to sustainability.

Through the deep understanding that Interface associates have gained on their journey to sustainability, many of them have participated in key initiatives for fostering a better understanding of the benefits of green building principles. One such initiative is through Interface's role in the development and growth of the US Green Building Council (USGBC). Interface was a founding member of the USGBC, and the USGBC Chairman is an Interface Americas employee. Interface employees at all levels have played key roles in the development of the USGBC's Leadership in Energy and Environmental Design (LEED™) Green Building Rating System, specifically in issues pertaining to materials resources and indoor environmental quality. Interface associates have also held key leadership roles in developing numerous local USGBC chapters.

Additionally, associates from Interface Asia-Pacific have been nominated to various working committees of the Australian Green Building Council, and an Interface Asia-Pacific associate also holds a position on the Technical Committee Rulings Panel, the final arbitration body of the Green Star rating for new and refurbished buildings in Australia.

Associates from Interface Flooring Systems in Canada are also participating in the Canadian Green Building Council (CAGBC).

Redesign Commerce

Redesigning commerce is about focusing on the delivery of service and value instead of the delivery of material. It is about engaging external organisations to create policies and market incentives encouraging sustainable practices. It refers to creating new methods of delivering value to customers, changing purchasing practices, and supporting initiatives to bring about market-based incentives for sustainable commerce. It also focuses on the services delivered by the multiple life cycles of its products.

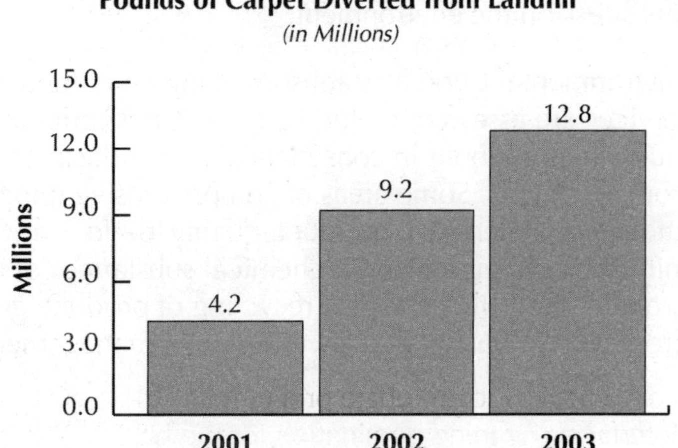

In redesigning its commercial model, the company has created Re:Entry, the carpet reclamation initiative for Interface Americas. This initiative has enabled the floor covering companies to divert more than 49 million pounds of material from landfills since 1994. In 2003, 12.7 million pounds of material were diverted from landfills; a 38% increase over 2002, and carpet tile recycling was up 51%.

Interface recognises that recycling is merely one component of the solution to a larger problem. The company is committed to continuing its work to develop new backing systems that can easily be recycled into the original material (closed loop recycling), and it is committed to continuing its research to identify and perfect a means for recycling other existing backing types, as well as nylon from the face construction.

Interface is also committed to certifying its products to those programmes that provide third-party validation for multiple environmental attributes that consider the full life cycle of the products. One such example is the recent certification of products from Interface Flooring Systems and Bentley Prince Street to the Scientific Certification Systems (SCS) Environmentally Preferable Product (EPP) programme for carpet.

Interface employees, using what they have learned through life cycle assessments of Interface products, have been integral in educating others on the full life cycle based approach to creating industry definitions, certifications and eco-labeling programs.

For example, Interface Flooring Systems was the first carpet company to certify its products to the Scientific Certification Systems' Environmentally Preferable Product (EPP) Certification for Carpet Products in August 2003. Bentley Prince Street certified products to this standard in 2004. The EPP programme has been instrumental in educating the industry, and the marketplace, on the importance of multiple product attributes and life cycle based evaluations in determining "environmental preferability" to meet the needs of various government orders and other specifications. It is expected that this approach will influence other initiatives such as LEED.

Interface Canada has certified its products to the Federal Ministry of Environment's Environmental Choice EcoLogo programme, a comprehensive national environmental labeling programme that helps customers make informed choices and encourages the supply of, and demand for, products and services which cause less stress on the environment.

Environmental Choice establishes stringent criteria against which products and services are assessed, including quality, performance, environment and safety. Guidelines are built in consultation with industry, relying on independent experts from all sectors. Some areas of comprehensive impact assessment include material and energy intensity of product, quality, performance, life, water usage, waste minimisation, air emission, chemical substances of concern, indoor air quality, product safety, recyclability, recycling of product, general design and delivery of product, and quality and environmental management systems.

The climb to the top of Mount Sustainability is an arduous, but rewarding, journey. Every foothold gained begins with a self-questioning analysis of the company's processes and materials, and the determination to achieve even better results with less, and ultimately, no impact on the environment.

At Interface, sustainability is built into business decisions from the raw materials sourced – to the way the company reclaims its customers' used products.

Case 5

Novo Nordisk – TakeAction! Make the Triple Bottom Line your business

Sustainable development is about preserving the planet while improving the quality of life for its current and future inhabitants. Novo Nordisk uses the term "Triple Bottom Line" (TBL) to indicate sustainability in terms of financial, social and environmental responsibility. It is an important part of Novo Nordisk's guidelines for all company planning and decision-making processes, as it builds its business in a way that is financially profitable, environmentally sound and socially responsible. This involves being clear about its purpose and taking into consideration the needs of all its stakeholders – shareholders, customers, employees, business partners, governments, local communities and the public.

Throughout its history Novo Nordisk has initiated a large number of activities that reflect the Triple Bottom Line. To build on these initiatives, the company aims to integrate and embed TBL far more into the business than ever before. The TakeAction! programme is one way to enhance this integration – and in the long run – create a TBL mindset or culture. The many local initiatives made by employees should make them reflect on how they can do their daily work in a more responsible way. To that effect, Novo Nordisk wishes to obtain a much larger outcome than what it would obtain from individual activities.

Essentially, TakeAction! informs, inspires and supports employees to initiate and drive social and environmental activities, and allows employees to spend time doing these activities. It further serves as a platform for sharing best practices. As most activities under the TakeAction! umbrella are driven by employees, the task of the TakeAction! team is to serve as a clearinghouse and resource for all of Novo Nordisk's employee-driven social and environmental initiatives.

Novo Nordisk is a focused healthcare company and a world leader in diabetes care, with the broadest product portfolio in the industry, including the most advanced products within the area of insulin delivery systems. In addition, Novo Nordisk has a leading position in areas such as haemostasis management, growth hormone therapy and hormone replacement therapy. Novo Nordisk employs more than 18,000 people in 68 countries and markets its products in 179 countries.

Starting Blocks

TakeAction! was launched in January 2003 at Novo Nordisk's yearly International Meeting (IM) for top managers. 210 of the 300 participants signed a TakeAction! commitment sheet and agreed to seek ways to make their actions reflect the Triple Bottom Line. Lars Rebien Sørensen, CEO, encouraged them to present TakeAction! to their employees and inspire them to get involved.

All participating managers were supplied with TakeAction! posters, brochures, pins, and a presentation to help them inform their colleagues about the programme. They were urged to encourage others to sign the commitment sheet. Each employee signing the sheet, receives a TakeAction! pin, and when all employees in a department sign the commitment sheet the department receives a TakeAction! Plaque as a symbol of their commitment. By January 2004, the TakeAction! team had received signatures from 7% of all employees worldwide.

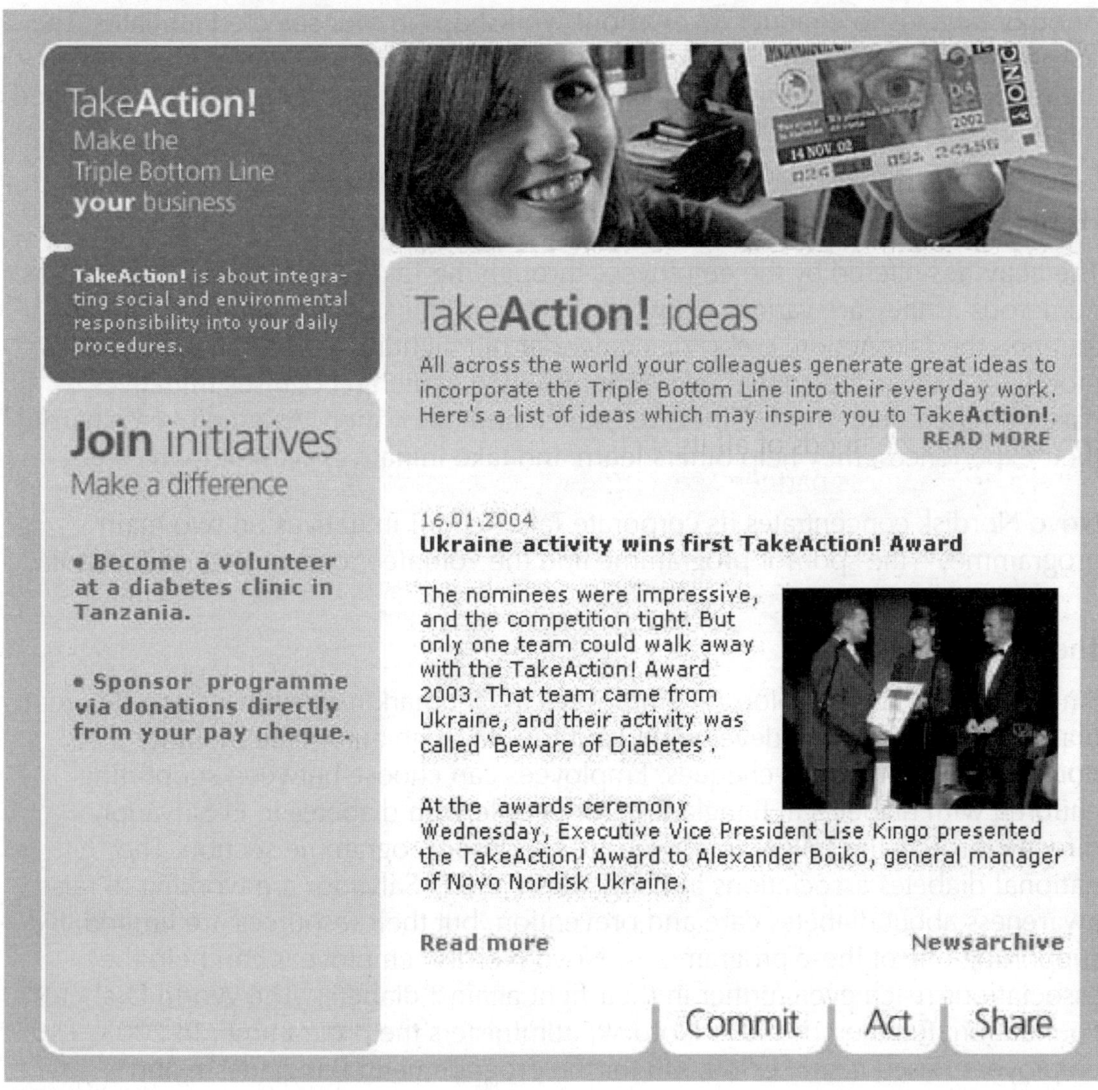

TakeAction! website – front page encouraging employees to share!

To further support its activities, the TakeAction! website was launched in January 2003, which aims to communicate general information about the programme and share best practices.

Employees are encouraged to send in their ideas to TakeAction! and report on already implemented activities.

The targets for the first year were: to have a successful launch with positive feedback; launch a sponsor programme and volunteer opportunity; receive 100 applications for the volunteer opportunity; inspire employees to initiate at least 10 new initiatives; and to share at least 10 already implemented initiatives.

Four targets have been identified for 2004. The first target was to present an award for the best TakeAction! activity for 2003 at the International Meeting 2004. Additionally, a "TakeAction! – the year in review" film was presented to all participants at the meeting, showing them the past year's activities.

Another target is to conduct TakeAction! workshops in four selected affiliates. The purpose is to give employees additional tools to engage in TakeAction! and to get their feedback and ideas for further development. Finally, a status report is planned for all VP's in December 2004.

Hitting the ground running

The activities offered by the employees through the TakeAction! programme are as numerous as they are varied. Activities are communicated through the company Intranet, the TakeAction! website, a calendar highlighting a different project every month, as well as the annual TakeAction! Award, which recognises initiatives based on their outcome, business relevance and innovation. As employees share their experiences, they help others learn and take initiatives of their own.

Novo Nordisk concentrates its corporate TakeAction! initiatives on two main programmes – the sponsor programme and the volunteer opportunity in Tanzania.

The sponsor programme

Since May 2003, Novo Nordisk employees in Denmark may sponsor two different diabetes programmes in developing countries through automatic monthly donations from their pay cheques. Employees can choose between supporting children with diabetes in Bangladesh, or people with diabetes in El Salvador, directly through the TakeAction! website's sponsor programme section. The national diabetes associations in Bangladesh and El Salvador are working to raise awareness about diabetes care and prevention, but their resources are limited. By supporting one of these programmes, Novo Nordisk employees can help the associations reach even further in their fight against diabetes. The World Diabetes Foundation, founded by Novo Nordisk, administers the programme. In 2003, 150 employees raised nearly US$9,000 for the programme in Bangladesh, and US$5,000 for the one in El Salvador. The sponsors receive regular updates on how their contributions make a difference.

The sponsor programme contributes to the TBL by raising awareness about diabetes in Bangladesh and El Salvador, while contributing to employee satisfaction and motivation at home. This is because Denmark does not have a long tradition of individual contributions to charity, due to its welfare system. The country is one of the largest public contributors of financial aid to developing countries (measured per BNP), and many have thereby felt that they pay their share via public taxes. However, this is slowly changing, as charity organisations receive more individual contributions than ever before. It is the aim of the sponsor programme to meet this increasing interest by giving the employees the possibility to support a cause that they – via their job – have a special interest in.

Volunteer opportunity (Tanzania)

In April 2003, Novo Nordisk launched a TakeAction! volunteer opportunity, where employees worldwide can apply to become volunteers for three weeks at a local diabetes centre in Dar es Salaam, Tanzania. Volunteers are invited to use their competencies to help develop the centre's processes and expertise in close collaboration with local staff. The clinic's staff determine the specific qualifications they need at a specific time, and the job offers are posted on both the TakeAction!

website and the internal Novo Nordisk job site. In 2003, the TakeAction! team received more than 100 applications and more than 200 inquiries from interested employees. This initiative contributes to the TBL by:

- Raising awareness about diabetes in Tanzania.
- Helping employees broaden their understanding of diabetes in developing countries (which is an increasing problem that the company aims to address).
- Giving a broader understanding of customers' needs.
- Promoting employee satisfaction, motivation, and loyalty, as volunteers are proud to work for a company that provides them with such an opportunity and which acts on its responsibilities.

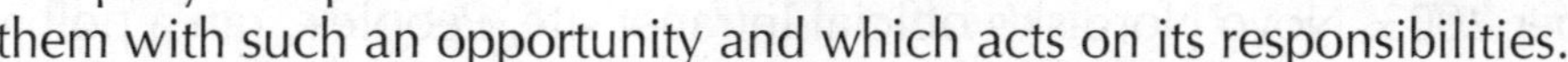

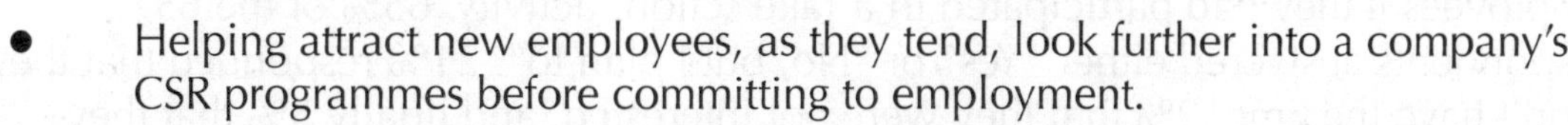

- Helping attract new employees, as they tend, look further into a company's CSR programmes before committing to employment.
- Supporting the perception of Novo Nordisk as leading the fight against diabetes.
- Building stakeholder trust among employees and partners in Tanzania.

The volunteer opportunity gives the volunteer (and their colleagues who hear about it) a unique insight into the severe diabetes situation in Tanzania. The volunteers have all been deeply affected by their experiences and many of them have stated that they look at their daily life with a whole new perspective after their return.

In addition to these two large programmes, Novo Nordisk subsidiaries around the world also organise events of their own. These initiatives have common bottom line motivations, including improving employee satisfaction and motivation, as well as the company's reputation, positively influencing stakeholder trust (employees and partners where the activities take place), supporting the perception of Novo Nordisk as socially responsible, supporting the perception that the company is leading the fight against diabetes, and increasing awareness about diabetes through articles etc. leading up to the event.

- In China, 75 employees and their families planted more than 100 trees at the foot of Miyun reservoir to increase afforestation to avoid sand storms.
- Employees in Denmark collected nine tons of clothes, linen and toys for a diabetes centre in Tanzania.
- South African employees held a walk-a-thon to raise money for the establishment of a local diabetes clinic.

- Indian IT department employees donated used computers to a facility for poor children and now plan to teach them to use them.
- Russian employees collected money for flu vaccine, toys, food and clothing for children in a Moscow orphanage.
- In Ukraine, employees held the "beware of diabetes" public awareness campaign, where they produced a leaflet about the disease and its complications, and distributed these on the streets of Bila Tserkva (winner of the TakeAction! Award 2003).

Measurement of success

Following the launch of the programme, the TakeAction! team has received positive feedback from employees. To follow-up on employee demands, employees have enhanced access to information on how to take action through news stories about future, current and past activities, as well as guidelines describing how to carry out various activities. A TakeAction! idea list was developed, providing concrete ideas (both team and individual) on how to take action.

TakeAction! Poll

In October 2003, Novo Nordisk's official Intranet site, People+, ran a poll asking employees if they had participated in a TakeAction! activity. 65% of the 657 respondents answered either "Yes" or "No, but I plan to". 21% responded that they didn't have the time, 2% that they were not interested, and finally 5% that they had never heard of TakeAction! The TakeAction! team will address the 21% that answered that they do not have the time by providing more concrete examples of how TakeAction! can be incorporated into their existing work programme.

TakeAction! Guide

In June 2003, managers received a TakeAction! Guide with practical information on the programme and a summary of the programme's status. The purpose of the guide is to provide an overview of the programme and some practical tools to get started on or continue their work with TakeAction! The questionnaire, which 11% of the managers returned, measured how well integrated the programme was and asked for ideas for improvements. Overall the answers were positive and the respondents all saw the value of TakeAction! However, the answers also identified some barriers standing in the way of TakeAction!, including lack of time and resources, and lack of support to daily business focus. The TakeAction! team will discuss how to overcome these barriers during 2004 and has commissioned a benchmark on this matter. Before the team makes any decisions it will investigate how other companies address the issue.

It is difficult to measure whether or not there has been a change of mindset – especially as the programme has only been running for one year. However, over the last year, the TakeAction! team has identified an increasing interest in diabetes in developing countries. Employees who have ideas on how their department can contribute to TakeAction! are continuously approaching the team. This often involves a break from old procedures, which can be seen as an indication of a change of mindset.

Living the values

The annual employee survey, eVoice, consisting of more than 100 questions, has been the benchmark by which the TakeAction! programme knows whether its initiatives are making a difference to the TBL. The tool assesses the working climate, with particular attention given to measuring how well management is translated into daily business practice. Each unit reviews its own data and takes action on low performance scores. At Novo Nordisk, "living the values" is one of the ten core global leadership competences and a key indicator of performance.

Values as an attraction factor

Changing demographics, an expected skills shortage, and changing employee expectations, are stretching companies' ability to attract and retain talented people. Novo Nordisk believes its commitment to sustainable development gives the company an advantage in a competitive labour market. Several studies show the importance of alignment between corporate and personal values. In 2003, for the second year in a row, Novo Nordisk was ranked the number one preferred employer among young professionals and business, engineering and science graduates, in a survey by the international consulting firm Universum Communications. 85% associated Novo Nordisk with a good reputation, and 53% named high ethical standards as one of the three most important characteristics that they associate with the company.

Sustainability approach as a retention factor

When Novo Nordisk employees were asked in the 2003 eVoice survey how they feel about the vision and the values of the company, three out of four consider Novo Nordisk's results within the social and environmental area to be important for the future of the company. To many Novo Nordisk employees, the translating of corporate values into the Triple Bottom Line approach, contributes to their job satisfaction and supports their decision to remain with the company.

Case 6

Veracel – Cultivating eucalyptus for pulp in Brazil

Veracel, founded in 1991, aims to cultivate and mill eucalyptus in previously deforested areas. The company's integrated project is composed of: a nursery for eucalyptus and native tree species; environmentally sustainable eucalyptus plantations; a road network for its operations; a maritime barge terminal; a mill for the production of 900,000 tons each year of bleached pulp; and a private Atlantic forest reserve.

The Atlantic rainforest in Brazil is one of the five most endangered forest biomes in the world. It once occupied 1.4 million km^2 or 15% of Brazilian territory, only 100,000 km^2 remain today. "With a deforestation rate of one soccer field every four minutes and an estimated 1.6 million species, 14% of the 1,371 known vertebrate species living in the forest risk extinction.[1] Although 42% of the species are endemic, less than 1% of the remaining area is protected. Significant deforestation of the Atlantic rainforest started after a road was built in the region after the Second World War and paved in 1974. In 1990, less than 5% of the original forest remained.

Despite an error in the initial phase of the project, which deforested 64 hectares of recovering forest (the area was subsequently replanted with native trees), Veracel has held an environmentally correct vision for its activities. The core of its environmental policy is the "mosaic landscape" that creates corridors of native forests interspersed among eucalyptus forest plantations. Veracel has currently acquired 149,807 hectares of land, but uses less than 50% of this amount for eucalyptus plantations. The remaining territory is destined for the maintenance and eventual recovery of the Atlantic rainforest (Mata Atlântica). The Veracruz Station, whose forestlands comprise 10% of the overall plantation area, and is the largest private forest reserve in the northeast of Brazil, complements these efforts.

Some 13 years into the project, Veracel is the main economic force in the region, providing over 1,400 direct jobs, and a new cycle of socio-economic development. It was created to produce, do business with, and generate opportunities for people in the region. 70,625 hectares (ha) of eucalyptus have already been planted, and harvesting started in 2001. Including its forests, the project's budget is US$1.25 billion and aims to produce 900,000 tons a year of bleached eucalyptus hardwood pulp.

Partnering for success

In the Atlantic rainforest, conservation requires: immediate actions and innovative strategies; work with private land owners; the involvement of all stakeholders. Conservation and recovery can be good business for companies and the communities in which they work, and the private sector has a role to play in creating capacity within the conservation community to interact with companies.

Veracel has been working in conjunction with several Non-Governmental Organisations (NGOs), including IBio, a Brazilian non-governmental organisation that was founded in 2002, and which is sponsored by Aracruz, Conservation International do Brasil, Veracel, DuPont do Brasil and Petrobras, to develop its integrated approach to working in the region. IBio was founded because companies and environmentalists realised the need to work together to conserve and recover the second most endangered forest biome in the world: the Brazilian Atlantic forest. Conversations evolved towards the creation of an independent organisation (IBio), which could, at the same time, take advantage of Conservation International's environmental conservation know-how, and the companies' commitment and assets (i.e. native forest fragments), to increase the efficiency and efficacy of forest protection and recovery and make its use an instrument for sustainable development.

As more than 80% of the Atlantic rainforest is privately owned, IBio has recognised the need to work with the private sector, and as such has developed a series of pilot projects aimed at significantly increasing the amounts of private land under protection, and a better connectivity between protected areas. The idea is to integrate the 20% of privately owned lands held in legal reserves into conservation areas. IBio is planning to work with Veracel to implement this on Veracel's own lands through The Conservar Project. Along with Aracruz, Conservation International do Brasil and The Nature Conservancy as partners and with US$250,000 in funding from USAID, the general objective of this project is to produce technology for Atlantic forest conservation and recovery in large scale. In order to do so, IBio and its partners are holding several field experiments, testing (i) carbon accumulation from native forest growth, (ii) connectivity between fragments, and (iii) biodiversity recovery, among other indicators. Based on the results of this project, IBio and its partners intend to use the technology to create ecological corridors, turning existing forest fragments into broader and more environmentally feasible structures for future biodiversity conservation and recovery of the Atlantic rain forest.

A local company with global standards

Veracel, owned 50/50 by Aracruz Celulose, the world's leading producer of short fibre eucalyptus pulp, and Stora Enso, the second largest paper producer in the world, is located in Eunápolis in the south of the state of Bahia. It is a typical case of a local company with global standards. Despite the fact that it is viscerally linked to its home state, the company is managed with an eye on distant markets and the most demanding standards in the world. Formed to develop, build and operate a pulp production facility, the project includes eucalyptus plantations, a world-scale mill supplied by its own tree-farming plantations, and related infrastructure.

Veracel was granted ISO 14001[2] certification in June 2003. Virtually all of its employees have attended excellence awareness and training programmes, and company policy states that its suppliers have to follow the social and environmental principles of the company (which are outlined in their integrated management system). These include:

- Raising awareness, training and developing people.
- Rationalisation of the use of natural resources.
- Minimising adverse environmental impacts stemming from processes and products.
- Conservation and recovery of the Atlantic forest. Promoting knowledge about the local biodiversity through partnerships with scientific institutions, and developing environmental education activities, using as its main agents the Veracruz Station and the Veracel Atlantic Forest Programme.
- The planning of plantations using the mosaic landscape concept, and making it a priority to acquire and manage land that already has been altered by mankind.

The environment

The land acquired by Veracel for its eucalyptus plantations has been previously degraded by several years of wood, agriculture, and intensive cattle raising activities. As of December 2003, Veracel owned 149,807 hectares (ha) of land. The area planted so far has reached 70,625 ha in 2004, and the company has a permit to plant 96,000 ha of eucalyptus. Veracel maintains 20% of the area, or about 31,000 ha, for legal reserves, as demanded by Brazilian legislation. In addition to the legal reserves, about 35,000 ha will be used as a preservation area, 6,026 ha for Veracruz Station, and about 7,000 ha for infrastructure.

The region has ideal growing conditions for eucalyptus trees – even rainfall, uniform temperature, which create excellent conditions for photosynthesis and year-round planting and growing. The warm Brazilian climate favours the fast growth of tree species, either by natural regeneration or by replanting new stands.

Tree cultivation protects the soil from erosion (through denser vegetation coverage) and raises organic material content in the soil, which favours soil fertility. In addition, permanent preservation areas (valleys, water springs, hillsides and forests) and remnants of native forest will be identified and protected. The application of the mosaic landscape concept will intersperse native forest, other crops and livestock, with eucalyptus plantations, generating a sustainable soil occupation model in an ordered manner, with a lower environmental impact then cattle raising activities. The land usage model will allow native vegetation corridor maintenance in valleys and on hillsides, protecting water springs and regional fauna and flora.

The people

Veracel's operations take place in an economically depressed sub-region of Brazil, where nearly 57% of the economically-active population receives only up to two minimum wages per month. The most significant activities outside of eucalyptus farming are cattle raising and some permanent crops, such as oranges, papaya and coffee.

The tree-farming programme aims to make wood production for the future industrial site possible through regional landowners. The idea is to involve the landowners by providing financing, technical assistance, and a sales guarantee for their final product (eucalyptus wood).

Additionally, Veracel currently employs 1,400 people – around 400 directly and 1,000 outsourced workers. The mill's construction will involve around 8,000 more people. The significant economic role that the company plays in the region through activity generation for related products and services will become even more important when the future pulp mill is built and enters operation, creating an estimated 8,000 additional jobs.

Veracel in numbers

Capacity of the future pulp mill	900,000 tons/year
Total investments foreseen for the project	US$1.25 billion
Investment foreseen for the mill	US$1 billion
Total area necessary	147,000 ha
Area destined for eucalyptus plantations	70,000 ha (own) and 23,000 ha forestry partners programme
Wood sale contracts	6 million m³
Wood delivered in 2002	1,044 million m³
Seedlings produced in 2002	23 million
Direct jobs generated (own and outsourced) until December 2002	1,422
Forecast of direct jobs (own and outsourced) with the mill in operation	2,000
Forecast of jobs during the peak of the construction project (temporary, direct and indirect)	8,000
External financial resources provided during the mill construction	US$670 million
Mill's foreseen annual billing	US$500 million
Investment already realised	US$300 million

The company favours the hiring of local workers and is working in partnership with SENAI, Brazil's worker apprenticeship service, to train a total of 5,500 people in areas including welding, electrical, piping, mechanics, operations, etc. In 2001, the programme trained 102 harvesting operators, 79 of whom were hired by the company. They all were awarded scholarships and, through the training they received, became leading candidates to obtain good jobs paying market-based salaries and fringe benefits.

The land acquired by Veracel was mostly used previously for cattle raising, employing some 300 people on the various farms bought by Veracel. The transformation of these farms into plantations created around 940 new job opportunities, providing employees with a dependable, regular wage. Veracel pays salaries that are higher than the regional average to employees on its direct payroll, and also offers good benefits. It requires its service suppliers to follow the same policy.

Veracel has a number of specific programmes designed for the region's farmers and entrepreneurs. The company encourages the harvest of non-wood products such as honey and piassaba in the areas near its plantations. It sells eucalyptus to small furniture makers, producers of doors and window frames, and eucalyptus is used for packing crates for fruit, for use in bakers' ovens, shoring up construction work and erecting temporary buildings on construction sites. These activities generate some 400 permanent and temporary direct jobs and contribute to the preservation of the native forests of the region.

The mill

Veracel's future bleached eucalyptus pulp mill, to be finished in the second half of 2005, will contain the largest single pulp production line in the world (in its category). It will also be one of the world's most advanced mills, both in terms of the modernity of its processes, as well as application of its environmental procedures to the highest international standards and energy self-sufficiency. Pulp processing will include two-stage oxygen bleaching, efficient washing and elemental chlorine-free bleaching. Debarking will be done directly in the eucalyptus plantations, thereby returning most nutrients to the soil (as they are mainly concentrated in the bark). The mill is duly licensed by the local environmental control agencies, and with a slim organisational structure, a maximised production scale, low fixed costs, and gains in logistics by building the mill close to a sea port, the mill will have the lowest manufacturing costs on the world market. This constitutes an important competitive advantage and will allow Veracel to remain healthy in poor market conditions.

Effluents from the mill follow strict environmental conditions, minimising water consumption and being a benchmark in terms of effluent quality. The socio-economical impact that the mill will have on the region is positive, and Veracel's investment is bringing a significant increase in the local economy that used to be largely based on low-return agriculture activities.

Eucalyptus plantations have existed in Brazil for more than 100 years, providing a proven and sound basis, which Veracel's use of the latest technologies has enhanced. Plantation development is centred on the fact that it is possible to reutilise the soil to replant trees immediately after harvesting, eliminating the need for additional land to keep up with production capacity.

Case 7

SC Johnson: Pyrethrum Sourcing from Kenya

Summary

Flowers, grown by subsistence farmers in the highlands of Kenya, are the key active ingredients for value-added products found in households around the world. Pyrethrum, a unique daisy, is the source for a naturally occurring insecticide that degrades quickly back into the earth. Over the past 30 years, US company SC Johnson has become one of the biggest single end-users of natural pyrethrins, for its RAID™ household insecticide products.

The Pyrethrum Board of Kenya (PBK), a parastatal agency that controls and operates the entire pyrethrum business in Kenya, manages the country's total supply of pyrethrum through a network of farmer co-operatives. SC Johnson has worked directly with PBK since 1970. This relationship has extended considerably beyond that of a normal supplier-purchaser relationship, and is characterised increasingly by a strong degree of knowledge and technology exchange.

SC Johnson has helped PBK develop planning and forecasting abilities through the sharing of best practice examples and on-going advice regarding the establishment and maintenance of a safety stock to help offset harvest shortages.

SC Johnson has also provided technical assistance to PBK. The company has provided bio-efficacy testing protocols and tools to allow for a better comparison of results between products tested at PBK in Kenya and at SC Johnson in the US. In addition, SC Johnson has collaborated in the development of up-to-date analytical chemistry methods that have aided the identification of new and different pyrethrum extracts.

As a result of this long-term capacity-building effort, there has been a notable improvement in product quality and a rise in production standards. PBK have made continuous improvements in their quality control programmes, and they have passed supplier audits from SC Johnson. Standards continue to rise and PBK is now seeking ISO certification.

Introduction

SC Johnson

SC Johnson is a 116-year-old family-owned and family managed business that manufactures home-cleaning products and products for home storage, insect control, and personal care. Annual sales are estimated at more than US$4.5 billion, and the company, based in Racine, Wisconsin, US employs 9,500 people and markets its products in over 100 countries worldwide.

Country Profile: Kenya

The Republic of Kenya lies on the Indian Ocean coast and forms part of the East African region. Whilst it is the most developed economy in East Africa, Kenya's population of over 30 million has a GDP per capita of only US$300.

Employment in Kenya is largely dependent on the agricultural sector. The major export commodities in Kenya include: tea, coffee, horticultural products (including cut flowers), processed petroleum products, pyrethrum, and other miscellaneous chemicals such as fluorspar, soda ash, sodium carbonate and diatomite.

Kenya's development challenges are not unlike those of other developing economies. Long-term barriers to growth, such as the dominance of key sectors by the government, endemic corruption, and a high population growth rate, continue to hold back development.

Natural Pyrethrum and Synthetic Pyrethroids

Pyrethrins are the class of insecticides derived from the dried flowers of the pyrethrum daisy (Chrysanthemum cinerariaefolium). Natural pyrethrins are not used widely in agriculture because they degrade easily upon exposure to sunlight.

For this reason, several pyrethroids (synthetic chemicals with a molecular structure and biological activities similar to natural pyrethrins) have been developed for use in agriculture. The largest use for natural pyrethrum is in the manufacture of consumer household insecticides. Pyrethrum was introduced to the highlands of East Africa in the 1920s, and by 1938 Kenya had become a major world producer. It has been the largest source of natural pyrethrum for the last 60 years and currently produces over 70 per cent of all pyrethrum traded in the world. Pyrethrum provides valuable economic and social benefits to more than 200,000 subsistence and low income farmers in Kenya.

Pyrethrum is a perennial crop that requires renewal once every five years, and is grown in highland areas enjoying moderate, well-distributed rainfall, cool night temperatures, and rich volcanic soils. In some areas where pyrethrum is grown the climate and soil structure cannot support other cash crops such as tea or coffee.

Other advantages for farmers are that it grows with limited inputs (such as fertilisers and pesticides) and farmers can rotate it with other crops to compliment land use and avoid disease difficulties. The size of the land owned by pyrethrum growers in Kenya averages 3 to 5 acres, in which the homestead is located and where the pyrethrum and food crops such as maize, potatoes, cabbages and kales are grown.

However, some growers do not own the land on which they grow pyrethrum, and have to rely on either hiring land from neighbours, planting on government-owned forest land, or even using road reserves.

For many Kenyan farmers, pyrethrum represents an important entry point to the monetised economy, and provides considerable social benefits to farmers, their families and communities. The price remains stable for a one-year period, and for over 200,000 subsistence farmers it is the only reliable source of cash. It is well suited to the economic circumstances of smallerholders, as input requirements consist only of readily available planting material and labour for planting, weeding and picking. Chemical inputs are not required. Pyrethrum has a favourable environmental profile in that very little chemical and fossil fuel inputs are consumed.

The Pyrethrum Board of Kenya

The Pyrethrum Board of Kenya (PBK) is a parastatal agency that has been mandated to oversee all activities related to the production of pyrethrum in Kenya for the benefit of growers and consumers.

PBK is a co-operative body established in 1934 through an Act of Parliament. The Act gives PBK the responsibility of licensing and providing extension services to growers, and mandates the Board to purchase all pyrethrum grown in Kenya.

Growers are paid monthly and PBK processes the entire crop into suitable products for sale to companies such as SC Johnson.

However, other government legislation limits the Board's ability to source bank credit and thus better manage pyrethrum inventory and supply. For instance, PBK must seek government approval for funding from the parent ministry (the Ministry of Agriculture) to finance a buffer stock, which would bring the much-needed stability to supply. Such approvals are needed quickly to maintain the quantity of supply, but the bureaucratic approval process is often too long to achieve this. Further, the Act demands that PBK remit all surplus earnings in a given year to growers, thus leaving little working capital to provide for reserves.

PBK provides a high level of transparency and consistency in crop pricing for growers. The annual price level is publicly announced in the media at the beginning of each year and remains constant for 12 months.

The crop grown by farmers is delivered to PBK through intermediaries, such as co-operative societies, self-help groups and PBK collection centres. These co-operatives operate at different levels. Growers deliver the flowers to individual co-operatives who form a union that subsequently supplies PBK. The intermediaries between the grower and PBK deduct commissions for their services.

This lengthy and complex supply chain is inherently inefficient, and PBK is looking for ways to increase efficiencies into the structure. PBK is working with farmers and co-operative management to develop new and better ways of managing the supply chain, and to encourage transparency within each co-operative structure. This is of particular importance as these co-operatives enable individual growers to consolidate their often meager flower output into viable quantities for delivery to PBK, as well as providing communities with an opportunity to learn business skills and a reason to collaborate across tribal lines.

The industry is preparing for liberalisation in line with current government policy (as a result of IMF rules and directions). This is expected to change the ownership and the way parastatals are managed. The PBK looks forward to the day it can operate as a self-sufficient commercial entity, unfettered by government bureaucracy. It desires to operate as a market-oriented enterprise that is able to seek investment capital for property, plant and equipment, and to build a suitable inventory to stabilise supply through the creation of buffer stocks. While this will mean that farmers will be able to grow pyrethrum without requiring PBK licences, the processing and refining equipment of the PBK is necessary to produce the saleable product. Unless an alternative group invests in this technology, the growers are likely to remain with the PBK.

Industry structure

Initially, ground pyrethrum flowers were used as a raw material input for making mosquito coils and powdered insecticides, resulting in a limited customer base. Success in the extraction and refining of purified pyrethrins from the flower gave this natural insecticide much broader applications, such as the water-based aerosols that SC Johnson pioneered. There has been increasingly wider recognition of the value of natural pyrethrum and pyrethrins for use in household insecticide products. The US is the single biggest market today. Only 6-7 major American buyers of purified extract remain, most of which are distributors, who purchase from the PBK and later resell to manufacturers.

During periods of shortage, some pyrethrum consuming companies have shifted supplies, in full or part, to synthetic pyrethroids to reduce their supply risk on the natural product and save costs. Currently the market is consuming approximately 60 per cent synthetic pyrethroids and 40 per cent natural pyrethrins.

Project Drivers and Objectives

SC Johnson produces a variety of household insecticide product forms under the RAID name, which utilises natural pyrethrin and synthetic pyrethroids. Due to corporate environmental objectives, SC Johnson prefers the use of natural pyrethrins if an adequate supply can be reliably sourced. Less expensive, high-quality synthetic pyrethroids are also a viable option for product formulas, since regulatory agencies governing the safety and marketing of insecticides characterise and regulate the natural and synthetic as the same.

PBK processes and markets all of Kenya's pyrethrum, of which over 95% is exported. Kenya's production constitutes more than 70% of global supply. The reliance on a single supplier in any business presents a certain risk, so a high level of reliability and consistency of supply is required. For SC Johnson's RAID business, this stability of product supply is essential. The company needs to determine product formulas years in advance of actual manufacture and sale, due to the rigorous and lengthy government registration and approval processes for household insecticide products worldwide. As a result, in some instances, product formulas have been based on access to a stable supply of either natural pyrethrins or synthetic pyrethroids. For PBK, the more reliability they can provide, the more likely natural pyrethrins will be included in formulas, thus securing a higher level of sales.

While the supplier of synthetic pyrethroids has proven to be able to provide a very reliable, consistent level of supply, Kenya has not. PBK has not always been able to provide reliability, and following an audit process, it was identified that there was considerable room for improvement before PBK could become a satisfactorily rated SC Johnson supplier. As long as this remained the case, the issues of reliability and consistency would always pose a threat to keeping natural pyrethrins in product formulas.

Therefore, as a result of SC Johnson's long-standing relationship with PBK and the preference for natural pyrethrins, an ongoing capacity-developing effort was undertaken to assist PBK in developing its capabilities as a global supplier.

Project Detail

History of involvement

Over the years, SC Johnson has become one of the biggest single end-users of natural pyrethrins. As a result, the company developed a direct purchasing relationship with the PBK, rather than purchasing through an intermediary. From this has developed a 30-year relationship.

SC Johnson has worked directly with PBK since 1970. The relationship has extended considerably beyond that of a normal supplier-purchaser relationship. SC Johnson has developed a strong commitment to this relationship and the provision of capacity building to address a range of issues and practices. In the early days there was a focus on exchanging skills and knowledge pertaining to pyrethrum growing, crop husbandry, laboratory maintenance and pyrethrin analysis. Education and training were offered to PBK's personnel in this area in the late 1980s. There has also been dialogue and exchange of views and technical information, with SC Johnson helping PBK to develop and maintain a state-of-the-art manufacturing and quality assurance programme in its factory. This collaboration is ongoing.

In addition, SC Johnson has helped a major PBK customer set up a factory to manufacture mosquito coils in Kenya, utilising Kenyan pyrethrum. SC Johnson purchases the pyrethrum-based coils from this PBK customer for sale in Kenya and surrounding countries. For this, SC Johnson provided a company scientist to work in Kenya with PBK's customer, and has provided on-going periodic technical support over the years.

The focus of the efforts shifted however in the last ten years, predominantly as a result of shortages experienced, as well as the increasing competitiveness of synthetic pyrethroids.

Initially SC Johnson was sourcing primarily natural pyrethrins. However, during the supply shortage of pyrethrum in the early 1980s, SC Johnson turned to synthetic pyrethroids that had improved in quality, price, and availability. A supplier was identified in Japan, which provided very high levels of customer service, efficiency and professionalism, which made them an appealing supplier.

On one hand this made the task of sourcing the input materials easier for SC Johnson Global Purchasing and Procurement Group, and the R&D Group were able to alter and register product formulas for this synthetic input.

However, the company maintained a preference for using natural pyrethrins and felt strongly that the relationship established with the PBK should be maintained. While formulation with only natural pyrethrins was not possible (due to the shortages only to be expected from any naturally sourced ingredient), the company looked to PBK to maximise their input. The decision to work with only one supplier entailed a certain level of risk, and it was in the company's best interests to consider how productivity of the output of the PBK could be improved, especially in relation to quality standards and reliability of supply.

The challenge then was to help PBK to reach higher standards as a supplier. The company had to address why PBK could not offer the same level of service that came from the synthetic suppliers, and consider what actions could be taken to improve the situation.

SC Johnson introduced its Quality Assurance Audit to PBK in 1995, and at this time their processes were significantly below the established criteria to be considered an SC Johnson "Partner in Quality." Efforts were then directed at helping PBK reach this global standard. This effort is still ongoing.

Understanding each organisation

An important part of this knowledge transfer and capacity building has been the initial and ongoing process of exchange that has enabled each organisation to better understand each others' business, as well as the operating constraints faced. Business and cultural differences and the structure of each organisation have resulted in a clear disparity between the way in which each organisation approaches the relationship and the resulting expectations that emerge.

PBK do not operate with the same level of understanding of customer service that SC Johnson may be more familiar with from other suppliers. PBK differ from many of SC Johnson's other suppliers in that they are a parastatal organisation, based in rural Kenya, and reliant on the output of 200,000 growers operating within co-operative social structures. Therefore they face different challenges and have different needs as a supplier. Due to a range of operational and institutional constraints, PBK requires for example a considerably longer lead-time for orders, which has in turn required adjustments from SC Johnson.

SC Johnson on the other hand operates in a considerably different environment. The company is largely driven by the need to have consistent supply levels to enable effective planning of production. It has therefore been helpful for PBK to spend time with SC Johnson to understand how product formulas are developed and how large-scale production of RAID is planned. PBK also needed to better understand issues such as impurities and how they affect products.

Understanding and adapting to these factors has required reciprocal learning on both sides. In one effort, there was the opportunity for the Chief Chemist of PBK to spend 3-4 months with SC Johnson in the US. Internship exchanges that see PBK employees spending 3-5 days at SC Johnson in Racine, as well as SC Johnson employees spending time with PBK in their Nakuru research laboratories, have been valuable in building skills and understanding for both PBK and SC Johnson personnel.

There are regular visits by PBK personnel to the US. This often includes two visits a year to SC Johnson's headquarters. SC Johnson personnel also visit PBK in Kenya, on average twice a year. This provides an opportunity for SC Johnson to examine the operations of PBK and the pyrethrum growers, and better understand the hurdles they face. SC Johnson staff spend time in the fields, with farmers and with officials of co-operatives, field extension staff, and other employees of PBK.

In addition, the process of conducting quality audits has brought a better understanding and direction to PBK regarding improvements necessary to upgrade their performance level.

Helping with planning and forecasting

Strengthening PBK's ability to provide a reliable level of supply has become a focus of the capacity-building efforts. This has required different levels of involvement and support, largely in an informal nature, rather than through a highly structured capacity-building effort.

SC Johnson has helped PBK develop planning and forecasting abilities through sharing of best practice examples and ongoing advice regarding establishment and maintenance of a safety stock to help offset harvest shortages.

During visits to PBK, SC Johnson experts have helped PBK learn how to better and more accurately forecast yields from dried flowers, which is necessary for ensuring a reliable level of supply.

Recognition of the need for a greater understanding and appreciation of each organisation's position, has led to a situation of constant feedback between the groups. Planning and purchasing personnel from SC Johnson conduct monthly teleconference calls with PBK to address supply quantity, pricing, and quality issues, and these issues are further addressed during the visits made by SC Johnson personnel to PBK and vice versa.

SC Johnson has also worked with PBK to help develop a more customer service oriented mindset. While there are many limitations faced (as they operate in rural Kenya as a parastatal organisation), it is important for them as a supplier to adopt more customer-oriented practices to enhance their competitiveness.

Technical assistance

SC Johnson has also provided technical knowledge to PBK. The company discusses the limitations of various bio-efficacy testing methods to enable PBK to ensure that biological performance matches the analytical quality of their production.

SC Johnson has shared bio-efficacy testing protocols to allow for a better comparison of results between natural pyrethrin products tested at PBK in Kenya and at SC Johnson in the US. The company has also collaborated in the development of up-to-date analytical chemistry methods that have aided in the identification of new and different pyrethrum extracts, as well as enabling the more accurate determination of active ingredient levels in pyrethrins shipped to Racine from PBK. Information on new product formulations utilising pyrethrins has also been shared with PBK. This has been accomplished by SC Johnson scientists visiting PBK; by PBK scientists and representatives visiting the company's Entomology Research centre in Racine; and by discussions held at various international meetings.

Project Outcomes

As a result of this long-term capacity-building effort, there has been a notable improvement in product quality, and a rise in production standards. PBK have made continuous improvements in their quality control programmes, and they have passed supplier audits from SC Johnson, as well as by other buyers such as Aventis. Standards continue to rise and PBK is now seeking ISO certification.

PBK is now recognised as an SC Johnson "Partner in Quality." The company's quality audits rate supplier performance from 1.0 to 5.0. A 4.0 is the minimum audit score required for a Partner in Quality status, which PBK achieved after only three audits, by working in collaboration with the SC Johnson Supplier Quality Audit team.

The planning systems SC Johnson introduced to PBK were something they had not used previously, and have led to an increase in the stability of supply levels. SC Johnson has also benefited through continued consumer-preferred products; more efficient use of the active ingredient; new product ideas that utilise natural pyrethrins; and access to a continued supply of this natural ingredient. While supply has become more stabilised, continuous improvements should be addressed and a diligent effort made to maintain consistency.

The most recent shortage experienced may have created the most significant shift away from natural pyrethrin formulations than any time in the last decade, and it can take years for the industry to fully recover.

The company is working to develop a sustainable business model for RAID, and recently conducted a detailed field survey in Kenya to evaluate the financial and non-financial capital being gained by pyrethrum farmers. The total life cycle analysis of pyrethrum was a first step in designing a model for all SC Johnson businesses that values the financial and non-financial impacts of raw materials. Such a commercialisation model will build on a foundation of Economic, Environment and social Equity ("3E"), including supply chain and external stakeholder partnerships. This may have further potential impact on the SC Johnson/PBK relationship.

Clearly, pyrethrum is a complex crop and industry, yet the PBK and SC Johnson have done well to bring so many subsistence farmers up to a high standard and given them the ability to manage this crop effectively and profitably.

Social benefits

200,000 farm families are now benefiting from pyrethrum as their primary cash crop, and PBK directly employs 680 people, with an increasing number of women in management. Overall, approximately 300,000 jobs are attributable to the growth and stabilisation of the industry.

Pyrethrum has been generating economic benefit for communities, with part of the income generated being utilised for social developments, such as being a major contributor to the building of schools, health centres, roads and other rural infrastructure. In addition, the profits from pyrethrum are having a considerable impact on schooling levels. The income derived from two acres of pyrethrum is sufficient to pay the school fees for three children in primary school and one child in secondary school or college. It is estimated that the school fees of more than 300,000 children are paid from pyrethrum earnings each year.

Pyrethrum in Kenya: Financial and non-financial capital impacts		
Economic Capital	**Environmental Capital**	**Social & Human Capital**
US$25 million in export sales value to Kenya.	Rotation crop helps maintain soil in 17,600 to 32,000 hectares on Kenya highlands.	200,000 farm families can educate up to three or four children each year through elementary and high school.
Natural compound. Broad bio-efficacy and food handling approval.	Little chemical and fossil fuel inputs versus other cash crops like coffee, tea and flowers.	680 direct employees at PBK makes it the largest employer in Nakuru. Over 300,000 direct jobs are created by the pyrethrum industry.
200,000 farm families rely on pyrethrum as their primary cash crop.	Grows in the highlands, and does not tie up the land like other cash crops.	80% of proceeds returned to farmers via a co-operative structure.
900,000 Kenyans (farm families and day workers, PBK employees) have economic access through pyrethrum.	Marc, a production by-product once considered waste, is sold as mosquito coil filler. Remaining vegetable waste by-product is used as animal feed.	Primary support in agricultural husbandry, technical support for pyrethrum growing and co-operative business management.
A cash crop that enhances food security by growing in rotation with subsistence crops (potatoes, corn, beans and dairy).	Pyrethrum crop does not require irrigation. Relies on natural rainfall.	Women (and children) have primary role in pyrethrum harvesting. Women are beginning to be represented in management positions in PBK and co-operatives.

This cash crop is of enormous value to subsistence farmers, and a measure of success can be gauged by evaluating the increase in numbers of children attending schools in the areas where pyrethrum is now being grown, as well as the overall standard of living enjoyed by pyrethrum farmers.

The co-operative structure, while problematic as a tool for managing the marketing of pyrethrum at a community level, contributes positively to a sense of cohesion. Co-operatives are also bringing community members together to determine how funds should be allocated for investments such as building new schools – bringing about a sense of participative decision making to the communities. Pyrethrum is also having a positive impact on families, as it is often a family enterprise that involves women and children as well. Many PBK employees have fond memories of picking pyrethrum after school, and have pyrethrum to thank for their education. They stress how the children's role of weeding and picking pyrethrum is important in their social development as responsible members of their family and community. Pyrethrum is also grown in schoolyards and tended by students and teachers to raise funds to purchase supplies and equipment and to improve facilities.

Environmental impacts

Environmentally, the impact of this crop is considerably lower than most other cash crops, especially in comparison to other agricultural industries in Kenya.

Chemical use is high for flowers, but negligible for pyrethrum. The crop grows well without fertiliser inputs, which in any case many farmers cannot afford or easily access. Weeding is generally done by hand and the plant itself is a natural insecticide, plus it is relatively easy for growers to rotate their way out of problems.

Farmers that shift to pyrethrum are often moving away from such environmentally damaging activities as deforestation for charcoal burning, so it offers an environmentally preferable source of income for these individuals.

Project Challenges

Reliable supply

This natural agricultural product will always be subject to the vagaries of weather. Technological advances have made the pyrethrum plant more drought tolerant and able to be cultivated in a wider range of altitudes, but the impact of weather continues to loom as a critical variable. A predictable, consistent supply of high-quality pyrethrum will likely continue to be the number one challenge facing this partnership.

Value proposition and cost competitiveness

A challenge for the industry remains regarding the value of natural pyrethrum. As long as natural pyrethrins and synthetic pyrethroids are considered "equal" by the EPA (US regulatory agency responsible for oversight on pesticides,) and synthetic pyrethroids are available at a much lower price than natural pyrethrum, the growth of the pyrethrum industry is threatened.

It will require the market to consider environmental and social value throughout the supply chain and in the calculation of the value proposition to conclude that a higher cost naturally-sourced material is competitive with synthetic analogs. The challenge for PBK as a long-term raw material source is to create greater awareness and demand for the natural product, in conjunction with increasing production of the crop. In the long-term, an inability to do so may threaten the overall sustainability of the industry and the ability for SC Johnson to retain natural pyrethrins in product formulas.

Macroeconomic and social stability

Kenya continues to be left behind by the global community due to the slow progress of economic market reforms. While there is no past history of pyrethrum supply disruptions due to these factors, Kenya is facing problems of real and perceived corruption and slow economic growth, bringing into question the PBK's ability to provide a reliable supply of natural pyrethrins to the world market.

Currently the US EPA and other regulatory agencies consider natural pyrethrins and synthetic pyrethroids to be equal. As a result, differential labeling cannot be used on product packaging, and advertising cannot highlight the use of natural pyrethrum. This limits the ability of the marketer to provide the necessary facts about natural pyrethrins to the broadest consumer audience. The PBK's ability to grow the market would be greatly enhanced by a shift in the current position held by these agencies.

Success Factors and Lessons Learned

Focus on a market orientation

In an environment filled with subsidies and closed market policies, it is important to rely on open market principles and a competitive value proposition. Transparency, efficiency, technology and reliability will be the key success factors to gain global market share. Once liberalised, the PBK will be empowered to manage itself as a private business, provided they make much needed changes in staffing levels and pursue growth-oriented investments. As a private business, it will no longer be tied to government constriction, and will be better positioned to promptly seek investment capital whenever needed.

Face-to-face meetings

No number of written reports can replace the learning that occurs both ways when business partners meet on each other's soil, especially with partnerships that transcend culture and economic resources. A one-way road, with the supplier always meeting at the buyer's home turf, is not sufficient. In this case, SC Johnson's knowledge of actual conditions faced in the growing, production and exportation of pyrethrum has been key to finding opportunities to become better business partners. A common understanding of each other's strengths and weaknesses is one path to a synergistic partnership. For instance, SC Johnson shared detailed production planning, whereas PBK shared growing and harvesting data, so both partners can work to achieve the best "just in time" production, and make effective use of PBK's limited working capital.

Proactive and frequent communications

Many traditional supplier-purchaser relationships are still based upon limited information sharing, perhaps in the hope of protecting a negotiating position. However, true supplier partnerships go beyond this to up-front and rapid information sharing. This is especially key to allow advance warning of potential problems. An environment must be created where potentially "bad news" can be delivered early on in the process without fear of losing the business.

Creativity and innovation work both ways

For the multinational partner, don't expect to have all the answers, but be prepared to be both the teacher and the student. This is the best way to find the most effective solutions as well as to leverage the unique creative solutions that generally come from living in developing countries with somewhat less predictable conditions. The PBK's clever uses for pyrethrin production waste as animal feed and by-products as mosquito coil filler are but two examples.

Long-term commitment

The major challenge in working with PBK has been their lack of a reliable predictor of pyrethrin supply and demand. Equally problematic has been their difficulty in responding to shortfalls in production given the nature of the cropping system. However, SC Johnson's relationship with PBK can certainly be characterised as successful. One of the quintessential success factors in such a relationship is the necessity of a long-term commitment from both the supplier and the customer. Trust, mutual respect, and a quality product are key ingredients in any successful relationship.

Summary

These case histories relate to the ways in which companies can work in harmony with various stakeholders and operate responsibly and ethically. Over time it will be interesting to see how effective these strategies are in making a better and safer environment for all. Thus instead of lowering expectations of consumers by pushing simplier living, many companies are attempting to boost consumption by being socially responsible. By doing this they are also benefiting a range of consumers in poorer countries and the locations where some of the products are produced. Companies wishing to become 'good' companies will have to work in a holistic manner, otherwise any shortcomings are likely to be picked up by NGOs and consumers alike.

The material within this booklet has been reproduced by kind permission of **The World Business Council for Sustainable Development (WBCSD).** CIM thanks WBCSD for the help and co-operation, without which this case study would not have been possible.

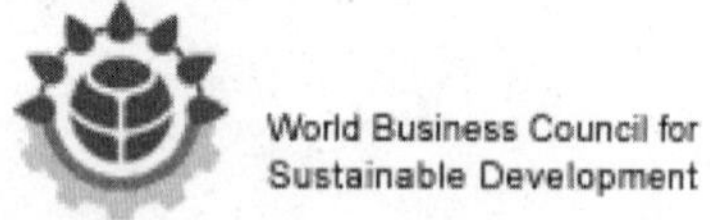

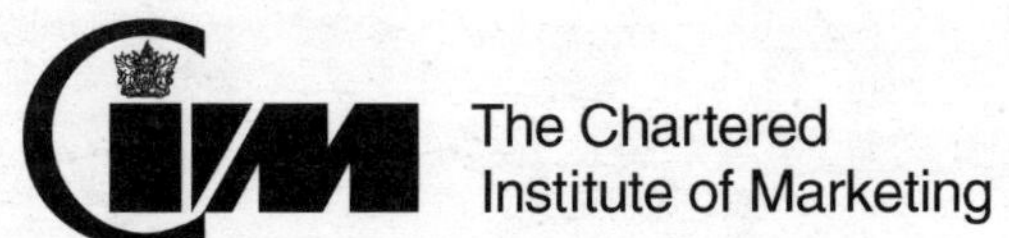

Moor Hall, Cookham
Maidenhead
Berkshire, SL6 9QH, UK
Telephone: 01628 427120
Facsimile: 01628 427158
Web Site: http://www.cim.co.uk

appendix 1 specimen answers and examiner's marking scheme

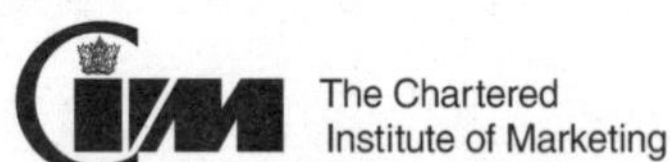

Professional Postgraduate Diploma in Marketing

Strategic Marketing in Practice

64: Strategic Marketing in Practice

SPECIMEN ANSWERS FOR DECEMBER 2004 EXAMINATION PAPER

Examination Papers

Each subject differs slightly from the other, and you need to make sure that you are familiar with the style of question and the requirements of the different examinations.

There are three basic question types:

1. The mini case or scenario or article
Part A of all papers (except Analysis & Decision) has a mini case, scenario or article, with compulsory questions. This represents only part of the paper, but students are required to make marketing decisions based on the information given. Spend time evaluating the material given in the case, but do not rewrite this for the examiners. You will gain credit for the decisions and recommendations you make on the basis of the analysis, but nothing for the analysis itself. This is a compulsory part of the paper designed to evaluate practical marketing skills. Make sure you allocate enough time to it, but do not ignore the other part of the paper.

2. The straightforward exam question
You are expected to make a choice from a number of questions. There is some skill necessary in selecting the questions which you are best prepared to answer. Read the questions through carefully before making your choice. Think about how you will tackle the question. Check you are answering the question in the context in which it has been set, then make a rough plan before you start writing. Remember that examiners are interested in quality answers.

3. Analysis & Decision (Diploma)
This final paper is an open book examination. The Case Study is sent out 4 weeks before the paper is sat. Students should complete their analysis and preparation before the examination takes place. The questions asked will include extra information about the case which will have to be used to obtain best marks.

Common Mistakes

Reports from examiners are published regularly and are available to students. Even a casual look through these reveals the same concerns and problems coming up time and time again across all subject areas. Most of these common mistakes are caused by a lack of exam technique and examination practice.

Not answering the question set
The examiners are looking for both relevant content and its application in an appropriate context. You must be able to work flexibly with the material you have studied, answering different questions in different ways, even though the fundamental theory remains the same.

Both of these essential business skills are of great importance to a marketing practitioner. The examiners expect work to be presented in a well-written, professional manner. 'Report' style, using sub-headings and indented numbering for points etc is not only acceptable, but looks much more commercially credible than academic essays.
This approach allows you to break the work up, highlight the key points, and structure your answer in a logical way. Take care with your grammar and use of language; small errors can change the sense considerably.

The scarce resource in an examination is time. You must control the allocation of this resource carefully. Read the instructions to the paper carefully, and identify what has to be done and how the marks are allocated. Spread your time proportionately to the mark allocation, ie if the mini case = 40% of marks, allocate 40% of your time to it. Allow a few minutes at the end to read through your work.

It is no good only completing four questions when you should have done five. It is so much harder for you to pass on just four questions. Have a clock or watch with you and be ruthless in your timekeeping. If you find you are spending too long on an answer, you are probably not answering the question specifically enough.

The examiners expect relevant theory to be illustrated with practical examples and illustrations. These can be drawn from your own marketing experience, or observations, or your reading. A theory paper without evidence of practical application is unlikely to be successful.

Introduction

The specimen answers provide examples of answers that can be reasonably written within the allocated time. The answers demonstrate what is required to achieve a good pass mark, unless otherwise indicated in the Comments.

Remember when revising from these examples that there are no right or wrong answers. The examiners are looking for you to apply your own marketing knowledge and skills to the question set. These answers should be indicative of the content and format that the examiners expect to see.

To give you the best chance of passing your exams, these specimen answers can be used in conjunction with the examiners' reports, in which the senior examiner for each subject outlines best practice. The examiners' reports are available from CIM Direct and on the CIM student website, www.cimvirtualinstitute.com.

We hope you find these specimen answers useful and informative. Although we cannot enter into correspondence, we would welcome comments or feedback, which should be sent to cimdirect@cim.co.uk or to CIM Publishing at the Moor Hall address.

CIM Specimen Answers

Professional Postgraduate Diploma in Marketing

PART A

Sustainability and Marketing Case Study

Introduction

This is a new style of case study and a new style of examination. In the future it is envisaged that the examiner will use a variety of formats for the case study, ranging from mini cases, sectoral cases and major cases based on one company to comparative cases looking at two companies. For this particular examination candidate have to analyse a range of case studies to formulate their answers. The theme is based around the title. The cases range from multi-nationals producing products as part of their CSR policies to companies working with local communities to create employment. One of the companies also looks at the Life Cycle Analysis of its products. Candidates need to grapple with the range of differing situations in order to pick some of the best ideas for the future development of CSR strategies.

In order to answer the questions candidates were allowed to analyse the case study four weeks in advance of the examination. Candidates were also asked to bring six sides of materials to augment their answers. For this reason each specimen answer is accompanied by the analyses produced the candidate. The answers have been chosen to indicate good practice and are some of the very good answers received by the examination team.

The key issues are:

(a) The role of sustainable action in developing marketing strategies
(b) The general role of Corporate Social Responsibility
(c) The way in which societal marketing operates
(d) Linking educational marketing to social improvement
(e) Measuring success
(f) Incorporating social issues within marketing strategies
(g) Understanding Life Cycle Analysis when developing products.

The Answers

This case is fairly complex and candidates need to understand the market sector that the company is operating in. It is important, therefore that the following issues are considered:

1. The application of theory.
2. The amount of CSR theory and application that the students can apply to the case (s).
3. The candidates should be thinking strategically not tactically.
4. The answers given must be realistic and practical.
5. A degree of innovation and lateral thinking should be rewarded.
6. It is important that the questions are answered within the given context.
7. The candidates should analyse this particular case to understand the problems associated with it.

Question 1

(a) Drawing from your examples, critically assess key ways in which an established company can implement CSR strategic marketing policies.

Marks 25

In answering this question, candidates should be able to draw from the various cases that have been given. They need to cover the following:

(a) The problems of 'adding-on' sustainable policies
(b) The different ways in which the other companies have dealt with the issues and relating this to the FMCG sector.
(c) Understanding issues of lifecycle analysis and its appropriateness to the FMCG sector.
(d) The need for the company to reorganise to make sustainability a feature of its marketing strategy.
(e) The need to market internally and get employee support.
(f) Utilising their strategies for generating PR.
(g) Understanding how green strategies could help the bottom line
(h) Understanding where the company stands in terms of its sustainability credentials by utilising matrices such as the ethics/sustainability matrix.

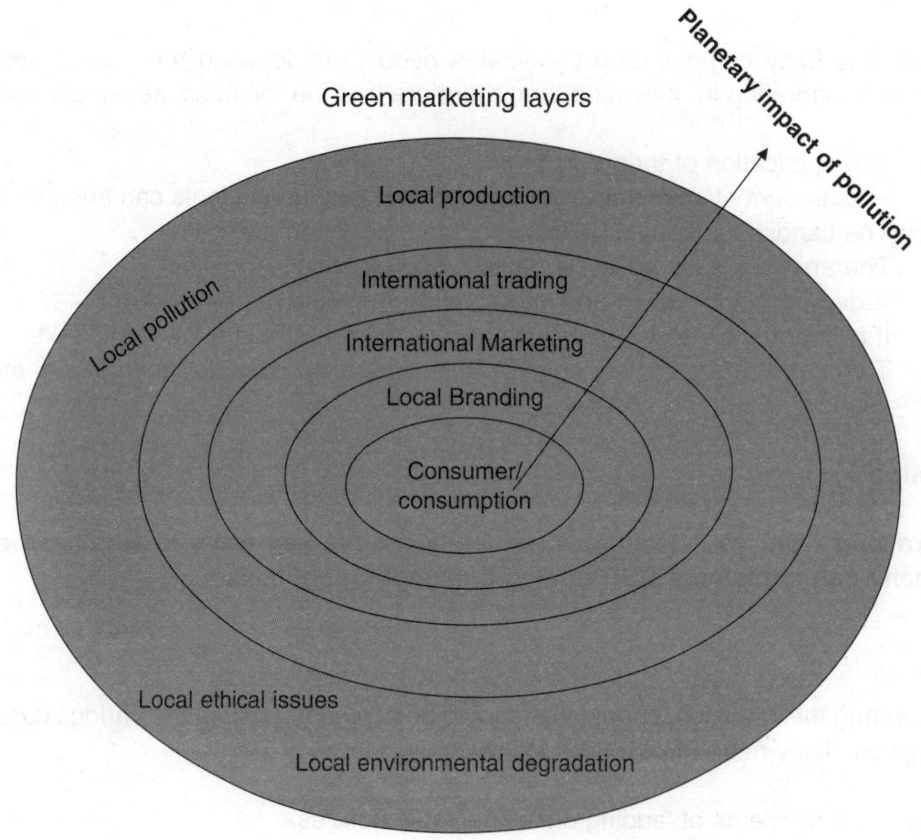
Green marketing layers
Planetary impact of pollution
Local production
International trading
Local pollution
International Marketing
Local Branding
Consumer/ consumption
Local ethical issues
Local environmental degradation

(Ranchhod, 2004)

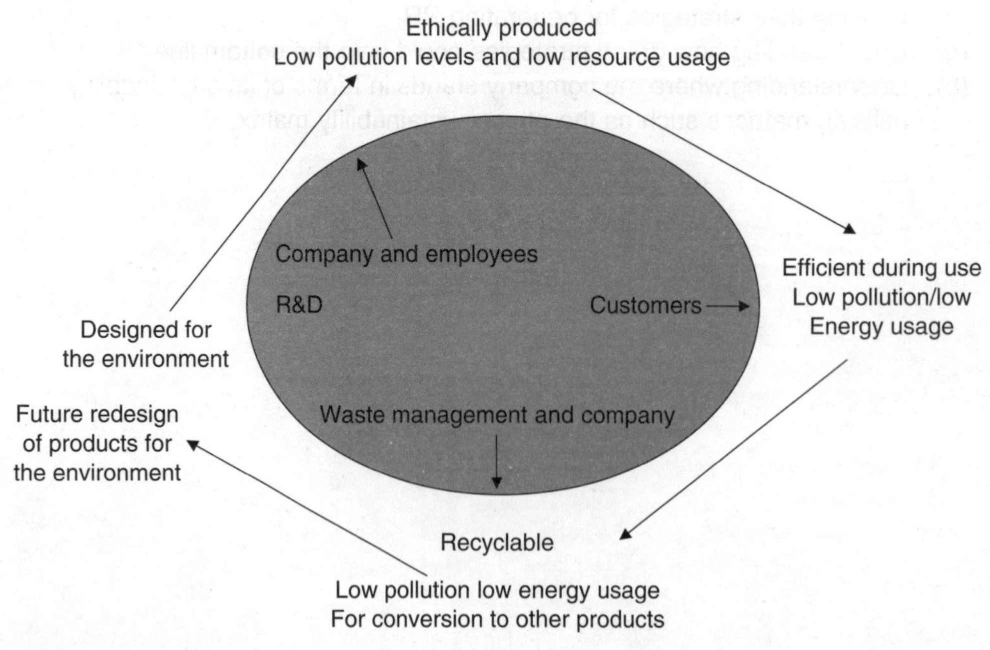
The virtuous, sustainable green circle for product management
Ethically produced
Low pollution levels and low resource usage
Company and employees
R&D
Customers
Efficient during use
Low pollution/low
Energy usage
Designed for the environment
Future redesign of products for the environment
Waste management and company
Recyclable
Low pollution low energy usage
For conversion to other products

(Ranchhod, 2004)

Sustainability and ethical strengths

Ethical stance \ Sustainability strengths	Low	Medium	High
Low	Cheap production systems exploitative of nature and humans		Production based on the care of the environment Human costs of little interest
Medium			
High	Often small ethical Companies who may not possess the technical know how for process improvement		The ideal company Does it exist?

(Both axes scaled 0, 20, 40, 60)

(Ranchhod, 2004)

Candidates should also consider the international and the localised effects of developing ethical and sustainable marketing strategies.

Any number of approaches are possible to answer this question and a good answer will develop both the depth and breadth required, together with a critical analysis of the answers.

Outcomes covered 9.64.1/2/3

(b) Marketing communications play an important role in developing company reputation. Explain how the case examples illustrate the various ways of developing communication strategies meeting the needs of differing customers.

Marks 25

In answering this question, candidates should be able to show how reputations can be developed by the use of sustainable and ethical values in marketing strategies. The communication strategies can be based on the following premises:

(a) Developing social marketing stances and overcoming barriers as shown in the table below.
(b) Working closely with stakeholders as in the case of Interface Inc.
(c) Working closely with communities in order to improve the environment as in the case of Veracel and Sonae.
(d) Adopting educational marketing as in the case of NutriStar and PuR.
(e) Communicating the benefits of helping to sustain communities in the developing world – SC Johnson.
(f) Offering customers a 'green' product that has undergone Life Cycle Analysis.
(g) Communication can be in various forms-leaflets, word-of-mouth, PR through newspaper articles, radio and television.
(h) Communicating sustaianable strategies through labelling as indicated by the EC.

Possible collaboration of approaches to social marketing given the sources acting as barriers to action

Problem	Barrier	Role for social marketing	Role for community mobilisation	Role for structured change approaches
Motivation	Individual	Creating awareness; promoting great benefits at a low cost	Urging media cooperation	Building web links to hard to reach individuals
	Community	urging opinion leaders to motivate others	Creating awareness raising public concern	Creating incentives for group organisation
	Structural	Urging change in structural rewards/ penalties (e.g. taxes)	Holding briefings	Changing structural rewards penalties (e.g. taxes)
Opportunity	Individual	Creating awareness of behavioural opportunities	Urging business and political cooperation	Changing economic barriers to individual action
	Community	Urging businesses to provide access to change agents	Changing repressive social norms	Eliminating antitrust restriction on business cooperation
	Structural	Urging use of government facilities for programmes	Bringing pressure to bear on legislators	Providing government subsidies changing physical environments
Ability	Individual	Providing modelling of ideal behaviour	Pointing groups members to individualised change tools	Allowing government agencies to provide training
	Community	Providing communication tools for outreach	Conducting group training	Allowing government premises (e.g. schools) for group training
	Structural	Urging removal of public disincentives	Changing community structures	Removing public disincentives

Excerpt from the EU rules on CSR

The consumer right to information is founded in the EC Treaty. Information should be accurate and accessible to be useful to consumers. As Consumers express a growing preference for socially and environmentally responsible products and services, access to relevant information about the social and environmental conditions of production is crucial to help them to make informed choices. Such information is available in different forms and from different sources, including claims made by the producer, information from consumer organisations and 3rd party verified labels.

Adherence to commonly agreed criteria for making and assessing social and environmental claims of a self-declaratory character would contribute to improve the effectiveness and credibility of these claims. Monitoring of claims by Member States and stakeholders is essential. The Commission is finalising guidelines for making and assessing environmental self-declared claims by producers or distributors, based on the ISO 14021:1999 standard, with the objective of preventing misleading claims and encouraging good ones.

Consumers also receive information through recognition schemes, such as listing of awards, prizes, labels, etc., which identify good practices on specific subjects. The EU-Ecolabel (6) as well as fair trade and ethical trade initiatives and labels are examples of 3rd party verified product labelling schemes. They are, however, only available for a limited range of product categories. For most consumer products, relevant social and environmental information is not easily accessible.

Both the ethical and fair-trade movements are now aligning themselves under common initiatives aiming at developing transparent and verifiable criteria for labeling and certification. The Commission welcomes these efforts as well as the rationalisation of existing labels through initiatives such as the new common fair trade label launched by the Fair-trade Labelling Organisations (FLO) and will examine the need to adopt further measures to promote fair and ethical trade. Participation in labelling schemes should be voluntary. Labels should be implemented in an objective, transparent, credible and non-discriminatory manner, respecting EU international obligations and applicable competition rules. The ILO core labour conventions should constitute a minimum baseline for such schemes. The EU supports the work of the ILO with regard to private voluntary initiatives.

By teaching the practice of making informed product choices, education could help develop a better understanding of the need for socially responsible products and services.

This excerpt offers some ideas surrounding labelling.

Finally students should also consider communications to the investment community and show how useful CSR policies can be.

A good answer will therefore be comprehensive taking into account most of the issues raised above. An average answer will cover these but not in the requisite depth and will only use some of the cases. A poor answer will fail to meet any of the key points made.

Outcomes covered: 9.64.1/3/4/5

(c) Show and explain in detail the main marketing metrics that could be developed by companies wishing to develop Corporate Social Responsible strategies.

Marks 25

This answer needs development of detail surrounding how measures can be developed. It needs candidates to realise that there are no measures that fit all the cases and different measures will be needed for different cases.

Marketing metrics is an emerging discipline and this needs to be discussed by individuals. They could utilise the following diagrams:

This table (Ranchhod, 2004) would be useful for Interface.

Environmental	Related EPI's	Examples of indicators
Crisis-oriented	o Output indicators directed at compliance	o Environmental discharges to air and water, efficiency of pollution treatment equipment, quantity and disposal conditions of waste per type
	o Environmental management indicators directed at compliance	o Number and frequency of complaints, fines and penalties, their nature and impact intensity extent and effectiveness of corresponding corrective programmes
Process-oriented stage	o Eco-efficiency indicators at the company level for product inputs resource conservation	o Energy, water, material (raw material/packaging) consumption efficiency related to volume, number of employees or financial returns per category
	o Eco-efficiency indicators at the company level for outputs (impact minimisation pollution prevention valorisation)	o Emissions per substance/effect/media concerned, waste by type/originating activity/production quantity o Environmental expenditures, costs resulting from environmental non-compliance and litigation, environmental costs and savings avoidance of the current year and previous years
	o Environmental accounting indicators directed at the environmental management system	o Degree of implementation of specific codes, internal policies or standards, number of training programmes and participants, improvements achieved, return on investment for environmental improvement projects, number of levels of management with specific environmental responsibilities, community relations (complaints, negative press reports, formal reports)
Chain-oriented stage	o Output indicators on a product chain level	o Environmentally harmful substances in the product chain (toxic dispersion) using life-cycle assessment (LCA)
	o Input indicators on a product chain level	o Materials intensity with the idea of closing material loops through re-use, recycling, product durability, resource conservation and energy intensity, along the chain (including extraction/supply and use phases)
	o Social performance indicators	o Employment generated, labour productivity (value added to the national GDP/number of employees), relationship between employee and company (personnel fluctuation rate, average duration of contract), education to build and maintain human capital (time invested for education and training), disabling illness, income level and distribution investments made outside the company in benefit for the community, sustainable metrics

For others it may be related to the factors such as:

(a) the number of individuals nursed to good health
(b) the number of individuals aware of the products (e.g. NutriStar)
(c) The number of jobs created
(d) Amount of pollution prevention
(e) Awareness of the benefits to the environment-by the general public
(f) The effect on the ROI

A framework for selecting marketing measures

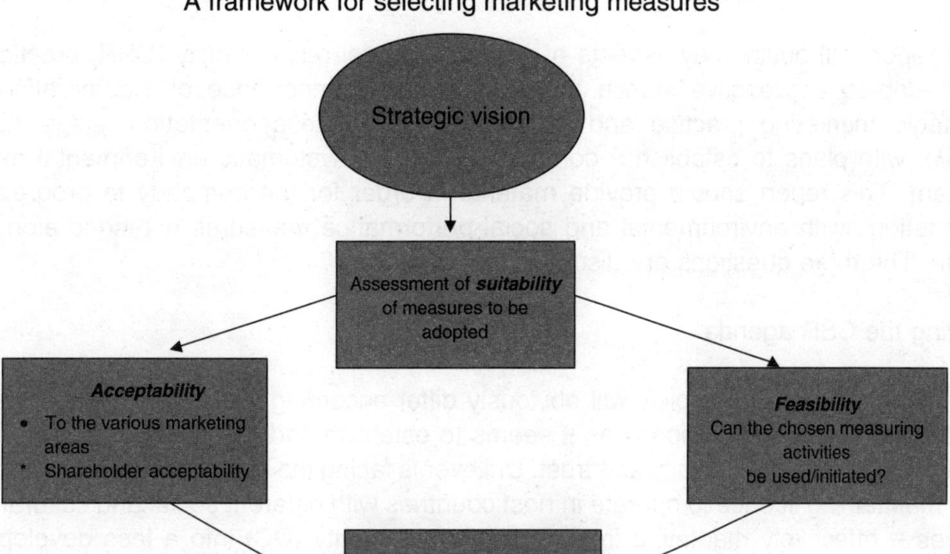

The above framework could be used to select suitable marketing measures. Candidates will need to be fully aware of the difficulties of measuring success for each company.

The good candidates will also consider the following:

(a) Customer loyalty
(b) Customer awareness
(c) Number of communities helped out of poverty
(d) Amount of pollution contained

And a range of other measures.

For this answer good candidates will take into account a range of options as indicated above. They should also refer to the cases to provide illustrative answers. Average students are likely to take a more piecemeal approach and not really analyse any of the cases or provide any framework for assessing measures. Poor students will be generally weak in the area of marketing metrics.

Outcomes covered: 9.46.2/6

All the questions will be marked out of 25. The other 25 marks will be allocated to each student depending on the level of analysis that have been carried out and how they have been applied. The marks will then be distributed equally across the three questions.

SPECIMEN ANSWER ONE

Question 1

Report for Board members; Unilever
From: Prospective Strategic Marketing Manager
To: CSR – Implementation, Communications and metrics
Date: 10 December 2004

Introduction

This report will outline key aspects of corporate social responsibility (CSR) practice. Unilever has adopted a proactive stance in recognising the importance of incorporating CSR into strategic marketing practice and is currently at 'process orientation' stage (Scherpereel *et al.*), with plans to establish a comprehensive and systematic environmental management system. This report should provide material in order for the company to progress to 'chain orientation', with environmental and social performance measures extended along the value chain. The three questions are discussed as *one report*.

Setting the CSR agenda

Implementation of CSR policy will obviously differ according to the original policy set and the challenges facing the company as it seems to establish and maintain competitive advantage, built through customer loyalty and trust. Unilever is facing the complex challenge of establishing and maintaining licence to operate in host countries with different social and cultural norms and values – effectively marketing from a developed county (DC) into a less developed country (LDC). Other examples provided in the case study are sourcing materials from LDC's for the manufacture of FMCb goods to sell in DC's, for example S C Johnson. All companies will begin from an initial audit position in order to establish (or review) their CSR policy and this would include:

- Recognition of the importance of stakeholders and their relative power and influence (ref. No 3).
- SWOT analysis of the strength, weakness, opportunities and threats facing the firm (4).
- Identification of the level of 'green' and 'ethical' behaviour currently. (refs 5&6).

It is important to recognise that successful implementation of CSR policy is dependent on it being part of the quest for effective and efficient strategic marketing orientation, and Kotler's Marketing Effectiveness Review (MER) has been incorporated into the benchmark analysis of the six case study companies (ref. 7) accordingly.

Implementation of CSR policies

It is recommended that Unilever sets at a corporate responsibility agenda and implements this from the top of the organisation, with full *commitment to the Board* and involvement of employees (to be discussed in communication section of the report). This involves giving shareholders full details of adjustments made, to comply with the Higgs Review of the role of non-exec Directors and assessing the role of corporate governance in CSR. Interface recognised the importance of top management commitment in 1994, with their Chairman acting as spokesperson. They have adopted a *Business Process Re-engineering* approach, reorienting the entire organisation towards CSR, placing ethical relationships with stakeholders at the heart of their social responsiveness process and products.

To discuss the *product* element of the implementation process in more detail, both Interface and Veracel are working towards a 'cradle to grave' approach, incorporating the 'green life cycle' – considering the CSR implications of product from birth to death. This can be examined in terms of the value chain, and Veracel is illustrated in point 8 of my analysis.

The consideration of supply chain and 'place' (or distribution) is of paramount importance, highlighted by Ranchod's recommendation to adopt 'a systems approach'. In order to enter new International communities, Delta Cafes established a 'competitive community' in East Timor, in fact creating it's own diamond (Porter ref. – no. 2). This is a good example of a company recognising that good CSR practice requires truly sustainable business, generating opportunities in new regions by working *with* the community to create a 'win – win' relationship. In this case it is not just a case of 'implementing' a CSR policy but rather recognising the competitive advantage to be gained from creating a new 'solidarity' market and placing ethical and sustainable behaviour at the heart of their business mission.

S C Johnson and P&G are both companies that have recognised their own competences, searched for partnerships that offered extra benefits, and implemented CSR practice in their distribution. Both organisations are motivated by the need for shareholder value and S C Johnson is recognised as the more transparently ethical and sustainable of the two, focusing on the establishment of a long term relationship as opposed to focus on potentially short term profit gains from distribution assistance for new products (P&G). P&G do, however, use *price* as a key differentiation, offering P&G PUR sachets at acceptable local market price, thereby reducing accusation of profit from suffering.

Implementation of CSR policy requires the recognition that employees, customers and your overall supply chain are all involved. Novo Nordisk recognises the importance of employee involvement but does not achieve buy-in of core 'TBL' values.

All companies could improve in the recognition of customer involvement in implementation. Tue 'responsible behaviour' branding means not only implementing CSR policies that both leverage competitive advantage and preserve the communities operated in and the planet, but also encouraging customers to adopt responsible practices. For instance, McDonalds now issue pedometer tokens with Happy Meals and Saab include a 'breathalyser check' as part of the new key ring of their latest car products. The true 'cradle to grave' approach for CSR implementation must extend through all 7P's of a company's implementation process, through all stakeholders and include the customer.

Comments

This answer starts off well but is somewhat limited in its approach. The diagrams in the analysis are utilised but the substance of the question answer lacks a little depth and detail. This is a good illustration of great detail provided in the analyses but not really utilised to good effect in the text. The analyses are very good and the application is good.

Question 2

Marketing Communications

Marketing communications (to differentiate, inform, remind/reassure and persuade) is a vital component of a company's CSR strategy. Again, approaches differ according to whether a company in the case study example is marketing into or at a LDC, or potentially communicating CSR just to a domestic audience. All organisations must meet the needs of stakeholders and communicate not only what business they're in, but how they do their business. This forms part of a company's segmentation, targeting and positioning practice and in order to develop communication strategy, companies must recognise the communication challenges facing them such as:

Developed countries

- Many consumers of ethical products are 'ethical invisibles', meaning that they do 'not label themselves as ethical consumers'.
- The total market share is currently only around 2 per cent of the total market – with companies needing to seek to turn 'Basic Browns' into 'Greenback Greens' potentially. Awareness of need recognition is required even more so in order to encourage trial and purchase. Delta Cafes has achieved this with the creation of a profitable 'isolation market'.

LDC's

Challenges relate to the need for education, in terms of need recognition (to be the product) and the provision of educational packs – a tactic employed by P&G.

These challenges are referred to Figure 19 and a suggested segmentation criteria for Interface is illustrated in Figure 15, with 'Attitude to Green' prioritised second.

The development of communications strategy in forming company reputation must be reviewed in three spheres – Doole and Lowe provide a useful model for this:

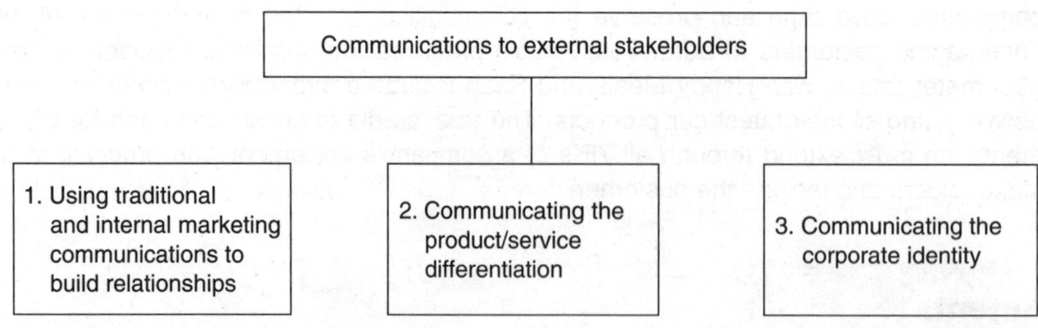

1. Using traditional and internal marketing communication
   S C Johnson recognises the importance of establishing networks to make connected stakeholders such as suppliers like PBK intrinsically *involved* in the maintenance of company reputation, and a 'win-win' relationship based on two way communication, speed and openness of into sharing and a consistent flow of communications.

   Figures 18 and 18.1 illustrate this point. S C Johnson initially adopted a push communications strategy but investment in the relationship has led to a 'communication loop' strategy. Unfortunately, there is little information on the end customer and this is indicative of most of the case studies, with customer feedback and constant communication a vital tracker in the pursuit of true market orientation incorporating CSR.

   Novo Nordisk is an example of a company attempting best practice internal communications, incorporating profile strategy in its use of management meetings and push strategy through creation of the 'Take Action!' intranet site. More information is required relating to the company's external communications and as Figure 17 indicates, the company has not succeeded in embedding CSR internally.

2. Communicating the product/service differentiation
   The establishment and communication of brand values (that incorporate CSR best practice) is a vital part of successful marketing communications and this will be discussed in part (3) relating to the corporate identity. However, many of the companies have recognised that in order to build trust and loyalty for all customers, products must reflect these values in order to be credible. Splitting this issue into two section:

   End users – Developed countries
   Delta Cafes has partnered Sonae and achieved successful communication through packaging and product placement/paint and sale materials in-store. This is in recognition of the challenge that customers must understand claims made; achieve esteem from purchase of the product (Maslow) and choose to purchase the CSR-friendly product over other coffee alternatives. The coffee is of medium quality but ha achieved a 'prestige' or aspirational positioning for consumers of the solidarity market wishing to demonstrate their attitude to green.

   End users – Lesser developed countries
   P&G learnt through experience (being a large enough multinational to spread the risk of projects) and offer lessons from their communication strategy that Unilever – as a direct competitor – could learn from. Their attempt to 'do everything themselves' was quickly replaced with partnerships with key NGO's and local experts and a two way communication partnership approach emerged, including the provision of education materials alongside the product, recognised the importance of visible signals, endorsed products and advocacy. (Figure 19 illustrates this point.)

3. Communicating the corporate identity
   Companies that are successful in their communication strategies develop trust and loyalty through two-way symmetrical PR, with 'mutual understanding and cooperation between and organisation and its public' (Grinig 98). More information is required as to how these organisations relate to their customers, but Interface is a good example of a company that has built ethical, dialogical partnerships with its community and has used public relations to build an ethical and sustainable corporate identity.

   Brand is of vital importance in the adoption of a profile strategy and Figure 16 illustrates an aspirational approach to the creation of a brand triangle for P&G PUK, based on lessons learnt from their project.

As a final line on this topic, consumers are increasingly discerning and have greater expectations, with brands needing to benefit from positive country of origin perceptions and overcoming negative perceptions (of poor CSR practice) in order to succeed. In order to proactively meet the needs of different customers it is important that communications are tangible and believable, consistent and integrated. Delta Café's approach of 'Do first, speak later' is a good example of ensuring that a company gets its CSR policies and practices right before talking about it.

Comments

This is a good answer taking into account most the key points concerned with regards to communications such as differing needs and the importance of branding. The analyses are utilised well and the examples from the cases are highly relevant.

Question 3

Marketing Metrics

To discuss the application of marketing metrics for this section, a case example for Unilever can be created. This is intended to provide discussion and is based on learning from examples of best practice in the case study companies and where they could be improved.

Firstly, it is important to recognise that the development of metrics relating to CSR strategy must form part of Unilever's strategic planning and control process (set targets, measure performance, corrective action). Ranchod provides a useful diagram to illustrate the overall approach:

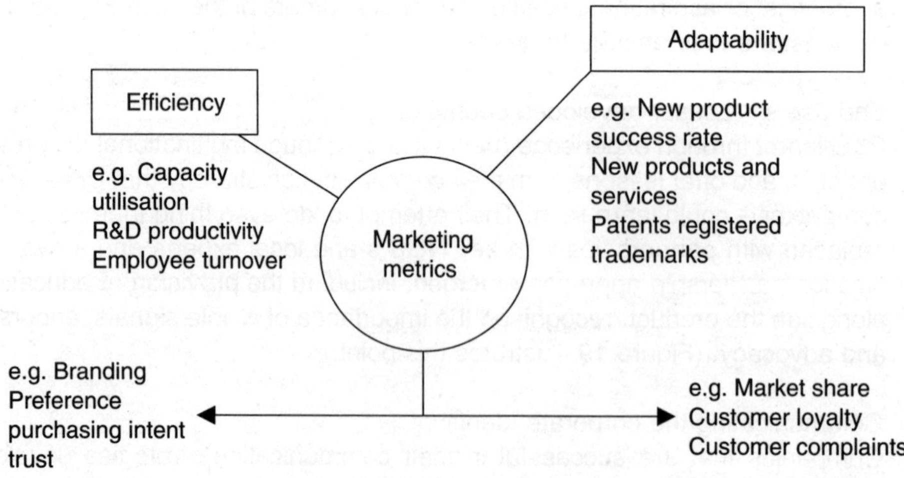

It is an assumption that the development of marketing metrics incorporating CSR will include the measurement of customer satisfaction, and awareness (for internal and external customers) and financial performance measures, etc. This report will now outline some of the stages and related metrics.

1. Unilever must set targets and build CSR into corporate strategies, including reporting in processes such as the Annual Report. At this stage the company can seek to adopt an industry standard – for instance the Dti has a CSR Competency Framework, with 5 levels of CSR attainment from basic awareness to 'leadership' – or create its own as indicated by Novo Nordisk's 'TBC' approach. It is important that this standard applies for Unilever's international markets, where exceeding basic compliance (regarding ethical and sustainable practice) is an obligation – it is viewed as unethical to take advantage of a country's lack of laws in this area.
2. Assess company operations overall. As outlined, the adoption of CSR may require business process re-engineering. Figure (9) illustrates how the TBL approach can be applied to the value chain (adapted to show from product birth to death). A more detailed approach is shown in Figure 20, which uses Ranchod's Total Quality Environment Management (TQEM) approach, with TBL to measure across financial, social and environmental responsibilities. The bottom of the chart indicates some of the measurement tools adopted by the different case study companies. It is recommended that Unilever examine the approach of P&G in detail (both cases), from the setting of the Millennium Declaration Goal to the recognition of 'the determination to achieve even better results with less, and ultimately, no impact on the environment'.
3. Measurement in this respect can still include two vital aspects of traditional performance measures:

   (a) Financial performance can be measured in terms of payback' (Novo Nordisk). Unilever will require support for CSR initiatives in terms of cash flow and resource commitment. Just as the case study companies seek a 'climate neutral' approach with their products (Interface) so they seek to recoup expenditure by achieving customer loyalty – that the customer purchases the product and adds it is to their evoked set because it offers perceived advantage over competitive products, rather than just a purchase in aid of esteem or to ease the conscience.
   (b) Performance standards from suppliers and employees. Setting standards, training and measuring on quality (zero defects – Figure 20), work at pit and measurement. These should be monitored continuously and success stories leads part of Unilever's marketing communications strategy.

4. A benchmarking approach is vital, including internal benchmarking, functional benchmarking and competitive benchmarking. Figure 20 outlines this in detail and the six-page document provides additional benchmarks in terms of:

   (a) Corporate ethical stance
   (b) 'Sustainability'
   (c) Both of the above, including measurement of the Marketing Effectiveness Rating.

   Again, benchmarking consultancies exist for this purpose and it is recommended that Unilever use *third party* verification of performance for profile strategy and to avoid being too internally focused. There is an organisation called the SERM Rating agency that will combine measurement of CSR performance with assessment of critical business risk, for example in Unilever's supply chain in less developed countries.

5. Establish and environmental management system.
   Ranchod's TQEM system has already been discussed, but the importance of creating process and procedures and measuring these with systems such as ISO 14001 (Veracel) must not be overlooked. This must be in addition to the establishment and continual updating of Unilever's Management Information Systems (MIS) and Marketing Information Systems (MkIS).

6. As already noted in brief, companies may establish their own standards and awards if they do not exist already (Interface) or could be improved upon.
7. In reference to this report, the effectiveness of any marketing communications strategy must be measured with respect to CSR. Tactical approaches include, for instance, take-up of internal marketing programmes and volunteer opportunities. Of vital importance is the brand equity gained from a CSR programme and increase in customer awareness and commitment (financial implications included).

Conclusion

Finally, as part of the strategic planning and control process, Unilever must build in measures throughout the cycle to continually evaluate performance (double-loop control) – seeking to be a learning organisation. This might include the disclosure of social/ethical/sustainable performance even when not favourable – as part of Unilever's reporting systems. However, the adoption of CSR practices will be a learning experience and is a necessity not a choice. Measurement is required to prove and communicate effort and potential success. As highlighted in the case study, only 4 per cent of customers strongly agree that companies listen to the public and respond to public concerns on social and environmental issues (page 5). By working to embed CSR into products and services, measuring out efforts and communicating strong brand values and ethical/sustainable good practice, Unilever can differentiate itself and achieve competitive advantage (Figure 9).

This report could form the basis of discussion for additional meetings as part of the recruitment process. Further information can be provided upon request.

Comments

This answer indicates a good understanding of marketing metrics. It is good to see a detailed breakdown of possible metrics that could be used by companies. The classification system proposed is good. It is also useful to understand that metrics can vary for each company. Another aspect of the answers is the useful link between each question, providing an interesting and coherent approach each area.

The analyses are interesting and varied taking into account the range of cases in a methodical and coherent manner. The candidate has also used the analyses to illustrate the answers very well.

Analysis

1. Introduction

'Corporate Social Responsibility' means open and transparent business practice that is based on ethical values and respect for stakeholders – including employees, communities and the planet. As companies become increasingly global, leveraging new technology to access new markets, the adoption of good CSR practice (for the total life cycle of their products or services) is a necessity.

Sales of ethically marketed goods and services are growing, with a 13% increase between 2001 and 2002. A key communication challenge for companies searching for competitive advantage however (in hostile markets such as FMCG), is that although ethical products are now close to being the product of consumer choice, many customers do not class themselves as 'ethical' and greater publicity will arise from the boycotting of unethical brands by ethical innovators/opinion-formers.

In this climate, it is vital that companies establish ways of measuring and benchmarking their CSR activity, whether as yet it relates to pilot projects (P&G) or full scale company operations (Interface). To gain stakeholder trust and build customer loyalty, CSR must be embedded into the entire value chain and culture of the company as part of its strategic marketing planning process; demonstrated through financial and performance measures and communicated internally and externally. This report will highlight examples of the approaches of six companies (for seven case studies), either on an individual basis as an example of good or bad CSR practice, or benchmarked against each other.

2. Porter's Diamond for Delta Cafes (adapted)

Firm strategy, structure and rivalry	Factor conditions/Demand conditions	Related and supporting industries
The president of East Timor is seeking to develop comparative advantage in coffee. Delta Cafes is market leader and has looked for expansion. The company has an 'early mover' advantage, creating a new 'solidarity market' for coffee in Portugal without cannibalising sales of other coffee products or as yet inviting hostile competitor response in Portugal or East Timor.	East Timor has a plentiful supply of raw materials and cheap labour, but lack of infrastructure. Investment from Delta Cafes has created a win-win sustainable community, with a competitive 'product origin community business model that Delta can take to other countries. In this respect, Delta must take care to recognise the CSR implications of pulling out of the region (despite political risk etc.) in the future.	Coffee growers are incentivised – staying close to their families and given a guaranteed buyer. Delta has established NGO and cooperative partnerships, plus a crucial link with Sonae. Initial barrier to entry will lower as Portuguese coffee manufacturer competitors seek to copy Delta's success and may approach Sonae as additional solidarity product lines.

3. Stakeholder power/strategy analysis for SC Johnson (Ranchod – adapted)

SC Johnson has recognised the value of a long-term partnership with PBK. SC Johnson must adopt a more proactive stance to lobby the EPA for labelling change, plan for contingency/crisis (e.g. pressure group action) and take a systems approach regarding the total green life cycle of it's products (and partners).

Stakeholder	Interlists at stake	Response risk	Power	Analysis of current strategy adopted	Current performance (3 high, 1 low)
RAID customers (USA)	Product	Switch to competitor's product/substitute	High	Accommodating	2
PBK supplier	Business	Will fail to deliver	High	Proactive – partnership	3
Our employees	Pay, security, expertise	Strike action, resignation	High	Proactive?	3
Kenyan Government	Election success, economic interest in business.	Prevent access to pyrethrum fields, tax, bureaucracy	Medium	Accommodating	3
Bankers (has no shareholders)	ROI, loan security, profits	Refusal to continue lending	Medium	Accommodating	3
EPA	Pesticide regulation, USA	Refusal to recognise labelling/ new toxicity measures	High	Defensive	1
Press/pressure groups	Headline news	Lobbying, activity	Medium	Defensive	1
The Planet	Protection of environmental resources	Depletion of natural resources/ environmental harm	High	Accommodating	2

4. SWOT analysis. Ranked by importance from 1 (high) to 4 (low)
4.1 SC Johnson (communication issue – can't promote natural ingredient through labelling)

Strengths	Weaknesses
1. Global distribution network and bargaining power. 2. Strong relationship with PBK based on knowledge-sharing and collaboration. 3. Transparent pricing, open and honest communications – fostered through PBK.	1. Weak strategic marketing orientation (CSR) plus lack of info c/o MKIS or focus on end user's needs. 2. Reliance on single supplier for natural pyrethrum. 3. Cultural difference between SC Johnson and PBK.
Opportunities	**Threats**
1. Lobby EPA re: labelling products (natural pyrethrum), whilst making contingency plans also (contamination etc.) 2. Work towards introducing strategic marketing planning (including MKIS) for PBK partnership, based on potential commercial opportunities from liberalisation in Kenya. 3. Capitalise on increasing consumer awareness of 'green products' by considering alternative labelling solution – e.g. 'fair trade product'. 4. Consider the provision of additional technology/training to PBK supply chain for JIT/fast response to market and stock management.	1. Continued lack of EPA recognition re: labelling of natural pyrethrum. 2. Political/economic instability or poor weather damages crops in Kenya – shortage of natural pyrethrum. 3. Product contamination (or accusations of RAID as insecticide being anti CSR) leads to pressure group action. 4. Competitive/substitute products marketed as 'humane' pest control or similar.

4.2 Interface (measures total green life cycle of product and creates awards to promote)

Strengths	Weaknesses
1. Leading manufacturer with multinational distribution network, bargaining power, relationships and resources. 2. Business Process Re-engineering – 10 years experience to reorient re: 5 Dimensions of Sustainability 3. 'Closed Loop' approach as recognition of Green Life Cycle of product.	1. CSR product-focused, not market focused. 2. Limited product portfolio and product suited to cooler climates could limit targeting of new markets. 3. No MKIS system at present.
Opportunities	**Threats**
1. Work towards introducing strategic marketing planning (including MKIS) to prepare for additional market entry options from success of pipeline. 2. Use technology competence to develop new CSR product extensions such as eco-friendly flooring. 3. Enter new communities with government support based on key integration skills (capitalise on trust and loyalty earnt for referral).	1. American market and carpet product ageing. Change in customer buying behaviour or substitute products through change in fashion – e.g. wooden flooring. 2. Decline in fossil fuels used for production and inabilty to source alternative power source. 3. Pressure group action.

5. Benchmarking of corporate ethical behaviour

Companies were first benchmarked by their corporate ethical stance. Johnson and Scholes define this as a 'the extent to which an organisation exceeds its minimum obligation to stakeholders.'

	Amoral	Legalistic	Responsive	Emerging ethical	Developed ethical *but some way to go
Delta			X		
P&G		X			
Novo Nordisk		X			
Interface					X
Veracel					X
SC Johnson					X

6. Benchmarking using Sustainability & Ethical Stance Matrix (Peattie & Charter *et al.* 1997)

Companies were rated through the Green Management Questionnaire. Veracel and Interface are the most ethical and sustainable ('green') currently.

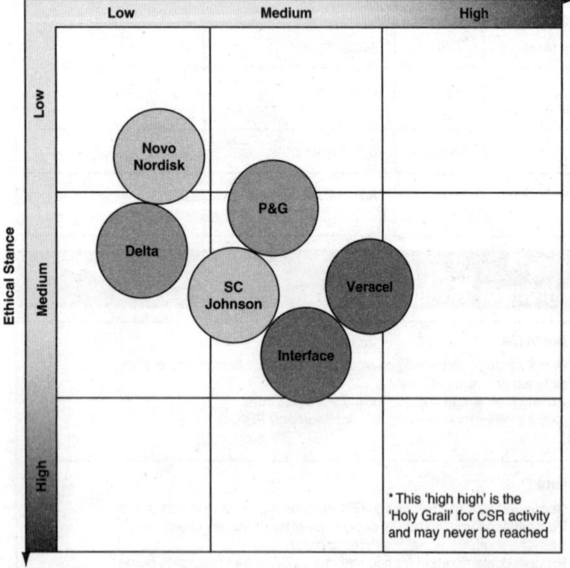

7. Benchmarking Marketing Effectiveness (Kotler) and CSR matrix (Peattie & Charter *et al.* 1997)

CSR must be part of a company's strategic marketing orientation. All companies have some way to go. Despite it's size, P&G learnt from experience of failure – they didn't plan, segment or target effectively.

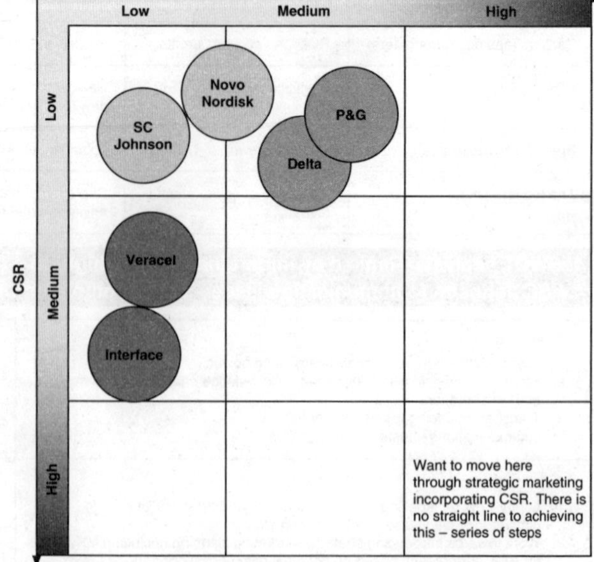

8. Value Chain for Veracel (Porter) for competitive advantage Life Cycle Analysis for measurement (3 high, 1 low or unknown)

Veracel has an environmental management system and has considered the life cycle of its own products, but has yet to consider responsibilities towards 'product death'. Expansion of the new mill requires strategic marketing orientation and the development of stock management/MKIS systems (and training) across the total life cycle.

SUPPORT ACTIVITIES

Firm Infrastructure Vertically integrated production and infrastructure. Eco-efficiency and self-sufficiency. ✓					
HR Management SENAI partnership brings fast recruitment from trained apprentices ✓	All employees receive excellence awareness training ✓				
Technology Development US AID funding for technology to aid conservation/ recovery ✓	Advanced pulp mill with maximised production, low costs ✓	Logistics value from sea port. Effluents meet envntal, conditions. ✓	No evidence of customer databases/ MKIS ×		
Procurement At top of supply chain and controls the source, with virtuous cycle of replanting ✓					
Raw materials and inbound logistics Suppliers adhere to ISO ✓	**Operations** (ISO 140012) certification of integrated envntal management system ✓	**Outbound logistics** Proximity to sea port and road links. ✓	**Sales & Marketing** No evidence of strategic marketing planning or KAM. ×	**Service** More information/ measurement required re: service levels/ SLAs. ×	**Product death** No info on whether customers recycle end product ×
Raw materials and inbound logistics TBL objectives FINANCIAL / SOCIAL / ENVIRONMENTAL 3 / 3 / 2	**Operations** TBL objectives FINANCIAL / SOCIAL / ENVIRONMENTAL 3 / 3 / 3	**Outbound logistics** TBL objectives FINANCIAL / SOCIAL / ENVIRONMENTAL 3 / 3 / 2	**Sales & Marketing** TBL objectives FINANCIAL / SOCIAL / ENVIRONMENTAL 1 / 1 / 1	**Service** TBL objectives FINANCIAL / SOCIAL / ENVIRONMENTAL 1 / 1 / 1	**Product death** TBL objectives FINANCIAL / SOCIAL / ENVIRONMENTAL 1 / 1 / 1

CURRENT PERFORMANCE

MARGIN

PRIMARY ACTIVITIES

9. Sources of Competitive Advantage achieved through CSR (Davidson – adapted – 3 high, 1 low)

	GOOD CASE EXAMPLE(S) OF ADVANTAGE GAINED	COMMENT	CURRENT PERFORMANCE
Superior product benefit	P&G PuR Delta Timor	Breakthrough product Organic product has opened up solidarity market	3 3
Perceived advantage	Delta Timor	Solidarity (has captured hearts and minds)	3
Low-cost operations	Interface Veracel	Payback possible Cheapest manufacturing costs	3 3
Legal advantage	Delta Timor Interface	Auditing via principles of Business & Social Accounting Setting the standards. Prepared should law change in their favour.	3 2
Superior contacts	P&G Nutri SC Johnson	Governments and NGOs support them Strong supply chain communication	3 3
Superior knowledge	Delta Timor P&G PuR Interface	Product origin communities as new markets First to market breakthrough product, learning curve effect 10 year's experience	2 3 3
Scale advantages	P&G PuR Interface Veracel	Market access via partnerships – bulk distribution Category dominance Size of owners, main force in region – expansion	2 3 3
Offensive advantages	Interface	Category dominance – barrier to entry	2

10. Competitive strategies (Porter) – Current position achieved

COST

Veracel pulp — Lowest cost product in industry. Has economies of scale.

P&G PuR — Low cost, breathrough product. Requires more widespread consumer habit change.

S.C.J. RAID — Stuck in the middle (labelling problems and natural version more expensive).

P&G Nutri — Unique product but trying to appeal to large market.

Delta Timor — Portuguese 'solidarity market'.

Interface Cool Carpet — New product. Still only appeals to 'True Blue Greens'.

DIFFERENTIATION　　FOCUS

11. Shell Directional Policy Matrix – mapping Delta's progress

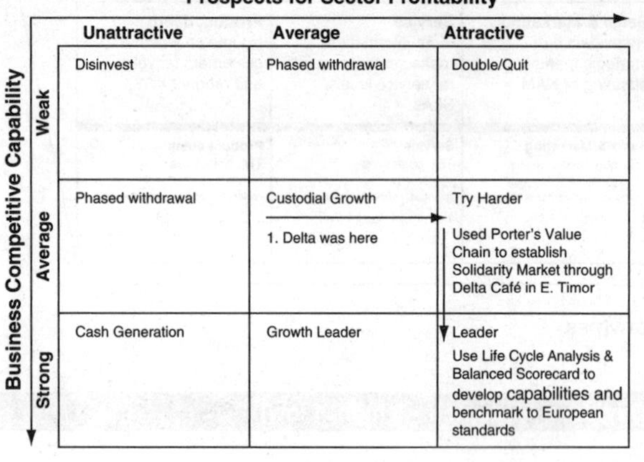

Prospects for Sector Profitability
Unattractive
Average
Attractive
Business Competitive Capability
Weak
Average
Strong
Disinvest
Phased withdrawal
Double/Quit
Phased withdrawal
Custodial Growth
1. Delta was here
Try Harder
Used Porter's Value Chain to establish Solidarity Market through Delta Café in E. Timor
Cash Generation
Growth Leader
Leader
Use Life Cycle Analysis & Balanced Scorecard to develop capabilities and benchmark to European standards

13. Growth and Product Capabilities: P&G strategic options (Ansoff adapted)

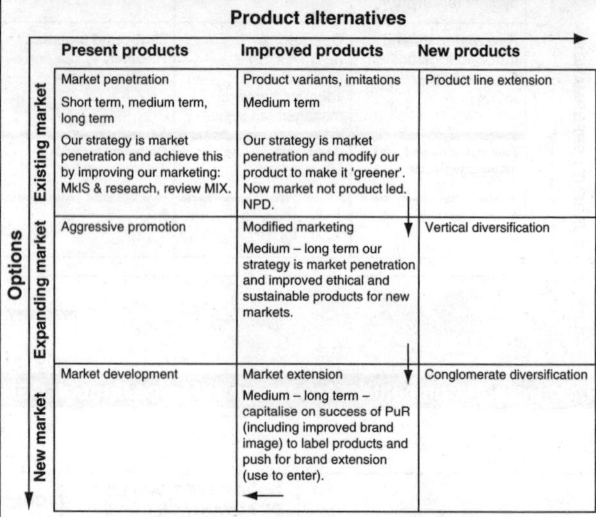

Product alternatives
Present products
Improved products
New products
Options
Existing market
Expanding market
New market
Market penetration
Short term, medium term, long term
Our strategy is market penetration and achieve this by improving our marketing: MkIS & research, review MIX.
Product variants, imitations
Medium term
Our strategy is market penetration and modify our product to make it 'greener'. Now market not product led. NPD.
Product line extension
Aggressive promotion
Modified marketing
Medium – long term our strategy is market penetration and improved ethical and sustainable products for new markets.
Vertical diversification
Market development
Market extension
Medium – long term – capitalise on success of PuR (including improved brand image) to label products and push for brand extension (use to enter).
Conglomerate diversification

12. International Product Market Assessment Matrix – Gilligan and Hird

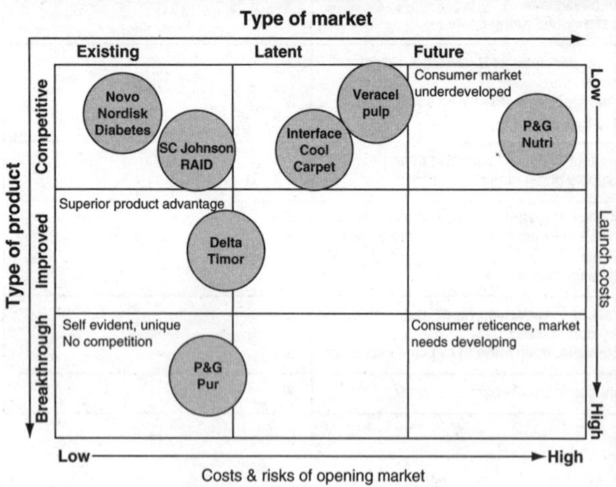

14. International Market Entry Modes – current position

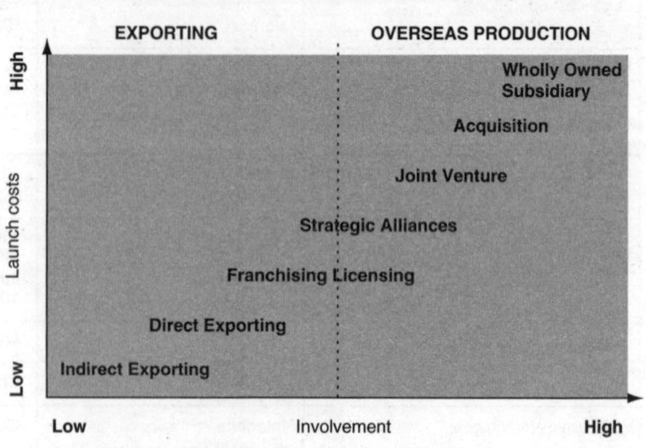

Direct Exporting - P&G PuR, Novo Nordisk
Licensing - P&G Nutri
Strategic alliance - Sonae & Delta, SC Johnson & PBK
Joint Venture - Veracel (owned 50/50)
Wholly owned - Interface

15. Segmentation Criteria for Interface – US market (Grant 2002 – adapted)

Industrial Buyers (order of priority)	**Size of organisation** – commercial B2B carpet wholesalers, residential bulk buyers – e.g. housebuilders **Attitude to 'Green'** – Interface is a True Blue Green org, therefore True Blue Green or Greenback Green buyer – incl. technical sophistication of green processes (work towards closed loop) **Location** – proximity to manufacturing site. High cost of transportation for carpet.
Individual household buyers (order of priority)	**Purchasing power/demographics** – high income full nesters. Likely to move home and/or refurnish carpet. **Attitude to Green** – True Blue Greens or Greenback Greens, with high degree of community involvement.
Distribution Channel	Exclusive hauliers as green distribution network. CSR involvement in packaging, arrival and disposal of carpet etc.

16. Aspirational Brand Triangle (Kotler) for P&G PuR (focused on end-user)

First motivation to buy for P&G comes from bottom of Maslow Hierarchy (physiological needs). To build trust and loyalty need to first educate for need and change attitude – ongoing basis.

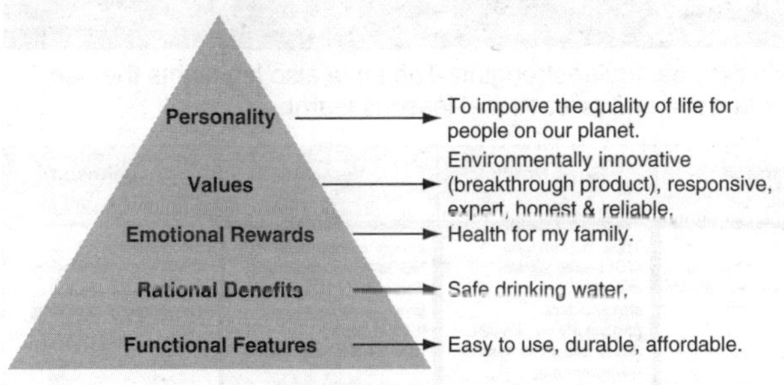

17. Communication – Internal marketing

Novo Nordisk has recognised importance of internal buy-in of TBL, but has not achieved internally or leveraged externally.

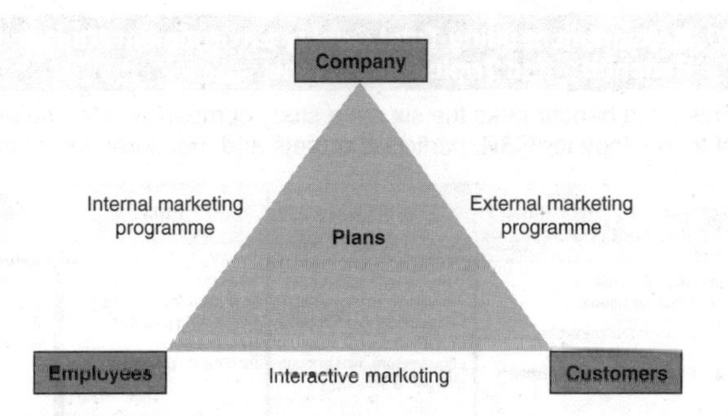

18. The Supply Chain/Communication Loop – SC Johnson

Black arrows show movement of product. Dotted lines show communication loop. There is no evidence of end customer feedback.

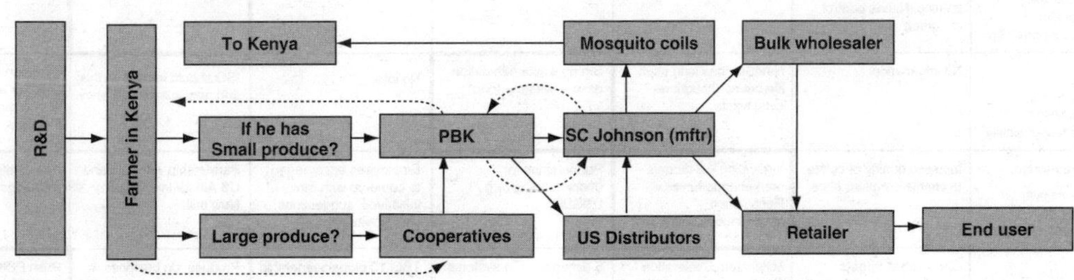

18.1 Communication based on two-way, long term relationship and partnership – SC Johnson. Via the Key Account Model (Cann)

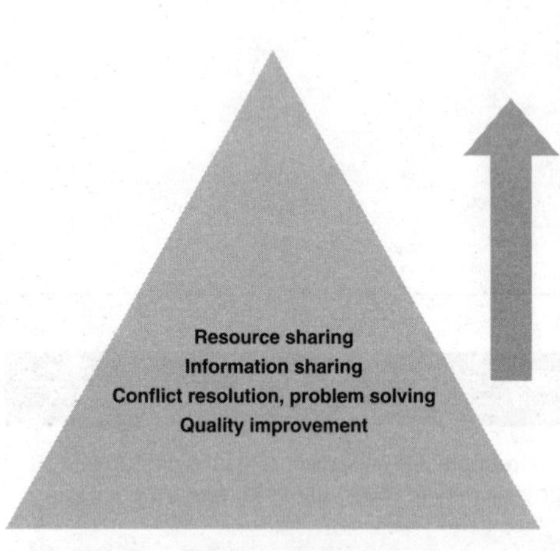

19. P&G Nutri – communication lessons learnt for the end user – Kotler & Anderson (adapted). Initial strategic approach was Profile (of P&G company brand to NGOs) and push through NGOs/partnerships to end users

EDUCATION	If you want to enter a market, make sure you **educate yourself first**. P&G failed in their strategic marketing orientation – with a lack of research, segmentation/targeting and positioning. **Need to avoid self-reference criteria (staff feedback from the ground?)** and be a learning organisation Sufficient planning and **continuous feedback loops** at every stage (to MKIS) are required – this is a **pilot project**. For your target market, **need recognition is required** re: micronutrients. This should be handled with partnerships and **third party verification**. Education may be required for basic skills such as reading & writing first. Good CSR policy means that you'll make this investment for the long-term.
VALUE CHANGE	**Build trust**. NGO Partnerships and local experts are required to give credibility and local, educational support networks.
ATTITUTE CHANGE	It's about investing in continuous education and targeting parents of families and opinion-formers – being able to **demonstrate the rational benefit**. You must understand the culture and ensure that your product and marketing respects local values and customs!
MOTIVATE TO ACT	Achieving the above should create latent demand and licence to operate. Only now may you be able to launch your product to the end-user, so note the amount of work/investment to get to this stage. **Encourage trial** with free sachets. Ensure product is available in small quantities and affordable for your actual target audience (not just middle class). Rational health benefits on packaging/advertising and mention of info re: long shelf life/durable in the heat/for travel. Feature you logo on the **packaging** and build local credibility.
TRAIN & REINFORCE	Continual reinvestment and education so that people start to be self-sufficient in recognising need and solution – **build loyalty**. Distribution problems will mean **lack of reach**, and **lack of patent** will mean that copycats get there first and undermine your credibility with false-claim products. Measurement should run throughout the project and accreditation **(industry accreditation or set up your own standards)** would have completed the process and perhaps led to additional licenses/new markets and given strength to government lobbying.

20. Measurement using Total Quality Environment Management (TQEM) – Ranchod – and Triple Bottom Line

This table benchmarks the six case study companies. Red boxes indicate particular strengths. The table also highlights the use of technology for CSR, particular targets and measurement of those targets, and promotional lessons learnt.

Total Quality Environment Management (TQEM)	Delta Cafes	P&G	Interface	Novo Nordisk	Veracel	SC Johnson
Identify customers/ stakeholder needs: 1. Financial responsibility 2. Social responsibility 3. Environmental responsibility	Demand for 'green coffee' Transparency of pricing Coffee bought at fair price Invest in education & infrastructure. Not enough thought re: Planet.	3 models Low price for end user Bulk & single sachet Not enough thought re: planet.	Five dimensions recognise stakeholders (including planet) Benefits to local community	Triple Bottom Line (TBL) – recognises importance of stakeholders, particularly employees. Social initiatives, less on environmental.	Integrated approach with NGOs (IBio), community. Focus on biodiversity, Employees paid market-based salaries & fringe benefits.	Recognition of partnership/relationship marketing with PBK. Transparency of pricing
Take a systems approach, people, equipment, processes. 1. Financial responsibility 2. Social responsibility 3. Environmental responsibility **Technology examples**	Invest profits back into region Principle of Environmental Accountability in audit process Not enough thought re: planet – Green Life Cycle. Technology to int'al spec.	3 models Network approach with partnerships Ref to local partnerships in supply chain. Not enough thought re: product. Innovation: R&D PuR sachet	Reorient entire org (Business Process Re-engineering) including suppliers, staff transport to work etc. e.g. plant trees to offset emissions. Set awards to show 'new' green products	Locking to integrate TB into business – info on products/supply chain required. Uses website as focus of comms plan. Intranet & eVoice survey	Considers environmental impacts from process to product. Systems mgt of forest renewal. Apprentices become employees – recruitment cycle. New mill, evtal management system	Partnership for planning and forecasting of crops to delivery through supply chain. Global Purchasing Group. Technology will be path to success for PBK
Do the job right first time – zero defects. 1. Financial responsibility 2. Social responsibility 3. Environmental responsibility	Quality control processes Invest in technology & training. Needs control re: 'green'.	Strong R&D & test	Maximising resource productivity	No info.	ISO 14001[2] for processes	Quality assurance process
Eliminate waste. 1. Financial responsibility 2. Social responsibility 3. Environmental responsibility	No information	NutriStar has long shelf life but no thought re: evtal waste.	Strong waste elmination drive – 'waste = food'	No info.	ISO should impact on this, and new mill for efficiency.	Pyrethrin production waste used for animal feed & mosquito coil by products.
Continuous improvement. 1. Financial responsibility 2. Social responsibility 3. Environmental responsibility	Increase quality of coffee to charge premium price	Innovation – 3 models – market opportunities. Recognition of continuous education.	Partnerships for understanding (e.g. USGBC).	Employees encouraged to come up with new initiatives, suggestions via website etc.	Partnership with IBio and US Aid for innovation New mill.	ISO certification, idea exchange
Example targets	Cooperation targets	Millennium Declaration Goal	5 dimensions, 4 systems conditions.	TBL, 10 global leadership competences	Produce, do business with and generate opps for region – measure?	Push PBK towards market orientation. Quality targets
Example measurement tools	Audit, process spec. quality control	Sales targets NGO verification.	Payback, certification systems, testing protocols	Employee survey External survey (Universum) Taking in activity.	No of emps attending training, effluent quality	Bio efficacy testing ISO certification 'Partner in Quality'
Example promotional tool or lesson learnt.	'Sustainable communities' logo. Sonae product placement	Health benefits on packaging but patent needed & education.	Third party verification. Create their own awards Label their products	No segmentation, TBL not embedded. Mktg activity unsuccessful.	No marketing as such, except word of mouth 'partnerships.	No labeling!

SPECIMEN ANSWER TWO

Question 1

To: Managing Director
From: Alan Walker
Subject: How to incorporate CSR policies into your organisation
Date: 10 December 2004

Executive summary

There is an increased focus for multinational organisations to incorporate CSR marketing policies into the organisation's strategic plan and culture.

Multinationals need to focus on the Triple Bottom line with regard to financial, social and environmental responsibility if organisations are considered to be unethical consumer boycotts can cost firms £2.6 billion per annum. According to Research International findings.

98 per cent of UK and USA consumers were aware of at least one cause related marketing programme.

83 per cent of UK consumers participated in at least one cause related marketing programme, an increase of 10 per cent.

68 per cent over two thirds demanded companies to increase their involvement in cause related marketing programmes.

The ethical market place is currently worth £19.9 billion but this only represents 2 per cent of the overall market, thus there is a huge growth potential for firms to increase their share of the ethical market place.

Introduction

This report will be divided into three sections:

Section 1 will identify the strategic methods multinationals can adopt to incorporate CSR strategic marketing policies.
Section 2 will discuss the organisation's promotional strategy and coordinated promotional mix when developing communication strategies.
Section 3 will evaluate the key marketing performance controls companies can utilise to measure the success of their CSR strategy.

1.0 ORGANISATIONS STRATEGIC ANALYSIS

To understand and appreciate where your organisation is positioned it is necessary to conduct a strategic analysis.

This reviews the External *market place*.

- Internal Analysis of the company
- Customer Analysis
- Stakeholder Analysis
- Competitor Analysis
- Key Issues Analysis
- Market Analysis

1.1 STEEPLE PLC – EXTERNAL ANALYSIS

Firstly to understand the external forces affecting the CSR concept it is important to review the:

- Social/cultural
- Technological
- Ethical
- Environmental
- Political
- Legal
- Economic

implications on CSR.

Please refer to page 1, section 1.0 STEEPLE ANALYSIS in my CSR analysis report to review the current issues surrounding CSR.

1.2 INTERNAL ANALYSIS

Having reviewed the external influences impacting and affecting CSR implementation it is useful to analyse the current organisational situation to identify whether your organisational culture, structure and style will allow CSR to be embedded or whether a change management process is required.

To review what a successful CSR strategy requires please refer to page 5 sections 6 Internal Analysis specifically 6.1 McKinseys > 5 frame work and 6.2 Calon and Sarnin's organisational culture frame work.

1.2.1 Change Management

Should elements of your internal analysis require altering you could adopt a *change management process.*

- Encourage right attitude
- Create a culture that embraces Innovation and Creativity
- Implement reward and recognition programmes
- Increase flexibility
- Increase employee involvement.

1.3 CUSTOMER ANALYSIS

To analyse your customers CSR needs and wants, it is useful to analyse their:

- *Buying behaviour* in relation to level of involvement with a product and degree to differences between brands.

- It is then useful to identify their *motivation* for purchasing a product based upon *Maslow's Hierarchy of Needs.*

Finally you can position your customers in relation to *Christopher's Relationship Marketing* ladder whilst also identifying the main participants from the decision making unit.

Please refer to page 3, section 3.1, 3.1.2 and 3.1.3 for further information.

1.4 STAKEHOLDER ANALYSIS

CSR strategies will influence and impact all an organisation's stakeholders. It is therefore important to review the CSR indicators that are of most importance to your stakeholders. Please refer to page 4, section 5 for an overview of the generic CSR indicators that impact on stakeholders wants and needs.

1.5 COMPETITOR ANALYSIS

Organisations need to review their competitors CSR performance to ensure that their offerings match and exceed what is currently offered to maintain competitive advantage within the CSR market place.

Useful models to analyse competitors are Porter's forces framework and strategic group analysis. Please refer to page 3, section 4.0 for Porter's 5 forces and page 4 section 4.1 for strategic group Analysis.

1.6 KEY ISSUES

It is useful to identify the key areas companies need to address and ensure they utilise to successfully incorporate CSR. A few are listed below:

- *Partnerships* with NGO's, governments, local manufacturers and distributors
- ISO Quality certification to trade internationally
- *Brand Leverage* to incorporate CSR
- *Supply chain reconfiguration*
- *Inspirational leadership.*

For further key issues, please refer to page 6, section 14.

1.7 MARKET ANALYSIS

Finally to review the CSR trends, potentials and challenges that will affect multinationals please refer to page 1, section 2.1 – CSR market size. 2.2 for CSR trends, potential and challenges – follows on to page 2.

1.8 FORMULATE YOUR CSR STRATEGY

Having conducted a thorough analysis, this information will assist you in developing a CSR strategy. You will need to segment, target and position your customers and company to gain a Competitive Advantage.

1.8.1 Segmentation

Please refer to page 3, section 3.2 for a useful segmentation model based upon green consumer behaviour. It is also possible to segment markets by *customer characteristics.*

- Demographic
- Geographic
- Geo-demographic
- Psycho-graphic.

Or behavioural characteristics

- Benefits sought
- Usage frequency
- Usage status
- Purchase occasion
- Attitude towards the product
- Buyer readiness stage.

Having reviewed the approaches from the six companies I based my research on, I would recommend using demographic, psycho-graphic especially lifestyle analysis based on the VALS study and the benefits sought and buyer readiness stage.

1.8.2 Targeting

According to Kotler Multinationals can adopt four targeting approaches:

- Undifferentiated
- Differentiated
- Focused
- Customised.

I would recommend the differentiated approach especially if companies wish to trade on a global basis as it considers and allows changes to be made to the following categories:

- Language
- Culture/tradition
- Legal/regulatory requirements
- Buying habits
- Motivational factors
- Standards of living
- Media availability and usage
- Competitive environment.

1.8.3 Strategic choices

Companies can also utilise *social model* non profit organisations.

- *Commercial model* – Private sector
- *Emergency relief model* – relief organisations

Multinationals can review *Porter's generic strategies* to identify whether they want to adopt a cost leadership, focused or differentiated strategy in relation to CSR. In relation to Growth Strategies multinationals can review *Ansoff's Growth* matrix and position their product ranges into the four segments.

With regard to analysing their product portfolio and product lifecycle they can utilise the BCG matrix.

Please refer to page 2, sections 2.3, 2.4 and 2.5 to review these models in more detail.

1.8.4 Positioning

Lastly in section 1, multinationals need to successfully position their CSR offerings in their consumer's minds and can opt for a number of the following methods:

- Product attributes
- Usage occasions
- Users activities
- Personality
- Origin
- Competitors
- Product class
- Symbol.

Having reviewed the context analysis, considered CSR goals and objectives and strategic choices the next stage concerns communicating your CSR proposal to stakeholders via your promotional strategy and promotional mix.

Comments

The candidate has tried to answer the question very much in the style of a plan. The question asks for the incorporation of CSR strategies. It is difficult to see how Porter can be applied to all seven cases from different sectors and make much sense. There are some good points covered such as CSR trends and stakeholder issues. The analyses however are far too messy as the candidate has almost tried to answer the question within the analyses. This is a good example of how analyses should be based on models and diagrams and where necessary bullet points rather than detailed wordy paragraphs. This actually detracts the candidate from providing a good answer.

2.0 PROMOTIONAL STRATEGY

There are three marketing communications strategies can adopt.

- Pull
- Push
- Profile

Please refer to page 6 section 13 for a diagram of the strategies.

2.1 PULL STRATEGY

A pull strategy focuses on demand coming from customers consumers pull a product or service through the channel of manufacturer → wholesaler → retailer → customer.

This strategy was adopted by Interface as they differentiated their carpets from competitors by focusing upon their climate control process. Interface also focused on differentiation through their seven fronts for approaching sustainability specifically highlighting to customers their use of green energy, their drive to reduce harmful emissions – cool fuel programme.

Delta Café's utilised a full strategy as they created a logo to highlight their coffee was produced to benefit sustainable communities thus they draw on pack recognition at point of purchase.

All of the cases draw upon the tangible, social and emotional attributes P&G utilised the nutritional benefits on the nutri-star packaging.

Pull strategies enable companies to:

- Differentiate their product
- Remind customers of the products benefits.

Utilise opinion formers as in P&G water – CDC, WHO, UNICEF, *Nutri-star* Micronutrient Initiative and Cornell University.

Opinion leasers can then educate customers regarding the product uses examples from P&G case studies are local doctors and international councils for nurses.

2.2 PUSH STRATEGY

Companies utilise this strategy to influence their market channels to take and hold their stock – S C Johnson uses a push strategy with their suppliers as they have a buffer stock in case natural pyrethrum reserves run low.

Delta Cafes adopted a push strategy when they created the relationship with Sonae a leading retailer.

Veracel to get furniture producers and construction sites to purchase their eucalyptus.

As push strategy must focus on a core message as in high quality goods affordable prices – it needs to tell the different channels what is required of them. A push strategy should adopt/ provide.

- Information
- Support
- Long term focus
- Enable coordination
- Increase loyalty
- Decrease emission and conflict.

2.3 PROFILE STRATEGY

This is the strategy the majority of the case companies adopted as this address all stakeholders. It projects a corporate identity to build and maintain a good reputation whilst shaping stakeholders perception of an organisation.

2.3.1 Corporate personality

This draws on the internal culture of an organisation – P&G and S C Johnson draw on the values of being family corporations.

Delta Cafes, Interface and Novo Nordisk all have strong visionary leaders.

Corporate personality illustrate the strategic purpose i.e. to create sustainable communities.

- The organisation strategy must be communicated to all employees – Novo Nordisk take Action website, meetings collateral packs and news bulletins.

2.3.2 Corporate identity

This is how organisations show consumers who they are via cues:

- *Symbols* – Delta Café created Delta Timor brand and sustainable communities logo.
- *Interface* – cool carpet and cool fuel trade marks
- *P&G* – branding – PUR and Nutristar
- *S C Johnson* – RAID trademark
- Behaviour
- Comms style.

2.3.3 Corporate image

Customers view from identity cues;

P&G – Branded approach series of brands unrelated to Novo Nordisk

Corporate image – Monolithic single name and visual style Delta Cafes, Veracel/Interface.

Endorsed separates subsidiary company and activities but endorses by adding group name – S C Johnson.

2.4 MARKETING MIX

Please refer to page 5 section 8.0 for an overview of what each company's core, actual and augmented product entails.

Page 6, section 12 for pricing.

Page 6, section 9 for a successful distribution method via Porter's value chain.

And then page 6 section 10 and 11.0 for branding considerations.

Having reviewed your promotional strategies and promotional mix the final stage is to incorporate marketing performance and measures.

Comments

This is a somewhat mixed answer. By using examples from the cases and the type of communication that they undertake indicates the possibility of the range of communication strategies available to a company. The analyses are used well, but quite often the candidate uses lists and does not justify all the possible strategies. Particularly strategies surrounding the promotion of green issues are not discussed in detail.

3.0 PERFORMANCE METRICS

In order to ascertain multinationals achieve their CSR objectives it is important to implement performance measures to identify any gaps that may need to be addressed.

There are 3 components to effective marketing metrics.

1. Set targets and objectives so performance can be measured.
2. Measure performance and apply corrective action in case you are not meeting your objectives.

All control systems should relate to corrective action it is important marketing plans are evaluated to influence future decisions thus incorporate a feed back loop for the most effective control.

Companies need to evaluate their intended CSR strategies as opposed to what actually happened.

3.1 Factors to consider

Hierarchy – level in organisation you are evaluating.

- Interim/financial control
- Whether control is measuring efficiency or effectiveness.

3.2 Control characteristics

- *Involvement of participants* in development and process of measures
- *Target setting* – quantifiable and achievable – agree them in advance
- *Focus* – difference between source of problems and symptoms
- *Effectiveness* – measure correct things
- *Management by exceptions* – tolerance zone corrective action
- *Action* – effective system to promote actions.

Financial ratios allow multinationals to incorporate them into trend analysis and industry comparisons.

Activity ratio is useful in analysing CSR effectiveness of activity.

3.3 BENCHMARKING

Review:

1. Precise process to be benchmarked and how you will measure
2. Select organisations to benchmark against
3. Identify differentiation performance and reasons for under performance
4. Plan how to improve create best practice
5. Implement a motivation and assessment programme.

3.4 Marketing metrics

Please refer to page 5, section 7.1 to review how multinationals can control their marketing activity.

7.2 for the appropriate Balanced Scorecard model created by Kaplan & Norton.

7.3 for the more recent corporate responsibility indexes that have come into force to specifically report on CSR performance.

4.0 CONCLUSION

This report has identified the stages multinationals need to go through to implement CSR strategic marketing policies, the marketing communications strategies and mix as can be adopted and utilised to generate awareness and finished by identifying useful marketing metrics for evaluation purposes.

Comments

This is a reasonable attempt at addressing the role of marketing metrics in a generalised manner. The cases are hardly explored and the triple bottom line approach used by Novo Nordisk is not explored. Some of the points made in the indicative answer scheme are not considered. The suitability of metrics for different types of companies is not even touched.

The analyses are rather general. Some of them actually address the points in the case. As the student has tried to second-guess the questions by writing a lot (the wrong way to approach analyses), he/she has not really produced good detailed analysis pertaining to the issues discussed within the case studies. The candidate has tried to utilise the analyses in the answers but because the analyses are as general as the written answers there is a certain lack of depth and detail.

Analysis

Date 10th December 2004 Alan Walker's Corporate Social Responsibility Analysis, for FMCG companies that wish to incorporate CSR into their Marketing Strategy.

1.0 STEEPLE Analysis

Social/Cultural	**Political/Legal**
• CSR awareness increasing between the 18–24 and 45+ segments • 68% of consumers demanded cause related programmes/fair trade • 48% of consumers positively altered their behaviour – switched to more ethical brands • Pressure groups forcing firms to focus on CSR – WHO, UNICEF (P&G) Green Power Market Development Group (Interface) Addocere (Delta Cafes) Ibio (Veracel) • Increase in social accountability – Delta Cafes improve working conditions Interface cleaner air, P&G food supplement and cleaner water, Novo Nordisk increase awareness of Diabetes, Veracel preserving the rainforest, SC Johnson maintained natural Pyrethrum supplies • Increased need to educate consumers, manufacturers and suppliers about CSR	• Dr Kim Howells CSR UK Government Minister-Legislation enforcing Multinationals to incorporate CSR – P&G Millennium Declaration Goal • International Barriers to Entry • ISO Certification required for foreign trade regulations – Delta Cafes, Vcracel, Interface, SC Johnson • Employment laws in countries wishing to enter – Human rights • Are Government's backing CSR as in Delta Cafes, Interface and P&G or are they corrupt SC Johnson case and Delta Cafes prior to breaking free from Indonesia? • Consider countries Taxation policies – Interface controlled by Emission Reduction Credits • Legislation regarding the reduction of CO2 emissions • Exchange Controls – Non-Tariff Trade Barriers • Absence of intellectual property rights
Technological	**Ethical**
• Technology allows Multinationals to decrease harmful gases and emissions – Interface emissions decreased by 46% • Distribution – Internet decreases transportation waste • R&D improved so increase number of new CSR products launched • Multinationals can donate older equipment to developing countries – Novo Nordisk Indian IT department donated computers to a facility for poor children and taught them how to use PCs • Intranets improve communication along supply chains and internally amongst employees • Technical Innovation utilising the LCA Concept	• Develop Corporate Marketing Ethics Policies • Increase Fair Trade, AMT coffee, Delta Cafes created solidarity market • BitC research when price is equal 80% of Western consumers would change brands – illustrates increased demand to be ethical providing price is right • Enlightened Philosophy Companies should have a 'Social Conscience' • Increased need for 'Ethics Education' Programmes • Focus on producing products that benefit the whole community • Increased focus on Societal Marketing – improve the lives of people in countries companies trade with
Environmental	**Economical**
• Kyoto Agreement – EU Legislation • Global Warming and rain forest destruction – companies need to be environmentally responsible • National Environmental Labelling Programme – Customers can choose products that put less stress on the environment • Environmental Accountability and Eco-Efficient Practice – Veracel, SC Johnson • Increase use of Green Energy – Interface • Decrease CO2 Emissions – Waste Processing • Rationalisation of natural resources • Efficiently use Emission Reduction Credits and Renewal Energy Certificates – Interface • Use recyclable packaging for products	• There is an Economic market for CSR as market share of the Ethical Goods Market represents only 2% of the total market • Decrease costs use a local manufacturer so the cost of production matches target markets disposable income • GNP low in most cases – SC Johnson population of over 30 m GDP capita of US$300, Veracel only 57% of the population gets a minimum of 2 wages per month – implications on pricing • Boycotts cost Multinationals £2.6 M per year • Currency fluctuations important when looking at International markets • Consumers in developed countries willing to spend more on CSR/Fair Trade products • As a result of CSR initiatives a number of jobs have been created for the Community, which will boost the local economy – Veracel main economic force 1,400 jobs, Delta Cafes employ 63% of the population, P&G created jobs

2.0 MARKET ANALYSIS relating to CSR

2.1 Market Size for CSR – According to Business in the Community (BitC), the CSR Market is growing, the value of UK Ethical Consumption 2002 was £19.9 bn. Consisting of 28% 'Ethical Invisibles' consumers who shop to support their local community and avoid unethical brands contribute £5.6 bn 35% Ethical Consumers contribute £6.9 bn an increase of 13% from 2001 and 37% Ethical Bankers, creating £3.9 bn (a rise of 16%) whilst the value of ethical investments declined by £3.5 bn, less than the actual market decline. It can be assumed the Ethical Marketplace will have grown since 2002, however please note the Ethical Marketplace represented 2% of the total market so a CSR market opportunity of 98% existed.

2.2 CSR Market Trends Potential and Challenges

According to BitC Business leaders have responded to CSR in 3 ways

Reactive – Minimal Legal Compliance, react to peer pressure, companies report on CSR activities

Conviction – Business leaders believe their company should be a 'good corporate citizen' – CSR partially implemented

Commitment – Business Leaders are committed to their company being a good corporate citizen, they use CSR to drive benefits and embed it into company's culture. Whilst measurement systems review CSR inputs and impacts

CSR Trends	CSR Potential	CSR Challenges
• Consumers switching brands for ethical reasons costs £2.6 bn • 132 leading FTSE250 companies reported performance in at least one CSR area 2002/03 • Visionary Business Leaders are implementing CSR • Increased need for partnerships/networks with Govt, NGO's and local firms to implement CSR successfully • Key focus on educational programmes • Larger organisations buying out smaller organisations Retailers have power over manufacturers • Consumers are demanding more cause related programmes – Tesco Computers for Schools, AMT fair trade coffee, Co-op Bank ethical banking and Day Chocolate Company fair trade chocolate 'Divine' • Increased focus on Green Marketing • NGO's and Governments driving CSR focus – part of the societal marketing concept • More retailer's are supplying organic, fair trade and non GM products Iceland key example • Companies are reducing the harmful effects their activities have on the environment whilst creating products that benefit less deprived countries and societies – Interface, SC Johnson, P&G • Increased need for ISO Certification for quality control and foreign trade regulations • Reconfigure the supply chain – draw the on skills of local firms to educate society in promoting the sustainability of the industry they work in	• Opportunity to embed CSR into company's brand values through a profile strategy • Highlight CSR initiatives to recruit and retain higher calibre employees – BP mention CSR in graduate recruitment collateral – BT study 25% of their image relates to CSR • Convert the 28% Ethical Invisibles to Ethical Consumers • Delta Cafes – Develop product origin communities in Angola, Columbia increase awareness of their sustainable communities logo • P&G Increase penetration into developing world, focus on innovation in product design • Interface – Teach others how to utilise renewable energy and launch similar manufacturing projects around the world • Novo Nordisk – requires Lars Rebein Sorenson full commitment to incorporate CSR successfully • Veracel – Enhance the local economy through the additional 8,000 jobs created, increase the geo-graphic area under protection as only stands at 10% currently and look to protect further sustainable resource • SC Johnson – Opportunity to increase R&D into further CSR projects, find additional partners	• Companies have to align their practices to CSR codes of conduct and certification • How can you differentiate products against competitors • Overcome criticism that CSR is an attempt to cover poor business performance and practices • Getting Shareholder's backing • UK has structural problems • Low unemployment in countries • Stable inflation environments • Rule-based fiscal regimes • Corrupt Governments • Educate consumers to use products – P&G Water and nutritious drink • Imbed and integrate CSR into business culture • Supply Chain Management • Credibility of communicator to raise awareness • Products copied but not to the same standard as Multinational's version and sold for cheaper price

2.3 ANSOFF GROWTH MATRIX

Market Penetration (*existing markets existing products*) Delta Cafes increase size of the 'Solidarity Market' and sales of the Delta Timor range Novo Nordisk Increase awareness and sales of product portfolio, address 21% who haven't got time to participate and 5% who haven't heard of Take Action Veracel increase penetration of rain forest currently own 10%	**Product Development** (*new products same markets*) P&G create more innovative healthcare products Interface current strategy – 'Carpet Cool' range & new supply of green energy Novo Nordisk opportunity to create further health care products that will assist the developing world SC Johnson growth of pyrethrum is threatened need to create new products that aid the environment
Market Development (*Existing Products new Markets*) Delta Cafes – potential to enter global markets Angola, Columbia & Europe Interface look to sell 'Carpet Cool' in new markets & implement green energy projects globally Veracel – adopt integrated project in other endangered forests SC Johnson sell synthetic pyrethroids to global markets	**Diversification** (*new products and new markets*) P&G should continue to create new commercial models and distribute them to new markets – use strategic partnerships to decrease risk SC Johnson potential to create insect control for the developing world to decrease spread of disease

2.4 PORTER'S GENERIC STRATEGIES (*Model adapted from Porter 1980*)

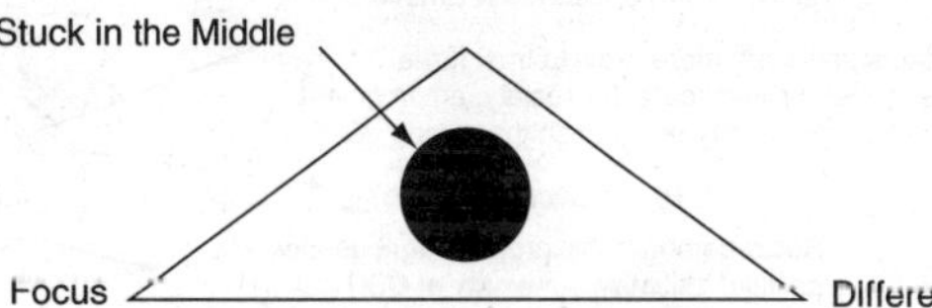

Cost Leadership – Veracel maximised scale of production, decreased costs, and focused on logistic gains and low manufacturing costs
P&G provided POU drinking water to reduce disease and a low cost nutritious drink. Reduced cost base by licensing production and distribution locally, gained Economies of Scale due to size, utilised strategic alliances to their advantage and globalised their operations

Focus – Novo Nordisk focused health care company – world leader in diabetes care. Company sponsors two diabetes programmes and offers employees volunteer opportunities in Tanzania

SC Johnson on the basis of this case study is focusing on the use of natural pyrethrin and synthetic pyrethroids. Relationship with sole supplier PBK lasted 30 years
SC Johnson is biggest single end user of natural pyrethrin

Focus Differentiation – Delta Cafes certification of origin 'Timor Coffee' differentiation through solidarity and fair trade, special logo in support of sustainable communities

Differentiation – Interface focuses on energy efficiency and increased use of renewable energy. Created strong brand identities – 'Carpet Cool', Cool Fuel and is a high performer in green power market illustrated by awards

2.5 Boston Consultancy's Group Matrix

Star – High Market Share/High Market Growth Delta Cafes – Market Leader 38% P&G NutriStar – fully national in Nicaragua Interface – Market leader in climate neutral carpets Novo Nordisk – broadest Diabetes portfolio	**Question Mark** – Low Market Share/High Market Growth P&G Water process simple acceptable price need to create consumer habit change Veracel – only own 10% of the forest Delta Cafes – sustainable community Delta Timor brand only 3.2% market share
Cash Cow – High Market Share/Low Market Growth SC Johnson – Pyrethrum Sourcing Interface – traditional carpet portfolio	**Dog** – Low Market Share and Low Growth

3.0 CUSTOMER ANALYSIS

3.1 Customer Buying Behaviour (*Model adapted from Assael 1987*)

Customer's degree of involvement with the product

Degree & Significance Of differences Between brand alternatives	Low	High
Low	**Repetitive Buying Behaviour** Novo Nordisk – Sponsorship programme automatic monthly payment into 1 of 2 diabetes programmes	**Behaviour designed to reduce buyer dissonance** P&G Point of Use Water Purification system to reduce diarrhoeal diseases Veracel – Sell Eucalyptus to furniture makers, construction sites and manufacturers of doors and window frames
High	**A search for Variety** Delta Cafes – Delta Timor blend – logo identifying it has been produced to support sustainable community – consumers prepared to pay more P&G – Nutritious food supplement – consumers bought competitor's cheaper imitation – price obviously key factor SC Johnson – natural insecticide	**Complex Buying Behaviour** Interface – range of carpet choices

3.1.2 Maslows Hierarchy of Needs
(*Model adapted from Maslow 1940*)

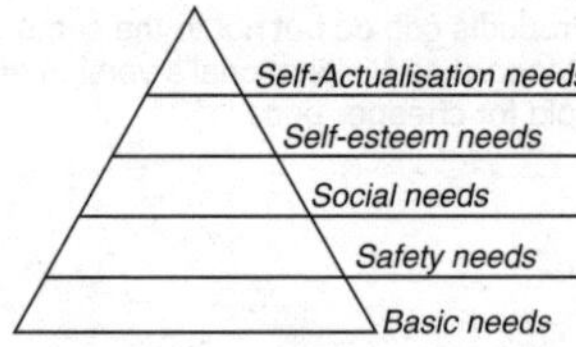

The majority of customers related to the self-esteem category as purchasing a fair trade or environmentally friendly product, allowed them to feel they had contributed to the well being of a developing country or the earth's atmosphere. However P&G need to educate their target audience to focus on their basic needs & increase awareness of problem

3.1.3 Relationship Marketing Ladder
(*Christopher et al. 1993*)

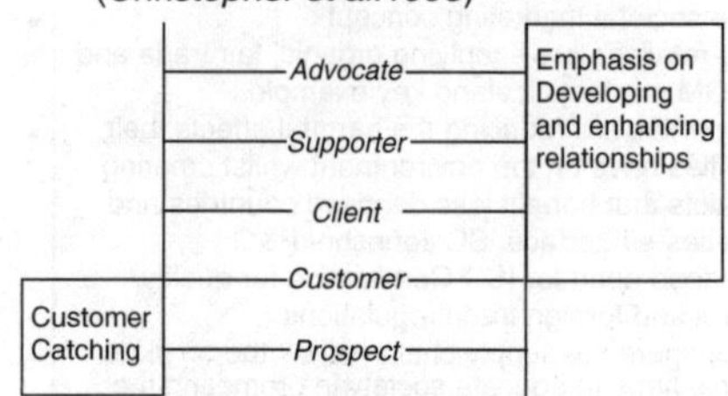

Ethical criteria is more significant in consumer's purchasing and brand loyalty decisions therefore need to encourage ethical consumers to become advocates

3.2 Customer Segmentation based upon Green Consumer Behaviour (*Model adapted from Wagner 2001*)

Green Consumer Behaviour

- Knowledge & understanding of environmental issues
- Ethical, Religious and spiritual dimensions
- Cultural Climate – influencing it & being influenced by it – Educational programmes are required as consumers unaware of medical problems they face on a daily basis
- Impact of media & pressure group campaigns e.g. foot & mouth, BSE
- Lifestyle Choice
- Peer group and social network
- Socio-demographic profile – age, gender, political affiliation – majority of CSR purchasers are between the ages of 18–24 and 45+ some are prepared to pay more for a fair trade product, others will opt for cheapest version
- Part of a counter-culture?
- Values, Motives, Desires & Emotions – Consumers are more likely to trust firms who they believe 'care' for society, environment staff & community and punish those who don't

Consumers more likely to participate in a cause related programme when there is – clear affinity between the brands, the company lives and breaths the relationship, it is easy for consumers to participate in and the programme communicates the company's commitment

4.0 COMPETITOR ANALYSIS Porter's Five Forces (*Model adapted from Porter 1980*)

This analysis reviews how easily it is for FMCG competitors to enter the CSR market place

POTENTIAL ENTRANTS – High
- Government Minister appointed for CSR more FMCG companies starting to review their business activities in relation to the triple bottom line
- First Mover advantages if develop new low income market products for consumers and communities
- More companies are introducing Cause Related marketing programmes
- International players may enter the CSR arena – ISO certification
- Barriers to entry tend to be low
- Strategic Alliances with local manufacturers/distributors, NGO's and key Opinion Formers aid firms

SUPPLIER POWER – Low
- FMCGs outsourcing manufacturing to global suppliers/local companies
- More FMCGs are recruiting suppliers that adhere to their CSR values and rules of conduct
- Advantageous to source components from developing countries where suppliers have less bargaining power than European countries where product quality likely to be higher but so are costs as supplier bargaining power higher
- Companies are reconfiguring their supply chain to successfully incorporate CSR policies

COMPETITIVE RIVARLY – Low
- In all seven case studies level of competition is relatively low – companies are first movers in a market or and products are nearly all stars – however Delta Cafes, Interface, P&G food supplement & SC Johnson's insecticides face competition as other versions available

SUBSTITUTES – Medium
- Tea, wooden flooring, nutritious soups & snack bars
- Consumers may choose to spend their disposable income on other items – holiday instead of a carpet
- Internet is a substitute to traditional distribution outlets – River Ford Organic deliver orders to your door
- Consumers may grow their own fruits & vegetables rather than buying organic products.

BUYER POWER High providing product ranges exist
- Consumer Boycotts on unethical companies cost firms £2.6 bn/annumn
- Retailers have power to choose whether they stock FMCG merchandise
- FMCG power to choose suppliers that adhere to strict CSR codes of conduct
- Consumers have the choice to switch between brands
- Consumers are demanding more fair trade, organic and socially responsible products – shop where these are provided

4.1 Strategic Group Analysis (*Model adapted from Meek and Meek 2000*)
Case study examples are placed into groups based upon range of CSR products offered and scope of business

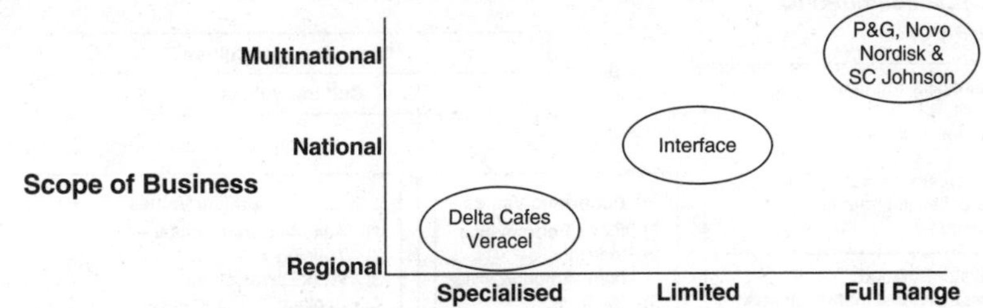

5.0 STAKEHOLDER ANALYSIS – Identifies the key CSR indicators that impact each stakeholder

Stakeholders

	Shareholders/ Directors	Employees	Customers	Suppliers	Government	NGO's	Communities
Values & Governance	Profile & turnover of Shareholders & investor's perception	Adherence to Values Employee perception of CSR programmes	Transparent about values, customer awareness & satisfaction	Code of conduct, supplier relations, incidence of code breeches	Values being part of governance, stakeholder perception	Disagreement re responsibility & complaints	Ethical importance Stakeholder perception
Regulations & Control	Conflict over controls & values, trends in shareholder feedback	Use/abuse of perks, incidence of disciplinary procedures	Meeting specifications, incidence of customer complaints	Presence of Bribery, number of disciplinary procedures	Compliance Non compliance, incidence of fines, regulatory audit	Use/abuse of legal protection	Compliance/non compliance with planning regulations, incidence of infringements
Business Operations	Alignment of operations with values & shareholder perception	Performance appraisal, % of employees assessed on CSR criteria	Investigations by advertising standards agencies, no of ads withdrawn	Pricing methods, supplier satisfaction, price differentials	Commercial espionage claims & litigation	Price dumping, claims & litigation	Safety of process, incidence of near misses/accidents, H&S audits
Accountability	Rigor of reporting, trends in shareholder feedback	Data protection, incidents of employees complaints	Appropriate information, customer satisfaction, reduction in customer requests for CSR products	Clarity about ongoing relationships, stakeholder perception	Reporting complaint standards, standard certifications	Appropriateness of measures, indicators & stakeholder acceptance	Disclosure of information, clarity & accessibility of information
Human Rights	Compliance with international codes, proof of policy statement, stakeholder perception	Respect for ethical/ local culture, license to operate withdrawn, protest incidents, boycotts	Monitor supply chain human rights, customer perception, boycotts, third party review	Equity of opportunity, profile of suppliers – size, gender, ethic origin	Investment Criteria, level of adherence to human rights regulations	Giving a voice to pressure groups, stakeholder perception	Adequacy of disaster planning/response no. of incidents, accidents 3rd party audit
Employee Rights	Relevant pay-earnings ratios	Freedom of association, frequency of committee meetings, training & development	Child Labour – no. of employees under 15/18 if hazardous work ILO convention 138	Tied contracts, incidence of complaints	Adherence to standards, incidence of breaches	Sweat shops pressure incidence of breaches	Support for community education programmes, level of investment time & money
Business Context	Types of alliances, satisfaction of non executive directors	Clarity of contractual terms, stakeholder satisfaction	Contract terms, customer satisfaction, customer retention	Payment terms, complaints, surveys of supplier satisfaction	Use/abuse of monologue, incidence of investigations	Ethical Sourcing adherence to voluntary code	Market power in local community, market share, market profile
Product Impact	Unethical products inclusion rate in ethical funds	Harmful process & substances accident rate, lost time due to injury, H&S procedures	Labelling, customer satisfaction, breeches of industry regulations & market share	Involvement in R&D, innovation, life cycle analysis & use of results in design process	Product stewardship, hazardous NPO returned to process/market	Safety of products, incidence of NGO regulatory targeting	Harmful emissions, releases to land & water of non-product output
Social Investment	Meeting Guarantees, complaint level	% of employees volunteering for CSR projects	Spend on cause related marketing, market share	Proportion of local suppliers	Joint Programmes	Adequacy of measures, indicators & monitoring	LT commitment to community investment, trends in local investment
Impact on others	Impact of investment assessment	Ethics of animal testing, employee concerns	No of boycotts, quantity of organic products sold	Breaches of government/ Industry regulations	Quality of research, controls, compliance with Govt standards	Quality of conversion programs, comments of independent expert	Quality of impact assessment and third party review results
Impact on Environment	Disaster planning/risk assessment % employees trained	Resource consumption, quantity of resource saved through employee action	Customer awareness about product use/disposal customer trends	Promoting high environmental standards in suppliers	Meeting standards, third party ratings & awards	Effective use of expertise, investment in Environmental research	Impact on local environment air pollution

6.0 INTERNAL ANALYSIS

6.1 McKinseys 7s framework

This framework illustrates the concepts companies need to enforce to implement a successful CSR strategy

Strategy	Focus on the Triple Bottom Line show sustainability regarding Social, Financial, and Environmental responsibility Develop a social infrastructure fosters desire for education Quality focus – ISO certification Develop strategic alliances and partnerships especially with NGOs Create a Cost Leadership, or Focused Differentiation strategy Develop economically sustainable local industry
Skills	NPD, Innovative products and distribution systems, Good communication skills to generate awareness, train local manufacturers in Technical skills they require to produce quality products
Staff	Trained, motivated, innovative workforces who can act as brand ambassadors, good calibre of marketing personnel, need staff to embed CSR into their day-to-day job. Holistic approach between departments is required for successful implementation. Staff need to offer good levels of service
Structure	Visionary Leader, departmental interaction, team work, Democratic management structure, effective internal & external communication
Systems	Incorporate CRM, MKIS, BiE Index, Corporate Responsibility index long stock turnover
Style	Various from family owned multinationals to regional and national businesses – strong leader is evident, focus on long term CSR projects, respect individuals and adopt either Commercial, Social or Emergency relief model
Shared Values	Strong vision and mission, CSR needs to be incorporated into corporate objectives so employees are measured on its success and have something to work towards – project must be mutually beneficial to partners and society improve the well being of developing countries

6.2 ORGANISATIONAL CULTURE FRAMEWORK

(*Model adapted from Calori & Sarnin 1993*)

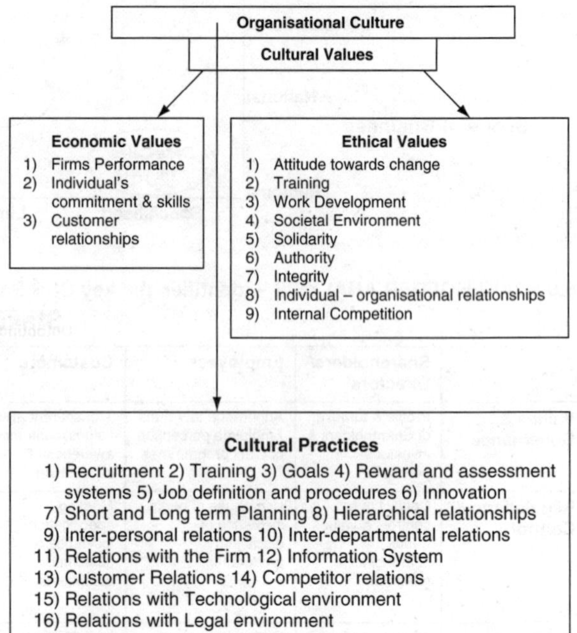

Cultural Practices

1) Recruitment 2) Training 3) Goals 4) Reward and assessment systems 5) Job definition and procedures 6) Innovation 7) Short and Long term Planning 8) Hierarchical relationships 9) Inter-personal relations 10) Inter-departmental relations 11) Relations with the Firm 12) Information System 13) Customer Relations 14) Competitor relations 15) Relations with Technological environment 16) Relations with Legal environment 17) Relations with Societal Environment

7.0 CSR PERFORMANCE MEASURES

7.1 Control of Marketing Activity (*Model adapted from Drummond & Ensor 2001*)

Product Market Share Sales Volume Sales by segment Number of new products Warranty Claims ROCE Repeat Purchase Customer Satisfaction	**Price** Profit Margin Price relative to competition Return on Sales Profitability Cash Flow
Place Channel Costs/volume/growth Delivery Time Stock levels Market Penetration level	**Promotion** Market Image and awareness levels Cost per contact Share of Voice Enquiries Generated

7.2 Balanced Score Card (*Model adapted from Kaplan & Norton 1996*)

Financial Return on Capital CashFlow Profitability and Growth Reliability of Performance	**Customer** Value for Money – Customer Ranking Survey Competitive Price – Pricing Index Customer Satisfaction – Customer Satisfaction Index/Mystery Shopper
Internal Marketing – Product & Service Development Manufacturing – Lower manufacturing Costs, improve project management Logistics – reduce delivery costs, inventory management	**Innovation and Learning** Innovate Products and Services – % revenue Time to market – Cycle time vs. Industry Empowered staff – attitude survey Access to Strategic Information Continuous improvement

7.3 CORPORATE RESPONSIBILITY INDEXES

BitC Corporate Responsibility Indexes improve organisations' performance by providing a systematic process to compare their management processes and performance against others in the same sector. Companies are given an overall score for Strategy, Integration, Management Practice on Community, Environment, Marketplace and Workplace and Performance in 7 impact areas – 3 Social and 4 Environmental

The High Performance Index considers – Shareholder Value, Product Service Diversity, Collection of Market Intelligence, Prioritising Customer needs, Product Service Quality, Stakeholder focus, Innovation, Attraction of Good Employees and Workforce training Business in the Environment (BiE) Index benchmarks companies' performance against their peers and industries against each other, on the basis of their environmental management and performance in key impact area.

8.0 PRODUCT ANALYSIS (*Model adapted from Kotler et al. 1999*)

1) **Core Product** – Fundamental need being met – Delta Cafes Staple goods purchase P&G clean water, nutritious drink, Interface floor covering, Novo Nordisk diabetes treatment, SC Johnson – Insecticide treatment & Veracel – Manufacturing Materials
2) **Actual Product** – Specific Offering aimed at meeting core need includes packaging, price, branding, performance features, styling, design – Delta Cafes – Delta Timor Brand, Logo for sustainable communities awareness, quality qualification
   P&G – Brand names PuR (point of use water system) & NutriStar (Nutritious drink), packaging – PuR small sachets easy to store Price NutriStar US$0.30 and PuR US$0.10 Interface – Cool Carpet and Cool Fuel trade marks, ISO certification – Novo Nordisk branding via their Take Action website, SC Johnson – RAID brand name utilises natural pyrethrin and synthetic pyrethroids Veracel Sell Eucalyptus with ISO Certification
3) **Augmented Product** – enhances actual product by offering additional services and benefits – Before, During and After sales service, Warranties, Add-ons, Finance packages, Maintenance, Advice – P&G provide demonstrations for their PuR product, all of the companies held educational forums either to increase awareness of health problems, the products available to help reduce the problems, how to utilise green energy, and how to improve production techniques. I also assume Interface's products come with a guarantee and after sales service.

9.0 PORTER'S VALUE CHAIN (*Model adapted from Porter 1985*)
This is an example of what a CSR value chain needs to address

Support Activities

Firm's Infrastructure – Visionary Leader – employees willing to follow, democratic management style where employees are involved in the planning & implementation stages of CSR, culture that embraces innovation and change, systems to track customer satisfaction, competitor intelligence system & CSR performance indexes

HRM – CSR strategies allow organisations to recruit higher calibre employees, staff need to be motivated and rewarded for focusing on CSR. Employees require training on new CSR policies & structures to become brand ambassadors and fully understand their roles & responsibilities

Technology – Require up to date systems for R&D into new products & processes, need process improvements to decrease harmful emissions, Internet strategy for distribution, review ways to increase use of green energy, to create replacement products for natural resources

Procurement – Purchase Emission Reduction Credits & Renewal Energy Certificates, ensure inputs are purchased at competitive rates without compromising quality, focus on supply chain management

Inbound Logistics	Operations	Outbound Logistics	Marketing & Sales	Service
Implement a Stock Management Process Reconfigure the supply chain Review relationships with suppliers	Create relationships with local Manufacturers to ensure costs/Product price matches disposable income	Focus on local distributors as they have useful knowledge and can decrease costs Distribute based on demand	Need extensive advertising, PR and educational programmes to increase awareness – consider promotional mix for internal markets	Train manufacturers, distributors & employees Develop service network for international markets

Primary Activities

Margin

10.0 BRAND ONION

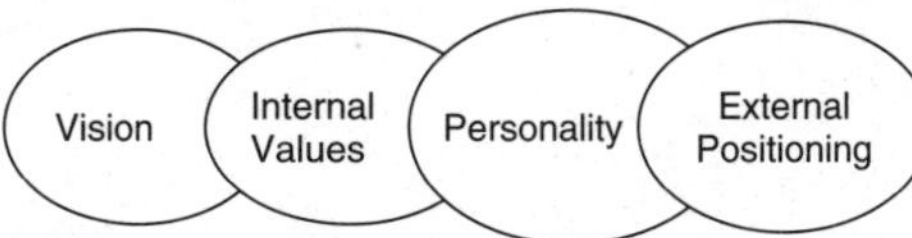

Vision – Snapshot of the Future
Values – A belief System – Way of working/communicating
Personality – Informs all Communications and Consumer Perception
Positioning – A summary of the Brand in relation to competition in the Consumer's mind

11.0 CONSTITUTES OF BRAND EQUITY
(*Model adapted from Aaker 1995*)

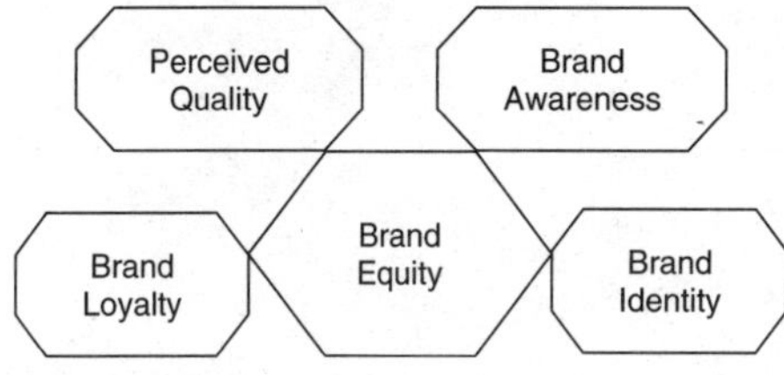

12.0 PRICING STRATEGIES

External Factors affecting Price

- Consumer Attitude & Behaviour
- Level of Market Supply & Demand
- Market Segmentation
- Competitor Prices
- Consumer Types

Internal Factors

- Production Costs
- Policy Decisions

Cost Plus Pricing – Calculate expected output, total fixed Costs are divided by expected output to create fixed cost per Unit, which is added along with the % profit mark up to give Price
Contribution Pricing – Marginal cost method of pricing – Calculate the contribution to total fixed costs made by each Product sold – selling price – variable cost = contribution
Skimming Strategy – Charge a high initial price when a New product is introduced especially if you have a temporary Monopoly situation because helps regain initial expenditure
Penetration Strategy – focus on lower prices & profit margins Appropriate if products – high volume, long-life, price sensitive Also if firm is planning to become market leader, has cost Advantage and can benefit from economies of scale

13.0 MARKETING COMMUNICATION STRATEGIES

Pull Strategy – To reach customers – consumers and business

Communication Flow

Manufacturer – Wholesaler – Retailer – Customer

Flow of Goods and Services

Push Strategy – To reach members of the Marketing Channel

Communication Flow

Manufacturer – Wholesaler – Retailer – Customer

Flow of Goods and Services

Push Strategy – To reach all relevant stakeholders Corporate Personality, Identity and Image

14.0 KEY ISSUES ANALYSIS
Key things to address when incorporating CSR are:

• Develop a CSR Strategy and integrate it into the business process • the marketplace appears to be the least understood aspect of CSR – define and manage responsible practice • Incorporate Performance Measurement for social & community impact • Reconfigure your Supply Chain Management • Little Brand Leverage • Credibility of Communicators • Require a Committed & Visionary Leader • Strategic Alliances and Partnerships with NGO's Governments local manufacturers, suppliers and distributors and communities • Active involvement is required across all organisational Departments • Culture must Allow for Innovation • Are Quality Certification Measures Required • Govt Corruption • Need for Education • Lack of Awareness.

appendix 2
examples of other analyses

I Candidate analysis

Strategic Marketing In Practice: Case Study Analysis

Fig. 1: 7 keys to Sustainability success: scaling 'greenness' by ranking degree of commitment by organisations to key Sustainability success factors. Weighting 1 (low) to 3 (high)

#	Case Study	Keys to Sustainability Success							Total score	How green?
		1	2	3	4	5	6	7		
4	**Interface (Carpets)**	3	3	3	3	3	3	3	21	95%
6	**Veracel (Eucalyptus Pulp)**	3	3	3		3	3	2	17	80%
1	**Delta Cafes (Coffee)**			3	3	3	2	3	14	67%
7	**SC Johnson (Pyrethrum)**			3		2	2	2	9	43%
2	**P&G (Drinking Water)**	1		3	1				5	24%
3	**P&G ('Hidden Hunger')**			3	2				5	24%
5	**Novo Nordisk (TarkeAction! TBL)**	2				3			5	24%

A fully integrated, eco-efficient programme. Ethical and moral issues addressed. Self & eco-efficient. Influence all parties in value chain.

Shareholder satisfaction is main objective but understand and enact eco-efficiency and social standards and rules.

Low on ethical and social issues i.e. child labour but chooses natural before chemical products.

Respect for ethics and just at start of CSR policy. Little respect for the environment

Fig. 2: Scale of 'greenness'

90%

50%

0%

A fully integrated total environment programme. Ethical and moral issues addressed.

Shareholder return rules but understand eco-efficiency and social rules

Low on ethical and social issues but does eco-sensitive

Some degree of respect for the environment but not concerned about social and ethical issues

Fig. 3: Stakeholder power analysis (Highlighted columns indicate those relevant to FMCG markets)

Case Study	Board of Directors	Community	Customers	Distributors	Employees	Government	Managers	NGOs	Regulatory Bodies	Shareholders	Suppliers	Total Score	%	Broad View	Narrow View
4	3	3	3	2	2	3	3	1	3	3	1	27	82%	✓	
1		1	3	3		3		1	1	3	3	18	55%	✓	
3			3	2		3		3	3	3		17	52%	✓	
2			1	3		3		3	3	3		16	48%		✓
5	3	1	1		3	3	3			1		15	45%		✓
7		1				3		3	3		3	13	39%		✓
6		3	1		1			2	2	1		10	30%		✓

(Stakeholders: Board of Directors to Suppliers; Summary: Total Score to Narrow View)

Fig. 4: Green Marketing – a holistic approach

Green marketing

Humanitarianism — Novo Nordisk Veracel

Equality — Veracel

Ecological — Interface Veracel

Eco-Conscious consumers — Delta Cafè Interface PG Hidden Hunger

Not for Profit — Novo Nordisk

Sustainability — Delta Cafè Interface Veracel

Political — Delta Cafè SCJohnson PG HH PG Safe Water

Conservation — Veracel Interface

Corporate & social responsibility — Delta Cafè Interface Veracel SC Johnson Novo Nordisk

Fair trade — Delta Cafè SC Johnson

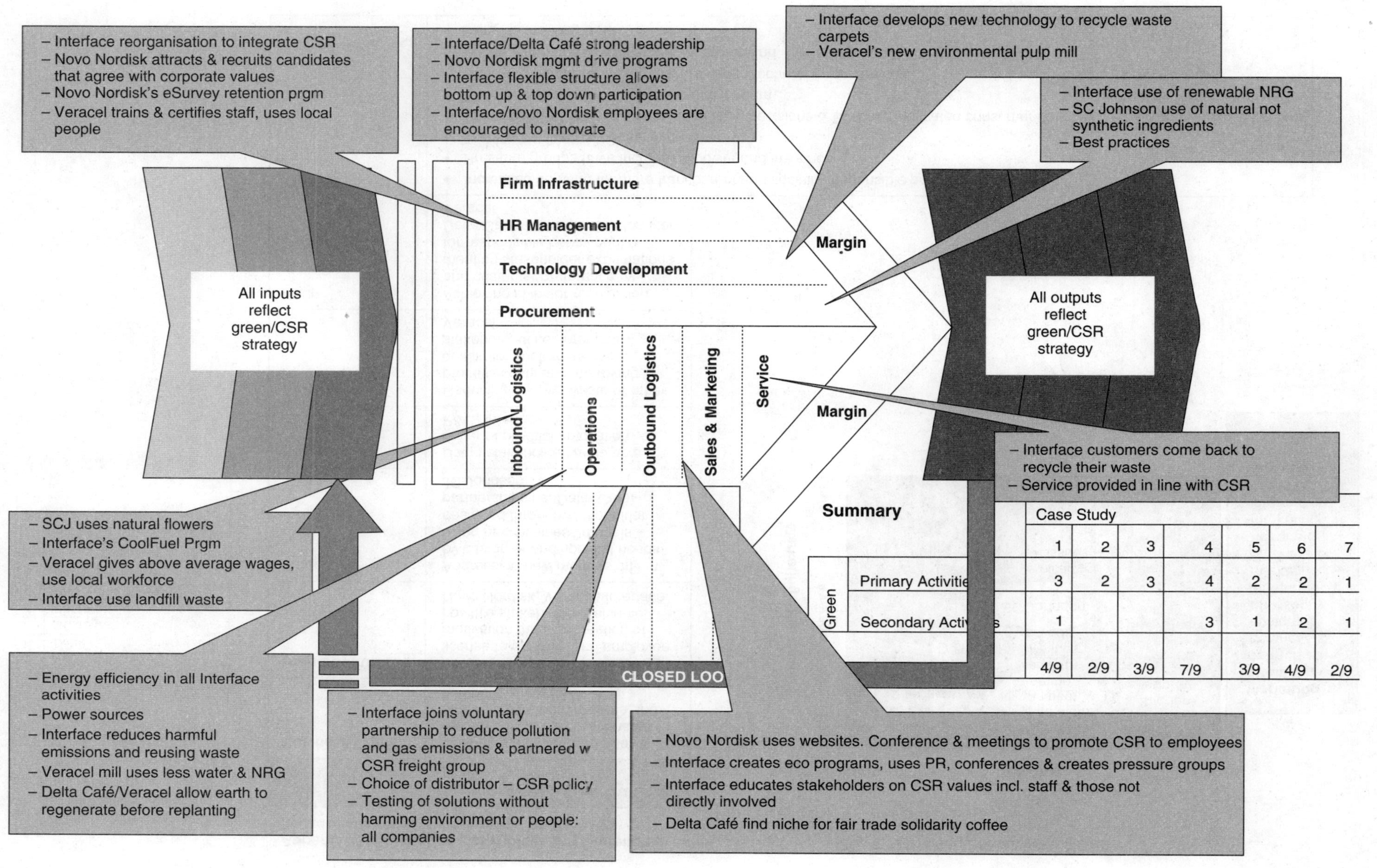

		Case Study 1	2	3	4	5	6	7
Green	Primary Activitie	3	2	3	4	2	2	1
	Secondary Acti s	1			3	1	2	1
		4/9	2/9	3/9	7/9	3/9	4/9	2/9

Appendix 1: Sources of stakeholder and shareholder value
Found at each level of the strategic focus

Level of Strategic Focus	Sources of Value/Opportunities at Each Level
Business Context	Changing the standard rules & regulations so that sustainable strategies are both feasible and competitive i.e. P&G.
Brand/Culture	Gaining competitive preference, license to operate, and employee motivation through creation of positive stakeholder Value i.e. Novo Nordisk, Veracel, Interface.
Market	Addressing new markets driven by customer and societal needs using new business models designed through stakeholder partnerships i.e. Delta Café, JC Johnson.
Product	Using stakeholder value as a driver of product innovation i.e. P&G, Interface, P&G.
Process	Reducing energy, waste or other process costs and improving quality for customers and stakeholders i.e. Interface, Veracel.
Risk	Achieving investor recognition and customer preference by meeting stakeholder expectations for responsible behaviour i.e. Delta Café, Interface, SC Johnson, Veracel.
Threats	• Increased demand for more transparent and socially-responsible practices • Pressure groups have increasing power and influence • Traditional energy sources in decline • Ethics shown to play a role in purchasing decisions & Ethically motivated consumer boycotts cost major brands 2.6 bn/year • Ethical consumerism moved into mainstream • Short-term profits compromised as Green technology can be cost • Green standards vague/open to interpretation = unreliable quality of source materials • Benefits are long term

Fig. 6: Marketing Effectiveness* Grid

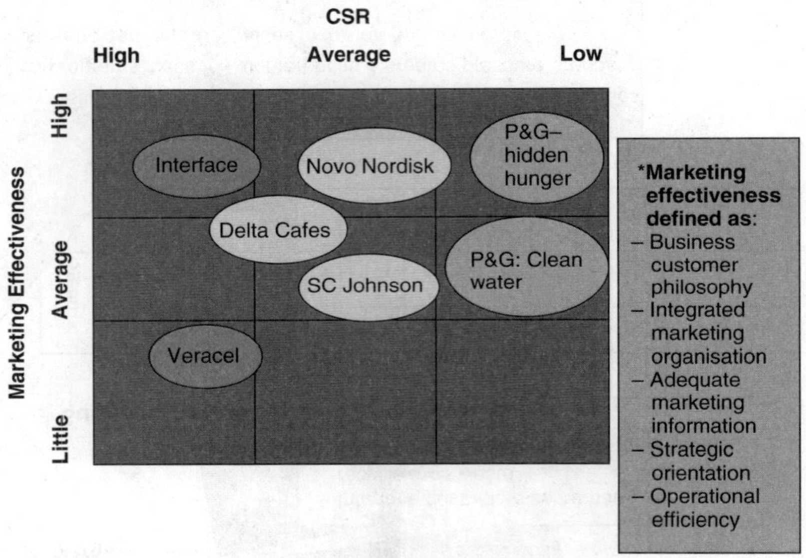

CSR
High
Average
Low
Marketing Effectiveness
High
Average
Little
Interface
Novo Nordisk
P&G– hidden hunger
Delta Cafes
SC Johnson
P&G: Clean water
Veracel

***Marketing effectiveness defined as:**
– Business customer philosophy
– Integrated marketing organisation
– Adequate marketing information
– Strategic orientation
– Operational efficiency

Fig. 7: **Porter's 5 Forces** Industry Analysis on CSR. Competitive environment

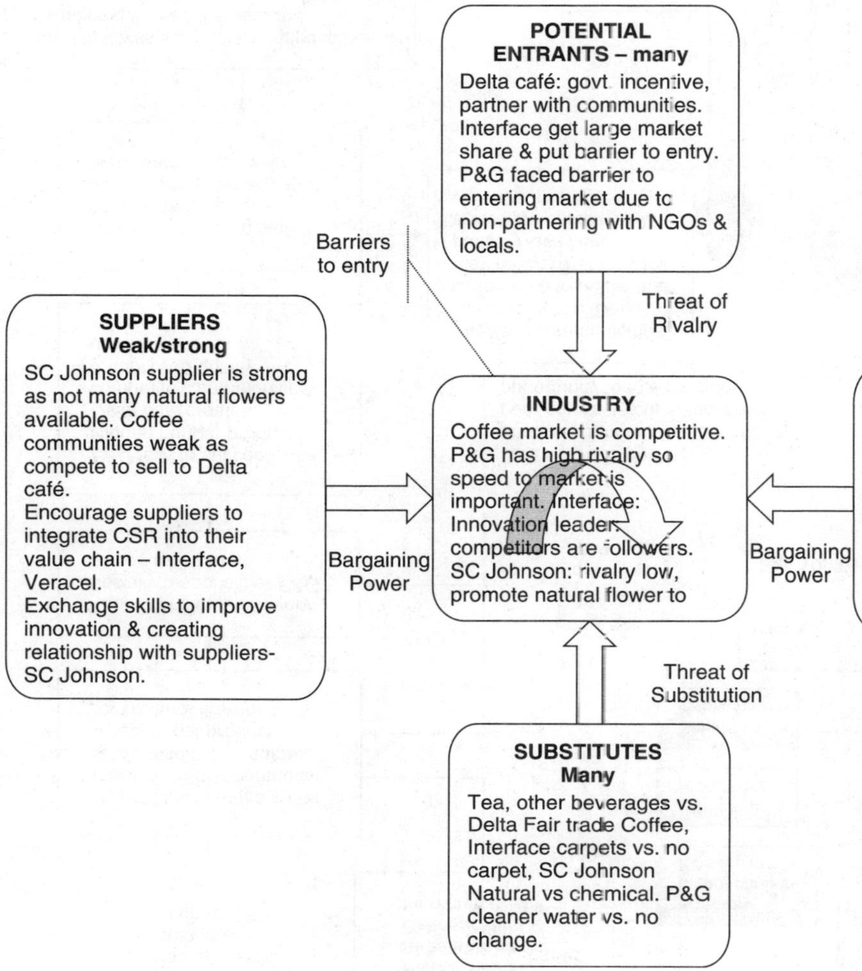

POTENTIAL ENTRANTS – many

Delta café: govt incentive, partner with communities. Interface get large market share & put barrier to entry. P&G faced barrier to entering market due to non-partnering with NGOs & locals.

Barriers to entry

Threat of Rivalry

SUPPLIERS
Weak/strong

SC Johnson supplier is strong as not many natural flowers available. Coffee communities weak as compete to sell to Delta café.
Encourage suppliers to integrate CSR into their value chain – Interface, Veracel.
Exchange skills to improve innovation & creating relationship with suppliers- SC Johnson.

Bargaining Power

INDUSTRY

Coffee market is competitive. P&G has high rivalry so speed to market is important. Interface: Innovation leader, competitors are followers. SC Johnson: rivalry low, promote natural flower to

Bargaining Power

BUYERS
Strong/weak

For Delta Café, Interface and Veracel the customer has many products to choose from.
Strong Power so CSR used as differentiator. P&G customer weak as no other product available.

Threat of Substitution

SUBSTITUTES
Many

Tea, other beverages vs. Delta Fair trade Coffee, Interface carpets vs. no carpet, SC Johnson Natural vs chemical. P&G cleaner water vs. no change.

Appendix 2: Dealing with CSR Communication Issues – DRIP:

D- Delta use ethical logo & appropriate packaging; P&G create 'visibly clean water'; Interface create 'Coolcarpet' brand; NN create 'takeaction!' internal branding campaign. SC Johnson promotes use of natural flowers to competitors as can't advertise on product itself.
R- P&G use further education to reinforce message to customers.
I- NN uses intranet to communicate to staff news & ideas & promote CSR program. P&G set up Educational programmes to inform customers.
P- Delta persuade community to trust by building school – sponsorship.

Appendix 3: Innovative CSR Strategies:

- Partnership: SC Johnson share skills & experience w/PBK: LT capacity factor
- 'a different PLC': Interface close the loop & become self-sustainable using waste to create products
- Technology: Veracel's economical mill uses less energy, creates less waste
- Positive competition: Delta set up competitive communities with equal opportunities
- P&G reinvent entry to market for success
- Veracel use of mosaic landscaping to protect land

Appendix 4: Measuring success of CSR strategy:

- Audits: DC café quality assurance improvements, SC Johnson perform quality checks. Veracel suppliers have to follow CSR policy.
- Financial analysis: Interface reduces cost through waster reduction.
- Feedback: NN launch eSurvey for employee feedback.
- Awards: Interface wins awards for high standard of CSR.
- Green/ethical metrics: Veracel reduces water usage, Interface reduces gas emission, Veracel creates jobs, DC provides labour.
- Recognition: P&G obtain support & trust from NGOs & local pressure groups.

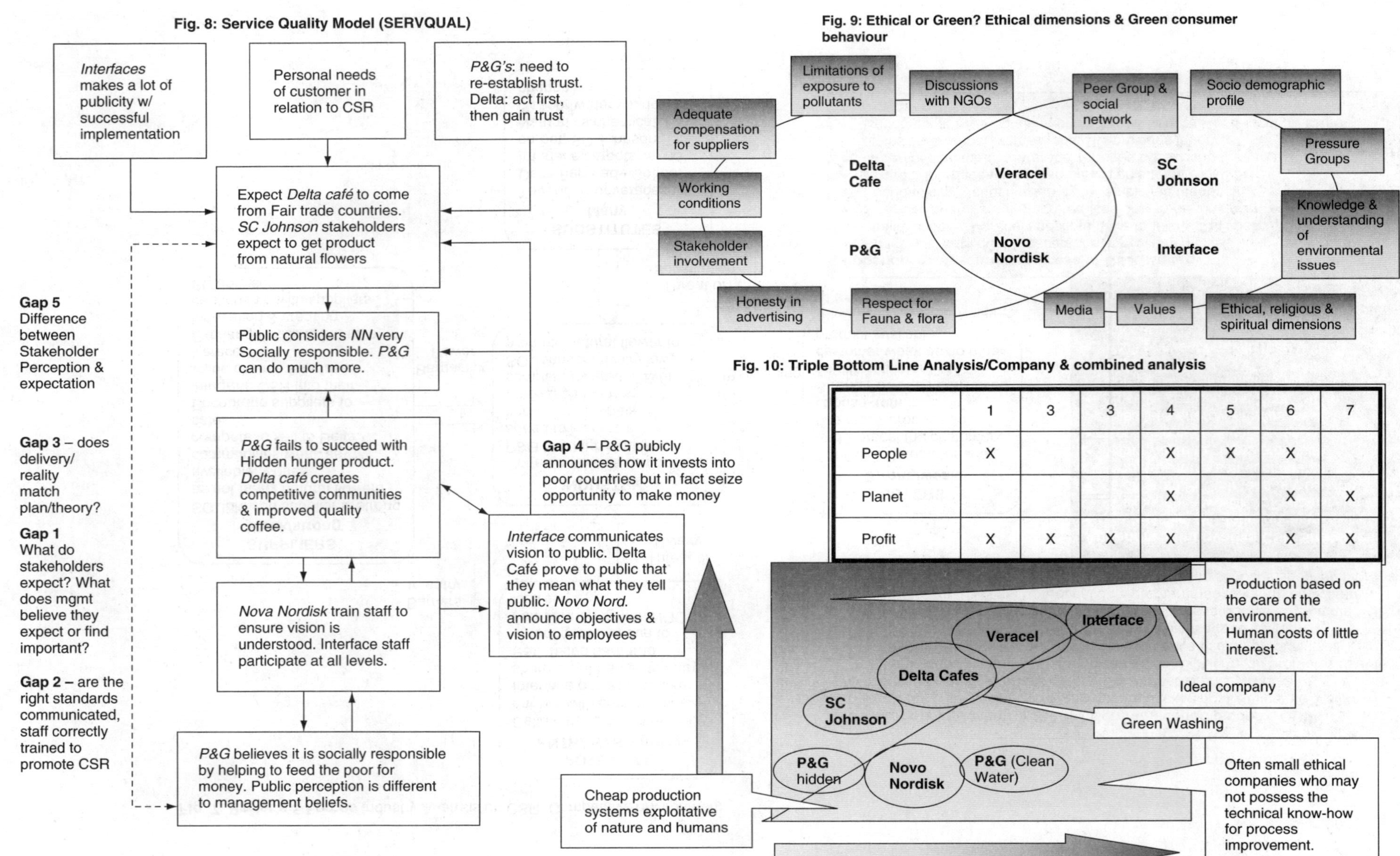

Fig. 8: Service Quality Model (SERVQUAL)

Fig. 9: Ethical or Green? Ethical dimensions & Green consumer behaviour

Fig. 10: Triple Bottom Line Analysis/Company & combined analysis

	1	3	3	4	5	6	7
People	X			X	X	X	
Planet				X		X	X
Profit	X	X	X	X		X	X

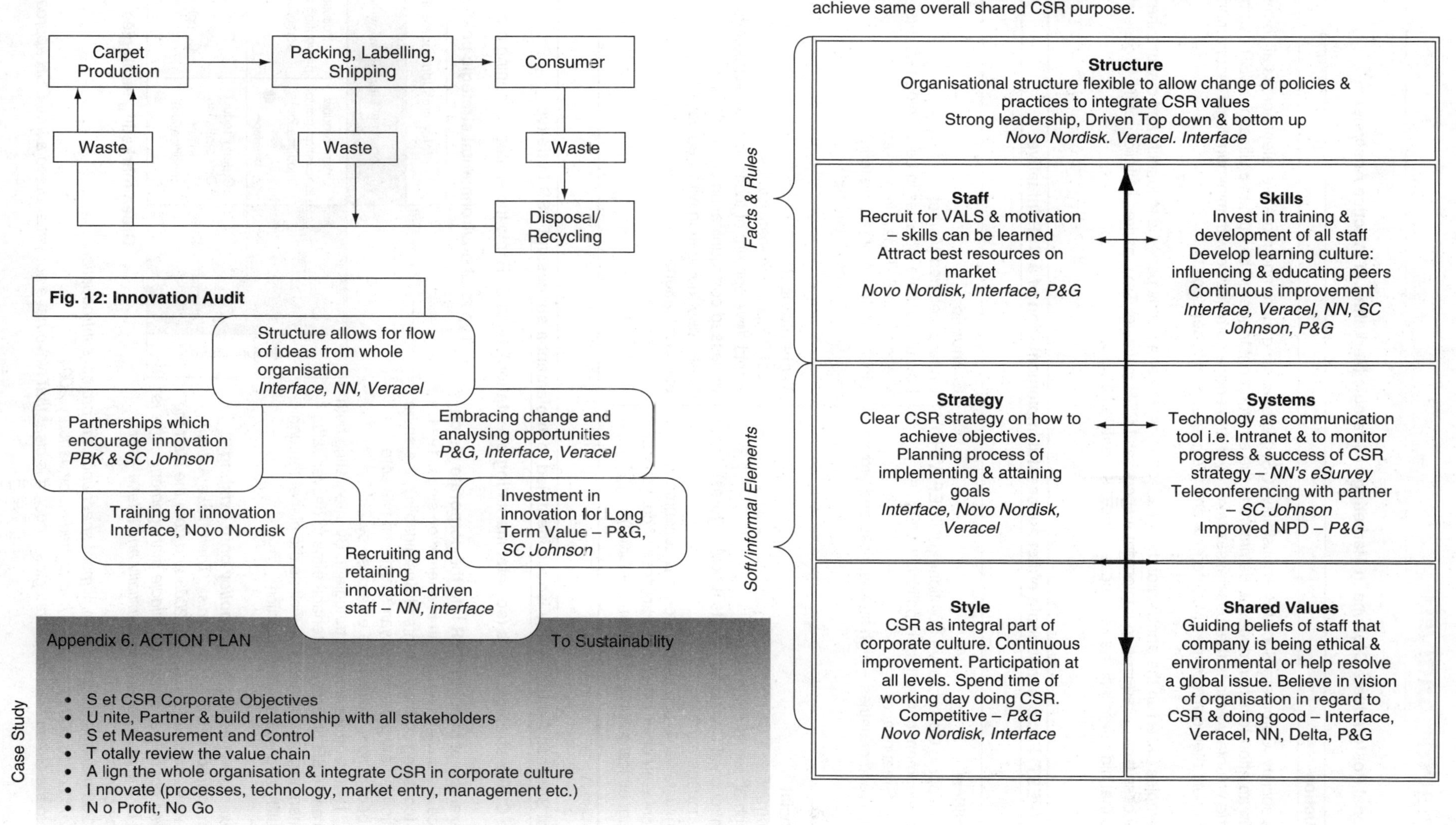

Carpet Production
Packing, Labelling, Shipping
Consumer
Waste
Waste
Waste
Disposal/ Recycling
Structure allows for flow of ideas from whole organisation Interface, NN, Veracel
Partnerships which encourage innovation PBK & SC Johnson
Embracing change and analysing opportunities P&G, Interface, Veracel
Training for innovation Interface, Novo Nordisk
Investment in innovation for Long Term Value – P&G, SC Johnson
Recruiting and retaining innovation-driven staff – NN, interface
To Sustainability
Facts & Rules
Soft/informal Elements
Structure
Organisational structure flexible to allow change of policies & practices to integrate CSR values
Strong leadership, Driven Top down & bottom up
Novo Nordisk. Veracel. Interface
Staff
Recruit for VALS & motivation – skills can be learned
Attract best resources on market
Novo Nordisk, Interface, P&G
Skills
Invest in training & development of all staff
Develop learning culture: influencing & educating peers
Continuous improvement
Interface, Veracel, NN, SC Johnson, P&G
Strategy
Clear CSR strategy on how to achieve objectives.
Planning process of implementing & attaining goals
Interface, Novo Nordisk, Veracel
Systems
Technology as communication tool i.e. Intranet & to monitor progress & success of CSR strategy – NN's eSurvey
Teleconferencing with partner – SC Johnson
Improved NPD – P&G
Style
CSR as integral part of corporate culture. Continuous improvement. Participation at all levels. Spend time of working day doing CSR.
Competitive – P&G
Novo Nordisk, Interface
Shared Values
Guiding beliefs of staff that company is being ethical & environmental or help resolve a global issue. Believe in vision of organisation in regard to CSR & doing good – Interface, Veracel, NN, Delta, P&G

Figure 11: Closed Loop Theory: INTERFACE

Fig. 12: Innovation Audit

Appendix 5: Elements of an organisation: McKinsey 7s – the different elements have to adhere to the same CSR settings & standards to achieve same overall shared CSR purpose.

Appendix 6. ACTION PLAN

- S et CSR Corporate Objectives
- U nite, Partner & build relationship with all stakeholders
- S et Measurement and Control
- T otally review the value chain
- A lign the whole organisation & integrate CSR in corporate culture
- I nnovate (processes, technology, market entry, management etc.)
- N o Profit, No Go

II Candidate analysis

Professional Postgraduate Diploma in Marketing - (Strategic Marketing in Practice Analysis)

1. Introduction

In today's society, Corporate Social Responsibility (CSR) is becoming more and more prevalent across all forms of industry, in an effort to help reduce the detriment to the environment triggered by human civilisation. CSR can be seen as the voluntary actions that businesses take, over and above compliance with minimum legal requirements, to address both their own competitive interests and the interests of wider society.

Using examples based on the analysis of the 7 case studies, the aim of this paper is to identify and discuss the critical success factors required to implement a successful CSR initiative. Text marked in italics refers to case study examples that did not reflect the key success factors identified below.

2. Macro (PEST) Factors that could effect successful implementation of a CSR initiative

Political	**Economic**
Developing Collaborative Solutions (UNICEF, WHO) Development of new highly political NGOs (e.g. Greenpeace) 3rd World countries – high stakes, risks and growth	Underdeveloped Market Low disposable incomes in developing markets Fragmented & disparate markets Global depletion of raw materials (e.g. China & Steel/Rubber)
Social Corruption & Civil Instability High 3rd world death rates Entrenched Consumer Habits (Local cultures) Language barriers Unsustainable population growth & consumption Increased environmental awareness of consumers (e.g. ethical buying – Monsanto – GMO)	**Technological** Poor 3rd world infrastructures Rapid development of technology in all markets Increased communication channels Faster communication with web based communications

3. Critical Success Factors & key issues identified to implement a successful CSR initiative

3.1 Make CSR a strategic issue (societal marketing orientation): build CSR into the strategic planning process

A good example of **building CSR into the corporate vision** is Interface. By developing a shift in orientation since, 1994, and now focussing on the 7 Fronts of Sustainability, the entire organisation is now proactive towards achieving its core vision of becoming a sustainable enterprise by 2020, (segment 1 – Green marketing strategies). By integrating both business and CSR objectives Interface aims to deliver value to customers through products as well as the planet through sustainability and eco-efficient practice.

Types of environmental strategic posture

Change orientation		Value creation approach	
		Benefit enhancement for customers	Cost reduction
	Proactive	Green product Innovation (major modification) ❶ Interface	Pollution prevention beyond compliance ❸
	Accommodative	Green Product Differentiation (minor modification) ❷	Pollution prevention Compliance ❹

Green marketing strategies

A Poor example of adding a ***CSR policy onto existing corporate objectives*** *is Novo Nordisk. Their 'Take Action!' initiative was launched in January 2003 and from the start the project was not fully accepted by middle management -, this is reflected by the poor buy-in levels initially and after 1 year across the company:*

- *210/300 managers signed commitment sheet upon the project's introduction*
- *Only 7% of 18,000 employees had signed up by January 2004*

Relating to the Green Marketing strategies model, it is clear that Novo have not yet adopted a true CSR approach.

Planning of strategy: examples of how the various companies used in the case study have integrated CSR into their corporate strategies:

- Delivered at core value: Interface's principles of business (refer to 3.1 - building into vision)
- Delivered at a new market: Delta Cafés whole entry into E. Timor is an integrated CSR project
- Delivered at a new market with new product: P&G PuR product in Guatemala and Nutristar product in the Philippines, Venezuela & Nicaragua
- Delivered at an existing market: a CSR project has been introduced by Veracel for their eucalyptus pulp mill in Brazil

CSR initiatives reflected by society's requirements: defined from Maslow's hierarchy of needs model – stemming from Physiological needs to Esteem needs

- Increasing global awareness of deforestation: targeted by Veracel working with INGO's to protect and redevelop world's 2nd largest biome (International need)
- E. Timor economy slowly being revived through redevelopment of their moribund coffee industry (and local community redevelopment) as part of Delta Cafés' initiative (National need)
- P&G working with local NGO's & Aid agencies as part of their initiative, to change local community mindset towards drinking cleaner water (through using PuR product) and therefore reducing death resulting from diarrhoea (Local need)
- Novo Nordisk's recognition of need for employee salary donation scheme as one aspect of their 'Take Action!' (Personal need)

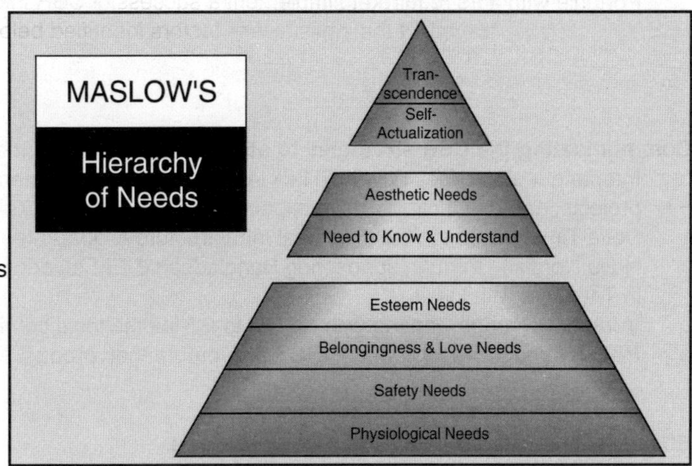

Defining objectives in relation to needs

Length of CSR strategy: how long will the CSR initiatives run

- Delta Cafés: 15 years to produce top quality coffee, thereafter, stabilised, self-sufficient local economy to manage initiative
- Interface: indefinite – total business process re-engineering to conform to continual sustainable development
- Veracel: indefinite? – re-forestation of previously de-forested areas. When targets are reached?
- SC Johnson – 30 years relationship to date; however with no EPA legislation change regarding differences between synthetic and natural pyrethroids; until project becomes unprofitable

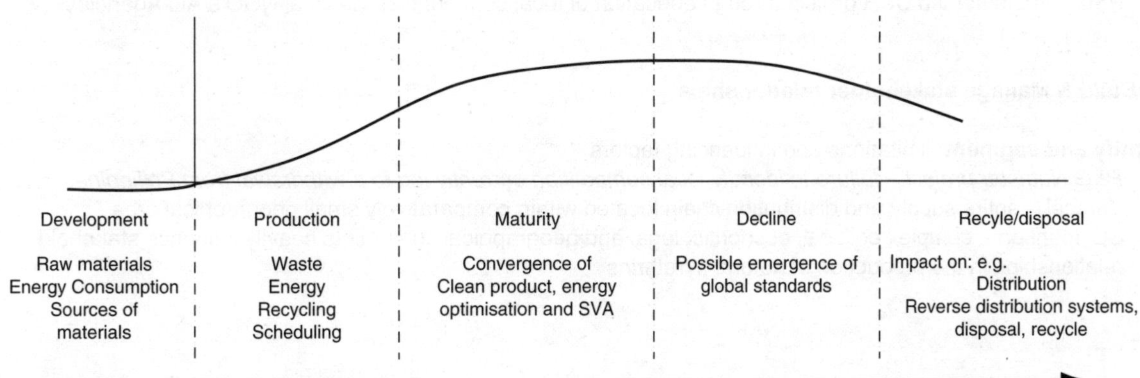

Interface CSR Life Cycle Assessment

3.2 Communicate Effectively: incorporate CSR into all forms of communication

Brand values: how the CSR policies fit the corporate brand

- Interface – entire products & brands (Cool Carpet™) have been built on green issues and sustainability
- Novo Nordisk – helping to fight diabetes (raising awareness of the disease – CSR initiative fits the brand very well)
- Delta Timor – by combining historical similarities in the way that Delta Cafés and Delta Timor were built around community regeneration and loyalty, the brand has been positioned as exclusively available and socially responsible, hence has created a solidarity market for the product in Portugal with a 3.2% market share).

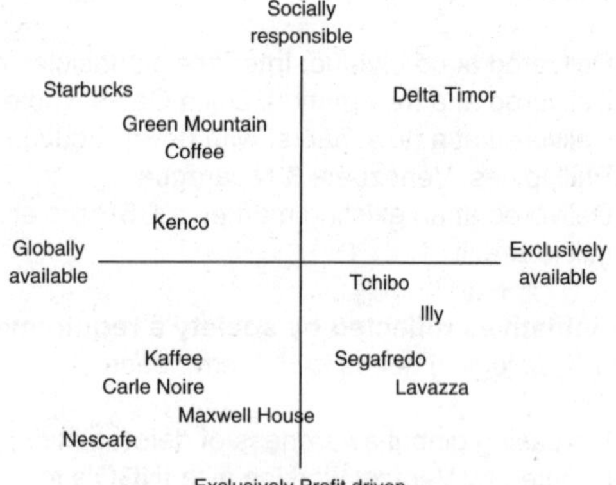

Brand positioning for Delta Timor Coffee

Communicating the CSR strategies to stakeholders: through messages and actions

- Interface – employees now hold key leadership roles in numerous local USGBC (US Green Building Council) projects, and use their Interface experience as building blocks for these external projects
- Delta Timor – through building local infrastructure & guaranteeing to buy coffee produced using Delta techniques
- Novo Nordisk– through sponsoring Bangladesh & El Salvador diabetes programmes and through working in Tanzania with locals
- Veracel – through working with NGO's to advice the local community of the importance of re-forestation
- P&G – through working with INGO's to promote their product and educate the local community

Effective integrated marketing communications

- *Novo Nordisk – although a management decision to undertake the 'Take Action!' CSR initiative it has had a poor take up (7% employees were signed up after 1 year)*
- Veracel – the commitment shown to the CSR initiative was translated throughout the organisation via the ISO 14001[2] certification
- Interface – through challenging their employees to find options for direct purchase of renewable energy, the organisation's commitment to their CSR initiative was widely communicated

Tactical Implementation: integration of CSR policy and business practice

- Interface – built CSR policy into principles of business (refer to 3.1 building into vision)
- Delta Timor – building competitive advantage into source of coffee production through CSR project
- *Novo Nordisk – introduced Take Action as a CSR initiative rather than as a corporate mission*
- P&G – implemented CSR project through education of local communities via local NGO's/Aid Agencies

3.3 Build & Manage stakeholder relationships

Identify and segment: limitations and influencing factors

- *P&G Nutristar project – failure to identify local competition correctly led to a withdrawal from Philippines*
- Veracel – entire supply and distribution chain located within comparatively small geographical area
- SC Johnson – complex political, economic, legal and geographical constraints heavily influence stakeholder relationships in the production of natural pyrethrins

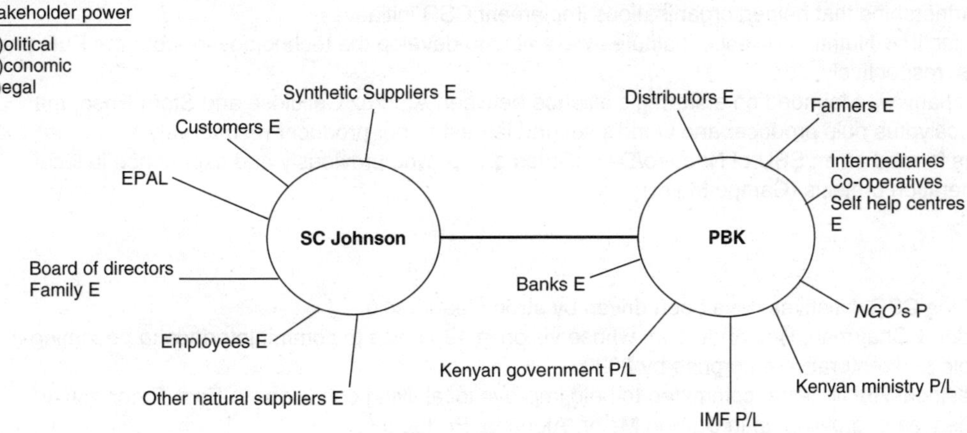

Stakeholder Power Analysis in the SC Johnson supply chain

Involvement of stakeholders: levels of involvement can influence the success of the CSR initiative

- SC Johnson – 30 year relationship with PBK and local farmers has led to knowledge and production technique sharing on both sides of the relationship
- Veracel – necessary to look across whole supply & distribution chain to avoid unethical uses of product
- Delta Timor – working with retailer Sonae from conception of project to integrate distribution into supply chain
- P&G – use of 3 distribution models to educate and motivate locals (Social, Commercial, Emergency relief), as well as deliver the PUR product

Feedback to stakeholders: various techniques are available for relaying CSR related information to stakeholders

- Interface – continual innovation has led to recognition from various external bodies via awards for use of green energy (Lone Star Award) as well as through products (Cool Carpet™)
- Novo Nordisk – ongoing activities reported on the Take Action! website
- SC Johnson – via knowledge management and sharing with PBK, local farmers and customers in Kenya
- Veracel – encouragement of harvest of non-wood products to regional farmers in nearby plantations

SCM/networks

- P&G – partnerships with the International Council of Nurses and Centres for Disease Control & Prevention
- Delta Timor – integrating local farmers at source & Sonae at distribution to form seamless supply chain
- Veracel – significant economic role in the region through activity generation for related products and services, however necessary to look across whole supply & distribution chain to avoid unethical uses of product
- SC Johnson – farmers' crops are delivered to intermediaries who form a union that subsequently supplies PBK

How CSR is reflected at Delta Cafés, using Porter's Value Chain

Internal partners: partnerships that helped organisations implement CSR initiatives

- P&G – the P&G Health & Nutrition Science Institutes were able to develop the technology for both the PuR and Nutristar products, respectively
- Veracel – the company was founded on a strategic alliance between Aracruz Cellulose and Stora Enso, the world's largest eucalyptus pulp producer and world's second largest paper producer respectively
- Delta Timor – was formed as an SBU of Nabeiro/Delta Cafés group, who previously had experience in local community regeneration projects (Campo Maior)

3.4 Manage Change

Leadership: many of the CSR initiatives have been driven by strong leadership

- Interface – Founder & Chairman, Ray Anderson, whose vision in 1994 was to commit Interface to becoming a leading sustainable and restorative enterprise by 2020
- Delta Timor – President Rui Nabeiro, committed to help improve local living conditions in East Timor, based on his own experiences of growing up in Campo Maior, Alentejo, Portugal
- Novo Nordisk – Lars Rebien Sørensen, CEO, encouraged employees to follow organisational sustainable development project, based on his drive to commit Novo Nordisk becoming a TBL enterprise

Internal marketing: how the CSR initiatives were reported within the organisation

- *Novo Nordisk – the Take Action1 Website was the main conduit for CSR reporting within the company. It proved to be reactive; hence poor employee buy-in levels were recorded*
- Interface – by proactively & continually educating its employees on the importance or reducing energy consumption, new levels of awareness were created throughout Interface
- Veracel – by introducing excellence awareness and training programmes to virtually all of its employees, the whole organisation has gained better insights into sustainable development

Organisation: how the organisation managed the ongoing change in relation to the CSR initiative

- Interface – the US EPA publicly recognised Interface for its continual change & ongoing commitment to purchase and use renewable energy and change
- *P&G – Nutristar product was withdrawn from the Venezuelan market; due to political and social instabilities*
- SC Johnson – over a 30 year period, flexibility was built into the supply chain relationship with the PBK to help manage the cultural differences more efficiently

Innovation & learning: how the CSR initiative inspired the organisation to innovate and learn from experience

- SC Johnson – gained valuable by-products knowledge from the PBK, and exchanged learning production techniques, training and support
- Interface – entire concept of sustainability within company mission is based on learning new and innovative ways to improve performance
- P&G – learnt that to successfully implement their CSR initiative, they would have to use 3 distribution models using external resources to deliver and market their PuR products to the local community

3.5 Measure the results: how the CSR initiatives were measured for success

Triple Bottom Line (TBL): balancing the financial, environmental and social objectives of the organisation

- Veracel – operates as an environmentally sound mill, a flat organisational structure with low manufacturing costs and a high production output
- Novo Nordisk – aims to build its business in a way that is financially profitable, environmentally sound and socially responsible
- Interface – sustainability built into business decisions from the raw materials sourced – to the way the company reclaims its customers' used products

Auditing: quantative measurement of CSR results as a control mechanism

- Delta Timor – specific production targets have been mapped out for the next 15 years, with product quality rising 27 points after only 2 years of production
- SC Johnson – the PBK is now recognised as an SC Johnson 'Partner in Quality', after only three audits since 1995

Benchmarking: competitor comparison as feedback indicator of the success of the CSR initiatives

- Interface – within the industry, it is now viewed by other competitors as the benchmark organisation in terms of sustainability development
- SC Johnson – by comparing natural and synthetic products in the supply chain, the PBK have dramatically increased their service and product quality, to match those of synthetic suppliers
- Veracel – benchmark environmentally sound production and supply techniques in world class mill

3.6 International issues: International influencing factors affecting the CSR initiatives

Management: how the CSR initiatives were managed across borders

- P&G – found that it had insufficient in-country infrastructure to deliver its product to the poorest communities, therefore resorted to using local help to produce, manage and distribute it's products (PuR & Nutristar)
- SC Johnson – leniency was shown in terms of supply lead times and customer service towards the PBK in recognition of cultural differences & working practices
- *Novo Nordisk – potential cultural issues implementing global sustainability drive, led to poor employee buy-in?*

Market development: how CSR experience will help organisations develop new markets

- Delta Timor – based on the success of the E. Timor CSR initiative, there are now plans to start similar projects in Angola, Columbia and elsewhere
- P&G – introduced faster and less expensive market entry system using local enterprises, which are internationally transferable

4. Conclusion

Having completed an analysis of the case study, it is possible to use the critical success factors (CSF) as indicators of Strategic, Operational and Tactical approaches to Corporate Social Responsibility.

From the analysis, Interface and Delta Timor can be seen to be the 'Greenest' organisations, with a total commitment to sustainability, reflected across the board in all their actions.

Veracel and SC Johnson have demonstrated a good understanding of eco-efficient practice, however are still dominated by shareholder value requirements, and therefore still have some issues to address before they can move into the greenest segment.

Moving further down the scale, although both P&G and Novo Nordisk have demonstrated willing, their actions can be seen to be those of a large multi-national corporation with a limited approach to practicing eco-efficient CSR initiatives. In such large organisations where objectives are frequently financial and shareholder driven, change invariably takes longer, consequently to integrate CSR fully will require continual review, reflection and response of the business climate.

Strategic
P&G - PuR
P&G - Nutristar
Novo Nordisk
Delta Timor
Interface
Veracel
SC Johnson

Operational
P&G - PuR
P&G - Nutristar
Novo Nordisk
Delta Timor
Interface
Veracel
SC Johnson

Tactical
P&G - PuR
P&G - Nutristar
Novo Nordisk
Delta Timor
Interface
Veracel
SC Johnson

'The Green Chart'

III Candidate analysis

Figure 1: PESTLE analysis across all seven case studies

	Delta Cafés	P&G PuR	P&G Nutri	Interface	Novo Nordisk	Veracel	SC Johnson
P	1. Gov Stability? 2. Partnerships with Gov, UN and NGOs	1. Developing countries different infrastructures	1. Stability (Venezuela) 2. Nicaragua – using collaboration model	1. Global market 2. Political infrastructures	1. Different political infrastructures	1. Local organisation 2. Partnerships with NGOs	1. Kenya 70% of production of Pyrethrum 2. Political control PKB
E	1. Market leader 2. Solidarity mkt	1. V poor target mkt	1. Correct split of funding required – low incomes	1. Slow market growth	1. High cost of diabetes treatment for LDC's	– Supporting network of infrastructures	1. Slow economic growth
S	1. Socially accountable 2. Local workforce	1. Educate to change 2. Low incomes	1. Educate to change-problem not known	1. Working within many different social groups	1. Awareness diabetes low 2. Need employee buy-in	– Local workforce – Increase employment	1. Fragmented supplier/ workforce
T	1. Quality standards 2. Educating process	1. Needed a simple process for product	1. Production skilled partners required	1. Advanced technology development		– Technology increasing (Veracel first mover)	1. Quality standards
L	1. Sustainability logo 2. Partner Sonae	1. Partnerships 2. Legislation for product	1. Lack of enforced patent rights	1. Emission reduction			1. Need for govt 'labelling' support for natural ingred
E	1. No contingency plan 2. Investing in eroded coffee fields.		1. Local manufacture using local supplies	1. Using renewable energy and ingredients 2. Being 'green'	1. Lack of local mfg	– Atlantic rainforest deforestation	1. One main source 2. Green product

Figure 2: P&G PUR Five FORCES Analysis (Porter)

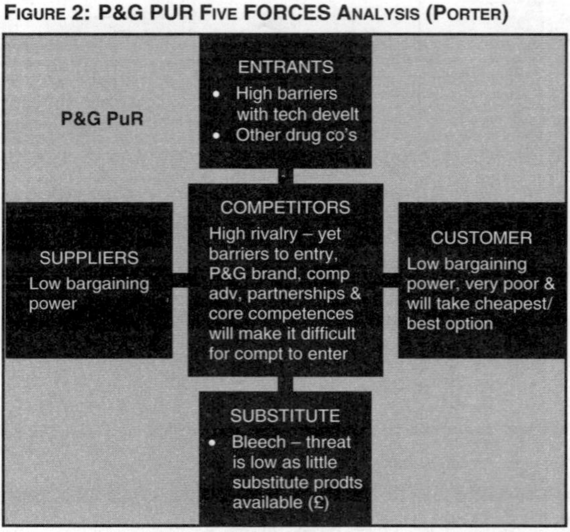

Figure 3: PORTERS VALUE CHAIN – P&G Nutri

Firm infrastructure: International organisation – 98,000 employees, works in 140 countries. Company goal of 'developing low income market products and business models'. Renowned for R&D.

HRM:	Specialists in R&D and expertise in food formulation	Investment from sales of NutriStar to education programmes	Education to raise awareness of issues and raise demand
Technology develt: Info from clinical study in Tanzania	R&D into micronutrients – Quality assurance		Packing was readdressed to lower costs
Procurement:			Sought partners with expertise on downtrade distribution

MARGIN: Failed Philippines/ pulled out of Venezuela

Inbound logistics:	Operations:	Outbound logistics:	Marketing & Sales:	Service:
• Inbound goods to be used in products • Infromation formed from clinical studies	• Nutri developed in collaboration with aid agencies • R&D in field research -needs of end-user • Sought partners with expertise in production	• Lack of control of outbound (failure in Philippines) • Reworked model to form partnerships with distributors	• Lack of enforced intellectual property rights mean that substitute products were easily launched in Philippines.	Provided through partner organisations to raise standards

MARGIN: now occuring in Nicaragua

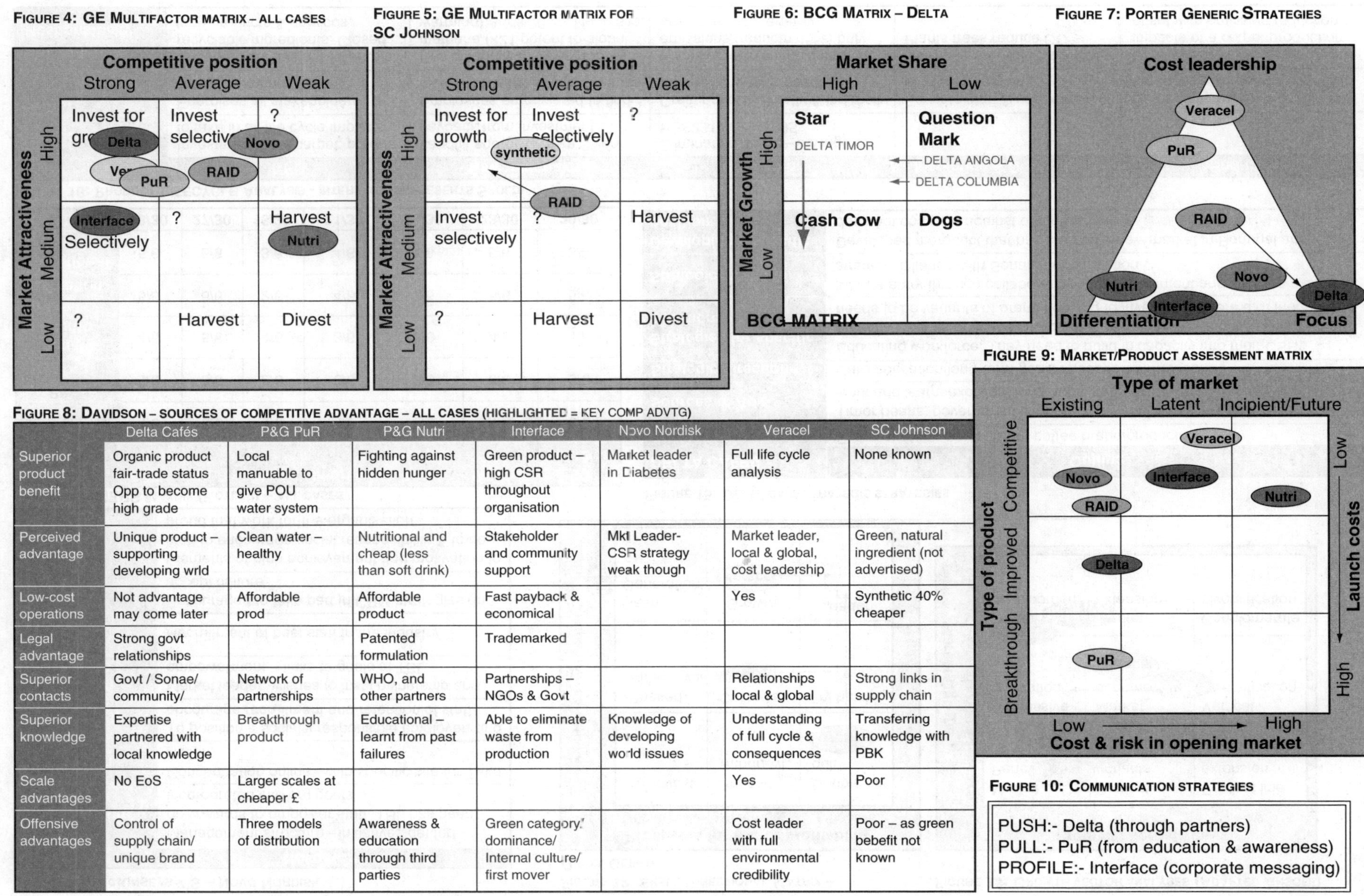

FIGURE 4: GE MULTIFACTOR MATRIX – ALL CASES

FIGURE 5: GE MULTIFACTOR MATRIX FOR SC JOHNSON

FIGURE 6: BCG MATRIX – DELTA

FIGURE 7: PORTER GENERIC STRATEGIES

FIGURE 8: DAVIDSON – SOURCES OF COMPETITIVE ADVANTAGE – ALL CASES (HIGHLIGHTED = KEY COMP ADVTG)

	Delta Cafés	P&G PuR	P&G Nutri	Interface	Novo Nordisk	Veracel	SC Johnson
Superior product benefit	Organic product fair-trade status Opp to become high grade	Local manuable to give POU water system	Fighting against hidden hunger	Green product – high CSR throughout organisation	Market leader in Diabetes	Full life cycle analysis	None known
Perceived advantage	Unique product – supporting developing wrld	Clean water – healthy	Nutritional and cheap (less than soft drink)	Stakeholder and community support	Mkt Leader-CSR strategy weak though	Market leader, local & global, cost leadership	Green, natural ingredient (not advertised)
Low-cost operations	Not advantage may come later	Affordable prod	Affordable product	Fast payback & economical		Yes	Synthetic 40% cheaper
Legal advantage	Strong govt relationships		Patented formulation	Trademarked			
Superior contacts	Govt / Sonae/ community/	Network of partnerships	WHO, and other partners	Partnerships – NGOs & Govt		Relationships local & global	Strong links in supply chain
Superior knowledge	Expertise partnered with local knowledge	Breakthrough product	Educational – learnt from past failures	Able to eliminate waste from production	Knowledge of developing world issues	Understanding of full cycle & consequences	Transferring knowledge with PBK
Scale advantages	No EoS	Larger scales at cheaper £				Yes	Poor
Offensive advantages	Control of supply chain/ unique brand	Three models of distribution	Awareness & education through third parties	Green category/ dominance/ Internal culture/ first mover		Cost leader with full environmental credibility	Poor – as green bebefit not known

FIGURE 9: MARKET/PRODUCT ASSESSMENT MATRIX

FIGURE 10: COMMUNICATION STRATEGIES

PUSH:- Delta (through partners)
PULL:- PuR (from education & awareness)
PROFILE:- Interface (corporate messaging)

Figure 11: McKinseys 7'S – Novo Nordisk

		Novo Nordisk
HARD	Structure	Management structure – initiatives get fed downwards to empower staff. TBL has been incorporated into org goals
	Systems	Concentration online – with specific site for Take Action
	Strategy	To position a socially responsible employer, and encourage recruitment and retention of staff
SOFT	Shared Values	Market leader, wishes to instil ownership and empowerment – links to goals of TBL
	Skills	Recruitment of best staff in the industry
	Staff	Encouraged to take part in CRM strategies and accept culture
	Style	Elements of high achievement and motivation to staff to encourage social responsibility & to be proud that work for the organisation

Figure 12: Shell Directional Matrix – Delta Coffee

Competitive capabilities \ Prospects for sector profitability	Unattractive	Average	Attractive
Weak	Disinvest	Phased withdrawl	Double or quit (Nutri)
Average	Phased withdrawal	Custodial growth (Delta)	Try harder
Strong	Cash Generation	Growth (Veracel)	Leader

Figure 13: Growth vector analyses (Adapted Ansoff)

Market Options \ Product alternatives	High	Medium	Low
Existing mkt	Market Penetration (Novo, PuR)	Product variants/extensions (RAID)	Product line extension
Expanded mkt	Aggressive promotion	Market segementation (Veracel)	Vertical diversification (Delta)
New mkt	Market development (Nutri)	Market extension (Interface)	Conglomerate diversification

Figure 14: MERS Matrix (Kotler) – all cases

MERS (kotler)	Delta	PuR	Nutri	Interface	Novo Nordisk	Veracel	SC Johnson
Customer philosophy	4/6	6/6	4/6	4/6	3/6	4/6	3/6
Integrated mktg org	5/6	5/6	2/6	6/6	3/6	5/6	5/6
Adequate mktg info	4/6	5/6	4/6	3/6	3/6	4/6	4/6
Strategic orientation	5/6	6/6	2/6	4/6	2/6	5/6	5/6
Operational efficiency	5/6	5/6	3/6	4/6	4/6	5/6	3/6
TOTAL	23/30	27/30	15/30	21/30	15/30	23/30	20/30

Figure 15: Delta cafe strategic strategies

DELTA CAFES	Outline
Generic strategies	Focus strategy on it's Timor coffee brand/product
Sources of Adv	Timor beans; government support; local workforces who are keen to work and learn; excellent land once restored
Strategic directions	Care/education/long-term goals to support infrastructure
Strategies for specific situations	Educating workforce. They need to build in capacity into their CSR coffee as risk as only one source of supply if there is a coup. There needs to be variants of brand (looking to invest elsewhere e.g. Indonesia)
Strategic methods	Market entry through collaboration with government and creating a strategic alliance with Sonae for distribution
Developing a specific position	Developed a product that has created a new market in Portugal and does not compete against other brands

Figure 16: Product Lifecycle Analysis – interface (represents Spold)

	NPD	Raw materials	Production	Marketing & Distribution	End-user
Finance	Investment Cool carpet; product to take in all life cycle impacts.	Landfill energy gives a 3 year payback from investment.	Eliminating waste – savings of US$231 since 1995.		
Social Responsibility	Energises all stakeholders around company vision.	Employees empowered to find local renewable energy sources.	Creating jobs directly & indirectly through energy production.	Educate staff & use resource efficient transport.	Community benefit from cleaner air; renewable energy sources.
Environmental Responsibility	Ensures max use of renewable/recyclable ingredients. Closed loop products & services.	Use of landfill for energy uses methane (×21 potent to global warming) Adds 20 yrs life to site.	Focus on eliminating waste/emissions (reductn 45%) only use renewable energy.	Deliver in recycled packaging. Plants trees reduce CO^2.	Cool carpet – all lifecycle impacts of a carpet production offset with emission reduction.

Figure 17: Seven keys to sustainability – develop a win-win solution

Value propositions	Delta Cafes	P&G PuR	P&G Nutri	Interface	Novo Nordisk	Veracel	SC Johnson
Innovate	Working practices & education of coffee production	New POU water – 3 distribution models employed	Fighting against 'hidden hunger' with marketable product	New ways of working from raw materials, prodn to distribn	Incorporating 'take action' into daily job routines (TBL)	New mill, concepts of working – creating chain of work	Using natural insecticide – though more expensive
Practice eco-efficiency	Rebuilding eroded coffee fields – investing in Timor	Profit whilst improving health conditions.	Profitable product whilst combating a growing issue	Investment in 'green' practices has shown economic return	Promoting organisation whilst proving care	Cost leadership whilst support green issues (ISO 14001)	Natural resource, supporting Kenyan farmers
Move from stakeholder dialogues to partnerships for progress	Partnerships with Sonae for distribution and E Timor govt for supply	ICN, CDC, WHO, UNICEF – working together to provide best solution	UNICEF, Cornell University, WHO, NGOs, Multilateral & local paediatric assc	NGO, Govt and local community partnerships	Empowering employees	NGOs, IBio, local partnerships	PKB, Farmers, Suppliers
Provide & inform consumer choice	Choice of premium or fair-trade coffee	Educating around issues & solution	Raising awareness of an unknown problem	Environmentally friendly products		Offering customer sustainable products	Need to educate to gain benefits
Improve market framework conditions	Rebuilding Timor infrastructure, invest in whole value chain	Working towards through ongoing education	Now developed a transferable model for implementation.	Introducing new processes, creating jobs & change		Creating jobs indirectly and directly	Invested in model around quality & supply
Establish worth of the Earth	Investment in new working procedures			Resource efficiency no 1 priority		ISO 14001 – creating green practices	Investment in natural resource
Make mkts work for everyone	Timor, Delta & Sonae all benefiting	End profit for P&G – reduction diarrhoea	P&G and developing world both benefit	Green products with envirnt improvement		Cost leader with econ & environt benefits	No economic benefit until recognised

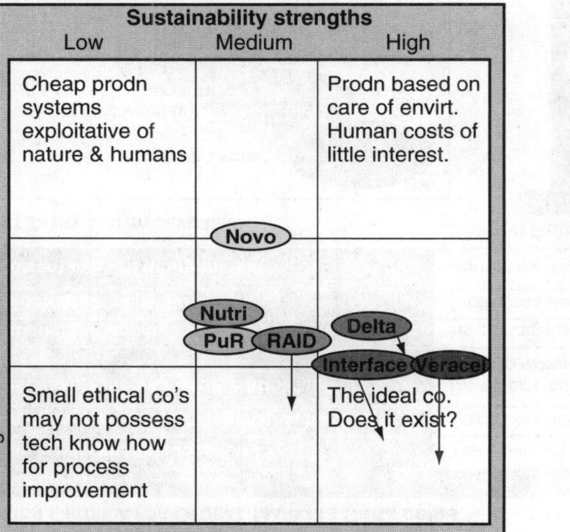

Figure 18: Sustainability and Ethical Matrix

Figure 19: Effectiveness Vs Efficiency of CSR

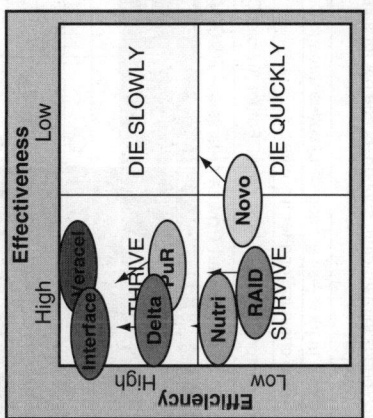

Figure 20: International Markets matrix: P&G Nutri

Figure 21: Selection Criteria for Global Markets Delta cafes

	Questions:	Delta Cafes
Accessibility	Can we access this location?	Yes – support form Timor Gov – distribution channels set. Need further research for Columbia and Angola.
	Any geographic, trade, legislative barriers?	Trade contracts set, quality levels need to be raised. Problems may occur as government is new and not totally stable.
Profitability	Disposable income levels? Affordability?	Developing country–needs infrastructure support–coffee not for sale in Timor. Portugal high disposable income – set customer base, plans to expend to Europe.
	Competitor activity? Currency? Payment?	No competition in Timor market – single source of coffee through Delta cafes. In Portugal Delta have highest market share.
	Repatriation of profits?	Profits invested in value chain for long-term profits.
Market Size	Current market, future market	Current market source from Timor sell in Portugal. Future Angola. Columbia source already sold across Europe.

Figure 22: Market entry and involvement

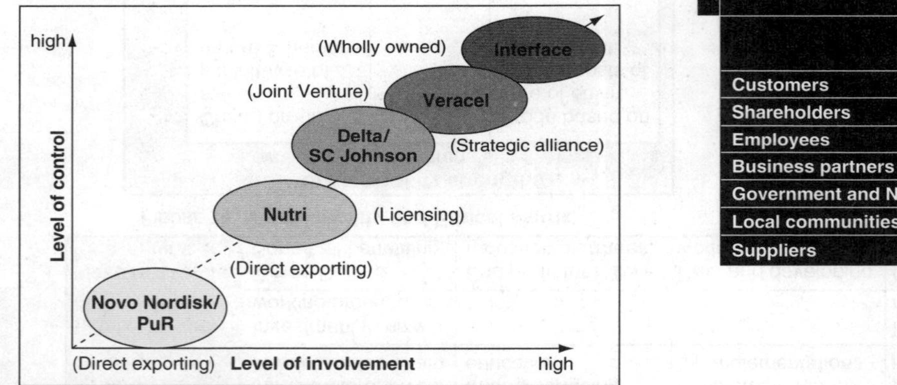

Figure 23: Stakeholder Power analysis – P&G Nutri

	POWER			STRATEGY			
	High	Medium	Low	Proactive	Accommodating	Defensive	Reactive
Customers	O						O
Shareholders	O				O		
Employees		O		O			
Business partners	O			O			
Government and NGOs	O			O			
Local communities & public			O				O
Suppliers		O				O	

Figure 24: KAM Model – SC Johnson

Level of interaction
Resource sharing
Information sharing
Conflict resolution/ Problem solving
Quality improvement
Synthetics
PBK
Farmers
Mosquito

Figure 25: Brand hierarchy

Delta
Interface
Personality
Values
Veracel
Emotional Reward
RAID
PuR
Nutri
Rational Benefits
Novo
Functional Benefits

Figure 26: Stakeholder needs – Delta Cafes

STAKEHOLDER	NEED	RESPONSE RISK
Customers	Good coffee, easy to purchase, ethical values, reasonable price	Switch brands
Employees	Security, expertise, satisfaction at work. Empowerment, recognition and shared values	Strike action, resignation
Shareholders	Return on investment	Sell shares – co vulnerable to take over, refuse to invest more
Partner (Sonae)	Ensured supply of quality coffee	End partnership & distri channel
Suppliers	Good relations, knowledge if supply needs	Failure to deliver
East Timor Gov	Boost to countries economy, investment in infrastructure & long term strategic plans for recovery. Public interest	End contract and offer to another organisation. Take over operations internally
NGOs (Addocerre)	Community interest to spend funds effectively for education	Ineffective education
Community	Economic & social support. Work, good wages & education	Lack of support for project – campaign against co/sabotage
Environment	Sustainability	Inability to grow coffee

FIGURE 27: SUSTAINABILITY ASSESST – VERACEL

Assessment of Sustainability	Company competencies High	Med	Low
Financial (10%)			
– Size/profitability	○		
– LT capital investment	○		
Organisation (25%)			
– Staff trn, motivation		○	
– Staff retention		○	
Supply chain (10%)			
– R&D, Innovation	○		
– Supplier distn, loyalty		○	
Govt/Community			
– Political structure		○	
– Trading infrastructure	○		
– Resource availability	○		
Ecological (15%)			
– Renewable sources		○	
– Pollution control		○	

FIGURE 28: SWOT ACROSS ALL CASES

	Delta Cafés	P&G PuR	P&G Nutri	Interface	Novo Nordisk	Veracel	SC Johnson
S	1. Partnerships (Sonae/Gov) 2. Unique brand 3. Supply chain 4. First mover	1. P&G brand 2. Breakthrough product 3. Prodt mktg QA, Prod develt.	1. Learnt from failures 2. P&G Brand 3. Partnerships 4. Prodt develt	1. CSR/green issues inaugural 2. Leader in innovation	1. World leader in diabetes 2. CSR part of crop objs 3. ntl presence	1. Cost & market leader 2. CSR integrated 3. Strategic relationships	1. PKB relation 2. Qual standards 3. Established models 4. Green prodt
W	1. Learning curve 2. Portuguese not Euro brand	1. Lack of own distribution channels	1. Arrogance 2. Lack knowledge mkt	1. First mover, needs to educate and learn	1. Lack direction 2. Buy-in to CSR is pushed	1. Privately owned land 2. Legislation	1. Fragmented supply chain 2. Diff to forecast
O	1. Expand distribution across Europe 2. Transfer model to countries 3. New market	1. Distribution models 2. Need for clean water 3. Packing	1. Partnerships/ using other channels for education and distribution	1. New markets/ Global presence 2. Stakeholders support 3. Energy efficiency/cost $	1. Superior staff 2. To market & supply to develg countries	1. Drive for green processes 2. Boost local economy & hence value chain	1. Huge opportunity if recognised from synthetic prodt 2. Niche market
T	1. Stability of country 2. Reliance on distribution through Sonae 3. Compt entry	1. Stability of countries 2. Need for ongoing education 3. Copycat prods	1. Lack knowledge of hidden hunger 2. Copycat prodts 3. Individuals needs	1. Consumer interest	1. External view programme is PR rather than CSR	1. Environmental legislation for working within the Atlantic rainforest	1. Market collapses have to use synthetics/ no contingency 2. Synthetic prodts cheaper

FIGURE 29: KAPLAN & NORTON: BALANCE SCORE CARD – INTERFACE EVALUATION OF PERFORMANCE

Financial Perspective

GOALS	MEASURES
Return on capital - invested	– Investment of waste elimination a return of US$231 (1995) – LaGrange landfill - 3 yr pay-back, cost savings $20,000
Sustainable priced product	– Commercially priced and accepted product

Internal Business Perspective

GOALS	MEASURES
Marketing	– Focus on cosumer perceived benefit (eg low pollution) – Energising & educating workforce (LaGrange/USGEC)
Manufacturing	– Reduced emmisions by 46% absolute – Improved energy efficiency (RECs) – Renewable energy sources (LaGrange landfill) – Reduced waste (cyclical material) 20% prodt non-petro
Distribution	Trees for travel 45,000 planted/Clean Co2mmute/Cool fuel
NPD	Cool carpet – complete lifecycle

*Interface also has own measurement goals – Four Systems Conditions of The Natural Step

Customer Perspective

GOALS	MEASURES
Customer satisfaction	– Reduced emissions (quality air/pollution) – Reduced need for fossil fuels
Customer partnerships	– Working with local communities to support infrastructure
Community support	– Providing work/revenue for LaGrange landfill US$30m – Energising stakeholders
Sustainability	– Educating community about recycling used carpets

Innovation and learning

GOALS	MEASURES
Technology leadership	– Cool carpet (lifecycle impacts offset) – Lonestar award 'New supply green energy' (LaGrange) – US EPA, Climate protection award 2004
Manufacturing learning	– Landfill site (Lower emissions, renewable energy, ROI) – Sustainability sharing knowledge & resources to educate – Re:Entry, carpet reclamation initative

appendix 3 curriculum information and reading list

Aim

Marketing has to be firmly rooted in both theory and practice. Practice informs theory and vice versa. The Strategic Marketing in Practice module is designed to allow participants to put strategic marketing into practice. As the final module at Postgraduate Diploma, it not only builds on the knowledge and skills developed in all the preceding modules, but also looks for an overall competence in marketing that encompasses all the various subject areas covered in Professional Certificate and Professional Diploma level. As marketing is constantly evolving, continuously informed by both academic and business research, one of the aims of this module is to explore the latest trends and innovations relevant to marketers who are operating at a strategic level within organizations. One of the other aims is to understand marketing as an activity, which is important in all contexts (profit, not-for-profit, societal, global). It is expected that participants undertaking this module will be able to add value to both their marketing experience and marketing knowledge. This module therefore does not have a specific syllabus and draws from all the preceding modules and syllabi.

Related statements of practice

- Ad.1 Define intelligence requirements and lead the intelligence gathering process.
- Ad.2 Develop a detailed understanding of the organization and its environment.
- Bd.1 Promote a strong market orientation and influence/contribute to strategy formulation and investment decisions.
- Bd.2 Specify and direct the marketing planning process.
- Cd.1 Promote organization-wide innovation and cooperation in the development of brands.
- Cd.2 Distil the essence of brands and direct/coordinate a portfolio of brands.
- Dd.1 Develop and direct an integrated marketing communications strategy.
- Dd.2 Lead the implementation of the integrated marketing communications strategy.
- Ed.1 Promote corporate-wide innovation and cooperation in the development of products and services.
- Ed.2 Direct and maintain competitive product/service portfolios.
- Fd.1 Promote the strategic and creative use of pricing.
- Fd.2 Lead the implementation of the strategic and creative use of pricing.
- Gd.1 Select and monitor channel criteria to meet the organization's need in a changing environment.
- Gd.2 Direct and control support to channel members.

Hd.1 Promote and create a customer orientation and infrastructure for customer relationships.
Hd.2 Direct and control information and activities that deliver customer relationships and service.
Jd.1 Establish and maintain a project management framework in line with strategic objectives.
Jd.2 Direct and control the delivery of programmes and projects.
Kd.1 Establish and promote the use of metrics to improve marketing effectiveness.
Kd.2 Create a system of critical review and appraisal to inform future marketing activity.
Ld.1 Provide professional leadership and develop a cooperative environment to enhance performance.
Ld.2 Promote effective cross-functional working linked to brands and the integration of marketing activities.
Ld.3 Promote and create an environment for career and self-development.
Ld.4 Contribute to organizational change and define and communicate the need for change within the department.

Learning outcomes

Participants will be able to:

9.64.1 Identify and critically evaluate marketing issues within various environments, utilizing a wide variety of marketing techniques, concepts and models.
9.64.2 Assess the relevance of, and opportunities presented by, contemporary marketing issues within any given scenario including innovations in marketing.
9.64.3 Identify and critically evaluate various options available within given constraints and apply competitive positioning strategies, justifying any decisions taken.
9.64.4 Formulate and present a creative, customer-focused and innovative competitive strategy for any given context, incorporating relevant investment decisions, appropriate control aspects and contingency plans.
9.64.5 Demonstrate an understanding of the direction and management of marketing activities as part of the implementation of strategic direction, taking into account business intelligence requirements, marketing processes, resources, markets and the company vision.
9.64.6 Promote and facilitate the adoption and maintenance of a strong market and customer orientation with measurable marketing metrics.
9.64.7 Synthesize various strands of knowledge and skills from the different syllabus modules effectively in developing an effective solution for any given context.

Knowledge and skill requirements

There is no formal specification of knowledge and skills requirements for this module. Participants are required to demonstrate a full understanding of, and to satisfy the knowledge and skills requirements specified in, the syllabus modules at Postgraduate Diploma, Diploma and Certificate level. The emphasis in this module is more on applying the knowledge and practical skills acquired in the previous modules. The essential skills assessed as part of this module are:

- Analysis, interpretation, evaluation and synthesis of information, including the ability to draw conclusions.
- Identification, exploration and evaluation of strategic options.
- Selection and justification of an appropriate option using decision criteria.

- Establishing the activities, resources and schedule needed to implement the chosen strategy.
- Working with others to implement and control the strategy.

Participants will be expected to demonstrate their awareness of current issues and an ability to make recommendations for a given context. From time to time CIM will publish a list of trends and innovations to guide tutors and participants in their preparation for assessment. Participants will be expected to read widely in the area of strategic marketing as part of their studies at this level.

Assessment

CIM will offer a single form of assessment based on the learning outcomes for this module. It will take the form of an invigilated, time-constrained assessment throughout the delivery network. Candidates' assessments will be marked centrally by CIM.

Strategic Marketing in Practice

Core texts

Collier, P.M. (2003) *Accounting for Managers: Interpreting Accounting Information for Decision-making*, Chichester: John Wiley & Sons.

Doole, I. and Lowe, R. (2004) *Strategic Marketing Decisions*, London: Thomson Learning.

Doyle, P. (2000) *Value Based Marketing: Marketing Strategies for Corporate Growth and Shareholder Value*, Chichester: John Wiley & Sons.

Little, E. and Marandi, E. (2003) *Relationship Marketing Management*, London: Thomson.

Ranchhod, A. (2003) *Marketing Strategies: A Twenty-first Century Approach*, Harlow: Pearson.

Syllabus guides/Workbooks

Ranchhod, A. and Marandi, E. (2005) *Strategic Marketing in Practice*, Oxford: BH/Elsevier.

Supplementary readings

Aaker, D.A. (2001) *Strategic Market Management*, 6th edition, Chichester: John Wiley & Sons.

Bartlett, C.A. and Goshal, S. (2002) *Managing Across Borders: The Transnational Solution*, 2nd edition, Harvard: Harvard Business Press.

Doole, I. and Lowe, R. (2004) *International Marketing Strategy: Analysis, Development and Implementation*, 4th edition, London: Thomson.

Fill, C. (2002) *Marketing Communications: Contexts, Strategies and Applications*, 3rd edition, Harlow: Pearson.

Gilligan, C. and Wilson, R. (2004) *Strategic Marketing Management: Planning, Implementation and Control*, 3rd edition, Oxford: Butterworth-Heinemann.

Gowthorpe, C. (2003) *Business Accounting: for Non-specialist*, London: Thomson.

Hankansson, H. *et al* (2004) *Rethinking Marketing: Developing Understanding of Markets*, Chichester: John Wiley and Sons.

Hooley, G.J., Saunders, J.A. and Piercy, N.F. (2003) *Marketing Strategy and Competitive Positioning*, 3rd edition, Harlow: Prentice Hall.

Johnson, G. and Scholes, K. (2004) *Exploring Corporate Strategy: Text and Cases*, 7th edition, Harlow: Prentice Hall.

Kotler, P. and De Bes, F.T. (2003) *Lateral Marketing: New Techniques for Finding Breakthrough Ideas*, US: John Wiley and Sons.

Stacey, R.D. (2003) *Strategic Management and Organisational Dynamics*, 4th edition, Harlow: Prentice Hall.

Overview and rationale

Approach

This new module has been introduced to practise the knowledge and skills on formulating a strategy and dealing with implementation issues learned about during Stage 3 and, as such, to provide a vehicle for summative assessment. For those participants who undertake the work-based project, it is intended to add value both for employer as well as participants in applying generic marketing principles at the strategic and global level to their own organization.

The emphasis on trends and innovations in marketing is a mechanism to keep the topics current. These trends, which may be highlighted by CIM from time to time, will be drawn from the marketing literature and other business and marketing publications. It will be the responsibility of participants and their tutors to ensure they are prepared for assessment in this area. They are expected to read widely in the area of strategic marketing as part of their studies at this level.

Syllabus content

The syllabus focuses on strategic marketing practice in organizations and how the trends and innovations in marketing affect it. It is important that participants understand that marketing is not fixed in time and that new developments within academia and business have a profound impact in the way business is conducted. Apart from the guidance given by the Senior Examiner and the CIM, it is up to the participants to keep themselves abreast of current trends and innovations in marketing. The learning outcomes specify the analytical and creative steps involved in identifying challenges, evaluating potential solutions and making decisions that will resolve challenges faced by an organization and take advantage of innovations.

This syllabus is based on the syllabus for the other three modules at this level, to which tutors and participants should refer for additional guidance.

Delivery approach

The delivery approach for this module can be flexible. However it is likely to follow through the key issues considered within a particular organizational problem or case study. Tutors will need to demonstrate a clear ability to impart knowledge on trends and innovations in marketing. It is likely that three hour sessions will be used to cover some of the key areas in marketing. At a later stage, once the case study is distributed as well as the assignment tasks, more detailed consideration of various aspects of the elements as they relate to the problem in question (case or organizational problem) can be debated within the class.

Index

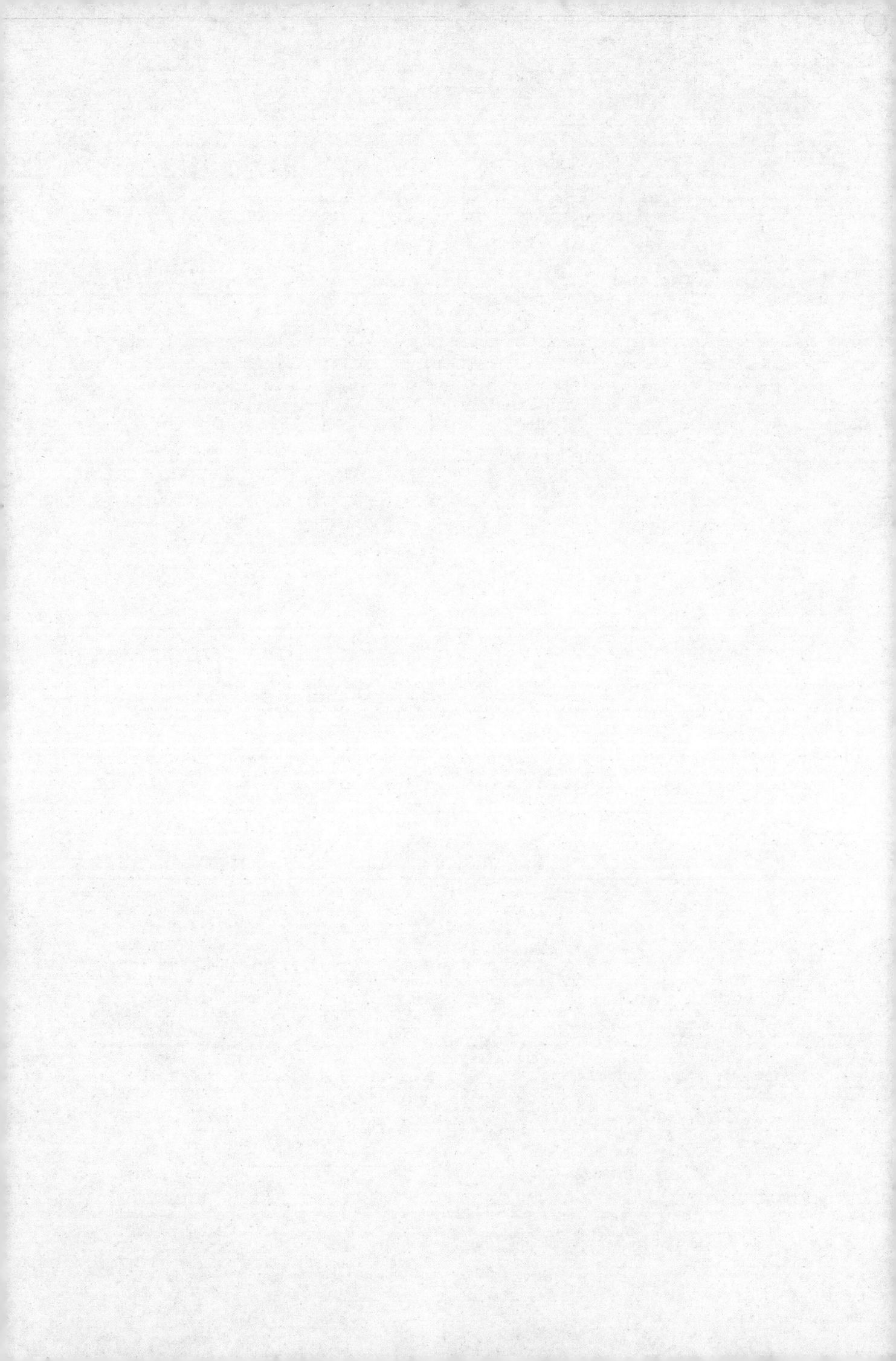